6118

THE VORY

THE VORY
RUSSIA'S SUPER MAFIA

MARK GALEOTTI

YALE UNIVERSITY PRESS
NEW HAVEN AND LONDON

For information about this and other Yale University Press publications, please contact:

U.S. Office: sales.press@yale.edu   yalebooks.com
Europe Office: sales@yaleup.co.uk   yalebooks.co.uk

Set in Minion Pro by IDSUK (DataConnection) Ltd
Printed in Great Britain by Gomer Press Ltd, Llandysul, Ceredigion, Wales

Library of Congress Control Number: 2017963166

ISBN 978-0-300-18682-6

A catalogue record for this book is available from the British Library.

10 9 8 7 6 5 4 3 2 1

CONTENTS

ILLUSTRATIONS

PREFACE

I was in Moscow in 1988, in the final years of the Soviet Union, as the system was sliding towards shabby oblivion even if at the time no one knew how soon the end would come. While carrying out research for my doctorate on the impact of the Soviet war in Afghanistan, I was interviewing Russian veterans of that brutal conflict. When I could, I would meet these *afgantsy* shortly after they got home, and then again a year into civilian life to see how they were adjusting. Most came back raw, shocked, angry, either bursting with tales of horror and blunder, or else spikily or numbly withdrawn. A year later, though, most had done what people do in such circumstances: they had adapted, they had coped. The nightmares were less frequent, the memories less vivid, they had jobs and girlfriends, they were saving up for a car, a holiday or a flat. But then there were those who could not or would not move on. Some of these young men collaterally damaged by the war had become adrenaline junkies or just intolerant of the conventions and restrictions of everyday life.

Vadim, for example, became a cop, and not just any cop but an OMON, a member of the 'black berets', the feared new riot police who were to become the stormtroopers of reaction in the final attempts to hold the Soviet system together. Sasha became a firefighter, the closest thing to his wartime life as an assault-landing soldier, one of the helicopter cavalry. Their role was to be on standby until the alert came and then to pile into one of the big Mi-24 gunships the soldiers called 'hunchbacks', bristling with gun pods and rockets, whether to intercept a rebel caravan or, just as often, to rescue Soviet soldiers caught in ambush. The camaraderie of the fire station, the sudden alarm, the intense blast of life-threatening yet also meaningful action, the sense of being a larger-than-life figure apart from the grey realities of day-to-day Soviet life – all that helped recreate the good old days in Afghanistan.

And then there was Volodya, known as 'Chainik' ('Teapot') for reasons I never did learn (although it is a term sometimes found in prison for a bully). Wiry, intense, morose, he had an indefinably brittle and dangerous quality which on the whole I would have crossed the road to avoid. He had been a marksman in the war and about the only thing which could transform him into a relaxed, open and even animated human being was the chance to enthuse about his Dragunov sniper's rifle and his kills. The other *afgantsy* tolerated Volodya but never seemed comfortable with him, nor with talking about him. He always had money to burn at a time when the majority were eking out the most marginal of lives, often living with parents or juggling multiple jobs. It all made sense, though, when I later learned that he had become what was known in Russian crime circles as a torpedo, a hit man. As the values and structures of Soviet life crumbled and fell, organised crime was emerging from the ruins, no longer subservient to the corrupt Communist Party bosses and the black-market millionaires. As it rose, it was gathering to itself a new generation of recruits, including damaged and disillusioned veterans of the USSR's last war. Some were bodyguards, some were runners, some were leg breakers and some – like Volodya and his beloved rifle – were killers.

I never found out what happened to Volodya. We were hardly on Christmas card terms. He probably ended up as a casualty of the gang wars of the 1990s, fought out with car bombs, drive-by shootings and knives in the night. That decade saw the emergence of a tradition of monumental memorialisation, as fallen gangsters were buried in full 'Godfather' pomp, with black limousines threading through paths lined with white carnations and tombs marked with huge headstones showing idealised representations of the dead. Vastly expensive (the largest cost upwards of $250,000, at a time when the average wage was close to a dollar a day) and stupendously tacky, these monuments showed the dead with the spoils of their criminal lives: the Mercedes, the designer suit, the heavy gold chain. I still wonder if some day I'll be walking through one of the cemeteries favoured by Moscow's gangsters, maybe Vvedenskoye to the south-east of the city, or

Vagankovskoye to the west, and will come across Volodya's grave. It will no doubt feature that rifle.

Nonetheless, it was thanks to Volodya and those like him that I became one of the first Western scholars to raise the alarm about the rise and consequences of Russian organised crime, something whose presence had, with a few honourable exceptions (typically émigré scholars[1]) been previously ignored. Human beings are slaves to overcompensation, though, and perhaps inevitably the 1990s saw ignorance about Russian organised crime turn to alarmism. Western delight at winning the Cold War soon became dismay: Soviet tanks had never seriously posed a threat to Europe, but post-Soviet gangsters seemed to be a much more real and present danger. Before we knew it, chief constables in the UK were predicting that Russian mobsters would be having gunfights in leafy Surrey suburbs by 2000 and scholars were talking of a global 'Pax Mafiosa' as organised-crime gangs divided the world between them. Of course, this didn't happen, nor did the Russian gangs sell nuclear bombs to terrorists, buy up Third World countries, take over the Kremlin or accomplish any other of the outlandish ambitions with which they were credited.

The 1990s were the glory days of the Russian gangsters, though, and since then, under Putin, gangsterism on the streets has given way to kleptocracy in the state. The mob wars ended, the economy settled, and, despite the current sanctions regime in the post-Crimea Cool War, Moscow is now as festooned with Starbucks cafés and other such icons of globalisation as any European capital. Russian students continue to flock to foreign universities, Russian companies launch their IPOs in London, and those wealthy Russians not under sanctions rub shoulders with their global counterparts at the Davos World Economic Forum, at the Venice Biennale and on the ski slopes of Aspen.

In the years since meeting Volodya, I have been able to study the Russian underworld at home and abroad as a scholar, as a government adviser (including a stint with the British Foreign and Commonwealth Office), as a business consultant and sometimes as a police resource. I've watched it rise and, if not fall, then certainly change, becoming increasingly tamed by a political elite far more ruthless in its own way than the old criminal bosses. All the same, I am still left with the image of that particular war-scarred gunman, at once victim and perpetrator of the new wave of Russian gangsterism, a metaphor for a society about to be plunged into a maelstrom of almost unrestrained corruption, violence and criminality.

ACKNOWLEDGEMENTS

This is a book, in a way, almost three decades in the making, and thus it has accumulated debts and obligations like a wannabe drug dealer down on his luck. The first draft of part of the manuscript was completed in Prague in 2013, and my thanks go to Jiří Pehe and New York University's Prague centre for their welcome and support, and to NYU's Provost's Global Research Initiative for enabling my stay. Another tranche, fittingly enough, was hammered out in Moscow, courtesy of the NYU Center for Global Affairs, which allowed me to parlay my way to a semester away from my office and closer to the action. The work was concluded while back in Prague, in my current position at the Institute of International Relations Prague.

Part of that 2013 draft was originally commissioned by the International Institute for Strategic Studies for a project which never came to fruition, but I would like to thank the IISS in general and Nicholas Redman in particular for their kind invitation in the first place and their willingness for me to draw on that manuscript for elements of this work. I would also like to note that sections of this book plunder articles of mine published over the years in *Jane's Intelligence Review* and by Radio Free Europe/Radio Liberty, and I am grateful for their permissions, too.

From those *afgantsy* who first alerted me to the emerging issue, to all the other Russians, on either side of the law, who have helped me with my research, my humble thanks. Their assistance was invaluable, even if for obvious reasons not something usually to acknowledge publicly. I should note that in a number of cases I discuss criminals using a first name or nickname only and there are other details which may well have been changed from the original. In some cases, this is to protect their identity; in others, it is to protect me from being sued (or worse) by figures whose misdeeds have yet to be successfully proven in a court of law.

Likewise, my thanks go to those equally anonymous sources within Western security and law enforcement communities with whom I have discussed Russian gangsters and their exploits. With relief, let me turn to others whose names can be listed and who, over the years and knowingly or unknowingly, have contributed to this book: Anna Arutunyan, Kelly Barksby, Serguei Cheloukhine, Martha Coe, Antonio De Bonis, Jim Finckenauer, Tom Firestone, Stephen Frank, Jordan Gans-Morse, Yakov Gilinsky, Misha Glenny, Alexander Gurov, Kelly Hignett, Valery Karyshev, Petr Pojman, Joe Serio, Louise Shelley, Svetlana Stephenson, Federico Varese, Vadim Volkov, Brian Whitmore, Katherine Wilkins and Phil Williams. Varese and Volkov have had an especially important role in shaping the field, in my opinion.

I received invaluable research assistance at the Center for Global Affairs from Andrew Bowen, who will go far. Gabriela Anderson cast a keen editorial eye over the manuscript and sanded off many a rough edge. At the Institute of International Relations Prague, Klára Ovčáčková was indispensable in helping to compile the bibliography, and Francis Scarr helped tighten up some chapters. At Yale University Press, thanks are due to Heather McCallum for her enthusiasm for the book and patience at my progress, and Marika Lysandrou for her valuable suggestions. Jonathan Wadman was a first-rate editor, sympathetic and truly meticulous in his work. Plaudits must also go to both the anonymous reviewers of the manuscript, who provided very helpful comments that helped address a few rough points in the draft.

That said, the most heartfelt acknowledgements must go to everyone, not least Penny the dog, who had to suffer my distractions and abstractions while following this particular obsession, and also provide in turn the distractions and abstractions I needed to remind myself that there is a world beyond shoot-outs, sit-downs and set-ups.

Mark Galeotti
Prague, 2017

A NOTE ON TRANSLITERATION

As this book is intended to be accessible to the general reader, in the main text I use a simplified transliteration, without soft signs, '-yi' endings and the like, and using 'yo' for *ë*. The exceptions are those cases where a word or name is so familiar in one form – such as Gorbachev, rather than Gorbachyov – that this would seem perverse. However, the references do use full, conventional transliteration, to ensure researchers can most easily find the sources in question. On the other hand, I have kept the Russian plurals, which typically end in '–i' or '–y', to avoid too much mixing of English and Russian.

INTRODUCTION

The wolf may lose his pelt, but never his nature.

Russian proverb

In 1974, a naked body washed up on the coast at Strelna, to the south-west of Leningrad (as St Petersburg was then known). It was not a pretty sight, having been floating in the Gulf of Finland for a couple of weeks. This body may not have been contending with land's issues of bacteria and insect ravages, but the denizens of the sea had snacked gleefully on the corpse, especially its eyes, lips and extremities. A series of deep knife wounds in the man's abdomen represented a fairly good indicator of the cause of death. Yet with no fingerprints, no clothing, and with his face bloated, battered on rocks and partly eaten away, there were none of the conventional clues to identify him. Checking dental records was a possibility, but this was before the true age of the computer and in any case most of his teeth were cheap metal replacements after a life apparently lived on the rough side. There had been no missing-persons notification filed for him. He didn't even come from the Leningrad region.

Nonetheless, he was identified within just two days. The reason: his body was liberally adorned with tattoos.

The tattoos were the mark of a *vor*, the Russian word for 'thief', but a general term for a member of the Soviet underworld, the so-called 'thieves' world' or *vorovskoi mir*, and life in the Gulag labour camp system. Most of the tattoos were still recognisable and an expert on 'reading' them was summoned; in this case, a former prison warder turned police investigator. Within an hour, they had been decoded. The leaping stag on his breast? That symbolised a term spent in one of the northern labour camps. They were known for their harsh regimes and thus survival was a mark of pride in the macho world of the professional criminal. The knife wrapped in chains on his right forearm? The man had committed a violent assault while behind bars, but not a murder. Crosses on three of his knuckles? Three separate prison sentences served. Perhaps the most telling was the fouled anchor on his upper arm, to which a barbed wire surround had clearly been added later: a navy veteran who had been sentenced to prison for a crime committed while in service. Equipped with these details, it was a relatively quick matter to identify the dead man as one 'Matvei Lodochnik', or 'Matvei the Boatman', a former naval warrant officer who some twenty years earlier had beaten a draftee almost to death when his side-line in selling off quartermasters' supplies had come to light. He was cashiered and spent four years in a labour colony, drifting into the underworld and being sentenced twice more, including a stint at a northern tough-regime camp. He eventually became a fixture of the underworld in Vologda, some 550 kilometres to the east of Strelna.

The police never found out quite why Matvei was in Leningrad and why he died. To be honest, they probably did not really care. But the speed with which he could be identified attests not just to the particular visual language of the Soviet underworld but also to its universality. His tattoos were at once his commitment to the criminal life and also his CV.[1]

Of course, all criminal subcultures have their own languages of sorts, spoken and visual.[2] The Japanese yakuza sport elaborate tattoos of dragons, heroes and chrysanthemums. American street toughs have their gang colours. Every criminal specialism has its technical terms, every criminal milieu its slang. These serve all kinds of purposes, from distinguishing insider from outsider to demonstrating commitment to the group. However, the Russians are truly distinctive in the scale and homogeneity of their languages, both spoken and visual – striking evidence not just of the coherence and complexity of their underworld culture but also their determination actively to reject and even challenge mainstream society. Decoding the detail of the *vory*'s languages tells us much about their priorities, preoccupations and passions.

The *vory* subculture dates back to the earlier, tsarist years, but was radically reshaped in Stalin's Gulags of the 1930s to the 1950s. First, the criminals adopted an uncompromising and unapologetic rejection of the legitimate world, visibly tattooing themselves as a dramatic gesture of defiance. They had their own language, their own customs, their own authority figure. This was the so-called *vor v zakone*, the 'thief within the code' or, literally, 'thief in law' – 'law' referring to their own, not that of the rest of society.

Over time, the code of the *vory* would change, as a new generation were enticed by the opportunities in collaborating with a cynical and vicious state on their own terms. The *vory* would lose their dominance, taking a subordinate role to the barons of the black market and the corrupt Communist Party bosses, but they did not disappear in the grey 1960s and 1970s, and as the Soviet system began to grind towards its inevitable collapse, they emerged anew. Again, they reinvented themselves to meet the needs of the moment. In post-Soviet Russia, they blended in with the new elite. The tattoos disappeared, or were hidden beneath the crisp white shirts of a rapacious new breed of gangster-businessman, the *avtoritet* ('authority'). In the 1990s, everything was up for grabs, and the new *vory* reached out with both hands. State assets were privatised for kopeks on the ruble, businesses forced to pay for protection that they might not need, and, as the Iron Curtain fell, the Russian gangsters crashed out into the rest of the world. The *vory* were part of a way of life that in its own way was a reflection of the changes Russia went through in the twentieth century.

In the process, organised crime – which I have defined elsewhere as 'a continuing enterprise, apart from traditional and legal social structures, within which a number of persons work together under their own hierarchy to gain power and profit for their private gain, through illegal activities'[3] – truly began to come into its own in a Russia that itself was becoming more organised. Since the restoration of central authority under President Vladimir Putin from 2000, the new *vory* have adapted again, taking a lower profile, even working for the state when they must. In the process, Russian organised crime has become at once an international bugbear, a global brand and a contested concept. Some see in it an informal arm of the Kremlin, with Russia airily dismissed as a 'mafia state'. To others, the descendants of the *vory* are just an inchoate collection of troublesome but unremarkable gangsters. Watch Western media representations, though, and you would be tempted to see them as a global threat in every arena, the most savage of thugs, the most cunning of hackers, the most skilled of killers. The irony is that almost all of these perceptions are true in some ways, even if often misleading or mobilised for the wrong reasons.

The question remains: why, in an age when crime is increasingly networked, international and cosmopolitan, should any ethno-cultural fraction of the global underworld deserve special attention?

The challenge of Russian organised crime is a formidable one. At home, it undermines efforts to control and diversify the Russian economy. It is a brake on efforts to bring better governance to Russia. It has penetrated the financial and political structures of the country and also tarnishes the 'national brand' abroad (the Russian gangster and corrupt businessman are ubiquitous stereotypes). It is also a global challenge. Russian or Eurasian organised crime – however this may be defined – operates actively, aggressively and entrepreneurially around the world as one of the most dynamic forces within the new transnational underworld. It arms insurgents and gangsters, traffics drugs and people, and peddles every criminal service from money laundering to computer hacking. For all that, it is as much a symptom as a cause of the failure of the Russian government and political elite to establish and empower the rule of law, while much of the rest of the world remains willing, indeed often delighted, to launder the gangsters' cash and sell them expensive penthouse apartments.

This book is about Russian organised crime, or perhaps more accurately about organised criminals, and especially the extraordinary and brutal criminal culture of the *vory*. This criminal subculture has metamorphosed periodically as times and opportunities have changed. The tattooed thugs, whose experiences in the labour camps meant that modern prisons hold no fear for them, have all but adapted themselves out of existence. Modern Russian criminals often even avoid the term *vor*, ignoring most of the structures and restrictions that used to go with it. They no longer separate themselves from the mainstream, they eschew the tattoos that openly branded them as members of the *vorovskoi mir* (which is why Matvei would be harder to place these days). But to assume that this means that the *vory* have disappeared altogether, or that Russian organised crime is no longer distinctive, would be to make a serious mistake. The new godfathers may call themselves *avtoritety*, have business portfolios stretching from the essentially legitimate to the wholly criminal, get involved in politics and be seen at charitable galas. But they nonetheless are the inheritors of the drive, determination and ruthlessness of the *vory*, men of whom even a New York mafia boss said, 'We Italians will kill you. But the Russians are crazy – they'll kill your whole family.'[4]

The key themes of the book, then, are three. The first is that Russian gangsters are unique, or at least they were. They emerged through times of rapid political, social and economic change – from the fall of the tsars, through Stalin's whirlwind of modernisation, to the collapse of the USSR – which brought specific pressures and opportunities. While on one level a gangster is a gangster throughout the world, and arguably the Russians are becoming part of an increasingly homogenised global underworld, the culture, structures and activities of the Russian criminals were for a long time distinctive, not least in their relationship to mainstream society.

The second central theme is that the gangsters hold up a dark mirror to Russian society. For all that they often sought to present themselves as being outside the mainstream, they were and still are its shadow, defined by its ways and times. Exploring the evolution of the Russian underworld also says something about Russian history and culture, and is especially meaningful today, at a time when the boundaries between crime, business and politics are important but all too often indistinct.

Finally, Russian gangsters have not only been shaped by a changing Russia, they have also shaped it. Part of the value of this book is, I hope, to address the myths about criminal dominance of the new Russia, but at the same time to look at the ways that its 'upperworld' has been influenced by its underworld. As tattooed ex-convicts are replaced by a new breed of globally minded criminal-businessmen, does this represent the house-training of the gangsters or the criminalisation of Russia's economy and society? Is this a 'mafia state' – and what does that even mean?

Do the gangsters run Russia? No, of course not, and I have met many determined, dedicated Russian police officers and judges committed to the struggle against them. However, businesses and politicians alike use many methods that owe more to the *vorovskoi mir* than legal practice, the state hires hackers and arms gangsters to fight its wars, and you can hear *vor* songs and *vor* slang on the streets. Even President Putin uses it from time to time to reassert his streetwise credentials. Perhaps the real question, with which this book ends, is not so much how far the state has managed to tame the gangsters, but how far the values and practices of the *vory* have come to shape modern Russia.

Part One

FOUNDATIONS

CHAPTER 1

KAIN'S LAND

Even a bishop will steal if he's hungry.

Russian proverb

Vanka Kain, gangster, kidnapper, burglar and sometime informant, was the scourge of Moscow in the 1730s and 1740s. When Princess Elizabeth seized power in a coup in 1741, she offered amnesties to outlaws willing to turn on their colleagues. Kain eagerly seized the opportunity to wash away the taint of almost a decade's crimes. While officially becoming a government informant and thief taker, Kain actually continued his crimes, corrupting his handlers at the *Sysknoi prikaz*, the Investigators' Bureau. But such relationships acquire their own consuming dynamic. He began by simply gifting them a share of his loot, usually imported luxuries such as Italian scarves and Rhenish wine. Over time, his handlers grew greedier and more demanding, and Kain was forced into increasingly daring and dangerous crimes to satisfy them. Eventually this came to light and Kain was tried and sentenced to a lifetime's hard labour.

Kain became a romantic hero in Russian folklore. Of course, the criminal as hero appears in popular culture throughout the world, from Robin Hood to Ned Kelly. But unlike Robin Hood, the Russian thief is not fighting against an exploitative usurper. He is not misunderstood, not a victim of a deprived childhood, not a good man in a bad spot. He is just an 'honest thief' in a world where the only distinction is between those thieves who are honest about what they are and those who hide their self-interested criminality beneath boyars' capes, bureaucrats' uniforms, judges' robes and businessmen's suits, whichever best fits the times.

Kain's story could be that of a twentieth-century *vor*, or even today's: the gangster whom the authorities think they can control, yet who ends up corrupting them. Swap horses for BMWs, and fur capes for tracksuits, and Kain's story could be played out in post-Soviet Russia without a hint of anachronism.

Criminal histories

I am not a scholar, but I can tell you this: Russians have always been the best, the bravest criminals around.
                    'Graf' ('Count'), middle-ranking criminal, 1993[1]

Ironically enough, while there is a strong historical pedigree for the *vory*, it is one in which they have never shown much interest. Some criminals revel in their history, even if it is typically mythologised, romanticised or simply invented. Thus, the Chinese triads represent themselves as the descendants of a centuries-long tradition of secret societies struggling against unjust tyrants.[2] The yakuza claim their roots are not in the bandit *kabuki mono* ('crazy ones') who terrorised seventeenth-century Japan or the hired thugs of gambling and pedlar bosses, but the chivalrous samurai warrior caste and the public-spirited *machi yakko* ('servants of the town') militias formed to resist the *kabuki mono*.[3] By contrast, modern Russian organised crime seems to revel in its very ahistoricity, lacking even a folklorish interest in its past. Eschewing memorialisation of its culture (as opposed to its current members[4]), it places itself firmly in the today and turns its back on its history. Even the traditional criminal culture of the *vorovskoi mir*, rich in gory and brutal folklore and customs generated and transmitted within the Gulag prison camps, is being put aside, as a new generation of criminal leaders, the so-called *avtoritety* ('authorities'), disdain the tattoos and routines which marked out the old generation.[5]

For all this, though, Russia's modern underworld of sharp-suited criminal-entrepreneurs and their heavily armed bodyguards and leg breakers did not emerge full-grown from their country's tumultuous transition to the market after 1991 and the collapse of the Soviet system. Instead, they are heirs to a history which in its twists and turns reflects the wider processes shaping Russia, from centuries of rural insularity to the crass, state-led, crash industrialisation of the late nineteenth century and the Gulag-driven modernisation of Stalin's reign. Perhaps most striking, though, is the extent to which Russia's history, while full of vicious bandits and blood-stained murderers, is unusually heavily dominated by fraudsters, embezzlers and gangsters who understood how to use the system to their advantage, when to challenge it, and when to keep a low profile.

One of the lessons of the historical evolution of Russian organised crime is that it emerged from a society in which the state has often been clumsy, threadbare, deeply corrupt – but also fundamentally ruthless, unconstrained by the niceties of legality and process, and willing to use often extravagant amounts of violence to protect its interests when it felt challenged. In the 1990s, it may have seemed for a while that the criminals were in charge. However, under Vladimir Putin, the state has re-emerged with a vengeance, and this has affected both crime and perceptions of crime. Even before the anarchy of the post-Soviet transition, though, a blend of coercion, corruption and compliance was central to the Russian way of crime.

Can Russia be policed?

Never tell a cop the truth.

Russian saying

There were, arguably, two ways Russian organised crime could have evolved, two potential precursors, one rural and one urban. In the nineteenth century, rural banditry looked as if it might have the greater potential. After all, this was a country almost impossible to police. By the end of the nineteenth century, tsarist Russia covered almost one-sixth of the world's landmass. The population of 171 million (1913)[6] overwhelmingly comprised peasants and was scattered across this huge country, often in small, isolated villages and communities. Simply for orders or warrants from the capital, St Petersburg, to reach Vladivostok on the Pacific coast could take weeks, even by horse relay. The railway, telegraph and telephone were to help, but the size of this country has been an obstacle to effective governance in many ways.

Furthermore, the empire was a patchwork of different climates and cultures incorporated largely by conquest. Lenin dubbed it the 'prison of nations',[7] but the Soviet state willingly accepted this imperial inheritance and even today's smaller Russian Federation is a multi-ethnic conglomeration of more than a hundred national minorities. To the south were the unruly and mountainous Caucasian regions, conquered in the nineteenth century but never truly subjugated. To the east were the Islamic provinces of central Asia. Westwards were the more advanced cultures of the occupied Congress Kingdom of Catholic Poland and the Baltic states. Even the Slavic heartlands included the rich farmlands of the Ukrainian black-earth regions, the sprawling and overcrowded metropolises of Moscow and St Petersburg, and the icy Siberian taiga. In all, the empire embraced some 200 nationalities, with Slavs accounting for two-thirds of the whole.[8]

Law enforcement had to deal with a wide range of local legal cultures, often espoused by peoples to whom the tsarist order was an alien and brutal occupier, as well as the practical challenges of apprehending criminals who could travel across jurisdictions. This might have been mitigated if adequate resources had been deployed to this purpose, but this was a state that policed on the cheap. After all, Russia's state has historically been relatively poor, inefficient in its revenue collection and perched upon an often marginal economy. Spending on the police and the courts tended to take a distant second place to the military. By 1900, the proportion of the state budget spent on the police was around 6 per cent – well below European standards and possibly half the per capita expenditure in Austria or France and a quarter of Prussia's.[9] Russia's police had to do rather more, with proportionately rather less.

Successive tsars tried and failed to police their country. From the *Razboinaya izba* or Banditry Office established by Ivan the Terrible (reigned 1533–84)[10] to the rural and urban forces established by Nicholas I (reigned 1825–55), all proved unequal to the task and the state's grip on the countryside was always minimal, largely confined to suppressing uprisings, and dependent on the support (and hired guards) of the local gentry. The police – both urban and rural – tended to be an entirely reactive force, suffering from a lack of people and resources, poor training and morale, high turnover, endemic corruption (all in part symptoms of salaries worse than an unskilled labourer's[11]) and minimal popular support. Furthermore, they were burdened with a whole range of additional duties which distracted them from policing, from the supervision of church worship to organising military recruitment. The standard 'summaries' of police duties published in the 1850s ran to some 400 pages apiece![12]

Furthermore, the police were as corrupt as any of the institutions of the state, something of a Russian tradition. The apocryphal story is that when the moderniser and state builder Peter the Great proposed to hang every man who embezzled from the government, his procurator general gave the blunt reply that this would leave him with no officials because 'we all steal, the only difference is that some of us steal larger amounts and more openly than others'.[13] This was scarcely an exaggeration as even into the nineteenth century, although officially banned from doing so, Russian officials were often implicitly expected to practise what in medieval times had been called *kormleniye* ('feeding'). In other words, they were not expected to live off their inadequate salaries, but to supplement them with side deals and judicious bribe taking.[14] Legend has it that Tsar Nicholas I told his son, 'I believe you and I are the only people in Russia who don't steal.'[15] The first government inquiry into corruption was not conducted until 1856 and its view was that anything less than 500 rubles should not even be considered a bribe at all, merely a polite expression of thanks.[16] For the sake of comparison, at this time, a rural police commissioner was paid 422 rubles a year.[17] This became a particular problem when people overstepped the boundaries of 'acceptable corruption'. For example, Major General Reinbot, the *gradonachalnik* (police chief) of Moscow 1905–8, became notorious for using his position to extort exorbitant payments, setting a dangerous example to his subordinates.[18] Two merchants who testified before an investigation of Reinbot's graft noted that:

> the police took bribes before, too, but this was done in a comparatively decent way ... When the holidays came around, people used to bring them what they could afford, what they could spare – the police used to accept it and express their gratitude. But this extortion commenced since the [1905] revolution, At first, they grafted cautiously, but when they learned that the new General, that is, Reinbot, accepted bribes himself, they no longer took bribes but actually commenced to rob the people.[19]

Reinbot himself was dismissed amidst a public investigation, but most corrupt police officials kept a much lower profile. Besides, Reinbot's fate was hardly a deterrent: when he finally came to special court in 1911, beyond the loss of his special rights and titles, he received a fine of 27,000 rubles and a one-year prison sentence. The fine was little hardship – from one deal alone, Reinbot was alleged to have pocketed 200,000 rubles – and Tsar Nicholas II subsequently interceded to ensure he never had to go to prison.

Petty corruption was endemic within the police as a whole, from turning a blind eye in return for a consideration, to outright extortion. Even essentially honest officers saw no real problem in breaking the law in pursuit of their duties, manufacturing confessions or applying the 'law of the fist' (*kulachnoye pravo*) to teach miscreants a quick lesson with a beating. Their watchword was 'the more severity, the greater the authority of the police',[20] but authority did not mean respect or support. Alienated from the masses, feeling largely unsupported by a state which paid them little and expected much, it is perhaps unsurprising (if indefensible) that the police cut corners and lined their own pockets.

Peasant justice

He's our criminal, and it's up to us to punish him.

Peasant saying[21]

Russian culture is characteristically rich in its forms of peasant resistance to their masters, whether that be the state or the local landlords, grandees and officials who afflicted them. At one end of the spectrum came the sporadic explosions of rural violence known as *bunt*, which Pushkin characterised as 'Russian rebellion, senseless and merciless'.[22] Russia has faced widespread rebellions at various times, such as the Pugachev Rising of 1773–4 or the 1905 Revolution, but more common were localised cases of violence, such as the depredations of outlaws or the visitations of the 'red rooster' (slang for arson, a crime used by peasants as 'an effective weapon of social control and a language of protest within their communities, as well as against those they deemed outsiders'[23]).

Most of Russia was in practice policed by the community's fists and by the landowner's whip. Even the chief of the paramilitary Gendarmes was of the view in 1874 that local police lacked 'even the possibility to organize any police surveillance at all of localities with heavily populated manufacturing centers', so that they were but 'passive spectators of the criminal acts that are committed there'.[24] Instead, order in the village was largely the preserve of *samosud* ('self-judging'), a surprisingly nuanced form of lynch law, whereby the members of the commune applied their own moral code to offenders, regardless or even in defiance of the state's laws. This has been best studied by Cathy Frierson, who concluded that – contrary to the opinions of many police and state officials of the time – it was not mindless violence but a process with its own logic and its own principles.[25] Above all, this sometimes brutal form of social control was essentially geared towards protecting the interests of the community: those crimes which threatened the survival or social order of the village were dealt with most harshly. In particular, that meant horse theft, which threatened the very future of the village, by depriving it of a source of foals, power, transport and, in due course, meat and leather. Death was the usual penalty, and often in some notably painful and inventive way. There was, for example, the thief whose arms and legs were skinned before his head was split by an axe,[26] or another beaten to within an inch of his life and then thrown to the ground before a charging horse for a poetic *coup de grâce*.[27]

Was this a crime, or was it the commune policing itself? Needless to say, the state resented and feared the notion of peasants taking the law into their own hands, but there was very little it could do, given the strength of the peasants' own moral code and the practical difficulties of mounting day-to-day policing of such a huge country. The police were thinly stretched across the countryside, did not seem able to promise real justice or restitution (tellingly, only around 10 per cent of stolen horses were recovered[28]) and rarely made great efforts to win themselves friends in the village. The rural guards known as *uryadniki*, for example, while drawn from peasant stock, had, by taking on the tsar's uniform, aligned themselves instead with the state. (It is worth noting at this stage that the injunction against taking arms for the state would also appear in *vor* culture.) The peasants typically called them 'dogs', and the *uryadniki* returned the favour: a contemporary observer complained that they 'boast of their commanding superiority and almost always treat the peasants with disdain'.[29] It is thus hardly surprising that one contemporary source suggested that no more than one in ten of all rural crimes were ever reported.[30] Nonetheless, the internal control mechanisms of the village – tradition, family, respect for the elders and ultimately *samosud* – ensured that the absence of effective state policing did not mean outright lawlessness.

This is especially because the most common rural crimes, beyond petty interpersonal squabbles of the kind usually resolved by the commune itself, were those such as poaching or theft of wood from the landlords' or tsar's forests, with which the peasants' moral code saw nothing wrong. These offences accounted for 70 per cent of male property convictions in late tsarist Russia.[31] The Russian language contains two very distinct words for crime: *prestupleniye*, an essentially technical definition, a breach of the law, and *zlodeyanie*, which carries with it a moral judgement.[32] Tellingly, the peasant proverb had it that 'God punishes sins, and the state punishes guilt'.[33] Such poaching may have been *prestupleniye*, but the peasants certainly did not see it as *zlodeyanie* because the landlord had more than enough wood for his personal needs, and 'God grew the forest for everyone'.[34] It could even be interpreted as an act of social banditry, a petty redistribution of wealth from the exploiter to the exploited. In the eyes of the eighteenth-century traveller the Marquis de Custine, the serfs had to be 'on guard against their masters, who [were] constantly acting towards them with open and shameless bad faith', and so they in turn would 'compensate themselves by artifice what they suffer through injustice'.[35]

Policing the countryside

How was I to enforce the law over a population of 60,000 scattered in 48 settlements with but four sergeants and eight guardsmen?

Rural constable, 1908[36]

Of course, none of this could be considered 'organised crime' in any meaningful sense – even when such acts as serial *samosud* murders were undoubtedly crimes committed in an organised manner, they were not for private gain. Even long-term and organised poaching only marginally approaches the criteria, especially as it was generally managed within the context of traditional village authority structures. While Nicholas I's reforms had been a significant start, that is all they were. They certainly did not bring law and order to the deep forests, dark fields and unmarked frontiers of Russia. A force which by the turn of the century had grown to 47,866 officers of different rank and variety was expected to police a country of 127 million souls.[37] The cities may have been moderately heavily policed (although even this is open to debate, as will be discussed later), but the real problem was in the countryside. There, 1,582 *stanovye pristavy* (rural constables) and 6,874 *uryadniki* were expected to patrol Russia's immense rural hinterland and keep almost 90 million people in line.[38] On average, each *stanovoi pristav* was thus responsible for some 55,000 peasants!

As a result, the countryside was open to settled or wandering bandit gangs, sometimes rooted in a community and preying on outsiders, otherwise happy to rob from anyone and everyone. This was hardly new: banditry has long been a feature of Russian life. Earlier Russian banditry can rarely be considered organised crime. Although relatively little hard data is available, there is little sense of the kind of sizeable, autonomous criminal groupings operating for an appreciable period that Anton Blok identified in the eighteenth-century Netherlands,[39] for example, or as represented by the sixteenth-century Italian bandit-chieftain Francesco Bertazuolo, who commanded several hundred men divided into separate 'companies', as well as a network of spies.[40] Even the infamous Vasily Churkin, a highwayman who terrorised the Moscow region in the 1870s, was much less influential than popular folklore had made him out to be.[41] Rather than being the daring master of a sizeable bandit gang, he was actually a murderous thug who rarely had more than a handful of followers. This was the norm, and most gangs were small and often ephemeral collections of outlaws and misfits which individually posed only a minor threat to the rural order. The challenge was, rather, the very number of such small groups.

A particular exception to this exclusion of rural banditry from the definition of organised crime were the gangs of horse thieves, which represented such a concern to Russian peasants that they reserved for their captured members the most savage *samosud* murders.[42] The lifeless bodies of these victims of lynch law would typically be left at the nearest crossroads (sometimes symbolically festooned with bridles or horsehair nooses) as a warning to other prospective horse thieves to continue on their way. However, the threat of *samosud* also forced the criminals to organise.

Horse thieves and the bandit tradition

Periodic epidemics, crop failure and other disaster cannot compare with the harm that horse thieves bring to the countryside. The horse thief holds peasants in perpetual, uninterrupted fear.

Georgy Breitman, 1901[43]

The horse thief lived a violent, dangerous life, at risk from both the police and peasant lynch mobs. He would typically form a gang and take over a village, then establish complex networks for trading stolen horses into other regions where they would not be recognised. This is, incidentally, an interesting parallel to the modern Russian gangster, who typically tries to create a home base, by corrupting or threatening local populations and political elites, as the hub for often transnational criminal networks.

These horse-rustling gangs had to have the numbers, strength and cunning to evade not just the authorities but, far more dangerous, the peasants themselves. In some cases, they numbered several hundred members.[44] One investigator, for example, wrote of the gang led by a certain Kubikovsky, which included almost sixty criminals and had its headquarters in the village of Zbelyutka. There, they made their lair in an underground cavern within which they could hide as many as fifty horses at a time. If this was full or unusable, then each local village had an agent, known as a *shevronista*, who could be called on to hide horses or provide information.[45] Not that they usually had to conceal them for long. Given that horses, while greatly in demand, were also relatively identifiable, the gangs – much like modern car thieves – needed to be able to conceal their original ownership (typically by selling them to a horse trader who could rebrand them and hide them amongst his regular stock) or else resell them far enough away from their original owner that it would be impossible for them to be traced. Thus, a study of criminal networks in Saratov province found that:

> Stolen horses are taken on a certain road to the Volga or the Sura rivers; in almost every settlement along that road there is a den of thieves who immediately transfer the horses to the next village . . . All stolen horses end up . . . beyond the province's borders, transferred either across the Sura into Penza and Simbirsk provinces, or across the Volga into Samara, while Saratov itself receives horses from these three provinces.[46]

For a village to harbour horse thieves might bring it greater prosperity (not least as they squandered their gains on local alcohol and women) and perhaps even security. In some cases, the horse thieves operated as primitive protection racketeers, demanding tribute in return for leaving communities' horses alone.[47] Faced with the very real threat of such attacks and the economic costs to the community of having to mount constant guard on their precious horses, as well as the absence of effective state police, many regarded paying such 'tax' – or hiring a horse thief as a herder, which also gave him the opportunity to hide stolen horses amongst those of the village[48] – as the lesser evil.

Horse thieves were sometimes caught, whether by the peasants or the police, but overall they prospered, growing in numbers in the years leading up to the Great War as part of a wider tide of rural crime.[49] While this was a specialised form of rural banditry, in their rough-and-ready way the horse thieves did represent a kind of organised crime. They operated with a clear sense of hierarchy and specialisation, possessed distinct turfs of their own, maintained networks of informants, corrupted police officers, visited retribution on those who resisted or informed on them[50] and traded stolen horses with other gangs and corrupt 'legitimate' dealers.[51] The more successful ones operated for years, and while they may have developed links with local communities, whether through extortion or as neighbours and protectors, they undoubtedly were not *of* the community, and in many cases recruited broadly, drawing on runaways, ex-convicts, deserters and petty outlaws.

This particular organised-crime phenomenon would prove an evolutionary dead end, though, and not survive long into the twentieth century. The First World War made dealing in horses difficult and dangerous, given the extent to which they were being bought and requisitioned for the army, and the chaos of revolution (1917), and the consequent civil war (1918–22) and famine (1920–2), further disrupted their commercial networks. Rural gangs were able to thrive for a while in this period of relative anarchy, a few becoming virtual bandit armies.[52] In some cases individual bandits or even gangs ended up being coopted into the military or administrative structures of one side or another: just as Vanka Kain for a while worked for the state, so too did notorious criminals such as St Petersburg's Lyonka Panteleyev, who for a while served in the Cheka, the Bolshevik political police, before likewise returning to a life of crime (and being shot in 1923 for his pains).[53] However, as the Soviet regime began to assert its authority over the countryside, these bandits faced unprecedented pressure from the state. While rural policing as a whole remained a low priority, when more serious challenges emerged, the response of the revolutionary state was much more urgent and exigent. To suppress the larger bandit armies of the Volga, for example, the Bolsheviks deployed more than four Red Army divisions, along with aircraft.[54] The primal energies of *bunt* and banditry still remained, ready to break forth when the state seemed weak or when it put unbearable pressures on the countryside. In the whirlwind of Stalinist terror and collectivisation, for example, rural criminality once again became a serious challenge. In 1929, Siberia was declared 'unsafe due to banditry' and gangs roamed across much of the rest of Russia.[55] In Sheila Fitzpatrick's words, 'theirs was a harsh frontier world, where bandits – often dekulakized peasants [repressed 'rich peasants'] hiding in the forest – were likely to take potshots at officials while sullen peasants looked the other way'.[56] However, although bandits did often seek to steal horses, the specific phenomenon of the organised horse thief gang was not to survive long into the Soviet era.

The horse thieves already exhibited some of the traits of the later Russian gangsterism of the *vorovskoi mir*. They were a criminal subculture that deliberately held itself apart from mainstream society, but learned how to manipulate it. In the process, they became connected to that society through cooperation with corrupt officials and winning over the allegiance of disillusioned populations. When they could, the horse thieves would take over political structures and establish 'bandit kingdoms' from which to manage networked operations. Extravagantly violent when they needed to be, they were also capable of very complex and subtle activities. Nonetheless, for the real roots of modern Russian organised crime, the real ancestors of the *vory*, one needs instead to look to the cradle of its Kains, the cities.

CHAPTER 2

EATING KHITROVKA SOUP

The city is wonderful for the shameless.

Russian proverb

Not twenty minutes' walk from the Kremlin was the Khitrovka, perhaps the most notorious slum in all Russia. Levelled during the 1812 Moscow fire, the land was bought by Major General Nikolai Khitrovo in 1823 with plans to build a market there. He died before his designs could be enacted, though, and by the 1860s, following the emancipation of the serfs, the area had become a spontaneous labour exchange. It was a magnet for newly arrived hopefuls and dispossessed peasants, at once desperate for a place to seek work and prey for urban predators of every kind. Dosshouses and cheap taverns lined a maze of small, dark courtyards and alleyways, teeming with the unemployed, unwashed and usually drunk or drugged. It was perennially cloaked in a heavy and evil-smelling fog from the stagnant river Yauza and the cheap tobacco and open cooking pots of its denizens as they cooked the unsavoury mix of salvaged and spoiled food known as 'dog's delight'. The common saying that 'once you've eaten Khitrovka soup, you'll never leave' was as much a statement about the mortality rates as about the miserable chances for social elevation.[1] This was a living hell, a slum in which up to 10,000 men, women and children were crammed into lean-tos, shacks, tenements and four disease-ridden *trushchoby*: the Yaroshenko (originally Stepanov), Bunin, Kulakov (originally Romeiko) and Rumyantsev houses. In these dosshouses, they bunked down on double- and triple-decked wooden sleeping platforms, above infamous drinking dens including those tellingly known as Siberia, Katorga ('Penal Servitude') and Peresylny ('Transit').[2] The last was a particular haunt for beggars, Siberia for pick-pockets and their fences, and Katorga for thieves and escaped convicts, who could find anonymity and employment in the Khitrovka.

The urban gangster was a product of the slums of a rapidly urbanising late-tsarist Russia, the so-called *yamy*, where life was cheap and miserable. It was in the drinking dens and dosshouses of the *yamy* that the subculture of the *vorovskoi mir* emerged, the 'thieves' world'. Its code, of separation from and contempt for mainstream society and its values – nation, church, family, charity – became one of the few unifying forces within this milieu, and would become a central part of the macho beliefs of the twentieth-century Russian *vory*. It was not that the criminals had no codes or values, but rather that they picked, chose and invented them as best suited their needs.

For example, Benya Krik, the gangster hero of Isaak Babel's *Odessa Tales*, is in many ways the epitome of two intertwined folk archetypes: the wily Jewish community leader and the benevolent underworld godfather. Fictional, yet based on the real-life 'Mishka Yaponchik' ('Mishka the Japanese') discussed later, Krik leaps from this series of stories written in the 1920s with a zest and vigour that no mere page can contain. He is the product and symbol of the predominantly Jewish Moldavanka neighbourhood of Odessa, the Black Sea port – and smuggling hub – that was in its day as cosmopolitan and free-wheeling a city as one could find within the Russian Empire. The Moldavanka may not have been much to look at, with its 'unsavory terrain, a quarter filled with dark alleys, filthy streets, crumbling buildings and violence',[3] but it was known for its vitality, cunning, romance and opportunity.

Sins of the city: crime and urbanisation

A husky, unskilled village boy comes to the city seeking a job or training –
and the city gives him only street fumes, the glitter of shop windows,
homebrew, cocaine and the cinema.

L. M. Vasilevsky (1923)[4]

There can be little doubt that the countryside can seethe with the same violence, sins and greeds as the cities. However, urbanisation and its bedfellow industrialisation have a very different culture. Rural life is driven by the daylight hours, by the seasons, by the life experiences of the elders, and by a small and usually relatively stable community's need to pull together to survive. By contrast, the Russian town was to be reshaped by rapid industrialisation and expansion as waves of migrant workers flocked in from the villages. It was characterised by massive turnover in populations, anomie, a loss of old moral norms and a sense of invisibility amongst all these new faces. While breaking down the former patterns of hierarchy and deference, industrial life is undoubtedly also organised and it breeds a new sense of structure and discipline, in which leadership goes not necessarily to the old but the able.

Even in the eighteenth century, in Vanka Kain's days, the city had its own underworld. It was a realm of runaway serfs and army deserters, impoverished soldiers' widows (who often became fences, buying and selling stolen goods) and opportunistic bandits.[5] Institutions such as Moscow's Great Wool Court – the city's main cloth mill, and its largest single employer – and the Moscow Garrison School – established for the sons of fallen soldiers – appeared on the surface to be bastions of the social status quo, but also became recruiting grounds for street criminals, havens for wanted men and warehouses for stolen goods. But then Russia went through a belated but brutal industrial revolution from the mid-nineteenth century, accelerated by the need to modernise the country's defensive capabilities after the debacle of the Crimean War (1853–6). Between 1867 and 1897, the urban population of European Russia doubled, doubling again by 1917.[6] If some of these new workers were attracted to the cities by their opportunities for economic and social advancement, many others were pushed there by a growing pressure on the land. As Russia's population grew,[7] the proportion of landless peasants almost trebled.[8] For many, moving to the city for a season or even to start a whole new life was simply an economic necessity.

It is no coincidence that the cities provided the cradle not only of new political forces – including what was to become the Communist Party – but also new types of crime and criminals. Between 1867 and 1897, both St Petersburg and Moscow almost trebled in size, from 500,000 to 1.26 million and 350,000 to 1.04 million respectively.[9] In the main, workers lived in crowded, poorly ventilated and unhygienic barrack blocks provided by their employers, perhaps even sharing a bunk bed by shift.[10] Yet these were the lucky ones. In the 1840s, a commission investigating the conditions of the urban poor in St Petersburg painted a picture of mounting overcrowding and squalor, with a single tenement often holding as many as twenty adults. In one case, fully fifty adults and children were squeezed into a room six metres square.[11] By 1881, a quarter of the entire population of St Petersburg was reduced to living in cellars, with between two and three workers in the city for each available sleeping place.[12] Conditions were terrible, with hours long (a fourteen-hour day was typical, longer ones common), pay minimal and safety provisions almost non-existent.[13]

The new workers lived lives full of exploitation and misery, yet empty of the village commune's mechanisms of support and social control. In the village, tradition and family provided a context for life, while the elders represented authority. In the cities, rural traditions seemed meaningless, most of the workers were young and single, and the alternative stabilising factors (such as a trained 'worker aristocracy' or the responsibilities generated by starting a family) had not yet had time to emerge. Many turned to the bottle for escape. Perhaps one in four of St Petersburg's residents had been arrested at some point in the late 1860s, usually for a drink-related crime.[14] There were other escapes, too, for the generally unmarried young male workers.[15] Syphilis and other sexually transmitted diseases spread wildly, and prostitution – both by 'yellow card' registered practitioners and by amateurs – increased equally markedly.[16] Street gangs also formed, although we know relatively little about them. The Roshcha and Gaida gangs, for example, became temporarily powerful in St Petersburg's poor quarters, staging regular brawls. They emerged around 1900, but by 1903 they had already fragmented – some members gravitating to more serious, mercenary crimes, others growing away from this life of male bonding through vodka and violence – only for new and even more violent gangs to rise in their place.[17] This was a time of rapid turnover even in the underworld, as yesterday's kids become today's street captains, and then tomorrow's corpses lying unremarked in the snow.

The worst of the worst were the *yamy* ('pits' or 'depths'). These slums exercised a morbid fascination for Russia's writers. In *Crime and Punishment* (1866), Dostoevsky wrote of St Petersburg's Haymarket *yama* being 'thick with whorehouses' and full of 'dirty, fetid yards',[18] and in his *Slums of Petersburg* (1864), Vsevolod Krestovsky characterised it as a place of vice and villainy.[19] Alexander Kuprin's novel *Yama* (1905) rather coyly describes Odessa's slums as 'a place exceedingly gay, tipsy, brawling, and in the night-time not without danger'.[20] However, Maxim Gorky, himself a man whose family had fallen from middle-class affluence into poverty, and who lived life as a vagrant before his transformation into an iconic writer, presents a rather more hopeless picture in his play *The Lower Depths* (1902). In it, a *yama*'s 'tipsiness' is not so much 'gay' as born of a desperate and unredemptive search for oblivion.[21] Likewise Mikhail Zotov, a writer of the popular publications known as *lubki*, portrayed the 'hopeless drunkards and vicious thieves' of Moscow's Khitrovka.[22] Near enough every major city had its *yama*. These were indeed the lower depths, to which sank the lost and the destitute, the twenty-kopek whores, the raddled alcoholics and the drug addicts who would kill for their next fix.

To Communist agitator Leon Trotsky, Odessa was 'perhaps the most police-ridden city in a police-ridden Russia'[23] and certainly it proved a dangerous environment for revolutionaries – and yet it also became a byword for crime of every kind. The explanation for this seeming paradox is that the police, in Odessa and elsewhere, concentrated on political crimes and securing the well-to-do parts of the cities. In the poor neighbourhoods, they chose largely to turn a blind eye to many offences, unless the crimes were especially serious or impinged on the interests of the state or wealthier classes.[24] Mass brawls between rival gangs or workers' groups were quite a frequent and almost ritual occurrence, for example, and they were often allowed to play themselves out to their usual bruised and bloody conclusion: only when they were staged in the centre of town were they likely to be broken up.[25]

At least the police were present from time to time in the poor workers' districts, but, to a large extent, they left the *yamy* and their denizens well alone. What, after all, was a murder, beyond one less problem walking their streets? As it was, they often confined themselves to collecting the bodies of the dead every morning. When forced to go into the slums more decisively – usually only in response to some outbreak of serious violence which could be construed as having some potential political implication – they went as if troops invading hostile territory, in squads, with rifles at the ready.[26] Otherwise, though, as one St Petersburg newspaper noted about the notorious Harbour Fields quarter on the city's Vasilevsky Island, 'police, or more often Cossack, patrols pass this place without stopping, since this "club" is outside the range of their operations: they pass by only in search of sedition'.[27]

Russian rookeries

In the gloomy half-light of the dirty dives, in crowded, bug-infested flophouses, in the tearooms and taverns and the dens of cheap debauchery – everywhere where vodka, women and children are sold – I encountered people who no longer resembled human beings. There, down below, people believe in nothing, love nothing and are not bothered by anything.

Alexei Svirsky, journalist, 1914[28]

This official neglect was not simply because the authorities did not care what happened in the *yamy*, more that they lacked either the resources or the political support to do anything about it. Contrary to popular belief, the tsarist state was by no means staffed entirely by backward-looking fools and greedy paper pushers. Quite the opposite: it is striking how many clear-thinking officials rose within the system, and the Ministry of Internal Affairs (MVD) itself was historically sympathetic to the Russian workers' plight, even if for the most self-interested reasons, as a happy worker is rarely a rioting one. Although scarcely a radical, future interior minister Vyacheslav Plehve, while director of the Department of Police, bemoaned that 'before the rich capitalist, the individual factory worker is powerless', and even the Okhrana political police force was 'a long-time advocate of factory reform and improving workers' conditions'.[29]

The real indictment is that their assessments and proposals were too often ignored. That the growth of the cities would pose a political, criminal and even sanitary threat was apparent from the first. Major General Adrianov, the *gradonachalnik* or police chief of Moscow 1908–15, not only made efforts to improve the honesty and efficiency of his force, he appealed to the Duma (parliament) to bring down high meat prices, and later established anti-epidemic commissions.[30] Most such measures were, however, limited or blocked. Instead, this became a time of creeping martial law, as the tsarist state increasingly sought to side-step its own legal system by relying on emergency powers, through the declarations of 'extraordinary guard' and 'strengthened guard' provisions. These gave governors and *gradonachalniki* sweeping powers[31] but they were largely used in the suppression of protest, not in extending their role or redefining the notion of the maintenance of public order. By 1912, only 5 million Russians out of a total population of 130 million were *not* covered by such martial law provisions.[32]

The question of urban crime only became a truly important political issue at the turn of the century. Even then, this was stimulated not by a sensitive assessment of the real pressures bubbling away but by a moral panic, stoked by a rising tabloid 'boulevard press', about the threat so-called 'hooliganism' posed above all to the genteel folk of St Petersburg.[33] Young workers, who once would confine themselves to 'their' part of the city, began invading the well-to-do central neighbourhoods. Suddenly it seemed that everywhere, rowdies in their trademark greasy jackets and flat caps were crowding the pavements, drinking, whistling at the passing girls, jostling and catcalling and in due course graduating to vandalism, random violence and demanding money with knives and menaces. To Russian educated and elite opinion, this was regarded hysterically as evidence of the imminent collapse of the social order and, not seeking to engage with the underclass, they demanded that 'their' police do something about it: that is, keep the uncontrolled workers out of 'their' city and squander overstretched resources protecting their rights.

A policeman's lot was not a happy one

At present, the work of the ordinary police appears to consist entirely in worrying people about passports, regulating the street-traffic in daytime, and 'running in' drunkards and dissolute females at night . . . The St Petersburg policeman has no beat . . . He is posted at certain points, and only moves about to keep himself warm or from falling asleep.

George Dobson, *Times* correspondent to tsarist Russia[34]

The police were thus confined to deterring and dealing with crimes rather than preventing the development of conditions which generated them. At this they were not, it must be said, very effective. They were often overstretched, forced to rely on the hue and cry to summon cooperative cityfolk as well as their unofficial deputies, the *dvorniki*. These were porters employed by nearly every town apartment building; they were required to report crimes to the police and even the comings and goings to and from their buildings, and also provided occasional muscle for arrests. The *dvorniki* were very much a mixed blessing. While there were many incidents of them raising the alarm and assisting the police, they were also often insalubrious characters themselves. In 1909, the head of Moscow's detectives suggested that *dvorniki* themselves accounted for or assisted in fully 90 per cent of thefts from locked premises.[35]

The precise degree of police overstretch is hard to ascertain. There has been an interesting debate about the actual size of the Russian police force. Robert Thurston's figures suggest that, by the end of 1905, Moscow had one officer per 276 citizens, comparing well with Berlin (325:1) and Paris (336:1).[36] However, Neil Weissman has made a convincing case that such figures should not be taken at face value. The Russians' own ideal was to reach a ratio of 500:1 in the cities (reduced to 400:1 after the uprisings of the 1905 Revolution), but they admitted to problems in achieving such targets.[37] Official figures were often of *establishment* rather than *actual* strength: even in St Petersburg at the end of 1905, the Department of Police was short by 1,200 officers, leaving more than half of its police posts unmanned.[38] The figures also include 'dead souls' introduced by fraudulent commanders (so that they could pocket those ringers' pay) as well as policemen who never pounded the beat but were actually permanently appropriated by senior officers to act as their messengers, cooks and batmen. Weissman suggests that in the towns and cities beyond Moscow and St Petersburg, the ratio was often 700:1 or even worse, a situation exacerbated by rapid urbanisation.[39]

Not only were there not enough police, but the Russians failed to make the best use of them, keeping them badly trained and inefficiently deployed. The *gorodovye*, the basic street cops, did not often patrol like their European or North American counterparts. They simply manned guard posts, each generally within earshot of the next, and waited for trouble to be reported to them or just come by.[40] This essentially passive, static approach to policing meant that the police largely 'slept like hibernating bears',[41] at best resembling security guards more than active public protectors.

It is hardly surprising, then, that the *yamy* and other slums, essentially abandoned by the state, became criminalised enclaves akin to the rookeries and stews of early modern London, where burglars could plan their raids and fence their goods, where muscle could be hired at any tavern, and where life and death were equally cheap. Vladimir Gilyarovsky's study of the Khitrovka included this scathing assessment of its police station: 'The police guardhouse was always quiet at night, as if it wasn't even there. For about twenty years, the city cop Rudnikov ... ruled there. Rudnikov was uninterested in unprofitable night-time calls for help, and the guardhouse door stayed locked.'[42]

The *yamy* came to symbolise both the plight and the perils of the indigent urban poor – as Daniel Brower noted, 'in popular literature Khitrovka acquired junglelike qualities and became a sort of "darkest Moscow"'.[43] These slums also raised a growing concern that the criminalisation of their teeming and discontented population could lead not only to revolutionary ferment but also a professionalisation of the underworld. Odessa's predominantly Jewish Moldavanka district likewise saw law breaking increasingly characterised in the eyes of outsiders as 'professional, businesslike criminality'.[44]

Gangs of the city

Dear Comrade Pinkus: On the fourth of August at nine o'clock in the evening, please be so kind as to bring, without fail, 100 rubles to the tram station across from your house. This modest sum will preserve your life, which is certainly worth more than 100 rubles. Any efforts to evade this payment will lead to major difficulties for you. If you turn to the police, you will be killed immediately.

Extortion notice, 1917[45]

Despite the exaggerated courtesy of this typical demand, the gangs which had turned to extortion, kidnap and intimidation were hardly delicate or educated. Instead, they were products of the drinking dens and barrack housing of the urban slums. From them had emerged a new criminal culture which, unlike its rural counterpart of the horse thieves, adapted to thrive in the post-revolutionary era. This was the *vorovskoi mir*, the 'thieves' world'.

There had, of course, been crime gangs before the late nineteenth century. Many were in effect underworld equivalents of the *artel*, a traditional Russian form of work association already appropriated by beggars' communities.[46] An *artel* was a voluntary group pooling its labour and resources to a common end. Sometimes it was made up of peasants from the same village who migrated together to seek work in the cities, sometimes a work crew paid collectively for their overall production. In this way, the *artel* was a way of recreating the mutual support of the peasant commune, but in smaller and more mobile form. Typically, an *artel* would have an elected leader, a *starosta* ('elder' – although this was an honorific rather than chronological term), who negotiated with employers, handled common arrangements (such as renting accommodation) and distributed any profits.[47] *Artely* typically had their own customs, rules and hierarchies, often reflecting those of their home villages.[48] Likewise, criminal *artely* also probably had their own customs, although evidence is lacking to confirm this, let alone to prove any kind of common pattern. Andrei Konstantinov and Mal'kol'm Dikselius, for example, have claimed that even in the times of Vanka Kain, there was a criminal culture in Moscow that had such rules.[49] However, it has been impossible to back this up with independent corroboration beyond later stories which are apocryphal, intended as entertainment, and if anything probably reflect the perceived criminal culture of the narrators' times. However, the *artel* model was just one form of criminal social organisation which emerged in the cities.

Writing about the fate of the rootless and dispossessed young man in the late tsarist slums, the contemporary Russian criminologist Dmitry Dril lamented that 'he encounters the company of veteran tramps, beggars, vagrants, prostitutes, thieves and horse thieves'.[50] Or, as teacher and youth worker V.P. Semenov put it, he will in turn and inexorably pass 'through the school of the flophouse, the tearoom and the police station'.[51] Within the *yamy*, a new generation would be born into a life of crime. The children of the cohorts of prostitutes would, for example, be rented out when newborn babies as usefully heartstring-tugging accessories to the city's beggars, before eventually graduating into begging themselves. At least they had a parent and perhaps even a home: many of the genuine *besprizorniki*, the uncared-for children, lived truly on the streets, sleeping in rubbish bins or fighting over a discarded barrel for shelter.[52] The children would play 'thief', a common and popular game,[53] before in due course moving into more active participation in the underworld, from standing as a lookout to becoming a *fortach*, one of the wily and agile children used to wriggle through open windows to carry out burglaries.[54]

The presence of specialised varieties of law breakers, with their own distinctive modus operandi and title, is often a good index of the rise of an organised criminal subculture. The *yamy* certainly proved fecund breeding grounds for this culture, sufficient to maintain an increasingly specialised and varied criminal ecosystem. Although many crimes were carried out opportunistically, the thieves' world embraced a wide range of criminal trades. Indeed, there was a bewildering array of such specialisms, from the *shchipachy* and *shirmachy* (pickpockets) to the common *skokari* (burglars) and *poyezdoshniki* (who would snatch travellers' bags from the tops of carriages). With specialisation also came hierarchy, as underworld professions became increasingly differentiated. Unlike the purist *blatnye* who came to dominate the world of the prison camps in the early twentieth century, and who deliberately turned their back on legitimate society, for most within the *vorovskoi mir* of the late nineteenth century, the dream was to be a member of polite society, all the while mocking its values and robbing it blind. Even Benya Krik, the criminal hero of Isaak Babel's *Odessa Tales*, made sure that when his sister was married, the occasion was marked with a grandly traditional feast, 'in accordance with the custom of olden times'.[55] Perhaps as a result, the 'aristocracy' of the *vorovskoi mir* were its fraudsters and those able to pass as the well-to-do in order to carry out their crimes. In Odessa, for example, particular respect was due to the *maravikhery*, elite pickpockets who masqueraded as gentlemen while they worked the circuit of high society, from the theatre to the stock exchange.[56] Of course, there was also a practical reason for the authority of the fraudsters, as those who were successful could make a great deal of money, more than they could easily spend. As a result, some became virtual bankers of the *vorovskoi mir*, lending their dirty money and in the process gaining clients and investing in further crimes.

Indeed, the criminals could more generally avail themselves of an increasingly sophisticated range of criminal services. For instance, *raky* (crayfishes), were tailors who could take a stolen item of clothing and overnight turn it into something else, undetectable to the authorities and ready for sale. Bunin's *trushchoba* in the Khitrovka was known for its *raky*,[57] while St Petersburg's Kholmushi tenement quarter was a favoured place to fence stolen goods through ramshackle local shops, along with the Tolkucha market.[58] Likewise, just as, for example, the taverns of Odessa's port district acted as virtual labour exchanges, at which contractors and *artel* bosses could recruit whoever they needed for that day or week,[59] so too did the drinking dens of the *yamy* become places where loot and information were exchanged, muscle hired and deals struck. Meanwhile, tavern keepers cultivated profitable sidelines in their own right, as fences and bankers to their shadowy clientele.

The *vorovskoi mir*

You want to understand today's world of criminals? Read Babel, read Gorky, read about Odessa under the tsars. Today's thieves' world was forming then.

Soviet policeman, 1989[60]

Striking evidence of the coherence and complexity of this underworld culture is to be found in its two languages: the criminal cant known as *fenya* or *ofenya*, and a visual one, encoded in the often complex tattoos with which career criminals inscribed their bodies. The hierarchies, internal organisation and evolution evident in these languages, which are explored in more depth in chapter 5, reflected the *vorovskoi mir* as a whole. This pre-Revolutionary underworld was not yet dominated by substantial and durable criminal organisations, but consisted of myriad small gangs and groups. The parallel with the *artel* only increased with industrialisation, as it often provided the social structure through which peasants could travel to the cities to work, especially in its early years.[61] *Artel*-style collections of thieves worked together long term or else would form as the apprentices and minions of a veteran who would teach them their craft, such as 'Morozhenshchik' ('Ice-Cream Seller'), an Odessan Fagin who taught a gang of his nephews and other street children the arts of pickpocketing and burglary.[62] These groups tended to work within a specific criminal profession or at least within connected ones (so that a single group might include both conmen running shell games or similar street gambling scams and pickpockets who would prey on the crowds of onlookers), although the kind of group which later became known as a *kodlo* was often more heterogeneous, with perhaps as many as thirty criminals united by mutual interest and experience rather than specialism.[63] These criminal *artely* had their own rules and rituals, and from them the customs of the *vorovskoi mir* would emerge, such as the swearing of oaths to the collective and initiation rituals requiring evidence of a command of *fenya*.

This was a time of social ferment and one in which people could and did move from city to city as new economic opportunities arose or, in the case of criminals, as they made enemies or became too well known to the local authorities. Combine that with the way the penal system became a powerful channel for transmitting the codes and folkways of the *vorovskoi mir* and it is perhaps no wonder that not only the core criminal culture but also local crime phenomena proved infectious. Of course, there was massive variation in the scale and nature of organised criminality across this equally massive empire. Odessa for example, thriving and cosmopolitan, acquired a reputation for its flamboyant and entrepreneurial crooks: 'the registers of investigative police agents from St Petersburg and Moscow to Warsaw, Kherson and Nikolaev were heavy with the names of Odessa thieves, "kings" and "queens" of crime whose mug shots graced "rogues' gallery" albums circulated widely throughout the empire'.[64] Especially notorious criminals were not only wanted by the authorities across Russia, they even became celebrities within the national underworld. Figures such as Faivel Rubin, the notorious pickpocket,[65] and the bandit Vasily Churkin[66] were at once inspirations for the underworld and the subject of exaggerated concern and prurient fascination within the legal world.

'Mishka Yaponchik' – his real name was Mikhail Vinnitsky – was a particular such legend in his own lifetime. The son of a carter, given his nickname 'the Japanese' apparently for his bony face and dark, slanted eyes, he was an ambitious and audacious gangster from an early age, with the charisma to attract others of the same mould to his side. He soon acquired a formidable reputation in Odessa and the police would reportedly turn a blind eye so long as he avoided them and left the neighbourhoods of the rich be. As he rose to become the foremost mobster of the city, he became rich on tributes from other gangs and extorted from businesses. He made no efforts to hide this status, promenading through the most fashionable haunts in a dandyish cream-coloured suit, bow tie and straw boater, always accompanied by his bodyguards. He would hold court in Café Fankoni, where a table was always reserved for him, alongside the city's other successful businessmen. From time to time, like any magnanimous monarch, he would hold street parties, with tin buckets of vodka and tables of free food. 'Yaponchik' would end up a casualty of the post-revolutionary civil war, killed in Voznesensk in 1920, but for five years the so-called 'King of the Moldavanka' would stand as a symbol of the Odessan gangster made good. He would even inspire a successor in the late Soviet years, the notorious Vyacheslav Ivankov, the man sent to America as a virtual underworld plenipotentiary, who also took the nickname 'Yaponchik'.[67]

A rigidly hierarchical tsarist society, in which officials from clerks to station masters had their uniforms and place, was reflected in an underworld which not only had its own castes and ranks but also learned to turn the characteristics of the 'upperworld' against itself. The fraudsters were the acknowledged aristocrats of the *vorovskoi mir*, not only because they could pass as the well-to-do or even aristocrats, and then rob their betters blind. They were typically smart, sometimes very well educated – just as modern Russian organised crime includes people with PhDs – and demonstrated that the corrupt, oligarchic nature of tsarist Russia meant that, if you could persuade people that you had power, you could get away with anything. Again, the parallels with modern Russia are striking, especially as these conmen also acted as patrons, bankers and brokers for the thuggish gangsters, just as many contemporary Russian businessmen can, when they need to, whistle up a corrupt cop or judge or a handful of leg breakers in leather jackets. It is perhaps not too fanciful to suggest that in the 1990s, when going through a period of terrible social and economic turmoil and political disruption, post-Soviet Russia had more than a spoonful of Khitrovka soup.

CHAPTER 3

THE BIRTH OF THE *VORY*

Where God builds himself a church, the devil will have his chapel.

Russian proverb

There were pirates on the Black Sea. In 1903, the passenger steamer *Tsarevich Georgy* was just outside the Georgian Abkhaz port of Sukhumi in the southern reaches of the Russian Empire. Suddenly, more than twenty raiders swarmed aboard, looting the upscale vessel and its passengers before making off in their small boats. In 1907, even though it had six armed guards, the *Chernomor* was similarly plundered just out of Tuapse, further up the coast. Later that year in the Caspian Sea, sixteen bandits raided the *Tsarevich Alexander* on the Krasnovodsk–Baku route. Sometimes, though, more subtle means were necessary. In 1908, the *Nikolai I* was in harbour at Baku, its safe stuffed with money and bonds to the value of 1.2 million rubles (equivalent to some $30 million today). Three men in police uniforms boarded, claiming to be conducting an inspection. They were accompanied by a man who turned out to be 'Akhmed', reputed to be the best safebreaker in Europe. He was certainly good enough for the ship's strongroom, and they emptied it before making a clean getaway.[1]

In 1918, Julius Martov, a dissident revolutionary leader, claimed a key figure of the Black Sea pirates was one Iosef Dzhugashvili. The latter brought a libel case against Martov, who found himself disallowed from calling witnesses from the southern region to support his case, which was unsurprisingly thrown out of court. Martov would survive the setback, though, and eventually leave Russia in 1920, which was perhaps wise given that Dzhugashvili, who had taken the revolutionary nickname 'Koba', was by then much more widely known by his later pseudonym: Joseph Stalin.

In comparison with many of his fellow Bolshevik leaders, Stalin was not a product of the university or the salon. He rubbed shoulders with outlaws and gangsters, and as a revolutionary he was a key figure in the campaign of 'expropriations' – violent bank robberies – to raise funds for the Bolshevik Party. Stalin does not seem to have been a triggerman or safecracker himself, but rather a fixer who found common cause with 'thieves' in it for the money, not (or at least not only) for the ideology. In 1907, for example, he organised the ambush of a stagecoach carrying cash to the Imperial Bank in Tbilisi, in which almost forty people died under a hail of gunfire and improvised grenades. The gangsters fled with a third of a million rubles, although most of this haul ended up unusable because it was in large-denomination notes whose serial numbers were quickly circulated throughout Europe. The actual rough stuff was in the hands of a ruthless Armenian, Simon Ter-Petrossian, known as 'Kamo', who already had his own gang and was as much a *vor* as a revolutionary.[2]

More than just a bloody page in Russia's thoroughly gory revolutionary history, this underlines a key phenomenon: the extent to which the Bolsheviks – and Stalin in particular – were willing to use criminals as allies and agents. In the process, they would not only bargain away the soul of the revolution for immediate gain, they would also set the scene for the transformation of the country's underworld, a process that would even help shape the Russia that emerged from seventy years of Soviet rule in 1991.

War, revolution and crime

If Lenin had shot more criminals and hired fewer, we might have seen a very different Soviet Union.

Soviet police officer, 1991[3]

The *vorovskoi mir* would go through its own revolutions after the chaos of the Great War, the 1917 revolutions and the civil war. Banditry would rise and fall, contingent on the levels of control and poverty imposed on the countryside, and *bunt* would explode at times of greatest pressure, although only to be repressed with a savagery and, worse yet, efficiency the tsars had never managed. Fraudsters would remain the genteel aristocrats of crime – at least in the popular imagination, reinforced by Ilf and Petrov's tales of fictional 1920s conman Ostap Bender, preying on greedy wheeler-dealers and self-important bureaucrats alike – until the dead weight of Stalinist orthodoxy would push most such stories off the written page and back into the oral tradition.[4] *Samosud* would likewise re-emerge during the anarchy of revolution, not just in the countryside but also in Russia's cities. With horror (if also perhaps hyperbole), the author Maxim Gorky claimed at the end of 1917 that there had been 10,000 lynchings since the collapse of the tsarist order.[5] This too would be suppressed by the Soviets, albeit still able to survive hidden within other expressions of vigilantism.[6]

For all the subsequent myth making about the Bolsheviks' 'Great October Revolution', this was no broad-based mass rising with joyous streets full of mobs waving red flags and singing 'The Internationale'. Rather, it was more akin to a coup. Lenin, the keen-eyed political pragmatist, realised that after the collapse of the tsarist order in February 1917, the new Provisional Government was scarcely in power in any meaningful sense. As he apparently later put it, 'we found power lying in the streets, and we picked it up'.[7] The First World War had been a test for which tsarist Russia proved itself conclusively unprepared. Over 3 million Russian soldiers and civilians were killed; millions more became refugees, fleeing the front lines; starvation and disease stalked them on their long, hopeless marches. When the Provisional Government committed itself to continuing to fight, the Bolsheviks' slogan of 'Peace, Bread, Land' offered enough to the soldiers, workers and peasants so that at the very least they saw little reason to stand in their way. Lenin's Red Guard seized the main cities and declared a new government – and then the real problems began.

Although able to negotiate, at terrible cost, an end to Russia's involvement in the Great War, the new government would soon find itself embroiled in a vicious and confusing civil war. Against the Reds (and sometimes against each other) fought a motley array of monarchists, constitutional democrats, nationalists, anarchists, foreign forces, warlords and rival revolutionaries. The Russian Civil War of 1918–22 was the formative moment for the Bolsheviks and in many ways their abiding tragedy. Their reformist impulses and idealism were sacrificed in the name of survival, and, while the Reds won the war, they lost their soul. What was left was a brutal, disciplined and militarised regime, in which the cynical and the ruthless would rise fast and far.

No wonder that all manner of bandits and thugs joined the Bolshevik cause, and took to professing Marxism in the name of career opportunity. Even many Bolsheviks were alarmed to see the Cheka, their first political police force, becoming, in the words of Alexander Olminsky, a haven for 'criminals, sadists, and degenerate elements from the lumpen proletariat'.[8] To take one example, in 1922 the *ispolkom* or executive committee running the southern Russian village of Novoleushkovskaya was reportedly run by one Ubykon, an infamous horse thief of pre-revolutionary times, who had been imprisoned for raping his twelve-year-old sister. His predecessor, Passechny, had been one of his horse-thieving gang who had narrowly escaped being lynched in 1911, and other members of his committee included an exiled grain thief and a murderer.[9] Even the notorious 'King of the Moldavanka', 'Mishka Yaponchik', was sucked into the struggle. After the revolution, he was persuaded to join the Bolshevik cause. However, having helped muster a regiment for them, he then rebelled in 1920, in circumstances that remain unclear. He tried to get back to Odessa, but was ambushed and killed in a shoot-out with Bolshevik forces in Voznesensk, 130 kilometres north of home.[10]

Lenin's bitter compromise

The rich and the petty criminals, these are two sides of the same coin, these are the two main forms of parasites reared by capitalism, these are the main enemies of socialism.

V. I. Lenin, 1915[11]

Although meant polemically, there was some truth in Moscow kingpin Otari Kvantrishvili's claim in 1994, that 'they write I'm the mafia's godfather. [But] It was Vladimir Ilyich Lenin who was the real organiser of the mafia and who set up the criminal state.'[12] By identifying the rich and the petty criminal as the enemies of socialism, Lenin was implicitly exempting the not-so-petty criminal, making him a potential ally. This was just one of the compromises made during the civil war that would shape the rest of the Soviet era. Although the new government adopted draconian policies – the Military Revolutionary Committee warned that 'at the first attempt by dark elements to cause confusion, robbery, bloodshed or shooting on the streets of Petrograd, the criminal responsible will be wiped off the face of the earth'[13] – in practice 'confusion, robbery, bloodshed or shooting' abounded. In 1918, robberies and murders were at ten to fifteen times the prewar level[14] and Lenin himself was not immune to the lawlessness of the period. On 6 January 1919, he, his sister Mariya and his sole bodyguard, Ivan Chabanov, were being driven in his official Rolls-Royce when they were flagged down by men in uniform. Chabanov was wary, but Lenin insisted that they were as subject to the law as any and ordered they stop. These men turned out to be the notorious gangster Yakov Kuznetsov (known as 'Yakov Purses') and his associates, who needed a suitable car for a robbery. A long-standing criminal with no fewer than ten convictions under his belt, Kuznetsov was not au fait with the politics of the day and didn't recognise Lenin's name. Reportedly, when asked 'What's the matter? I am Lenin', the gangster replied, 'So what if you're Levin? I'm Purses, and I'm the boss of this city at night.' So Kuznetsov simply appropriated the car, various documents and Chabanov's gun. Shortly thereafter, looking through the papers, he realised he had passed up the chance to bag a valuable prize, and doubled back with the thought of taking Lenin as a hostage. By then, though, Chabanov had spirited him away. What followed was a massive manhunt, with Kuznetsov repeatedly slipping through the authorities' fingers, before finally falling to a hail of bullets in July. Here is his claim to fame, as the man who could have changed the course of Soviet history, had he only known who Lenin was.[15]

As it was, Lenin had it easy. The bitter violence, chaos and hardships of the civil war were piled on the existing woes generated by the Great War. Millions were displaced by both wars, and for years to come the country roiled with individual and group migration. This created whole new opportunities for criminals: to lose themselves in the human tides, and to prey on people adrift, whom no one knew or would miss. For instance, the bandit Mikhail Osipov, known as 'Mishka Kultyapy' ('Stumpy Mishka'), practised his murderous trade across Siberia for years, 'touring' as he put it from one city to the next, carrying out armed burglaries and house invasions, then moving on.[16] His particular trademark was the 'fan': laying out the bound bodies of his captives in an arc, feet together and heads apart, before methodically bashing in their brains with an axe. At least seventy-eight murders were ascribed to him and his gang, with no fewer than twenty-two in one especially gory 'fan'. Osipov was eventually brought to justice in Ufa in 1923 and put to death, but not before he had sent Filipp Varganov, the detective who ran him to ground, a note congratulating him for his skill and commitment, closing: 'My advice to you is this: do not change your tactics and put them into practice. Only in such ways is it possible to fight crime.'[17]

One particularly poignant challenge was what to do with the *besprizorniki*, the millions of homeless and abandoned children who often formed gangs simply to survive. There were already some 2.5 million of them by the start of 1917, but the perfect storm of revolution, epidemic, famine and war that then blew through Russia brought the figure to an extraordinary 7 million or more.[18] The new Bolshevik government was not unaware of the problem, nor uncaring. Indeed, in February 1919 it established a Council for the Protection of Children, intended to provide them with food, shelter and moral guidance, but the resources and experience at their disposal were entirely inadequate for the task.

The phenomenon of *besprizornost* would survive through the 1920s, and bring with it the associated challenges of begging, theft and even violence. Tales abounded – sometimes exaggerated, but sadly too often accurate – of gangs of teenagers or even younger children not only engaging in petty theft but mobbing and sometimes killing victims in gangs ten, twenty, thirty strong.[19] Joseph Douillet, the last Belgian consul to the prewar USSR, witnessed the endgame to a rising in the Persianovka children's camp, where some twenty-five youths from Novocherkassk armed themselves with knives and guns and took the camp, holding it for almost a week before soldiers came to restore order.[20]

Indeed, too often the authorities had to turn to tough measures to round up *besprizorniki* turned feral by their tragic experiences, many of whom had become habitual drug users even before they were in their teens, and who had begun to emulate the adults of the *vorovskoi mir* by their use of tattoos and nicknames. Although the official policy was rehabilitation, many at the time felt they were beyond redemption, as one policeman bluntly affirmed: 'Unofficially, my opinion is this: the sooner all your *besprizorniki* die, the better ... they are a hopeless bunch, soon to be bandits. And we have enough bandits without them.'[21] This also contributed to the pervasive fear of violence on the streets. Douillet, admittedly not the most sympathetic of observers, stated that 'in Soviet Russia, it is dangerous to venture out of doors in the evening. At dusk, the streets are entirely in the power of numerous gangs of hooligans.'[22]

Nor were the *besprizorniki* the only, or even the main, challenge. In 1922, in a desperate bid to revive the economy, Lenin signalled a reversal of the earlier policy of maximalist War Communism, based on nationalisation, grain requisitions and the militarisation of labour. The New Economic Policy (NEP) instead saw a liberalising step back towards the market: the state continued to control the so-called 'commanding heights' such as the banks and heavy industry, but peasants were now encouraged to buy and sell their produce and many other aspects of small-scale capitalism were allowed, and indeed encouraged. A controversial policy for the purists, which Stalin would reverse as soon as he could, it nonetheless proved surprisingly successful in its aims.

Bandits and '49ers'

I think the '20s would have been interesting times in which to work.
'Lev Yurist' ('Lev the Lawyer'), low-ranking *vor*, 2005[23]

The rise of private enterprise also generated its own criminal opportunities, from fraud and tax evasion through to bandit predation on the new class of 'NEPmen' entrepreneurs. A Bolshevik police force, called the militia to distinguish itself from its tsarist counterpart, would partially be able to draw on veteran officers and investigators from pre-revolutionary times, but it was hampered by a lack of resources and experience (most had no formal training).[24] Meanwhile, they were having to cope with the consequences of the opening up of tsarist prisons and the loss or destruction of many records from the time. Violent gangsters walked free, only to reprise their old repertoires. The gang of Vasily Kotov and Grigory Morozov, for example, terrorised Kursk province in 1920–2. They swooped on isolated estates and farms, murdered everyone inside – Morozov himself favoured an axe for this – and looted whatever they could find. In 1922, they came to Moscow and in a three-week orgy of violence killed thirty-two people before fleeing the city. The gang was finally rounded up in 1923 and executed by firing squad, but not before it was ascertained that Kotov had been released from prison in 1918 as a 'victim of the tsarist state.'[25]

This was thus a time again open to freewheeling banditry of a sort, largely now transposed from the countryside to the city, and again prone to generate anti-authority folk heroes. One such was Lyonka Panteleyev, a daring Red Army soldier and then Bolshevik secret policeman who was dismissed in 1922 – possibly on Stalin's orders. Embittered, he turned to a life of crime and gathered a gang which at its peak was launching twenty or more armed robberies in the Petrograd (St Petersburg) region a month. Unusually, the womanising Panteleyev not only relied heavily on maids and female servants as informants, but his gang also included a number of gunwomen. Arrested and tried, he managed to escape, consolidating his status as a mythic hero. Enraged, the Soviet authorities virtually locked down the city as he launched another twenty-three armed robberies. Eventually he was found and killed in a massive police assault – but so concerned were the authorities to kill off his memory as well, that they displayed his body just to prove to all that they had brought him down.[26]

In part as a response, once the immediate needs of the civil war began to recede, the Bolshevik state began again to take regular crime more seriously. Under the infamous Article 49 of the Criminal Code, introduced in 1922, people began to be rounded up on the basis of often quite petty crimes, such as shoplifting, or even their connections with what was called a 'criminal milieu', and banished from the six main cities (hence this punishment became known as 'Minus Six').[27] These '49ers' were deemed inherently socially dangerous, and their treatment reflected a central tension in the Bolshevik vision of policing. For all that they held often truly utopian notions of rehabilitation and of the extent to which crime was a symptom of class inequality and educational failure, many of the new leadership, battle-hardened veterans of revolution and civil war, continued to see themselves on a war footing. In 1926, for example, political police chief Felix Dzerzhinsky – the notorious 'Iron Felix' – had a simple solution to shortages in the supply of textiles, which he blamed on the presence of 'speculators' manipulating the market: 'I think we should send a couple of thousand speculators to Turukhansk and Solovki [labour camps].'[28] This was exactly the kind of unresolved tension Lenin's eventual successor would gladly and murderously exploit.

Stalin's children

Communism means not the victory of socialist law, but the victory of socialism over law.

                                        Pavel Stuchka, Bolshevik jurist, 1927[29]

The tattoos that were such a distinctive characteristic of twentieth-century professional criminals in the USSR included a number featuring Joseph

Stalin, dictator from the end of the 1920s until his death in 1953. This was sometimes satirical, and sometimes reflected a belief that no firing squad would shoot at their own master. But it was also a strangely fitting tribute to the man who was, in a way, their true progenitor. In the early Soviet era, despite hopes that it would prove simply a transitional phenomenon, crime burgeoned in an era of scarcity, uncertainty and weak state structures. By the 1930s, the terms of Article 49 were beginning to be adapted to Stalin's political agenda. In 1932, the political police (by that time known as OGPU) issued instructions to local authorities to give greater attention to 'criminal and social-parasitic elements' and to divide them into new categories which lumped together unemployed gangsters and homeless children.[30] Famine and chaos in the countryside, as a result of Stalin's collectivisation campaign (effectively seizing control of farmland for the state), led to a resurgence in *besprizornost*. Children as young as eight, unable or unwilling to prove their age, were casually dispatched to the labour camps as 'age around 12'.[31] Increasingly, though, a clear distinction was also being drawn between regular criminals and anyone assumed to have some kind of political motive. Mere thugs and bandits were 'socially near' workers who had gone astray. They needed chastising, correcting. But it was the political dissidents for whom the most savage treatment was reserved, and who in due course would be fed into the labour camps in their thousands and millions.

Stalin's whirlwind of terror, industrialisation and incarceration would revolutionise the *vorovskoi mir*. The Gulag system of labour camps – 'Gulag' was simply the acronym for *Glavnoe upravlenie lagerei*, Main Directorate of Camps – was the engine of his state-building project.[32] In part, this was practical: millions of *zek* convict labourers felled trees, dug canals and mined coal in the name of modernisation. How many? We do not really know, but Anne Applebaum suggests a figure of 28.7 million through the Stalin era as a 'low estimate'.[33] However, it was also political and psychological: the labour camps were places to exile those who resisted the state's collectivisation of farmland and those who showed undue independence of will, and also offered a cautionary tale to cow any who might question the Party. There was, after all, nothing secret about the arrests and the Gulag system, with convicts working even in the major cities (Moscow's sublime metro system was built on the backs of this hellish modern slavery) and 'Stolypin' prisoner-transport carriages with their armed guards and barred windows attached to the back of regular passenger trains. The principle of arresting people in the early hours was not only a matter of practicality, catching them when they were likely to be home and at their most vulnerable. It was also part of this whole theatre of terror: the arrival of a vehicle outside at a time when the streets were virtually empty except for the 'black raven' vans of the political police, boots echoing in the stairwell, a hammering on a door, the cries of children, protestations, the stern commands of the authorities. One person may be arrested, but a whole apartment block would be suffused with terror and the shameful relief that this time it was someone else.

Alexander Solzhenitsyn's compelling image of the 'Gulag archipelago', 'an almost invisible, almost imperceptible country' coexisting spatially with the Soviet Union, easily leads us to believe that there was a line dividing these two nations as sharp as barbed wire, but this was not the case. There were, of course, camps themselves with walls, fences, gates and guard towers. But there were also virtually open camps in the far wilderness, guarded by their very remoteness, as well as the labour gangs and encampments inside the cities. There were even so-called 'de-convoyed prisoners', granted the right to travel unescorted to and from their work assignments along certain set routes or even sometimes to live outside the camp, under the threat of losing the privilege or even summary judgement if they tried to escape.[34] There was a black market that saw food, medicine and other goods smuggled into the camps, and scarce camp supplies sold to the outside population. A prisoner at the Siblag camp, Yevsei Lvov, remembered, 'The nearby population is literally to a person dressed in the footwear, pants, padded jackets, pea-jackets, hats, blouses [and] quilted jackets of the camp type.'[35] Meanwhile, the limited assistance given former prisoners to return home meant that many camps coexisted with rough-and-ready townships full of 'a floating population of ex-convicts, marginals, and "pioneers" in search of quick earnings'.[36] In short, Stalin's labour camp system managed to be at once both a state-within-a-state and an inextricable part of the Soviet Union. It is thus hardly surprising that what happened in the Gulags did not stay in the Gulags.

Many *zeki* were '58ers', political prisoners swept up by the infamous Article 58 of the Criminal Code on 'counter-revolutionary acts', which could be anything from telling a joke about Stalin to being associated with someone who had just fallen out of favour. Others were either petty criminals, or so-called *bytoviki*, 'everyday-lifers', whose crimes were just those everyone ended up committing, from getting to work late to filching a little food in the middle of a famine. (Back in tsarist times, they were known as the *neschastnye*, the 'unfortunates'.[37]) In such times of universal hardship, it was so easy for people to end up on the wrong side of the law. The state sought to control movement, not least with internal passports that turned vagrants into criminals.[38] Others, struggling to find work in provincial cities and denied legal access to the slightly more prosperous metropolises, were forced into theft or off-the-books work to survive. Again, chaos in the country also encouraged a murderous migratory pattern of urban banditry, and groups sprang up such as the 'Black Mask Gang' and the 'Band of Forest Devils', notorious for committing often bloody crimes in one city and then moving to another. Some were formed from professional criminals but others, especially those involved in crimes such as organised shoplifting and burglary, were often really products of a desperate struggle for survival.

The thief within the code

The vor *is an honourable thief, a man who doesn't care about the law, but cares about his word, the code. The* vor v zakone *is the kind of man every* vor *wants to be.*

'Lev Yurist' ('Lev the Lawyer'), low-ranking *vor*, 2005[39]

But then there were also the true criminals, the *vory*, and the existing culture of the *vorovskoi mir* was magnified and communicated as they were thrown together in the camps, in *etap* (prisoner transport convoy) trucks and train carriages, and in the transit stations along their routes. Prisoners were, after all, routinely moved around, whether to disperse dangerous concentrations, relieve overcrowding or meet new economic needs. Through this constant mingling of criminals from across the Soviet Union, the *vorovskoi mir* became ever more homogeneous and interconnected, a veritable 'gangster archipelago'. In the process, the camp system strengthened and transmitted this distinctive subculture, at once enforcing and teaching underworld orthodoxy. Thus, for example, Vyatlag camp was described in its own prison newspaper, *Za zheleznoi reshyotkoi* ('Behind Iron Bars'), as 'a real school' offering 'courses of the second stage of moral training for future skilled, "stylish" criminals'.[40] This was not just about indoctrinating criminals into a common culture, it was also about the communication of professional skills. In its own vicious way, the Stalin regime was bringing about rapid urbanisation and industrialisation and, as during late tsarism, this generated increased specialisation and stratification within the underworld, just as for the rest of society. Such professional classifiers ranged from the *farmazonshiki*, counterfeit-currency dealers (who would also often palm *kukly*, 'dolls', onto unwitting marks: a bundle of fake notes or even just scrap paper, with real notes at the top and bottom to fool the eye), to the *gonsha* ('shoe'), a pickpocket working the crowded buses and trams at rush hour.

Nonetheless, they were all of the *vorovskoi mir*, and from this critical mass emerged a new breed of authority figure, the *vor v zakone* (which literally translates as 'thief within the law', but is perhaps best rendered as 'thief within the code').[41] These *vory v zakone* were not necessarily gang leaders, nor always the biggest, toughest or richest criminals, but instead the judges, teachers, role models and high priests of the *vorovskoi mir*, acclaimed by their peers. 'Valentin Intelligent', the *pakhan*, or 'boss', encountered by Alexander Dolgun was probably one such *vor v zakone*:

> In rank and authority, this guy has the status of a robber king. In the mafia he would be like a godfather, but I do not want to use that word because there is a godfather in the labour camps and that is an entirely different thing. Besides, a pakhan can arise anywhere and does not have to be linked to a particular family. He is a man widely respected in the underworld for his skill and experience and authority. To meet such a distinguished, high-class urka [*vor*] is a very rare event.[42]

Valentin treated Dolgun courteously, but a key part of the job of a *vor v zakone* was to be both an exemplar of the demanding code of the thieves and responsible for policing it by fierce and exacting means. If a wannabe *vor* acquired a tattoo to which he was not entitled, he might be killed, or simply have the offending piece of skin cut from his body. Often, though, the discipline was internal. A thief in the Kolyma camp, for example, lost three fingers on his left hand because he had failed to make good on a bet (an almost sacred obligation within the *vorovskoi mir*): 'Our council of seniors met to hand out my punishment. The plaintiff wanted all my left hand fingers off. The seniors offered two. They bargained a bit and agreed on three.'[43] The thief expressed no resentment at his treatment, as 'we have our laws, too', and the *vory v zakone* were thus mediators, moral authorities and enforcers all in one. An even more dramatic example of this cult of macho endurance and a refusal to bow to outsiders was witnessed in the camps by Michael Solomon. A young thief was accused of selling out his brothers to the authorities. He stoically said nothing in his defence, but when given the choice 'by cutting or by hanging' opted for the former. The senior of the three *vory* who had been his judges cut the thief's throat, then calmly washed his knife and hands of blood and banged on the door to attract the duty officer and face his own fate.[44]

This hard core of *vory* also called themselves *blatnye*, along with other terms, such as *urki*, *urkagany* and *blatary*. A minority even amongst the criminals, they contented themselves largely with preying on the petty and political prisoners. They terrorised and abused them, stealing their food and clothing, forcing them from the warmer bunks in the barracks, beating, even raping, with virtual impunity. We know of the *blatnye* largely through the memoirs of political prisoners, who in the main clearly had few reasons to write fondly of them, but their stark assessments also appear in official reports and even those few writings by camp officials. 'The criminals were not human', wrote Varlam Shalamov, and Eugenia Ginzburg likewise felt 'the professional criminals were beyond the bounds of humanity'.[45] Unsurprisingly, they also forced the other prisoners to do their work, as it was against the code of the *vorovskoi mir* to lift a finger for the state. A true *blatnoi* would, after all, feign illness, mutilate himself or as a last resort defy the clubs and guns of the guards before he bent before them. Ginzburg writes of a moment when she and her fellow politicals 'stood freezing for more than an hour while the argument went on, accompanied by songs from the ordinary criminals, who hopped around as they bawled at the top of their voices: We don't work on Saturday, on Saturday we don't work, and every day is a Saturday for us.'[46]

Even if they refused to bend to the rules of the Gulag – and, as will be discussed in the next chapter, many did refuse – they were nonetheless shaped by the experience. The rich and brutal *vor* culture, with its own slang, visual language and customs, will be explored in chapter 5. The key point is that the camp system was the crucible in which the loose *vorovskoi mir* that had emerged in late nineteenth-century Russia would not only become increasingly homogeneous, including embracing non-Slavic nationalities, but also acquire what it had always lacked, some kind of hierarchy. The dog-eat-dog struggle for daily survival in the Gulags, summarised in the precept 'you die today, and I'll die tomorrow',[47] only deepened the cultural ties amongst the *blatnye*, and the gulf between them and the rest of society.

CHAPTER 4

THIEVES AND BITCHES

It is a wicked thief who preys on his own village.

Russian proverb

After the Second World War, the Gulag system was to be torn by struggles between traditionalist thieves and those they considered traitors for collaborating with the state. The law of the *vorovskoi mir* was, after all, very clear as to what all 'honest thieves' should do with such apostates. As the traditional criminal song 'Murka' puts it:

> Days were replaced by nights of dark nightmares,
> Many of the gang were caught.
> But now we shall discover quickly who became a snitch,
> And punish them for their betrayal.
> As soon as someone finds out anything,
> We should not hesitate.
> Sharpen the knife, get the gun,
> Get the gun – lay it down ready.[1]

When one particularly large and violent revolt in the Gorlag camp was finally suppressed in 1953, for example, a *zek* who had been a colonel in the Red Army before his arrest and imprisonment stood by the column of captives as they were led away, identifying the ringleaders. He was marked for death. First he was kept in the camp hospital, where he avoided one attempt on his life only because he had switched beds. Eventually, he was sent to a solitary cell in a women's camp, but even there he was not safe and was stabbed by one of the inmates, even though it set her up for execution by the state. It didn't matter: as Michael Solomon put it, 'the execution order had been relayed through underground channels and nothing under God's sun could prevent the death sentence from being carried out once it had been issued by the convicts' own mafia.'[2]

Sentiment and personal bonds of fellowship and trust are all very well, but any encapsulated social community, especially one founded on transgression and self-advancement, also needs to have mechanisms to judge and punish those who break its rules and question its values. This is, as will also be explored in the next chapter, an especially significant element of the *vorovskoi mir*. Indeed, it is also visible in other aspects of Russian life, not least in the ceaseless, cannibalistic quest under Stalin for 'traitors' real and imagined, or even in Vladimir Putin's particular hatred of those who betray their state and their service today. Broadly speaking, mere dissidents will be harassed, silenced or expelled, but those whom Putin considers turncoats tend to find themselves facing much more direct retribution. Perhaps the highest-profile was ex-security officer turned defector and whistleblower Alexander Litvinenko, killed over twenty-two agonising days in a London hospital, having been covertly dosed with an intensely radioactive isotope called polonium-210.

If to the *blatnye* thieves, true to their code, the ordinary convicts were simply prey, then in due course their own culture would also spawn, thanks to Stalin, those who would likewise prey on them. If there was one crucial, and ultimately fatal, weakness in the code of the *vorovskoi mir*, it was the absolute ban on any form of cooperation with the state. This helped define the thieves and build their coherent subculture, but in an age of totalitarian dreams and massive state power, it was to prove increasingly untenable.

Bitch in law

Twenty percent of criminals keep in terror eighty percent of morally pure prisoners. Three percent of criminals (blatary) keep in blind obedience all the rest of the criminal world.

Alexander Solzhenitsyn[3]

Just as Stalin's policies unified the *vorovskoi mir* on one level, they also divided it on another, creating a new body of collaborators, the so-called *suki* ('bitches'), who were willing to help the state run the Gulags, but only in their own interests. The challenge for the Stalinist state was how best to manage the massive influx of convicts, and to do so cheaply and efficiently. While the primary initial motivation of the purges and the mass incarcerations was political, the state also sought to exploit this virtually enslaved workforce for economic gain. As a Polish-born *zek*, Gustav Herling, put it, 'the whole system of forced labour in Soviet Russia – in all its stages, the interrogations and hearings, the preliminary imprisonment, and the camp itself – is intended primarily not to punish the criminal, but rather to exploit him economically and transform him psychologically'.[4]

The answer was to co-opt the worst underworld elements as agents and trustees to keep the 58ers and the 49ers, the political prisoners and petty criminals respectively, controlled and working. There were, of course, still regular prison guards, but the lion's share of managing the Gulag population was in effect subcontracted to inmates. At first, bandits, corrupt officials and the like – criminals but not of the *vorovskoi mir* – were offered a preferential status within the camps, easier lives, perks and even eventually jobs, in return for keeping the other inmates in line and the production norms met. In due course, though, even *blatnye* were seduced by the opportunities.

Solomon said that while they were 'kept under lock and key, [they were] regarded by the authorities as their shock brigade against the political prisoners'.[5] Given that it was miserable work in terrible conditions, there was always a need for more Gulag staff – as late as 1947, the VOKhR armed guards were still 40,000 men short[6] – so much so that it was crucial to find ways to control the camps from the inside. Many camps effectively operated with an outer control zone watched by the VOKhR from their machine-gun towers, and an inner zone, known simply as the *zona*, where most day-to-day supervision was in the hands of these prisoners. As former *zek* Lev Kopelev put it, 'inside the camp – in the barracks, the yurts [tents], the dining room, the bathhouse, the "streets" – our lives were under the direct control of the trusties'.[7]

These trusties served as guards, technical specialists and administrators and could even rise to command camps – sometimes while still serving their sentences. They also acquired new opportunities for criminal activities. Trusties were much more likely to be put into administrative roles involving contact with the outside world, or allowed to move around 'de-convoyed' beyond camp walls. To some, this was an occasional chance to forage for food, to loaf or even to snatch a quick drink. For others, though, it was a chance to build criminal networks between worlds. A case from the Novosibirsk region epitomises this. In 1947, it emerged that a gang of trusties under one Mikhailov, a criminal who had been made camp senior accountant, had established a long-term scam in partnership with a couple of black marketeers in the city.[8] For months, they were able to smuggle food meant for prisoners into Novosibirsk, where it sold for ten times its official value, while Mikhailov simply cooked the books. Eventually, when the scam came to light, Mikhailov was shot and his partners in crime sentenced to longer prison terms. However, the opportunities to live a rather different life, even within the camps, meant that almost no amount of punishment prevented a constant flow of criminal deals through, into and out of the Gulag archipelago.

Cracks in the code

> 'Your Code has outlived its time. All the "Code men" have cracked . . .'
> 'I come from a long line of Russian thieves. I have stolen and will again.'
> Conversation between a prison guard and a *blatnoi*, in Sergei
> Dovlatov's novel *The Zone*[9]

At the end of the day, the rewards had to outweigh the risks. By taking such positions, thieves were breaking one of the fundamental taboos of their code. As a *blatnoi* known as 'Bomber' put it, 'a thief cannot squeal on another thief to a viper [camp authorities]. If he does, he's not a thief, he's a bitch.'[10] Nonetheless, especially by the later 1930s, even members of the *vorovskoi mir* became tempted by the opportunities of collaboration. The traditionalists within the *vorovskoi mir* despised these quislings. They became outcasts, the *otoshedshie* ('departed'), more commonly and vitrioli-cally known as *suki* ('bitches'). Their lives were forfeit in the eyes of the *blatnye*, who increasingly also called themselves *chestnyagy*, 'the uncon-verted'. As a *pakhan* explains in another popular criminal song from the 1930s, 'Music is Playing in the Moldavanka', when he hears that a former associate is now working for the camp authorities:

> We, small thieves, have our strong laws,
> And by these laws we live.

And if Kolka has dishonoured himself,
We will threaten him with the knife.[11]

Of course, to kill a *suka* was in turn to risk being killed by the state or by his fellow trusties. For criminals who treated prison terms as a mark of pride and already had long stints ahead of them, the thought of another sentence being added on top held few fears. However, there were other ways of visiting retribution, from a simple knife in the dark, to being locked up in a freezing cold punishment cell for a week, or forced to stand in sub-Arctic winds in wet clothes, or staked out overnight in a Kolyma summer, when mosquitos swarm in clouds thick enough to limit vision to a few metres. Criminals who did not fear a fight did not necessarily view frostbite, pneumonia, tuberculosis or being consumed by insects with quite the same nonchalance.

Through the 1930s, then, an uneasy stalemate prevailed between these two groups, as they ignored each other as far as blood enemies could. Solzhenitsyn's assertion above, that 3 per cent of the prison population would keep the rest of the criminals 'in blind obedience' is questionable, not least because of what we know about the violence that was such a constant factor in Gulag relations. More to the point, the *suki*, outnumbered but backed by the regime, knew better than to try to force the *blatnye* to work. They concentrated on the politicals and petty criminals, who represented a majority of the Gulag population. In turn, the *vory*, for all that they loathed the *suki*, knew that to visit the murderous revenge their code demanded on them would lead to the state's equally murderous response. They largely tried to ignore the *suki*, and likewise exploited the 58ers and 49ers. The authorities, eager to avoid direct confrontations and the violence that would entail, cooperated, trying to ensure that different groups were kept apart, both in the camps and especially on the *etap* transfers, where control and supervision were even lighter. So for a time, the Gulags saw a cold war far more volatile and visceral than the US–Soviet conflict would ever be, but one which ultimately could not last.

The balance of terror tilts

You were in the war? You picked up a rifle? That means that you're a bitch, a real bitch, and should be punished by the 'law'. Besides, you're a coward, too! You didn't have the strength of will to abandon the ranks – you should have accepted a new sentence or even death, but not taken the gun!

Traditionalist thief, in Varlam Shalamov, *Collected Works*[12]

This stalemate was brought to a violent end by the Second World War. When Germany invaded the USSR in 1941, many within the Gulags – including some *blatnye* – ended up in the Red Army, some willingly and some by force. People's Defence Committee Order No. 227, issued following the disaster that was the decimation of the Soviet defensive line in the initial German onslaught, envisaged that hundreds of thousands of convicts would be rushed to penal battalions, originally punishment units for deserters and malcontents. In the first three years of the war, almost a million Gulag inmates were transferred into the Red Army.[13] Some thieves resisted; Dimitry Panin, for example, recalled an infamous bandit known as 'Lom-Lopata' ('Crowbar-Shovel') who killed another prisoner simply to avoid being sent to a penal battalion, a classic example of a criminal whose sentence was already so long, another ten years added on top meant nothing.[14] Those who volunteered, though (or failed to commit further offences to avoid the draft), generally felt that they were simply doing their patriotic duty: they may have been criminals, they may have despised the Soviet regime, but a deeper loyalty to Mother Russia endured. Strictly speaking, however, they were breaking the code of the *vorovskoi mir*.

By 1944, as the tide turned, the Kremlin reconsidered its early promises of amnesty and parole. *Zeki*, conscripts and volunteers alike, began to be returned to the camps, only to find themselves all considered collaborators in the eyes of the traditionalists. The Gulag population, which had shrunk in the early years of the war thanks to military service, mortality and the need for labour in agriculture and industry, began again to grow, especially as Stalin sought to re-establish his grip on power by imposing a series of tough new laws and regulations on the country.

However, the convict population would acquire a rather different composition. The *vory* and regular criminals who had served in the army and were now considered to have broken their code were joined by maybe half a million former soldiers and partisans whose 'crime' had been to be captured by the enemy when Stalin expected – demanded – that they fight to the death. For them, 'liberation' meant an inglorious transfer from a foreign prison camp to a Soviet one. Over a third of a million Red Army soldiers ended up in the NKVD's 'verification and filtration camps', and while most were eventually freed to civilian life or returned into the military, at least a third of them ended up in the Gulag.[15]

Finding themselves in a world divided between exploited politicals, collaborators and career criminals, they tended to align themselves with the *suki*. In effect, these 'soldiers' or 'red hats' were forced into such an alliance, as the traditionalists either ostracised or tried to intimidate them, frequently with unexpected outcomes. In one incident in Norilsk, for instance, a gang of *blatnye* decided to persecute some politicals, who turned out to be former Red Army officers, who 'took them to pieces, even though they had no weapons. With wild screams the remaining thieves ran to the guards and the [camp] officers, begging for help.'[16]

The story is that in 1948, representatives of leaders of the *voyenshchina*, the 'soldiery', gathered at a transit point at Vanino and thrashed out a pragmatic compromise between the old ways and new opportunities. In what was in many ways a conscious alignment with the *suki*, they decided that they would accept the notion of a thieves' code, but that it would not bar collaboration with the authorities, and they would work within the system. In truth, the meeting was probably a reflection of an existing trend within this fraction of the *zek* population, rather than a dramatic new approach. Either way, the authorities reported a growing willingness to cooperate on the part of these *zeki*. Increasingly, they were recruited not just as clerks, foremen and guards, but also as informants.

However, the war had also encouraged anti-Soviet nationalist groups, from the Russians who joined General Vlasov's Russian Liberation Army and fought alongside the Germans, to Ukrainian partisans who joined the Ukrainian Insurgent Army. Those not killed out of hand ended up in the camps. Furthermore, as the Kremlin closed its fist on central Europe, there were waves of Balts, Poles and others who ended up in the Gulag, whether because they had fought against the Soviets or simply because they were patriots whose presence would be inconvenient as new puppet regimes were installed. When Joseph Scholmer – a German doctor and communist who had already enjoyed the tender mercies of the Gestapo – was arrested in East Germany in 1949 and sent to Vorkuta, he found himself in a cell on whose walls 'prisoners of every nation had cut their names. "SOS", the Star of David, the swastika, "*Jeszcze Polska nie zginęła*" (Poland is unconquered) and SS insignia were to be found alongside each other.'[17]

Many of these ethnic and national groups cohered for mutual support and defence within the Gulags, sometimes finding common cause with others, but not sharing in the existing culture of the camps. They were often able to turn the tables on the *blatnye*, who were accustomed to preying on outsiders as individuals, not anticipating that their compatriots would come to help them out. Unlike the *voyenshchina*, they had no interest in cooperating with the Soviet authorities, and they generally regarded the *suki* and *blatnye* as equally hostile. Often, indeed, violent interethnic struggles would supersede others, such as in the three-cornered struggle inmate Leonid Sitko witnessed, where a dispute between Russian, Ukrainian and Chechen labour gangs 'became war, all-out war'.[18] A Chechen gangster who had known Gulag survivors from the time recounted a similar case, when even Chechens who had been part of the *vorovskoi mir* broke ranks with the other *blatnye* to side with other Chechens: 'the code is important, but blood is everything'.[19] In other words, these ethnic groups were essentially wild cards, constantly destabilising forces in a camp system already under pressure.

Meanwhile, times were changing even for the rank-and-file criminals of the camps: the 49ers, the *bytoviki*, the petty crooks, the small-scale recidivists, often simply referred to collectively as the *shpana* (a term for habitual prisoners dating back to tsarist times) or *shobla yobla* ('rabble'). They were being squeezed between these power blocs within the Gulags. In the past, they had tended to look to the *blatnye* for moral leadership – if that is not too much of a contradiction in terms – even while having to obey the *suki* in many day-to-day issues. However, the old certainties and rules suddenly seemed no longer as clear, nor the hierarchies of camp power.

There was now a critical mass of collaborators, too many to be ignored by the *blatnye*, and no longer willing to be intimidated. There were new groups not easily controlled through the old mechanisms. The slow improvement of conditions in the camps after the desperate privations of the war years, remembered as the 'Great Hunger', was also, ironically, acting as a destabilising force. Less consumed with the day-to-day struggle to survive, the *zeki* were now able to organise: 'the Government had quite literally given them food for thought, and their thoughts were moving in the direction of rebellion'.[20] The writing was equally literally on the wall, and everywhere else: anti-government slogans were appearing carved on tree trunks in Gulag logging territories, scratched on the sides of Stolypin convict railway carriages, daubed on barracks in the night, and scribbled on scraps of paper thrown across barbed-wire fences.

Furthermore, at the very time when internal tensions were building, those managing the Gulag system as a whole began wondering if this was the time to deliver a lethal blow to the *blatnye* and the economic inefficiencies they represented. Increasingly, camp authorities actively began to seek to convert or break the traditionalists. Varlam Shalamov, for example, recounted the tale he had heard in 1948, of convicts arriving at Vanino transit prison forced to strip, so that the thieves could be identified by their tattoos.[21] They were offered the choice between ritually forsaking their code and death, with many choosing the latter. It is unclear if this actually happened, or whether it was just one of the myths that circulate in any information-scarce society, but the authorities certainly did use the *blatnye*'s own customs against them, not least identifying them by their ink. They also demanded that traditional-ists publicly recant their old ways, by carrying out some symbolic act of labour (such as raking the forbidden zone between fences, which was kept cleared to show footprints), locking the door of a barracks, and sitting and eating with other collaborators. That way, they were irredeemably 'departed' from the *blatnoi* community, and could not go back.[22] Together, the changing composition of the *zek* population and the government's policies would tear the Gulag system apart, and reshape the *vorovskoi mir*.

The bitches' war

A guard ran down the corridor and shouted 'War! War!' – whereupon all of the thieves, who were less numerous than the bitches, ran to hide in the camp punishment cell. The bitches followed them there, and murdered several.

Gulag inmate Leonid Sitko[23]

The late 1940s and early 1950s would see the Gulag system torn apart by the 'bitches' war' (*suchya voina*),[24] a battle for supremacy over the camps but also for the soul of the *vorovskoi mir*, and one the authorities initially encouraged but would come to regret. Indeed, the fact that a whole series of *suka*-on-*blatnoi* attacks happened near enough at once across the camp system in 1948 is strongly indicative of the government's hand (and possibly prompted by the *voyenshchina*'s Vanino decision of that year).[25]

For instance, at the Intalag mining camp, 150 *suki*, equipped with shovels, axes and other perfectly serviceable weapons, were deliberately delivered into the midst of 100 *blatnye*. The result was a massacre: ten of the traditionalists surrendered and turned, the rest were killed.[26] The aim was clearly to destroy the *blatnye*, or at least force them to abandon their code and their resistance. Broadly speaking, the war was fought between the traditionalists and the *suki*, allied with the 'soldiery'. In practice, though, the battle lines were often confused. There were national groups, there were factional splinters within both the *blatnye* and the *suki*, there were alliances of ordinary prisoners – the list continues.

This was a war fought as often in the shadows as in the open, typically its casualties in the ones, twos and threes, although sometimes in the dozens or greater. It was a war fought with savagery and desperation. Informants would have their heads cut off and laid before the guard posts; knives, shovels, iron bars, pickaxes and planks ripped from the sleeping shelves would be pressed into service as weapons, with fists and boots if all else failed. Just a partial summary of killings in a single camp, Pechorlag, in a single year, 1952, gives a sense of the ugly, close-quarter struggle: nine men suffocating a tenth, using a bed sheet; two smothering a third with a towel; five men hacking a sixth to death with a pickaxe; several group stranglings, typically a single victim throttled to death while being held down by four or more others; and so the tally of bespoke inhumanity continues.[27]

In terms of the big picture, the collaborators won, for a variety of reasons. They often had numbers on their side, and the ex-soldiers brought with them military experience: the *blatnye* might be tough individually, but so were their enemies, and many of them were used to fighting as units. Perhaps most importantly, the *suki* had the support of the regime. The authorities found a variety of ways to tilt the balance, whether by allowing them to dominate camp careers such as cook and barber – which meant knives and razors – or by giving them access to work tools such as axes and shovels. They could also move groups of prisoners like armies in the field, concentrating them in individual camps until they had wiped out the *blatnye* there, and then moving them on to the next.

Nonetheless, this shattered the rough and ready but brutally effective old control system. In particular, casualties amongst informants dramatically diminished the authorities' ability to control and even understand what was going on inside the *zona*.[28] Violence in the camps was the norm, and risings and strikes spread. The bitches' war essentially started in 1948 – although with no formal declarations, it is hard to unpick it from the general violence of the Gulags – and reached a peak around 1950–1, when reports were coming in daily of attacks. Having encouraged or at least allowed the conflict to begin with the thought of purging the Gulags of the *blatnye*, the authorities began to worry about it escalating out of control. The bloodshed between these groups cut dramatically into labour productivity: in 1951–2, not a single Gulag administration achieved its targets for the Five-Year Plan, and in 1951, a million man-days were lost to strikes and protests.[29] More to the point, the war created violent instability that encouraged wider protests and revolts, in a vicious circle. In 1952, a meeting of Gulag officials warned that 'the authorities, who until now have been able to gain a certain advantage from the hostilities between various groups of prisoners, [are] beginning to lose their grip on the situation . . . In some places, certain factions are even beginning to run the camp along their own lines.'[30]

Colonel Nikolai Zverev, a camp commander from Norilsk, even produced a memo on how to deal with the crisis, which deliberately pulled no punches. The system could be reformed dramatically, or else the number of armed camp guards, the VOKhR – which had never reached its full strength because the job was so unpleasant and difficult – would have to be doubled.[31] He must have known that, given the diminishing returns of the 'Gulag-industrial complex' and the other demands on the Soviet treasury, this would not be met with enthusiasm. His alternative proposal? Let almost a quarter of his camp's prisoners go.

After Stalin

The vast majority knew and understood what [Stalin] was made of. They understood that he was a tyrant . . . that the fate of every prisoner was somehow linked to the fate of Stalin.

Camp doctor[32]

It is ironic that after Stalin's death in 1953 it should be his last secret police chief, Lavrenty Beria, a man as evil as one might expect in such a job, who began lobbying for a scaling down of the camps. In a report, he wrote that of the 2,526,402 Gulag inmates at the time, only 221,435 were truly 'dangerous state criminals' and advocated an immediate amnesty for about a million *zeki*, which was approved. Later, most likely in an attempt – which proved unsuccessful – to distance himself from his bloody past, he proposed that the government 'liquidate the system of forced labour, on the grounds of economic ineffectiveness and lack of perspective'.[33]

The Gulags became a little less bestial, but, as is so often the case, a slight relaxation emboldened rather than satisfied. With new-found confidence, prisoners organised, visited retribution on informants, and in some cases plotted. Internecine camp violence increasingly gave way to mass strikes, protests and even risings. In 1953, the Siberian labour camps were to see a series of strikes that at their peak would involve more than 10,000 *zeki*.[34] In the Gorlag camp in Norilsk, the shooting of a prisoner during the march to work triggered strikes and demonstrations that escalated into a protest that engulfed the whole complex. Meanwhile, a similar process was taking place in the Rechlag camp in Vorkuta. In both cases, Moscow first blustered, then opened insincere negotiations, and finally sent in the troops. These strikes were crushed, but even so, there would be retribution meted out to those who had collaborated in the state's response.

Other strikes and protests would follow, especially spearheaded by Ukrainian nationalist prisoners. The largest and most dangerous of all would take place in the Kengir camp zone of the Steplag Special Camp in Kazakhstan in 1954. Eventually, this was crushed when soldiers burst into the camp zone behind T-34 tanks, some of which blithely rolled over prisoners in the way. Yet the whole Gulag system was demonstrably in crisis, and mass amnesties and rehabilitations would follow. By 1960, the size of the Gulag population was just 20 per cent of what it had been in 1953.[35]

So the *suki* had won, albeit at the cost of playing their part in rendering the Gulags virtually ungovernable. Nonetheless, win they did, and reshaped the *vorovskoi mir* in their own image. They retained most of the code, and the culture of brazen and merciless dog-eat-dog predation, but they rewrote the prohibition on collaboration with the state. It now became permissible, so long as it was in the criminal's interest. When the Gulags were opened, these collaborator-criminals were amongst the first to be released, and over the following decade they would impose their own vision of the code across the Soviet underworld, by threat, persuasion and violence. The way would be open for a new generation of *vory* to collaborate with dishonest Party functionaries when they felt it was in their interests. This was Stalin's toxic legacy to the Soviet Union.

CHAPTER 5

THIEF LIFE

One can get used even to living in hell.

Russian proverb

There is something seductive about ritual, about arcane knowledge, about insider jargon. It makes you feel special, builds communities, eases you into a world of mutual and possibly difficult and dangerous commitments. A relatively low-level gangster, 'Lev Yurist', once described to me how he felt on being accepted into the criminal fraternity in the mid-1990s.[1] He would not go into some of the details ('that's not for outsiders') but other aspects he was willing to discuss. He had had to prove himself, both by being a loyal and efficient *shestyorka*, a gofer or runner, for at least a year, and by undertaking some specific risky tasks. Some were probably connected with actual criminal acts, others – such as stealing a coat from the cloakroom at a restaurant run by Chechens – more about demonstrating bravery and élan. He had to have three established criminals willing to vouch for him. He had to be able to recite some declaration – I'd guess pledging himself to the group – in criminal slang. Then there was a ritual that involved blood, vodka and an icon.

It was fascinating to hear, but strangely ahistorical. Proving your long-term loyalty, engaging in criminal acts, showing bravery: these make sense and are expected of a new recruit by any gang wherever you are. Even so, these sounded relatively gentle demands compared with the unyielding ways of the camps. Stealing a coat from a restaurant in the 1990s would likely earn you a beating if you were caught, but a true *blatnoi* was expected to be willing to mutilate himself to avoid work, or murder an innocent bystander as a wager in a game of cards. Furthermore, I had never heard Lev use more criminal slang than the terms frankly on everyone's lips in those days, and he admitted he had had to memorise his catechism by rote. As for the rest of the ritual, without knowing the details it is impossible to pass judgement, but the implication is that it was essentially a reinvention of old rites from the glory days of the *vorovskoi mir*, the 1930s–1950s, blended with cinematic representations of mafia initiations and the like. The evidence suggests that the distinctive culture of the *vorovskoi mir* did not die out in the 1960s, but certainly became far less powerful and ubiquitous, only to be recreated as the *vory* reinvented themselves from the 1970s onwards. As such, their folkways would be a pallid and half-remembered reflection of the powerful, vital and brutal culture of the *vory*'s heyday.

Vor life

Being an inmate, I have chosen the thieves' path and swear before equals to be a worthy thief and never cooperate with the Chekists [political police].

Thief's oath[2]

Before the camps, the *vorovskoi mir* was about a subculture rather than a structure. Individual gangs had their own hierarchies, and cities and regions might have informal pecking orders, but there were no wider assemblages of power. The emergence of the *vory v zakone* as the authority figures, and the increasing homogenisation of criminal culture in the forcing houses of the Gulag camps, likewise did not create some nationwide shadow state. The *vory* were too independent minded, and Stalin's regime too paranoid about anything resembling a conspiracy, to allow that. Indeed, even individual *vory v zakone* were not necessarily gang leaders, and not every gang leader was necessarily a *vor v zakone*. Rather, the 'thieves within the code' represented moral authority within the *vorovskoi mir*: people to be listened to, people to be shown respect. Former Gulag inmate Marlen Korallov noted that one such *vor v zakone*, Nikola, was zealously protected and coddled by the other criminals: they gave him the only metal bed in the barracks, pushed it into a sheltered corner, masked it with blankets so he had privacy, and mounted guard on it even when he was gone, so that no one else could presume to lie on it.[3] The *vory v zakone* were, after all, a common good for the criminal community as a whole, the nodes around which a powerful and surprisingly effective network could be anchored.

As will be discussed below, the *blatnye* criminals of the thieves' world had their own languages, of tattoos, slang and even fashion. They also had their own rituals, each of which had its own practical value for the members. Prospective members, *patsany*, were quizzed informally, to ensure they were being honest about their criminal pasts and also to screen out informants. At least two existing thieves had to be willing to vouch for them, and eventually a *skhodka*, a criminal meeting, would be held to decide if they were worthy. A successful entrant with years of distinguished deeds under his belt might eventually hope to be considered a *pakhan*, a senior thief, simply as a mark of respect, but the process of being selected to be a *vor v zakone* was far more formal and intensive. Candidates had to be well known within their community, with sponsors willing to attest to their being upright exemplars of the criminal code. The regular transfer of criminals between camps, as well as the corruptibility of camp personnel, also made it easier for messages to flow between them, by word of mouth or on a small slip of paper called a *ksiva*. These were used to double-check a potential thief's pedigree and consult more widely, as well as to deliver edicts and death sentences where need be. Eventually, the successful candidate would be elevated in a ritual known as a 'coronation', presided over by existing *vory v zakone*, who in the process became responsible for their continued commitment to the thievish life and its code.[4]

The rituals were therefore ways of screening out those who were insincere or who failed to match the standards expected, even from behind the barbed wire of a Gulag. They also provided an aura of exclusivity and near-religious standing to the brotherhood of the *vorovskoi mir* and the authority of the *vory v zakone*. Likewise, the *vory v zakone* played a crucial role in the survival and prosperity of the underworld by resolving – when possible – disputes that otherwise could lead to violence, and also by administering the common funds eventually known as the *obshchak*. Gangs had their *obshchak* funds, as in some cases did the collected criminals of towns, regions or even camps, although really this is a term and a concept which only came into common usage in the 1950s. Originally such funds had been

mainly confined to the Gulags, to look after the dependents of jailed criminals, but they also came to be used to bribe camp officials, secure better
food, ensure the *blatnye* were not forced to work, and otherwise do what
they could to twist the everyday realities of Gulag life their way without
actually cooperating with the state.[5]

Most *vory v zakone* would have one or more henchmen known as *smot-
ryashchie*, 'watchers', who were their eyes and ears, checking up on potential
new *blatnye* and standing in for their boss if he were moved to a different
camp. Although some suggest they had other underlings, from advisers to
bodyguards, this was really a product of later times from the 1960s onwards,
when the *vory v zakone* were out of the camps and more likely to be running
gangs. In the 1930s through to the 1950s, though, they were simply big men
– very big men – within the Gulag underworlds, connected into nation-
spanning networks of information and allegiance, protected and respected
by the thieves, but generally neither seeking nor expecting any more institutional power.

Talking tough: thieves' language

*Fight resolutely against coarse expressions, swearwords, and the jargons
of professional thieves.*
            Boris Volin, People's Commissariat for Education, 1934[6]

For some of Stalin's Gulags, those deep in the northern wastes or thick
Siberian pine forests, the final layer of security was not the barbed-wire
fences, not guards' guns, not the specially bred dogs, not even the local indigenous people paid handsome bounties for runaway prisoners. Instead, it was
the very remoteness of the locations, the prospect of days and days on the
run, often in the most trying conditions, without finding human habitation,
anywhere to buy, beg or steal food. Hence in some cases *blatnye* desperate to
escape would befriend a fellow prisoner outside their culture and invite him
to flee along with them. Unbeknown to him, the companion's actual role was
to be a walking larder, eventually to be killed and eaten when needs must, in
a grotesque piece of inhuman pragmatism that truly put the *vor* into 'carni-
vore'. To be sure, reported cases in which this happened are few, but this was
either common enough[7] or remarkable enough, even by the standards of the
blatnye, that their slang acquired a term for the hapless prey: *myaso*, meat.

Now, languages are not just a medium of communication, they are also expressions of values, histories, cultural influences and social activities. They are alive, constantly changing meanings, assimilating new coinages and losing old ones. They embody the environment in which they emerge and develop, and both reflect and shape the thoughts, concerns and interests of those who use them. Studying a language is thus also a means of studying those who speak it.

One can, for example, expect a language to provide particular precision and nuance to those issues and activities central to its speakers' lives. The indigenous Sami Lapp people living in the very north of Russia's Kola peninsula, for example, have at least 180 words for various kinds of snow and ice, and perhaps a thousand for reindeer, including – surely the height of linguistic specialisation – the word *busat* for a bull with a single, oversized testicle.[8] In that context, it is hardly surprising that *fenya* could distinguish a theft on a bus (*marku derzhat*, literally 'holding the brand') from one at a train station (*derzhat sadku*, 'holding the cage').[9] Likewise, the need often to pass news between cells and barrack blocks by tapping code on the walls helps explain why *stukat* ('to knock') was used for 'speaking'.

Time and again, this language also emphasised the criminals' conscious and contemptuous withdrawal from mainstream society.[10] Ordinary people were *frayery*, a world derived from Yiddish where it means a 'john' – a prostitute's customer – or a sucker. The term *lyudi* ('people') was used specifically for *svoi* ('our own') members of the *vorovskoi mir*. Victor Herman, an American who spent eighteen years in the Gulag, recounted the tale of when he fought so hard against some thieves who tried to bully him that the camp's criminal godfather assumed he must be a *blatnoi*. The way he framed it, though, was to ask 'Who are you? . . . Are you a person? Are you an Urka? . . . Are you one of us?'[11] So only the *vory* were truly people; even the other criminals – known as *muzhiki*, 'peasants', or occasionally *zhigany*, 'whipping boys'[12] – were there simply to be used and exploited. Interestingly enough, this was echoed by the Gulag guards, who would often tell the *zeki*, the convicts, that they were *ne lyudi*, not people.[13]

This was not simply a collection of specialised jargon, though. Every profession, legal or illegal, has its technical vocabulary, from colloquialisms to terms of art relating to its particular activities. However, *fenya* did not confine itself to defining crimes and the underworld life, it even extended to provide substitutes for all kinds of day-to-day words, like *varezhka* ('mitten') for mouth.

Of course, there was a practical value to *fenya* in that it allowed criminals to communicate without fear of being understood by others. Some kind of thieves' cant even appears in the eighteenth-century tales of Vanka Kain. There is an account of the key to his fetters being smuggled to him in prison, baked in a loaf of bread, along with an explanatory note that the guards could not understand as it was couched in slang.[14] It was a safeguard, making it harder for the authorities to place agents in their ranks. It also represented a means of intimidating outsiders: even if they could not understand the cant, they knew what it meant when people used it. More than that, though, it was also a way of requiring and demonstrating a commitment to this alternative world, and those who hoped to rise within the *vorovskoi mir* had to learn and use *fenya*. This also helps explain the authorities' periodic and unsuccessful attempts to stamp *fenya* out: it represented another way in which the *blatnye* could live separately from the common folk. In 1934, Stalin warned that 'the person who speaks thieves' cant ceases to be a Soviet citizen'.[15] What he may have failed to realise was that this was precisely the point.

One world, one language

Know the language, know the world.

Russian criminal saying

The homogenisation of this criminal language speaks to the homogenisation of the Russian underworld. It is now widely known as *fenya* or *ofenya*, after an earlier beggars' cant dating back at least to the late eighteenth century, in which extra syllables, typically 'fe' and 'nya', were inserted between the syllables of regular words.[16] Thus *tyurma* ('prison') would become *tyurfemanya*. By the mid-nineteenth century this particular practice appears to have fallen into disuse, but the name remained.[17] However, it seems likely that in the period when *fenya* was most widely used, from the 1920s to the 1960s, it was more likely actually referred to as *blatnaya muzyka*, 'the music of the *blatnye*', or the more prosaic *blatnoi yazyk*, '*blatnye*'s tongue'. The other language is – or, as will be discussed below, now largely was – a visual one, encoded in the often complex tattoos with which career criminals inscribed their bodies. While neither is unique to the Russian *vorovskoi mir*, with criminal cants in Europe identified as far back as the fourteenth century,[18] they are distinctive in their spread and interaction. Even in the early twentieth century, the Russian language spoken by commoners was still fragmented, branched into countless local dialects. Yet both the spoken and visual languages of the *vorovskoi mir* were largely universal, promulgated not just in the *yamy* and the drinking dens but perhaps most importantly in the prison system. Tellingly, the slang term for a prison was to become *akademiya*, 'academy'.[19]

It was in the nineteenth century that this thieves' cant really became widespread within the underworld. There are certainly suggestions that it had become so by the 1850s. Vladimir Dal's ground-breaking *Explanatory Dictionary of the Living Russian Language*, first published in 1863, notes the distinctive jargons of groups such as the *mazuriki*, St Petersburg's criminal subculture.[20] Even so, it was at first a very fragmented argot, or rather a series of connected but distinct ones. It was never a true replacement for Russian: rather, it provided a parallel body of new words, existing words given new meanings, and phrases with commonly understood implications, with which criminals could pepper their conversations, and in doing so demonstrate their identity and allegiance.

Like so many such cants, *fenya* was a hotchpotch of borrowings from other, often more localised slang, from sailors' to merchants', as well as foreign languages and Russian words given new meanings. Thus, the *fenya* word *musor* for the police means 'trash' in Russian, but actually came originally from the Yiddish *moser*, for an informant. The Russian word for a lynx, *rys*, acquired the meaning of an experienced criminal wise in the ways of prison. The word *amba*, for death, was shared between both criminal and sailors' slang, while *shirman*, 'pocket' (hence *shirmachy* as one term for pickpockets), was found on the lips not just of crooks but also of some local traders.[21] *Fenya* also included numerous terms for particular criminal trades and acts. The German 'good morning', *guten Morgen*, for example, came to be used for a burglary carried out in the morning. It also had essential descriptors of different levels of social status, from the humble *shestyorka* ('sixer', from the lowest score in a card game) up to a *pakhan*, a boss, something essential given the prickly sense of status within the *vorovskoi mir* – it wasn't enough for a senior thief just to *be* senior, he needed to demonstrate it, and have others acknowledge his status.

In the first half of the twentieth century, though, *fenya* would achieve a level of standardisation that made it a genuine criminal lingua franca.

This was a perverse outcome of the increasing detention of criminals in prisons and labour colonies. In 1901, there were on average almost 85,000 prisoners in detention at any one time; by 1927, the figure had risen to 198,000; by 1933, it was 5 million.[22] The overwhelming majority were petty criminals and political prisoners, but many professional criminals were also swept into the system. The lengthy *etapy* on which the Gulag system relied could involve weeks or months of marching and being crowded into the notorious Stolypin railway carriages, with *zeki* being picked up and dropped off on the way. Even before they reached their labour camp, prisoners from different towns and regions were forced together, an experience repeated when they arrived. Furthermore, inmates would be shuttled from one camp to another, as bureaucratic or economic needs dictated.

With a far greater proportion of the professional criminals now assembled in the Gulags, and with the regular transfer of prisoners from camp to camp – as well as the tendency of those released to reoffend and be reimprisoned – *fenya* began to become increasingly homogenised through practice and intent. The fact that the professional thieves were often kept separate from the politicals, not least on *etap* transfers, also meant that they had greater chances to mix with their own kind. Facing both new opportunities and new temptations, the very identity of the *blatnye* became much more powerful and much more self-conscious. A central expression of that identity was the rise, transmission and use of their own language, one that increasingly merged with the wider world of Gulag slang, as well as *mat* – drawn literally from the root-word 'mother' – which is Russia's rich and distinctive language of obscenity.[23]

From the late 1950s, though, the Gulags would be opened and the code of the *vory* redefined in such a way that they lost their abhorrence of mainstream society and also of the *muzhiki* of the petty criminal world. As will be discussed, the later Soviet gangster derived his wealth and opportunity precisely from dealing with the corrupt officials and black marketeers who thrived as the system began to grind to a standstill. Slang still abounded, but it no longer divided two worlds so sharply. Moreover, the homogeneity and exclusivity that had characterised it was no longer as important, nor was it possible to maintain. By the 1970s, one could hear *fenya* and Gulag songs on the streets, but increasingly terms also cropped up which were distinctive to a particular city or region.

Tattoos: writing resistance on the body

Do you stand by your tattoos?
Usual challenge to new inmates when arriving in a cell[24]

Like *fenya*, the thieves' code of tattoos drew often upon traditional visual themes, not least religious iconography. However, given that classic motifs included naked and voluptuous Virgin Marys and angels enjoying oral sex, the intent was clearly deliberately sacrilegious. This demonstrated the criminals' lifetime commitment to their 'world' and a deliberate and defiant alienation from mainstream society. Later, new forms of blasphemy became popular: Nazi swastikas or obscene caricatures of Marx, Lenin or Stalin had a similar consciously iconoclastic intent. As Alexander Solzhenitsyn put it so evocatively in his *The Gulag Archipelago*, the *vory*

> surrendered their bronze skin to tattooing and in this way gradually satisfied their artistic, their erotic, and even their moral needs: on one another's chests, stomachs and backs they could admire powerful eagles perched on cliffs or flying through the sky. Or the big hammer, the sun, with its rays shooting out in every direction; or women and men copulating; or the individual organs of their sexual enjoyment; and all of a sudden, next to their hearts were Lenin or Stalin or perhaps both . . .[25]

The most extreme tattoos, such as barbed wire across the forehead or 'don't wake' on the eyelids, could hardly be hidden – and that was intentional. The extensive tattooing, often done in the Gulag with makeshift needles sanitised simply by being passed through a flame and using ink mixed from soot and urine, was done to symbolise not just a permanent commitment to the *vorovskoi mir*, but also manliness. It was painful and carried the risk of septicaemia. The aforementioned 'don't wake' tattoo involved sliding a spoon under the eyelid before starting the inking.[26] You needed to demonstrate your willingness to endure pain and risk your life, as well as your separation from the world of the *frayery* to be a true *vor*.

It is hard to be confident about dating a coherent 'language' of tattoos, not least because any conclusion rests largely on the negative data that while earlier police reports referred to criminal slang, they were essentially silent about a specific tattoo code. Nonetheless, it seems to have emerged around the turn of the twentieth century. Originally, the *vorovskoi mir* was simply a culture which arose amongst outsiders excluded from mainstream society by poverty and ill fortune. Increasingly, though, there emerged a strand within it that did not just accept but embraced and exalted this exclusion. It actively turned its back on the mainstream, starting a process which would lead to the rise of the *blatnye* criminals.

The tattoos that reflected this also encoded a criminal's career and rank, with designs denoting the kinds of crimes he had committed, where and how long he was imprisoned and his ascent within the underworld.[27] A *vor v zakone* might sport a star on his chest; a dagger denoted a killer for hire; shattered fetters on the ankle indicated someone who had broken out of prison; an onion-domed church marked the number of prison terms served, a cupola for each one. The hand was a virtual curriculum vitae, with tattoos marking criminal convictions and specialities, whether a second-storey cat burglar or a convicted armed robber. Others were acronyms whose meanings were well known, but also deniable. For example, KOT (literally 'CAT') stood for 'Native of Prisons', NEZh 'Fed Up with This Fucking Life', and ZLO meant 'Take Revenge on Informants'. Irony also played a part: NKVD, the abbreviation for the political police through much of Stalin's reign, was used to stand for 'There's No Friendship Stronger than Criminals''. Tattoos could have a declaratory purpose, expressing such sentiments as 'if you lose at cards, pay your debt' or 'life is short'. This could even be a way of communicating a very specific message: two bulls tattooed over the shoulder-blades, for example, symbolised an intent to challenge for gang leadership.

The language of the tattoos would also change over time. During the 'bitches' wars', declarations of renewed commitment to the traditional code were inked. Tattoos on the shoulders, for example, expressed a commitment never to wear epaulettes – symbols of military rank and also of the *voyensh-china* – while stars on the knees symbolised a refusal to kneel before the authorities.[28] This was, of course, fighting talk, or at least ink. Earlier generations of criminals may well have sported their own tattoos, but they were less prone to regard them as part of a formal language, less eager to use them as a permanent and defiant demarcation between their world and that of the legitimate sector. They were also less punctilious about the 'right' meaning of each image, something that would later become essential. By the 1930s, a *vor* who sported a tattoo encoding some distinction he had not deserved might find it being stripped from his skin by the traditionalists, eager to punish transgression and preserve the commonality of their visual language.

By the same token, Gulag tattooists were a privileged group, prized not just for their skill and their ability to scrounge and assemble the necessary ink and implements, but also their almost sacral role as the chroniclers on the flesh of thieves' identities, accomplishments and ambitions. Inmates with this talent might find themselves protected by the *blatnye* for this reason, even if they were *muzhiki* or politicals. This was, for example, the saving grace for Thomas Sgovio, an American Communist who moved to the USSR, buoyed by a sense of mission, and who was then arrested in 1938 when he tried to reclaim his US passport on seeing just how this workers' paradise was turning out. Sent to the Kolyma labour complex, he was fortunate enough to be able to demonstrate his skill as a tattooist, which helped win him food and protection from the criminals around him.[29] Conversely, a tattooist who dared ink someone with a design they had not earned could expect violent, even fatal treatment. After all, in a world where there were no paper records and honour and appearance were all, this was as close to an official record as the *vorovskoi mir* could have.

The brutal counterpart to this was the use of forced tattooing to demean, isolate and punish those who fell foul of the thieves and their code. Sometimes, *blatnye* would not be allowed to redeem their sins through physical punishment and yet had not done enough to be killed. One option was for them to be seized and either physically restrained long enough to be tattooed, or forced to undergo it on pain of death. Even more pernicious was the treatment meted out to inmates who had been sexually assaulted by other male thieves and were thus deemed 'debased' in the macho *vor* culture, considered to have been the victims of their own weakness. They were treated as pariahs, not even allowed to eat at the same time as the *blatnye*, and they might also be forcibly tattooed with eyes over the groin or the word 'slave' on their face. In this respect, the language of the tattoos was as brutal, complex and hierarchical as the underworld subculture which had spawned it.

Cultures, clothes and custom

They finished me, the bastards, they finished me.
They destroyed my youth,
My golden hair turned white,
And I am on the edge of ruin.

Gulag song[30]

When *zeki* were being mustered for a march to a work site or transfer, the guards would deliver the same murderous catechism: 'A step to the left or a step to the right will be considered an attempt to escape. The escort will shoot without warning.' There are other ways of forcing people into narrow paths, though, and for all their freewheeling airs, the thieves actually lived very constrained lives. Their crude 'honour amongst thieves' code was enforced by collective beatings and murder in a direct carry-over from *samosud*, the peasant lynch law of pre-Soviet times.[31] However, their values were also encoded in, and enforced through, the superstitions and rituals of the *vorovskoi mir*.

We have little evidence about the conduct and content of these rituals beyond hearsay, but Federico Varese uncovered a fascinating case of a *skhodka* that had to decide on whether or not a new recruit was worthy of joining the fraternity while locked down in a transit prison's isolation cells.[32] Unable to meet and talk, they had to communicate with each other by notes, notes which the police later found and impounded, representing a unique primary source. Two sponsors, as was required, recommended the candidate to the others, writing that 'his behaviour and aspirations are totally in accordance with the *vory* world view', not least because 'he defied camp discipline for a long period of time'. Eventually, of the other nine cells, two expressed themselves in favour ('if his soul is pure, let him in') and none of the rest demurred, so the application was successful. Grappling in their own way with the *patsan*'s 'soul' and his capacity for defiance took precedence over simply enumerating his crimes.

On joining the fraternity, a thief would gain his *klichka*, his criminal nickname, both as practical security and also as symbol of the start of a new life. Dmitry Likhachev, whose life spanned both time in the Gulag and a career as a distinguished scholar of medieval Russian, considered this 'a necessary act of transition to the sphere of the *vory*' akin to 'the taking of monastic vows'.[33] The choosing of this name was very important, for it generally could not be changed (although one could acquire several over time) and would become a central element of the thief's new identity. While presented during the initiation as something placed upon the new member, in practice it would typically be agreed beforehand by the prospective thief in discussion with his patrons. Most such nicknames were permutations of the criminal's original name or patronymic (the second, 'son/daughter of X—' name all Russians have), perhaps reflecting the way his new identity overwrote his old. Thus, Alexander Chapikin became 'Chapai' and Miriam Mamedov 'Miron'. Often, the person's place of birth or operations also featured: Eduard Asatryan became 'Edik Tbilisski' ('Tbilisi Edik') because he was born there, and Nikolai Zykov was 'Yakutyonok' because he was by birth a member of the Yakut minority. Others, though, were plays on words – Vadim Fedorchenko became 'Fedora', after the hat – or moral, physical or other attributes, such as 'Fierce', 'Cross-Eyed' or 'Lucky'.[34]

Luck mattered, after all, as gambling was central to life in the *vorovskoi mir*. It was not just to while away time spent in the camps, but was a metaphor for their intensely competitive ethos and a way of demonstrating skill, cunning and honour. It is no coincidence that *derzhat mast*, 'to hold the suit' – in the card-playing rather than sartorial sense – was a *fenya* term for holding authority over other prisoners.[35] To fail to pay one's debts was, as has been mentioned, a terrible crime against the code, sure to bring violent consequences. One classic form of atonement with honour was to scale the barbed wire of the outer zone and die by the guards' guns. Yet these debts were often themselves symbolic: two thieves might, for example, wager the possessions of another inmate, a *frayer* or a *muzhik*, and the loser was then expected to go and take them to hand them over to the winner. In this way, the game also reinforced the predatory relationship between the thieves and everyone else. Even more strikingly, jailed historian Anton Antonov-Ovseyenko recalled encountering a *blatnoi* whose forfeit had been to stay mute for three years. Even while transferred from one camp to the next, he knew he had to stay silent because word of his situation had spread on the underground grapevine and 'no one can evade the law of thieves'.[36]

Gambling could take many forms, from playing draughts with pieces moulded out of stale, wetted bread and a board scraped on the ground, to wagering on the weather or which guard would be on duty that night. But the true sport of the *vorovskoi mir* was cards, which assumed an almost mystical significance as portents of the future (and thus also appear disproportionately in tattoos). Even in the 1980s, in a more relaxed age when convicts could get hold of cards openly, a soldier whose brother had been in prison told me that one of his cellmates had hanged himself because he had drawn four jacks in a row and had considered it a most terrible omen.[37] In earlier times, even the making of a deck of cards was a complex exercise in scrounging and ingenuity. Rectangles of paper salvaged from any available source were glued together with wet bread to form the cards, then dried under a bunk until hard. Crude stamps fashioned out of the base of a tin mug or cut into a shoe heel were used for printing the pips; black ink was made out of ash, red out of clay, blood or streptomycin (an antibiotic often used in camps to address the frequent outbreaks of TB).[38] In particular cases, where the craftsman could get hold of pencils or ink (usually through a trusty working in the camp administration), the face cards would be hand drawn, occasionally with some artistry. These cards were, after all, more than just a pastime: they were a prized possession and symbol of the chance and honour that the thieves felt was at the heart of their life. As Vlas Doroshevich observed from his time in prison, 'the card game is the all-grasping, all-absorbing terror of *katorga* [penal colony]. I saw [thieves] lying in hospital because of emaciation: they'd gambled away their rations and eaten nothing for weeks ... [or] betting their medicine against other patients in the hospital.'[39]

Rituals, games and tattoos were not the only identifiers of this subculture. Senior *vory* often affected particular styles of dress to distinguish themselves from *frayery* and lesser criminals alike. This is something that predated the Gulag: military officers' caps predominated during the First World War, perhaps as another deliberate act of sacrilege, then flat trade-school caps like those of classic American newsboys in the 1920s. In the Gulags, demonstrating that you could still find and retain particular items of clothing had a particular significance, as it attested to your authority, protection, connections or outright toughness. According to political prisoner Varlam Shalamov, in the 1940s the Kolyma *vory* wore leather caps and home-made aluminium crosses, although according to Michael Solomon, whose time there followed Shalamov's, they later favoured raincoats, as much a mark of rank as a practical item, and a counterpart to the leather coats affected by the camps' political commissars.[40] The French-Russian Maximilien de Santerre, sentenced to the Gulag on espionage charges in 1946, also mentions the crosses, and that they would wear waistcoats and shirts not tucked into their trousers.[41] Caps, waistcoats and untucked shirts also featured in Georgy Feldgun's reminiscences of 1940s camp life.[42]

And they sang. In the days before Uber transformed the world of Moscow's taxis, anyone using a cab would likely be blasted by the throatily saccharine sound of *Radio Shanson*, a station specifically dedicated to the *shanson*, a genre of ballad not confined to but very heavily influenced by the music of the Gulags. By definition, this made it very much the music of the *vorovskoi mir*, and *blatnaya pesnya* ('thieves' songs') are a popular genre even today. The later popularisation of the genre is discussed in chapter 16, but for the thieves in the Gulag, music became a way to safely express their feelings, from their hopes and dreams of the outside, to their anger and despair inside the *zona*. Perhaps it is not surprising that one of the common terms for living a criminal life was *po muzyke khodit*, 'to move to the music'. Beyond ways to pass time and cope with life in the Gulag, the songs also became part of the oral history of the camps, a necessity given the perennial absence of writing materials and the inability to save and distribute accounts in any other form. The song 'Kengir', for example, is a detailed telling of the 1954 prisoners' rising there. 'Although the enemy is strong,' it warns, 'the masses are breaking their fetters.'[43]

Women in the thieves' world

The moral code of the professional criminal . . . prescribes contempt for women . . . This is true of all women without exception.

Varlam Shalamov[44]

Of course, the *vory* forged fetters of their own, and oppressed and preyed on those around them with less organisation but as much enthusiasm as the Stalinist state. To this end, perhaps it is worth concluding this chapter by looking at the role of women in the *voroskoi mir*, as it encapsulates the tensions between the crude machismo at its heart and the practical and emotional realities of any human collective. This was an unpleasantly, often horrifically misogynistic culture, exalting a caricature of manliness in which women were confined to the roles of idealised mother, wanton prostitute, helpless victim, gangster's moll or excluded outsider. From the portrayals of women in their tattoos – typically naked and sexualised – to the sentimental stanzas of their songs, the thieves might affect to revere or despise women, but never to respect them.

Although in many cases efforts were made to keep male and female prisoners apart, camp memoirs are depressingly packed with accounts of not just one-off rapes but women forced, through violence, intimidation or the prospect of slightly better – more survivable – conditions, into sexual relationships with *blatnye*, officials and those *zeki* whose occupations gave them even a slight degree of privilege and impunity.[45] In some cases, this was a ruthlessly deliberate strategy in literally murderous conditions, more often a reflection of the brutal social relations of the times.

For the thieves, these relationships were precisely meant to be unequal and meaningless. Varlam Shalamov, an outsider with a sharp axe to grind but no less observant for that, said that they learned 'contempt for women from childhood', a belief that 'woman, an inferior being, has been created only to satisfy the criminal's animal craving'.[46] He was, sadly, not wrong, and he also perceptively noted the saccharine but ultimately empty cult of the blessed mother in *vor* culture: 'There is one woman who is romanticised by the criminal world ... This woman is the criminal's mother ... [But] no criminal has ever sent so much as a kopek to his mother or made any attempt to help her on his own.'[47]

As ever, there was something of a gap between code and reality. Just as especially gifted storytellers, singers, even famous sportsmen, and those who just happened to catch a senior *vor*'s eye with their wit or spirit might find themselves sheltered under his wing, for all that they were *frayery*, so too could different relationships emerge between male criminals and women. The code of the pre-Stalinist *vorovskoi mir* had demanded that, when one joined the fraternity, one severed all existing ties – to church, to family, to wife – as a mark of one's new commitment. In practice, many remained married, but the unfortunate wife was considered within the underworld now to be little more than gang chattel: her husband's first, but that of another member of the gang were he to die or be imprisoned. She was lucky enough to be considered of greater status than a prostitute – arguably not the highest bar to vault – but in Valery Chalidze's words, 'the relationship of a thief and his wife is that of master and slave'.[48] Ex-convict Gustav Herling recounted a scene when Marusya, the lover of a thief called Koval, spat in the face of one of his fellows in response to an insult. Rather than defend her, he at once turned on his lover and forced her to submit to gang rape by the rest of the group in punishment.[49] Whether out of fear of the consequences for himself or a genuine outrage at this perceived transgression – as if it matters either way – Koval unhesitatingly placed his male comrades over his lover.

As ever, there were exceptions, such as thieves with genuinely loving feelings towards their spouses, and a very few female gangsters who gained a degree of respect within the professional underworld. These rare cases, though, in no way moderate the overall impression of a subculture where gender relationships were almost prehistoric in their imbalances.

This was also visible in the female underworld. Although formally there was no room for them in the *vorovskoi mir*, a women's equivalent of sorts had emerged even before the Gulag era, and anchored itself in their side of the prison *zona*. Just as the *vorovskoi mir* ended up defined by the Gulag, so too this female criminal subculture was essentially shaped by its masculine counterpart. Individually or in groups, the female thieves undoubtedly could be formidable. Eugenia Ginzburg describes her shocking encounter:

> But the worst was yet to come, our first meeting with real, hardened female criminals ... down the hatchway poured another few hundred human beings, if that is the right name for those appalling creatures, the dregs of the criminal world ... the mongrel horde surged down upon us, with tattooed, half-naked bodies and grimacing, apelike faces.[50]

For all that Chalidze claims such gangs 'are treated with respect', this seems hard to substantiate.[51] Instead, denied any official status by the men, the women were relegated to a subaltern role, which they seem to have embraced, following the male habits of swearing and *fenya*. Even their own tattoos to a large extent reflected the chauvinist aesthetics of the men's, with representations of women essentially confined to three archetypes: the Madonna, the mother or the whore.[52] In their loudly proclaimed freedom from the manners and values of regular society, the *vory* actually managed to create alternative, less extensive but much more fiercely policed constraints for themselves – but these were nothing to the ways they abused and distorted the subculture of their female counterparts. No wonder this was essentially a product of the *zona*, something that could only truly flourish in an artificial world of barbed wire and forced labour, casual violence and institutionalised abuse. When the thieves were let out into the wider Soviet world, a world of freedom and choice compared with the Gulags, this vicious society would change dramatically.

Part Two

EMERGENCE

CHAPTER 6

THE UNHOLY TRINITIES

Big thieves hang little ones.

Russian proverb

It is a perverse irony that the true midwives of organised crime in today's Russia are to be found in an unlikely and disparate trinity of Soviet general secretaries: Stalin the tyrant, Brezhnev the manager and Gorbachev the reformer. Stalin created the collaborator-criminal willing to work with self-interested elements of the elite. Brezhnev presided over a Soviet Union characterised by corruption and the black market, turning the new *vory* increasingly towards the informal economy. And Gorbachev shattered the state, but also unleashed new market forces that the *vory* would prove best placed to exploit.

The way their policies conspired to shape the *vory* is perhaps best illustrated by the career of Gennady Karkov, 'The Mongol'. In the late 1960s and early 1970s, his gang was the terror of Moscow's black-market magnates, and it would set the tone for the evolving relationship between gangsters, underground entrepreneurs and a corrupt state. It would also be the finishing school for a generation of future kingpins, including Otari Kvantrishvili, who in the early 1990s looked set to become the boss of Moscow's ganglands, and Vyacheslav 'Yaponchik' Ivankov, who brought Moscow's underworld to New York's Brighton Beach.

Karkov (sometimes also called Korkov) was born in 1930 in Kulebaki, 300 kilometres east of Moscow, a child of Stalin's charnel house industrialisation and the Second World War. By all accounts he soon fled the smog and shadow of Kulebaki's foundries and the workers' barrack blocks around them, and took to the underworld. He was smart, quick, ruthless and daring, a natural-born leader who was very willing to get his hands dirty, and he quickly adapted to the new, more permissive code of the *suki*. He was crowned a *vor v zakone* at the unusually young age of twenty-five, just two years after Stalin's death in 1953, and given the *klichka* 'The Mongol' on account of his Asiatic appearance. Later that year, he was arrested in Moscow on charges of theft. He served six years of a ten-year sentence before returning to the capital in 1962 and resuming his criminal activities, but now with a more ambitious plan. Before, he had simply been a robber; now, he would be a racketeer. In his absence, the black market in Moscow had grown exponentially, and the *tsekhoviki*, the 'shopmen', who ran it were doing well for themselves. He assembled a gang of some thirty criminals, and began to stalk these hidden capitalists. Initially, the gang would burgle the *tsekhoviki*'s apartments, confident that their victims could not go to the police lest they had to explain how they had accumulated the cash and luxuries that were taken. Then, they graduated to extortion, demanding payment in return for a peaceful life and kidnapping those who refused or who had hidden away their ill-gotten gains.

Having taken to wearing police uniforms to access people's homes without question, Karkov's men also began using the same tactic to seize their victims. The *tsekhoviki* would then be driven out of town, typically into the woods or to abandoned houses, and tortured with sadistic ferocity until they broke: burned with hot irons; hung from trees and only cut down when nearly asphyxiated; even nailed into a coffin, which the burly, drug-addicted thug bearing the imaginative nickname 'The Executioner' would then begin to saw in two, as if in a magic trick. For a while they did handsomely for themselves, and Karkov's gang doubled in size. Meanwhile, with the rise to power of General Secretary Leonid Brezhnev in 1964, the corruption of the Communist Party and the pervasiveness of the underground economy only deepened.

Karkov and most of his men were arrested in 1972 in one of the largest post-war operations mounted yet by MUR, Moscow's Criminal Intelligence Division. Most of the charges failed to stick as witnesses became strangely forgetful and documents vanished, but there was no way the authorities were going to let 'The Mongol' walk. He was convicted on two charges and sentenced to fourteen years in a strict-regime prison colony. He would end up serving his full term, only being freed in 1986, a year after Gorbachev had become general secretary, and in the earliest and most hesitant stage of his reforms. Karkov's time had passed, though. He tried to muscle his way back into the criminal big leagues, and built himself something of a fiefdom in Moscow's northern Tushino region, but this never amounted to much. He eventually died of cancer or cirrhosis – reports vary – in 1994.[1]

His decade-long reign in Moscow was punctuated by arrests and time in detention, but nonetheless 'The Mongol' became a legend. I can attest that in the 1990s, hardened MUR investigators and gangsters alike used him as a benchmark for assessing the underworld contenders of the time. Beyond his own talents, it was because he was the first seriously to appreciate the extent to which the rise of the black market, facilitated by the corruption of the Party, was creating a new class of underground entrepreneurs who were cash rich but protection poor, such that they were ripe for exploitation. Karkov had money, but he also accelerated the process leading to an understanding between *vory*, *tsekhoviki* and the state. This would finally be formalised in 1979 when a gathering of kingpins from across the Soviet Union decided the terms of the 'tax' they would expect from the black marketeers in return for protection.[2] Karkov's true legacy was not just a new generation of *vory* but also a whole new criminal world in which they would operate. This alliance would be crucial in the 1980s, when Mikhail Gorbachev's quixotic reform programme would in practice doom the state and empower the gangsters.

Stalin's legacy

In certain circles, criminal tendencies are even becoming fashionable. Thieves' slang and even thieves' tone of voice have become trendy.
Letter to the Party leadership from concerned citizens
of Chelyabinsk[3]

On 5 March 1953, Stalin succumbed to a stroke, cardiac haemorrhage and paranoia (the last because his suspicion of potential assassins meant he forbade unauthorised entry into his rooms and so lay dying for hours before anyone realised). The Soviet Union he bequeathed to his successor was a perverse collection of paradoxes. It was an unquestioned superpower, a nuclear one at that, with an empire in eastern Europe. It had industrialised and electrified, brought literacy to the masses, made the steppe sprout grain and the tundra give forth gold and timber. Yet this had been on the basis of murderous mass terror, and it left the countryside scarred with Gulags, prisons and mass graves, and the Soviet psyche shadowed with habits of collaboration, opportunism and automatic defensiveness.

It was also showing the signs of pressure. The elite were desperate not to deliver themselves to another Stalin, but at the same time were worried about retaining their grip on society. The Cold War was in full swing. The labour camps had become uncontrollable and uneconomic, hence their opening up. 'Theft of socialist property' was a serious crime, but also endemic. It was not just that in times of extreme hardship and shortage people had to steal from the state to get by, it was also a by-product of the alienation brought about by the stark juxtaposition of an official narrative of worker empowerment, shared plenty and comradely democracy, and the reality of corruption, scarcity and authoritarianism. If everyone owned everything, then surely no one owned anything, and how could it be theft if no one owned it? Everyone stole what they could, and even if they could not steal goods, they stole time, disappearing from work to queue up for food, or moonlighting off the books. Everyone knew it, and this was even the subject of much humour:

> 'I think,' says Ivan to Volodya, 'that we must have the richest country in the world.'
> 'Why?' asks Ivan.
> 'Because for nearly sixty years, everyone has been stealing from the state and still there is something left to steal.'[4]

Stalinism had been marked by a strange cognitive dissonance, a nation-wide Stockholm syndrome in which a bloody and wasteful tyranny could somehow coexist with continued belief in the Marxist-Leninist dream, or at least that there was some greater purpose to the suffering. Ironically, Nikita Khrushchev's denunciation of Stalin in his soon-leaked 'Secret Speech' in 1956 and the consequent programme of 'de-Stalinisation' knocked away many of the surviving ideological underpinnings of the Soviet state. If enduring Stalin had been for nothing, what else meant anything? From this anomie would emerge all kinds of different counter-cultural expressions. Amnestied *zeki* brought with them the music of the Gulag, such that, as dissident poet Yuli Daniel wrote, 'songs from the camps were becoming popular. They were gradually seeping through from Siberia and the Far North, and you kept hearing snatches of them in refreshment rooms at railway junctions . . . At last they marched into town on the backs of the "rehabilitated" offenders.'[5] Foreign-influenced youth fads emerged, such as the *stilyagi* beatniks and rockers of the 1950s and 1960s, the football-mad *fanaty* and the heavy-metal *metallisty* of the 1980s. They not only challenged the orthodoxy of the Party, but often expressed that through a quest for Western clothes and music.[6] Even theft from the state and corruption acquired a perverse, implicit legitimacy as blows struck against a hypocritical and exploitative elite. Change was coming, but no one could be sure quite what kind.

The *vory* found themselves within this strange new world. The irony was that, while the *suki* had won the cultural – and very physical – war in the camps, and were amongst the first to be released in the amnesties following Stalin's death, they were emerging into a USSR whose underworld was still dominated by the *blatnye*. The result was a renewed struggle, in which again their key assets – a capacity to organise and a willingness to work through and with the authorities – ensured that the *suki* won. It was a patchwork victory, a neighbourhood here, a township there. One retired police officer I spoke to recalled his early childhood in Yekaterinburg (then called Sverdlovsk), a city in the Urals that ever since the mid-1950s had been afflicted by so-called 'blue gangs' – called that because of their dense tattoos – of ex-convicts. At first this had meant vicious street battles between *blatnye* and *suki* groups on an almost daily basis.[7] It was not an easy victory for the 'bitches', then, let alone a bloodless one. Much of the dramatic increase in lawlessness across the Soviet Union – 552,281 recorded crimes in 1953, 745,812 by 1957[8] – was accounted for by the inevitable chaos when 5 million convicts were suddenly dumped into the country, with minimal assistance; it also concealed a nation-spanning underworld revolution. However, it was near-enough inevitable, given the circumstances.

Gangsters under pressure . . .

The real tragedy of the 1980s is that until then, the [criminal] authorities were kept under the state's thumb. We were winning. And then we threw it away.

Russian police officer, 1990[9]

After they had completed their reconquest of the Soviet underworld, though, the gangsters soon had to come to terms with their place in the new order. In 1957, Deputy Interior Minister Mikhail Kholodkov complained that 'often in the camp points it is not the administration but the recidivists who are in command'.[10] Outside the labour camp system, though, the biggest gang in town was undoubtedly the Communist Party and the opportunists who had risen under Stalin. With understandable hyperbole, David Remnick calls it 'the most gigantic mafia the world has ever known',[11] but this was a view shared in the underworld. As the professional pickpocket 'Zhora the Engineer' put it, 'there certainly is a Soviet mafia. And it's organised a hell of a lot better than the American mafia. But it has another name. It's called the Communist Party. We wouldn't dream of trying to compete with it.'[12]

The state was authoritarian and possessed – in the form of the *militsiya* (police) and the political police (from 1954 known as the Committee of State Security, KGB) – the undoubted capacity to crack down on the gangsters if ever they became a challenge or an embarrassment. Indeed, one of the key purposes of the 1956 Law on Measures for Improving the Performance of the USSR MVD (Ministry of Internal Affairs) was precisely to suppress the gangs that were erupting out of the Gulags, and a multi-vectored campaign was soon launched by the police, the KGB and the agencies of social and political control. Even *suki*, in what could be considered tough but ironic justice, might find themselves considered 'counter-revolutionaries' rather than mere hooligans if they tangled with the police or their volunteer auxiliaries, the *druzhinniki*. This was generally done to regain control over the situation and to reassure the public, but it was also implicitly part of the creation of a new set of *ponyatiya*, understandings between the state and the underworld.

Throughout the 1960s and 1970s, the *vory* were very much kept in their place, and the general consensus is that the gangs which had first emerged in the 1950s were largely dismantled. Organised crime was atomised back to relatively small-scale ventures and, despite continued sporadic cases of armed robbery and the like, often defaulted to activities such as fraud and illegal gambling. In the late 1960s, for example, an old man who had been a fabled card-sharp in the 1940s, and who went by the *klichka* 'Tbilisi', was persuaded to set up an informal academy in Moscow and pass on his skills to a new generation. As a result, in the early 1970s the capital saw a flowering of professional gambling, which spawned its own specialisms, each with its own place in their hierarchy, from the 'riders' who played in taxis roaming Moscow's streets, to the top tier, who had their own secret gambling dens in restaurant backrooms and apartments.[13]

Without a critical mass of members, spread as they were now across the country, without the Gulags as forcing houses for a new generation, and without the ability to operate openly, the *vorovskoi mir* as a distinctive subculture began to die. Of course, there was still much crime, a great deal of it organised. But the *vory*'s strong sense of being separate from the rest of the population, of their status as the only true *lyudi* ('people'), began to fade, along with the transmission of the code and folklore of the *vorovskoi mir*. The father of the police officer quoted above had himself been in the *militsiya* in the 1960s and, in his view, 'then the *vory* were already losing their way. Some believed in the old code, and remembered it well. They tried to teach it to the youngsters. But outside the camps, it was different. Just because they knew all the lyrics of Vysotsky, the youngsters thought they knew the code. They didn't.'[14]

Vladimir Vysotsky, an iconic singer-songwriter of the post-Stalin era, did indeed draw heavily on thieves' music for language and inspiration. But, as the retired policeman noted, the essence of the *vorovskoi mir* was not just a shared songbook. For perhaps twenty years, the thieves' world would fade, gaining a mythological status at the expense of authenticity and power. It had adapted to Stalinism, though, so it would be revived, reinvented and reinterpreted again in the later Brezhnev and Gorbachev years, from the 1970s. It would re-emerge in an underworld dominated by the opportunities to be found in the informal economy and corruption, but also one with far fewer opportunities to use violence openly without incurring the wrath of the state. Just as the *suki* used the same language as the *blatnye*, simply rewriting the code, so too the new generation of *vory* would seek to use that language and culture in new ways. Karkov's story, of the *vor v zakone* who found his chance preying on the underground economy, was indeed the harbinger of the next iteration of the *vorovskoi mir*, one shaped by the black market.

... street gangs on the rise

Say what you like, but there are now two battles being waged in Kazan.
One of them, with knifing and bloodshed, is in full view of the public.

But the other is even more awful. It is a hatred-arousing battle that has divided Kazan into 'rotten boys' and 'good ones'.

Ogonyok magazine, 1988[15]

One perverse irony of this situation was that it also contributed to the rise of marginalised and violent street gangs. Back in the day, many of the more aggressive and charismatic young street toughs would have drifted into the *vorovskoi mir* and the discipline that entailed. As it was, though, their anti-social proclivities, magnified by the absence of alternative outlets and activities beyond the stultifying banalities of the Young Communist movement, had to find other outlets. The so-called 'Kazan phenomenon'[16] – because it was first properly recognised in that city – followed a classic pattern, as adolescents clustered around territorial divisions, particular affiliations (such as following the same football team) or even large factories, to hang out and brawl. Indeed, this had been a staple of village life until the 1960s, and was simply transposed into the cities. Fights, often conducted with a kind of rough-and-ready ritual and rules, let young men blow off steam, demonstrate their masculine virtues and establish hierarchies. Fyodor Razzakov remembers being part of a gang in 1970s Moscow which claimed three streets in the north-east of the city – Kazakov, Gorokhovsky and Tokmakov – and whose allies were the kids from Bauman and Pochtovaya streets, while their blood foes were the lads from the alleys around Bauman Gardens less than half an hour's walk away. Even so, all these gangs would gladly unite for a grand brawl with their rivals from the central Chistye Prudy neighbourhood, which could sometimes involve up to a hundred young bruisers.[17]

Sometimes, street gangs evolved into organised crime groups, monetising muscle by turning it into territorial control, or at least the capacity to extort rents from the local informal economy. In Kazan, several street gangs ended up merging into Tiap-Liap, an organisation run by Sergei Antipov, an older ex-convict who masterminded a process of consolidation that saw more and more small gangs forced to join or be destroyed. By the end of the 1970s, Tiap-Liap had perhaps 200 members, with their own structure, a common *obshchak* fund and even a uniform: dark padded jackets and a badge (a crown with the letters TK, for Teplokontrol, the neighbourhood where it all began). They were involved in organised burglary, provided protection for the *tsekhoviki* black-market entrepreneurs, and escorted the movement of illegal goods. Their example encouraged or forced other Kazan gangs to go through a similar transformation, but the authorities were evidently reluctant to admit to such an open criminalisation of their city.[18]

Ultimately, though, Tiap-Liap would become a victim of its own success and its overconfidence. In August 1978, in a deliberate show of force against the rival Novotatarskaya Sloboda gang, they deployed perhaps fifty toughs with guns and iron bars and began shooting and beating at random in their territory. A seventy-four-year-old war veteran was killed, and ten others – including two police officers – were wounded. This the authorities could not ignore and so, as usual, they swung from wilful blindness to draconian repression. Thirty gang members were tried and convicted; two senior members were executed. While gang violence in Kazan persisted into the 1990s, Tiap-Liap itself was broken.

So even in its most primordial forms, organised crime endured, and it had a chance for a revival in the 1970s – to a large extent, ironically, thanks to the government that had tamed it. For all that it had the laws, the men and the guns, the state was also riddled with corruption and increasingly dependent on the black market to satisfy the needs of ordinary Soviets and elites alike. A second shadowy trinity emerged, of corrupt officials, gangsters and black marketeers. The Party was facing a prolonged period of stagnation and decay. Under General Secretary Brezhnev (1964–82), the scale of corruption within both the Party and society expanded dramatically. As the planned economy began to grind to a painful halt, the underground economy grew to compensate.

To an extent, this was a natural by-product of the failures of the system: people turned to bribery, the black market and *blat* – the economy of favours[19] – to fill in the gaps. However, it was implicitly also policy: under the social contract that Western Sovietologists came to call the 'little deal', the state granted the masses greater freedom to loaf, complain, steal and barter, so long as they did not challenge the status quo.[20] Likewise, the elite were pacified by perks, access to scarce goods and a quiet, safe life. This shabby compromise worked for a while, so long as the economy was growing at a sufficient rate to provide the resources to keep everyone content, but it would not last. Meanwhile, not only did organised crime benefit from the indolence and venality of the state, it acquired a new role as the indispensable middleman between corrupt Party figures and the *tsekhoviki*.

The fish that rotted from the head

Who is the most dangerous counter-revolutionary right now? The bribe taker.

Soviet propaganda poster, 1923[21]

In the 1970s, in particular, ordinary Soviets were being bought off by the fruits of early consumerism: a fridge, a television, maybe even a car. But the *vlasti*, the people of power, had from the first eagerly used their new latitude to feather their own nests on a much grander scale, building themselves summer palaces, dressing in imported clothes, and generally living often lavish, easy lives. As the Russian proverb has it, the fish rots from the head, and the institutionalised corruption of the Soviet elite not only increasingly made the state dysfunctional and ungovernable – and, as Gorbachev was to discover, unreformable – but it also contributed to the corruption of society as a whole.

The original Bolsheviks had considered corruption not just a moral failing, but also a symptom of pre- and anti-revolutionary attitudes and a practical threat. However, they were no more able to control it than Stalin. Indeed, under his reign the malign convergence of hunger and desperation on the one hand, and impunity and official omnipotence on the other, made it all the more integral to the system. James Heinzen has suggested that the Second World War was 'a largely unrecognized turning point in fuelling the kind of corruption that proved to be a hallmark of later periods of Soviet history'.[22] With their careers and bonuses dependent on the often unrealistic demands of the Five-Year Plan, managers and officials used illegal methods to meet their quotas (or at least to appear to). Most enterprises had their *tolkach*, their 'fixer', whose job it was to use his connections to get the labour, raw materials, spare parts, transport or whatever else was needed to reach the targets.[23]

Of course, within the workplace – from labour camp to government office – those with power also demanded tribute from those beneath them, for promotions, perks or just a quiet life. Meanwhile, ordinary Soviet citizens paid bribes to get what they were entitled to but which was in short supply, and also to get other goods, services and opportunities to which they were not. Samuel Huntington memorably once suggested that 'in terms of economic growth, the only thing worse than a society with a rigid, over-centralized, dishonest bureaucracy is one with a rigid, over-centralized and honest bureaucracy'.[24] Soviet citizens would probably have agreed. Bribery, connections and *blat* were ways in which citizens could exert some personal control over their lives and a world which were otherwise shaped by the Plan, the command economy and scarcity. But, while on a micro-scale they empowered the individual, overall they simply passed wealth upwards, to the gatekeepers who could control access to *defitsitny* goods (ones in short supply), grant a job or a promotion, or approve a medical treatment. The so-called 'socialist' system actually became a pyramid of predation, as those at the bottom paid those at the top, often for what was no more than their legal due.

Beyond the bespoke corruption at the individual level, there were also industrial-scale schemes which emerged thanks to the weaknesses and structures of the post-Stalinist state. The dependence on clientelism, the lack of independent checks and balances, and the pervasive culture of illegality allowed rings of officials, especially in the regions, to organise schemes which would plunder the greatest piggy bank of all: the state itself. Perhaps the crowning glory was the Uzbek cotton scandal, wherein local Party boss Sharaf Rashidov and a slate of Party and government officials in the central Asian republic of Uzbekistan, including the local KGB, were involved in a decade-long scam that embezzled some three billion rubles in payments for cotton that was never harvested, from fields and farms which did not exist. Claiming uncharacteristic efficiency and discipline, reports flowed back to Moscow of new irrigation networks dug, new fields planted and productivity records shattered. No wonder cotton was known as 'white gold', as thanks to the connivance of co-conspirators in Moscow – including Brezhnev's son-in-law and deputy interior minister, the grossly overpromoted Yury Churbanov – they were able to conceal the minor detail that none of this alleged harvest actually existed. So tight were the circles of mutual obligation and self-interest that, when Yury Andropov, the ascetic former KGB chief who became general secretary in 1982, began to try and get to the bottom of this plot, he had to turn to extreme measures. Spy satellites were redirected to photograph the Uzbek cotton lands, and soon revealed scrub and steppe where rolling fields were meant to be. This was the beginning of the end. Rashidov died in office in 1983 – some claim suicide – and hundreds of officials were swept up in the successive investigations. Sackings, prison terms and further suicides followed.

Yet while the cotton scandal may be an egregious example, the fact is that it reflected the general pathologies of the late Soviet era. Rashidov had been feted and honoured – including being awarded no fewer than ten Orders of Lenin – because of his real success in maintaining control over Uzbekistan through the reigns of three general secretaries and his apparent success in achieving and exceeding targets. Needless to say, his control had been largely for his own benefit and his successes often rooted more in fiction than fact. As one of the defendants in the cotton case rightly claimed, 'crimes like bribery and inflated production reports, and theft, have become the norm. There is no serious attempt to combat these things . . . Thus not a single question gets resolved without paying a bribe.'[25]

In an era when even the most powerful and highly praised figures within the system were deeply and enthusiastically involved in corruption to maintain their privileged existences, is it any surprise that ordinary citizens, experiencing a relative decline in their standards of living, likewise turned to illegal means? To an extent, this meant corruption. But it also meant an ever-deeper relationship with the underground economy.

The shadow men . . .

No one lives on wages alone. I remember in my youth we earned money by unloading railroad freight cars. So, what did we do? For every three crates or bags unloaded we'd take one for ourselves. That's how everybody in the country lives.

General Secretary Leonid Brezhnev[26]

Much of the underground economy was in the hands of petty *fartsovshchiki*, black-market wheeler-dealers, but it was big business, and could not have developed as far as it did without close ties with corrupt Party officials. The more powerful and ambitious *tsekhoviki* (or *tenevniki*, 'shadow men') needed these connections not just for their own survival, but often to gain access to raw materials, facilities and labour. Many *fartsovshchiki* dealt in illegally imported *defitsitny* goods, from clothes to decadent Western music, or ran illegal money exchange scams. The legendary Yan Rokotov, 'Cross Eyes', who was said to have amassed a fortune of 20 million rubles by the time of his arrest at the end of 1960, started earning serious money trading vodka for Western clothes off the backs of thirsty Finnish tourists, before he later went into more ambitious schemes dealing in foreign currency (with a side-line in outright fraud).[27] However, the greater part of the underground economy was accounted for by domestic goods, whether diverted from official production or made in underground factories.

Many of the black marketeers went out of business or were arrested: this was, after all, 'speculation', defined as unauthorised buying and selling for personal gain. It could get you up to seven years in prison under Article 154 of the 1960 Russian Criminal Code (which was the basis for the codes adopted in the other constituent states of the USSR) if considered a proper business, not just an isolated transaction. Indeed, Rokotov was shot in 1961, after Khrushchev had amended the law on currency speculation to allow capital punishment.

Many of those who built up business empires, which often prospered for years, did so working inside state structures and, frankly, making up for the failures of the planned economy. In 1981, a major scandal broke relating to underground businesses in the Chechen-Ingush Republic. An ambitious entrepreneur called Veniko Shengelaya, conscious of the demand for basic consumer goods and the miserably low productivity of the local economy, targeted an especially moribund enterprise. It had a fabric shop that made linen for industrial flour sieves, and thus every excuse to order materials. Shengelaya and a consortium of existing black marketeers brought the plant manager into their scheme and set up separate production facilities turning out shopping bags. Materials came from the state sector, workers moonlighting on this job were paid extra, and the bags met a market need. In its first two years, protected by judicious bribes to a variety of senior officials, all the way up to figures at the Ministry of Light Industry, the business made almost half a million rubles. At that point, like any good start-up entrepreneur, Shengelaya sold the business on to another for a hefty fee. It prospered and grew further, diversifying into knitwear, artificial leather and other markets. It was five years before it came to the attention of the authorities, and then only because one of the conspirators was sending money overseas, to his brother in Italy, whom he hoped to join.[28]

The conspirators ended up receiving sentences of up to fifteen years in prison, but what is striking is, in many ways, the very banality, even wholesomeness of the operation. Not only did it follow the same essential trajectory of any capitalist business, it did so wholly inside the system and did not compete with the official economy so much as supplement it. The workers were paid better; the consumers received good-quality merchandise they simply could not find in the shops. So what was the problem? Such businesses evaded taxes, of course. They also often could operate precisely because they acquired raw materials cheaply through state requisitions and squatted inside government facilities. But most dangerously for the regime, they demonstrated the failings of the planned economy compared with the dynamism of the market, and encouraged widening networks of corruption and compromise. Such networks could, and did, reach to the very pinnacles of the system, as the Uzbek cotton scandal had demonstrated.

The king of the *tsekhoviki*, though, was the notorious Otari Lazishvili. A Georgian, his business success depended to a considerable extent on his close, symbiotic relationship with Vasily Mzhavanadze, Georgian Party first secretary from 1953 until 1972. From the late 1960s, Lazishvili built up a business empire with resources diverted from the legal economy. He established a network of factories and workshops, many, like Shengelaya's business, on the premises of official plants, in which goods from shopping bags to raincoats were made for sale across the USSR with raw materials which managers overclaimed or wrote off as damaged or destroyed. While Lazishvili bribed lesser officials left and right, Mzhavandze was his true *krysha* ('roof'), his protection, and in return he received the steady stream of gifts and tribute he needed to live the kind of high-rolling life to which he and his wife Viktoria soon became accustomed. A high-ranking Party official could live like a prince, but they aspired to live like kings.

Lazishvili meanwhile enjoyed his wealth and his impunity. It was said that he had bath taps made of gold at a time when ordinary Soviet citizens could wait for years for new fittings, and he would fly to Moscow to watch the Dinamo Tbilisi football team, wagering thousands of rubles on a game, at a time when a nurse might earn 1,000 rubles in a full year.[29] Again, ultimately this cosy scheme foundered thanks to the general anti-corruption campaign Andropov launched while still head of the KGB. The apocryphal story is that Georgia's ambitious interior minister, Eduard Shevardnadze, spotted Viktoria Mzhavanadze wearing an enormous and distinctive diamond ring that Lazishvili had given her and which Interpol had reported as stolen. This is probably just a myth, though, not least as Lazishvili's businesses and the Mzhavandazes' venality were hardly secrets. In any case, with Andropov's enthusiastic support, Shevardnadze launched a campaign against Lazishvili's business empire and its protectors. Ultimately, Mzhavanadze was sacked in disgrace in 1972, and Lazishvili arrested soon after.[30]

Yet this relationship arguably foundered only because its protagonists were unusually flagrant and because of the political ambitions of Andropov (whose anti-corruption campaign was a useful weapon against his enemies within an elite where everyone had skeletons in their closets) and Shevardnadze (who replaced Mzhavanadze). From the 1960s, the underground economy had become an unacknowledged but crucial element of Soviet life, but to acquire this position, the *tsekhoviki* had had to reach understandings not just with officials, but organised crime.

. . . and their gangster friends

The gangsters left the black-market barons alone, even protected them. For a price, of course, because no one does anything for free. And over time, they got to see how the secret capitalists worked, and how they lived, and they came to see that they could do that, too, when they had the chance.

Russian police officer, 1990[31]

Few of the *tsekhoviki* were anything like as rich and powerful as Lazishvili, just as few Party bosses were quite as blatant and entrenched as Mzhavanadze. The latter had the power to punish or protect, and virtually absolute authority over their own fiefdoms. On the other hand, they often lacked the means to convert that into the money and consumer goods they craved. With their protection, the magnates of the underground economy could smuggle in foreign luxuries, deal in high-demand goods and set up workshops and factories to produce everything from counterfeit jeans to cigarettes. In the process, they became rich – but could not risk spending their ill-gotten gains unless they retained that protection. Furthermore, in most cases neither party could easily or safely talk to or work with the other.

First tempted to be predators on the *tsekhoviki*, following the example set by 'The Mongol', the gangsters then became their middlemen. Through the 1960s and 1970s, they were in many ways the weakest of the three: they needed the black-market businessmen's money and the Party bosses' protection. But they also became indispensable, and knew how to parlay that into greater leverage and freedom. By the late 1970s, the *tsekhoviki* had decided that it was better to make a deal. Representatives from both worlds met in the southern Russian spa town of Kislovodsk in 1979, in a gathering that undoubtedly was known to the authorities and may even have been brokered by them. Although I have never seen anything to corroborate it, one retired KGB officer who served in the Fifth Chief Directorate (responsible for domestic political policing) later claimed to me that the head of his unit had actually attended this so-called 'congress' as an observer. The outcome was an agreement that, in return for a tithe of one-tenth of their earnings, the *tsekhoviki* would be free from interference.[32]

Everything became increasingly institutionalised: black marketeers would pay local gangsters a tax, while the *vory*, possibly in conscious mockery of the Party but more likely assimilating its language and methods, began holding more such congresses of gang leaders on issues including whether to deal drugs, how to respond to changes in policing and even, at a meeting in Tbilisi in 1982, whether to get involved with politics.[33] (The result was inconclusive: Georgian *vory* wanted to get closer to corrupt officials, Russian traditionalists under the *vor* 'Vaska Brilliant' were reluctant, and the meeting ended without a firm decision.) The more they dealt with entrepreneurs, the more they had to come to understand the market and respond to new opportunities; the more they dealt with the state, the more they had to understand politics and demonstrate the capacity to resolve disputes and maintain discipline. Furthermore, in a foreshadowing of a process that would become much more important in the 1990s, what started as a simple exchange of a tax for a quiet life led in many cases to closer and more productive cooperation between the black marketeers and the gangsters. From being the outcasts of the Gulags, the *vory* were moving closer to the heart of the Soviet system. And Gorbachev, alas, would unwittingly let them all the way in.

CHAPTER 7

GORBACHEV'S GANGSTERS

The humble suffer from the folly of the great.

Russian proverb

While I was in Moscow in 1990, a callow PhD student watching the slow-motion train wreck of the Soviet system around me, I was able to line up a meeting with the deputy head of mission of one of the larger Warsaw Pact states. I felt very impressed with myself as I sat in his apartment, hearing tales of meetings in the Kremlin and classified briefings. After a while, though, he apologetically excused himself, picking up a clanking plastic bag full of bottles of spirit from his homeland. 'You'll have to excuse me,' he said, 'but I have a meeting with someone who has some toilet paper to sell.' He paused, and added reverentially, '*Soft* toilet paper.' For someone used to the reliable plenty of the West, it made a deep impression on me: that even one of the few dozen most senior diplomats in Moscow had to go *nalevo* – 'to the left', to the informal economy – just to wipe his bottom in comfort.

Poor Mikhail Gorbachev. When, after his accession to the general secretary's position in 1985, he launched his futile bid to reform the Soviet Union and create his own version of 'socialism with a human face', he – and everyone else – had no idea that in the process he would ensure a sudden and unexpected rise in the criminals' fortunes. His *perestroika* (restructuring) reforms would position them well to benefit from the very collapse of the USSR that his campaign would accelerate. Indeed, if anything, he began with a crackdown on corrupt officials that looked promising (or alarming, depending on which side of the fence you were on). For example, Vladimir Kantor, director of the Sokolniki *univermag* or department store, was an infamous profiteer who had assumed the patronage of Moscow Party boss Viktor Grishin would keep him safe. Until, that is, he was arrested on the first day of April 1985, while Grishin was on an official trip to Hungary. Behind what turned out to be the armoured door of his home was a trove of precious metals, jewellery, antiques and luxuries.[1] He ended up sentenced to eight years in prison, and had more than 600,000 rubles in possessions confiscated.

Three key aspects of the Gorbachev era were crucial in revolutionising organised crime. First, his well-intentioned but ill-conceived anti-alcohol campaign did for Soviet gangsters something a little like what prohibition did for their North American counterparts. Second, a limited liberalisation of the economy and the creation of a new form of private business (the so-called cooperatives) provided the criminals with new victims for extortion and opportunities to launder all the cash they were making through alcohol sales. Finally, the collapse in the authority of the state meant that just at the time when they were acquiring unprecedented financial and coercive resources – money and muscle – the criminals also faced no serious controls. They no longer had to rely on the payments of the black-market barons as they had their own sources of income; the corrupt Party bosses now needed their protection rather than the other way round. In short, the pyramid upended itself, leaving the gangsters on top for a while.

The Bootleg Revolution

Drinking is the joy of all Rus'. We cannot exist without that pleasure.
Apocryphal remark by Prince Vladimir of Kiev, 988[2]

The anti-alcohol campaign was a naïve and mishandled attempt to address a serious issue: the levels of drunkenness that were reducing labour productivity and burdening the health system. Soviet citizens were the world's heaviest drinkers, on average consuming the equivalent of 11.2 litres of pure alcohol a year, and by 1980 the typical family spent up to a half of its household budget on drink.[3] As a result, in 1995 Gorbachev – incidentally not much of a drinker himself, unlike bibulous predecessors such as

Brezhnev – pushed the Party's Central Committee to issue its Resolution on Measures to Overcome Drinking and Alcoholism. The idea was that coercive measures such as higher drink prices, limited supply and tougher penalties for public drunkenness would be combined with more imaginative public information campaigns and the provision of alternatives, such as non-alcoholic drinks and juice bars where people could still socialise. That was not allowing for the stodgy and essentially authoritarian habits of the system, though, and while vineyards were uprooted and alcohol barred from restaurants before two in the afternoon, the alternatives never really appeared and the propaganda remained as leaden and easy to ignore as ever. Gorbachev, *generalny sekretar* (general secretary), became known derisively as the *mineralny sekretar*, the mineral-water secretary.

There were some successes, to be sure. Time lost through alcohol-related disabilities fell 30 per cent between 1984 and 1987, and drink-driving deaths fell by 20 per cent.[4] However, for too many Soviet citizens, alcohol had become an increasingly important, though destructive, escape from the drabness and hopelessness of everyday life. Already accustomed to using the black market to make up for the shortfalls of the legal economy, they turned *nalevo* for drink too. The result was a demand that far outstripped the capacities of the *tsekhoviki*, not least because in the main they had never tried to compete with the state on quantity, just quality. Organised crime networks, which had for years become used to the ways of the informal economy, exploited the gap, gladly supplying imported, home-brewed, black market and stolen drink of every kind. Home brewing remained a cottage industry, with all kinds of vicious rotguts being produced in people's cupboards, in sheds, and even in the bath. The gangsters helped distribution for those whose production outstripped the market they could easily supply through their own informal networks. Indeed, so great was the upsurge in illegal production of alcohol that it led to a nationwide shortage of sugar, which was needed for the process. Arkady Vaksberg recalled that in Ukraine, in 1986 alone, the demand for sugar went up 24 per cent.[5] Elsewhere, the *vory* played a key role in using their contacts to divert alcohol stocks from those factories which still ran to sell for inflated black-market prices, or even in some cases selling on drink that had been earmarked for destruction. Sometimes this was stolen by the gangsters themselves, or more often corrupt officials would write it off, but as they needed help getting it onto the black market, they had to turn to the *vory*.

This illegal industry provided the criminals with not only a market but a constituency. Their submerged role within the Soviet state had meant that they rarely interacted directly with most of society; the days when ordinary people might encounter professional criminals in the Gulags were essentially gone, and the days of overt gangsterism on the streets had not yet arrived. For most people, the first time they ever knowingly encountered the *vory* was not as predators but as suppliers. The gangsters found themselves making more money than ever, in the unexpected role of friend and ally. One young man who was at that time a mere *shestyorka*, a gang runner or gofer, described the surreal experience of his first time accompanying an older criminal on his rounds in a housing estate in Moscow's southern Chertanovo neighbourhood: 'People were pleased to see us, they would smile and joke, offer us cigarettes. They would ask us what we had today, like we were shopkeepers.'[6]

Because of course that is what they were. The criminals who first sold people alcohol were connected to wider black-market networks that allowed them also to supply other *defitsitny* goods, from clothes and cigarettes to household goods and medicines, at a time of increasing scarcity and rationing.[7] Furthermore, their connections to corrupt officials meant that they could also broker deals. It was not, after all, as though ordinary Soviet citizens had not had connections with black marketeers before, or that they had not used corruption to ease their lives. Instead, the obstacles had more to do with networks and trust. Did a particular person know whom to bribe for a particular service, did they have access, did they know the 'right' rate, could they trust the recipient?

The gangsters emerged as ad hoc brokers able to make the necessary connections and also, implicitly and sometimes explicitly, guaranteeing the transaction. They had a reputational stake in the deal going smoothly, not least as future business would depend on this. Federico Varese has written incisively about the *mafiya* as a source of private protection and enforcement of contracts in post-Soviet Russia, and in many ways the genesis of this was to be found in the grimy halls and crumbling stairwells of Gorbachev-era housing estates.[8] In cheerless Chertanovo, for example, the young *shestyorka* remembered how early in the rounds people would take the initiative to encourage the gangsters into diversifying: 'Hey lads, thanks for the booze; how about finding some cigarettes for next time?' 'Do you know anyone at the polyclinic? I'm sure my daughter needs to be looked at.' For a rookie criminal it was a bewildering experience to suddenly be treated more like the local wholesaler. For his bosses, it was both enriching and a source of unexpected legitimation and revelation as they began to appreciate the new opportunities Gorbachev was unwittingly opening up to them.

Gangster-entrepreneurs

It was clear that the militia [police] would be of little use . . . so I got onto the crime boss, an authority, and even got to know a couple of vory v zakone . . . *We agreed that we'd admit them [to our restaurants], and they'd not hassle us.*

Entrepreneur, discussing arranging protection for
his new businesses[9]

Gorbachev's general programme of reform became more ambitious (and desperate) over time as he began to appreciate both the scale of the challenge and the degree of resistance from the corrupt elite. Early Plan-driven attempts to improve the economy failed, so he took a leaf out of Lenin's book and began his own version of his predecessor's liberalising NEP. In a comparable effort to tap the energies of the market, Gorbachev opened up the economy to cooperatives, small-scale private enterprises such as restaurants and services. A new generation of *kooperativniki* emerged, in a way a legal counterpart to the black market's *tsekhoviki*.

One might think this was an advantage, but in practice it proved a crippling weakness. They proved even more vulnerable than the *tsekhoviki* in the 1960s and 1970s, lacking their established contacts and protection, and soon ran into hostility from the public and authorities alike. The cooperatives typically offered greater quality and flexibility, but at a higher price. A public seeing their own standards of living decline perversely scapegoated these 'profiteers'. Admittedly, they were not always wrong. The management of the Yava cigarette factory in Moscow, for example, spotted an opportunity and, thanks to allies within the city's state distribution system, organised an artificial shortage. At the same time, they set up a chain of cooperative shops, through which they sold their cigarettes at inflated prices.[10] Meanwhile, this new generation of would-be entrepreneurs represented a challenge to both an ossified orthodoxy and also the sweetheart deals on which the elite had come to rely. Whatever the Kremlin may have wanted for them, the *kooperativniki* faced hostility from the public, obstruction from local authorities and a wilful refusal from the police to offer proper protection.

Looking for places to launder and reinvest their new-found wealth, and with the capacity to easily intimidate these vulnerable entrepreneurs, the gangsters were able to move into this sector on a massive scale. Protection rackets were rife, so much so that some gangs, desperate to exploit this new opportunity, had to learn how best to do this from scratch. One member of a Lyubery gang – discussed below – recollected that 'our major manuals were videos about the American and Hong Kong mafia: we watched them in video salons to get some experience'.[11]

Many businesses were taken over or driven into the ground. By late 1989, the criminals controlled or were being paid off by an estimated 75 per cent of cooperatives.[12] As a report in the magazine *Ogonyok* admitted:

> For a certain percentage, racketeers can provide a wide variety of services, from protecting cooperative property to obtaining supplies and ruining the competition … In the event that a racketeer's services are refused, all kinds of things can happen: a fire may break out in a cooperative café, or government inspectors may take a sudden interest in a sportswear manufacturer.[13]

In the process, the criminals – who until recently had depended largely on the black market and on black marketeers for their revenue – found themselves increasingly financially solvent. Criminals who had once run small-time rackets were now dreaming bigger. In Perm, for example, the gangster Vladimir Plotnikov ('Plotnik') had largely concentrated on fraudulent street games of chance until the mid-1980s, but then moved into black-market business, smuggling chainsaws from the local Dzerzhinsky plant across the USSR, 200 at a time.[14] In 2004, he went on to become a local parliamentarian. Other gangsters became service providers even more explicitly; the Muscovite *vor* Pavel Zikharov ('Pavel Tsirul') began as a pickpocket in the 1950s, but by the later 1980s he was living in a three-storey villa outside the city and lending money off the official record to *kooperativniki* who could not get commercial loans.[15] A thuggish generation of predators was having to evolve, or else it would be supplemented or replaced by a new breed of gangster-businessmen.

The new gangs

Do you know how difficult it was for us to get used to a peaceful way of life? There, during the fighting, you can see straight away who is who. White was white there, and black was black.

Afghan War veteran, 1987[16]

Even these gangster-businessmen needed muscle, though, and amongst all the expressions of the grass-roots entrepreneurialism of the Gorbachev era, few were as pernicious as the rise of the professionals of coercion. Russian sociologist Vadim Volkov called them the 'violent entrepreneurs', who monetised their muscle, turning the will and capacity to use or threaten force into a resource.[17] Many simply filled the lower ranks of the gangs, most of which could always find room for another *byk* ('bull', a heavy) or a *torpedo* (hitman). However, in other cases groups with a particular and credible capacity to deploy violence became the basis for organised crime gangs. Three particular examples were sportsmen, unofficial bodybuilders (*kachki*) and *afgantsy*, veterans of the Soviet Union's ten-year (1979–88) war in Afghanistan.

The Soviet Union spent considerable effort on its sportsmen, both to garner a rich crop of medals in international competition – which had become a proxy battlefield of the Cold War – and also to build the capacities for effective workers and soldiers. In the 1980s, the generous salaries and subsidies on which this industry had relied came under increasing pressure. Many fit young men, including wrestlers, boxers and martial artists, found themselves underemployed and unloved. Furthermore, there was a burgeoning official and underground fitness and martial arts scene, providing further potential recruits for the new racketeering outfits.

For example, from perhaps 1985 to 1987, Leningrad's foremost gangster was Nikolai Sedyuk, known as 'Kolya Karate' for his martial arts prowess, whose entourage included dozens of young men from his training club, the Ring.[18] Vadim Volkov notes that certain staff and students from all three of the city's specialised sporting training centres – the Lesgaft Institute of Physical Culture, the Military Institute of Physical Culture (VIFK) and the High School of Sports Mastery (ShVSM) – formed their own criminal outfits. The chief enforcer of the city's infamous Tambovskaya group was a sports coach and graduate of the Lesgaft. VIFK cadets formed Shvonder's Brigade, which extorted businesses around the nearby Finland station, while the ShVSM had its own Wrestler's Brigade.[19] Likewise, the Yekaterinburg Uralmash gang, discussed later, was formed on the basis of a core of these sportsmen.

An offshoot of the sportsmen's gangs was that some street gangs developed a particular cult of bodybuilding and martial arts training. Most infamous were the Lyubery, named after Lyubertsy, the miserable industrial east Moscow suburb from which they hailed. In the early 1980s, bodybuilding became a local fad, and the basements of housing blocks were turned into informal gyms. Some of the blue-collar young *kachki* formed gangs which combined low-level hustling with a confused ideology that somehow muddled Young Communist rhetoric, fascistic impulses and a heavy dose of racism and class envy.[20] One day, they might be heading into the city to throw their weight around and beat up non-Russians, or hippies, or any well-dressed young Muscovite *mazhory* ('privileged ones') who caught their eye. The next, they might be attacking neo-fascists or just brawling with a rival gang from the next street along.

At first, the police and authorities seemed to turn a blind eye to much of their violence. They saw in them a potential weapon against anti-government agitators, but the street gangs proved unwilling to be deniable stormtroopers of reaction. More to the point, as the phenomenon began to spread to other poorer Moscow suburbs, and, indeed, to other cities, the result was a moral panic that portrayed them as apocalyptic harbingers of brutish chaos. The parallel with the hooliganism crisis of late tsarism is compelling. An article in the influential magazine *Ogonyok* that presented them not as a disparate collection of muscle-bound thugs but as a movement with its own uniform and 'kings' who could muster a couple of hundred soldiers within a few hours did much to fan the flames.[21] By 1987–8, the police were beginning to crack down on them, but that only accelerated a trend that had already begun: the recruitment of these young toughs into organised crime gangs.

As for the *afgantsy*, they were typically marked by their experiences not only in war, but also in peace. Veterans of a conflict Moscow did not want to acknowledge (in the early years, the state flatly denied that there were Soviet soldiers in Afghanistan and veterans were ordered to keep quiet about it), they were often scapegoated by society and neglected by the state. Promises of proper medical attention, of jobs, of decent housing, all tended to be broken. This was less because of any real prejudice against them than because they were a politically marginalised group competing for resources in a time of extreme scarcity.[22] Nonetheless, for many this led to a degree of 'shadow socialisation' in which they actively turned against mainstream society and its values.

Most of the million-or-so *afgantsy*, of course, got over their experiences, but even so a fair number – perhaps a quarter – became involved in some way in the veterans' movement, joining the Union of Veterans of Afghanistan (SVA) or other structures. Many got jobs on this basis in military-patriotic education, a massive sector in the USSR, where every school had its military educator and there were all kinds of programmes to instil the skills and attitudes advantageous for future national service. The 1987 Law on Amateur Associations and Hobby Clubs laid the first foundations for genuinely independent groups, at which point some *afgantsy* moved much more actively into lobbying for veterans' rights. They were rarely especially successful, though, given the crisis then gripping the state, and as a result often went into business themselves, from making and selling records of Afghan War songs through to running their own cooperatives.

Cooperatives run by Afghan War veterans were, needless to say, rather less amenable to gangster shakedowns. One veteran, in 1990, told me what happened when two scrawny *shestyorky* tried to intimidate the one-legged shop assistant in the little kiosk his group ran in Leningrad: 'He just banged on the door to the storeroom, and I and my three mates came out and showed the punks what we'd been taught in the VDV [paratroopers]. They didn't come back.'[23] Especially given that one of the particular market sectors for which were suited was establishing and running gymnasia, martial arts studios and the like, the transition to private security on the one hand, and crime on the other, was a relatively obvious one. The SVA, for example, set up its own private security firm, Soyuznik.[24] The police also sought to recruit veterans, especially for their new OMON riot police units and similar special forces. In 1989, Interior Minister Vadim Bakatin said that their 'colossal authority and undiscovered potential must be made use of . . . to act against the affront of the bandits, speculators, racketeers and other crooks'.[25] However, an officer from the MVD's organised crime squad admitted that *afgantsy* were often the first choice when gangs were looking for muscle.[26]

For both the sportsmen and the Afghan War veterans, the post-Soviet 1990s would see their criminal careers at their peak. The combination of generous tax exemptions (which created opportunities for smuggling), struggling law enforcement and seemingly boundless opportunities for racketeering and corruption briefly opened up bloody new vistas for them, before they were again brought under the control of state and conventional gangsters in the 2000s. However, even in the later 1980s, already it was clear that new markets for violence and protection were emerging, and power and money would flow to those groups and individuals best able to secure and service them.

Tomorrow belonged to them

You can already see it in the regions, and it's probably here too, and in Moscow: organised-crime authorities are now people to look up to . . . Soon enough, officials will be inviting them to visit their dachas and offering them partnerships, because that's the way of the future.

Police officer, Kiev, 1991[27]

In many ways, though, the most dramatic development was the collapse of the Communist Party thanks to Gorbachev's liberal reforms. *Glasnost*, a new openness about contemporary affairs and past horrors, knocked away much of the legitimacy of the Party, and the economic hardships produced by botched economic reforms ate away at the rest. Facing growing resistance from an alarmed and self-interested elite, Gorbachev was simply radicalised, and turned to a limited democratisation campaign to give himself a power base independent of the Party, shattering its fragile unity. This liberalisation also encouraged local nationalist movements which, in turn, threatened the very existence of the Soviet state, which for all its notionally federative status was to a large extent a Slavic-dominated multi-ethnic empire.

In this context, the officials who once had held the literal power of life and death over the *vory* were generally too busy to be bothered with them. Sometimes they found themselves needing their services, whether getting out the vote or, more often, helping them amass the money they would need when their positions were no longer guaranteed. Even the central Communist Party, worried that it was seeing the writing on the wall, began salting away funds.[28] In 1990, a secret Central Committee decree ordered the KGB to start building a network of businesses and accounts covertly connected to the Party for the day when it might not be able to count on state funds. An unknown amount of money – billions of dollars – was spirited from the coffers of a state which could scarcely afford it and into hundreds of these accounts. Nikolai Kruchina, head of the Central Committee Administrative Department, was a key figure, and to some the only man who knew where all the money was. During the chaos of a short-lived anti-Gorbachev coup in August 1991, he fatally fell, jumped or was pushed out of his fifth-floor apartment window.[29] That money was officially never found, but no doubt many of the individuals involved, from KGB officers to Party accountants and managers, had little reason to mourn Kruchina's unexpected and precipitous passing.

Put together, all these processes meant that the contours of the overt gangsterism of the 1990s were already becoming visible in the late 1980s. Organised crime was increasingly powerful, wealthy and self-confident. The fragmented little gangs of the 1970s, spiritual successors of the tsarist criminal *artely*, were being replaced by or coalescing into large, powerful combines. The interethnic tensions which would explode with such violence soon enough were already growing. From around 1988, for instance, the division in Moscow between the Slavic gangs and those of the 'Chechen brotherhood' (*chechenskaya bratva*) and their allies from elsewhere in the north Caucasus was visible. Chechen-dominated gangs such as Avtomobilnaya and Ostankinskaya – named after the neighbourhoods they controlled – were beginning to be name-checked in public discussion.[30] The heavyweight newspaper *Literaturnaya Gazeta* admitted that year how things had changed: 'Even five years ago, the question as to the existence of the Soviet mafia caused the leaders of the USSR Ministry of Internal Affairs to raise their eyebrows. "You've been reading too many detective novels." '[31]

By the time Gorbachev was forced to bow to the inevitable and, at the end of 1991, sign the USSR out of existence, organised crime had become a visible and powerful presence in the streets, in the economy and even within the political scene. A few days before the dissolution of the Soviet Union, some thirty senior *vory* from across the country had gathered for a *skhodka* at a dacha near Moscow.[32] The aim was nothing less than to hammer out some understandings about the Soviet underworld, even as the whole Soviet state was near death. There was an agreement about a common front against the gangs from the north Caucasus, and tentative accords about dividing the country between them.

What on one level looked like a marvel of coordination, though, actually proved quite marginal in its real impact. For the collapse of the USSR would overturn old assumptions, throw open new opportunities, and plunge the Russian underworld into vicious struggles for markets, turf and precedence seemingly unheeding of the state and its forces. Before, the gangsters had been the weakest partner in an underworld triumvirate alongside corrupt officials and black-market magnates. Now, for a short while, they would appear dominant. To sum up, if Gorbachev was one of the midwives of Russian organised crime, the first president of post-Soviet Russia, Boris Yeltsin, was to prove its wet nurse.

CHAPTER 8

THE 'WILD NINETIES' AND THE RISE OF THE *AVTORITETY*

Two bears cannot live in the same den.

Russian proverb

Dangerous the life of the man who would be king, and whose life is worth, it transpires, a middle-sized Lada family car. Otari 'Otarik' Kvantrishvili was a powerfully built man, at the age of forty-six still showing something of the physical power that had made him a championship-standard wrestler, until a conviction for rape ended his sporting career. He was also a cautious man, known to wear a bullet-proof vest under his suit when out and about. Perhaps that explains why the sniper who shot him dead as he left his favourite bathhouse did so through his left shoulder, the three bullets bypassing the vest through the arm-hole and ripping into his torso.

This was April 1994, in the middle of Boris Yeltsin's presidency, when the new, post-Soviet Russian state was going through a time of violent turbulence, and when contract killings were commonplace. Even so, Kvantrishvili's assassination marked a turning point in the country's underworld history. An ethnic Georgian, Kvantrishvili and his brother Amiran had both been members of 'The Mongol's' gang – Amiran was a card-sharp, Otari muscle – but when that group was disbanded, 'Otarik' set up on his own. He gathered an assemblage of sportsmen including 'Alexander the Bull', a judo champion, and 'Ivan the Gypsy', a boxer, and embarked on all kinds of criminal activities, from protection racketeering to illegal currency dealing.[1]

However, Kvantrishvili soon moved into the ostensibly legal sector, as one of the entrepreneurial gangsters who took fullest advantage of the opportunities of the liberalisation of the 1980s. He established the Fund for the Social Protection of Athletes, which acted as a convenient front to recruit and maintain hired muscle, as well as being a smuggling and black-market organisation. Then, in 1988, he founded the XXI Century Association. This organised concerts and charity events and claimed to be committed to raising funds for sports, but was actually a holding company of sorts for a wide range of criminal businesses. Another of his enterprises, the Sports Academy – which despite its name was a closed joint-stock company – was granted freedom from import and export taxes in 1993 by Boris Yeltsin himself. It did no sports training, but did end up becoming the agent for deals involving hundreds of thousands of tonnes of Russian aluminium, cement and titanium sold abroad, and millions of dollars of consumer imports then retailed through networks of the sales kiosks that organised crime had so monopolised.[2]

Nonetheless, Kvantrishvili not only escaped prosecution, he became something of a celebrity, denying his criminal status, but always with a knowing nod and a wink. In 1990, for example, he was photographed at a tennis match close to Yeltsin.[3] He became a fixture in Moscow high society, and a friend of singer Iosif Kobzon, often called the 'Russian Frank Sinatra' for his close ties with alleged gangsters,[4] as well as *shanson* stalwart Alexander Rozenbaum, who attended his funeral and lamented that 'the country has lost – I'm not afraid of this word – a leader'.[5]

He proved an adept underworld politician, manoeuvring his way round the disputes raging between other gangs, notably Chechen and Russian ones, but this seems to have gone to his head. In late 1993, he declared that he would be entering legitimate politics, forming the Party of Sportsmen. At the same time, he made it clear within Moscow's criminal circles that he intended to assert a claim to being boss of the capital's underworld. He was undoubtedly the most powerful individual criminal in the city. However, he had failed to appreciate the essentially egalitarian, contrarian nature of the *vorovskoi mir*. In 1994, leaders of the other gangs in the city held a *skhodka*. They decided that Kvantrishvili had to go and charged Sergei Butorin, head of the Orekhovo–Medvedkovo gang, with arranging this. Soon thereafter, Kvantrishvili was gunned down by Butorin's right-hand man Alexei Sherstobitov ('Lyosha the Soldier'), as an object lesson that no one – and especially not a Georgian – was going to become the boss of bosses, Italian-style. As one of the hangers-on at that meeting later told me, 'Moscow is not Sicily.'[6]

Sherstobitov, who was convicted of the killing fourteen years later, was given that Lada for his marksmanship.[7] Everyone else got a resumption of the underworld struggles of all-against-all that mirrored the chaos in the country as a whole. Just as the 1990s saw Russia go through financial and political crises as it tried to define itself and its place in the world, its underworld spent most of the decade expanding rapidly into every corner of the economy and society but also getting involved in running turf wars as gangs rose, fell, united, divided and competed. This was a decade of drive-by shootings, car bombs and the virtual theft of whole industries, in which the forces of order seemed powerless. In 1994, President Yeltsin declared that Russia was the 'biggest mafia state in the world'.[8] He almost sounded proud of it; certainly he did not do much to stop it, and cronies of his were deeply involved in this arrant criminalisation of the country. From this anarchy, though, a new order would emerge, as major underworld combines formed, pecking orders emerged and territorial boundaries became established. As for the *vory*, it was time for another renewal, another reinvention to fit the very different needs and opportunities of the time.

Yeltsin's 'superpower of crime'

Russia is becoming a superpower of crime.

Boris Yeltsin, 1994[9]

Yeltsin's presidency offered organised crime the perfect incubator. This was a time of extraordinary change, including a massive widening of the gap between haves and have-nots. Moscow began to be decked in gaudy neon, and Mercedes-Benz was selling more armoured limousines in Russia than the rest of the world put together. But outside the metro stations you would see lines of desperate pensioners selling anything they had – a chair, a half-used tube of toothpaste, a wedding ring – just to try and make ends meet. The police, underpaid and outgunned, often lacked fuel for their cars and bullets for their weapons. Once, I was invited on a 'ride along' with a patrol through Golyanovo, in eastern Moscow, a long way away from the tourist sites and investment hotspots. It was alarming enough to be handed an army surplus bullet-proof vest; doubly so to realise it hardly lived up to the billing, as it had neat bullet-holes through both breast and back plates. No wonder, perhaps, that the 'patrol' was a high-speed rush through the main streets, blue lights flashing, the officer next to me clutching an AKR submachine gun, stopping for nothing until we were back in the safety of the police station. There was no sense that they regarded themselves as being in charge of the streets, and I was reminded of the accounts of tsarist police only venturing into the slums when they must, and then mob-handed.

The headlong rush to privatise state assets transferred many into criminal hands at bargain basement prices. Likewise, limited democratisation created corrupt local fiefdoms which resembled nothing so much as the snake-pit municipalities of interwar America, familiar from Dashiell Hammett's noir thrillers – but with Kalashnikovs and the internet. Perhaps most insidious and corrosive was the widespread sense of insecurity and uncertainty; the new laws were contradictory, the old certainties were gone. If you needed a contract enforcing or a debt collecting, to whom could you turn when the courts were corrupt and backlogged? If you needed protection and security, who could provide it when the police were corrupt and inefficient? The answer, needless to say, was organised crime, which emerged perversely as an entrepreneurial Robin Hood, offering these very services – for a fee.

This was a period of experimental state building on a massive scale and in the midst of economic crisis. Between 1991 and 1998, when Russia's stock, bond and currency markets collapsed, GDP fell by 30 per cent, unemployment rose and inflation hit 2,500 per cent in 1992 before falling to tolerable levels later in the decade – but only after wiping out savings and devaluing benefits.[10] By 1999, more than a third of Russians lived below the poverty line. The hurried and ill-thought-through crash privatisation campaign saw state assets being transferred into private hands at a fraction of their true value, a process exploited by those who already had cash and connections: corrupt officials, underground entrepreneurs and criminals.

Just as the gangsters had helped and in some cases suborned politicians as democracy emerged by providing street-level assets to hustle the vote and crowd out rivals, so too were they able to leverage their capacities during the privatisation campaign. Some of the more entrepreneurial ones simply used it as an opportunity to convert illicit earnings into legal assets. But during 1992–4, reformists desperate to move assets out of state hands adopted a voucher privatisation programme. Every Russian citizen was entitled to a voucher notionally worth 10,000 rubles – this may sound impressive, but it was perhaps equivalent to $8.30 by the end of 1993 – to exchange for shares in a range of companies that were being divested by the state. For many Russians, unsure whether they would have food on the table tomorrow, the promise of potential dividends at some time in the future offered little appeal. Instead, most sold their vouchers, for a tiny fraction of their face value, not least to the myriad street corner buyers who stood there with a sign saying 'I Buy Vouchers' and a pocket full of hard cash. Some of these may have been entrepreneurial individuals, but many were working for organised crime (and, as I observed on a visit to Moscow in 1993, were bussed to their respective corners in groups, and typically had a minder attached, whether watching out for them or simply watching them). The gangs aggregated the vouchers into meaningful batches and either used them or, far more often, sold them on to managers eager to take over their own enterprise, or to the rising oligarchs out shopping for bargains. Thus, Russian organised crime was from the first not just part of the emerging system but a stakeholder able to help shape its evolution.

Overall, this was a time of legal, cultural and social crisis. The laws were being rewritten on the fly and were thus often confused and contradictory. For example, although Russia was now supposedly a liberal market economy, the old Soviet law on 'speculation' – unauthorised trade for profit – remained on the statute books for years. The police and courts were overstretched, underfunded, demoralised and uncertain of their very role. 'Capitalism' was too often seen as a licence to make money through whatever means was available, and so much of the Yeltsin era was marked by economic anarchy. Gangs and corrupt officials alike plundered the economy on a massive scale. In particular, this led to the consolidation of local criminalised baronies and the hollowing out of surviving state institutions. Even charities often became nothing more than organised-crime fronts: two successive heads of the Afghan War veterans' union were murdered in bomb attacks in a struggle over the lucrative tax exemptions the association had been granted, for example. The boundaries between politics, business and crime were at best hazy, at worse meaningless, as criminals and politicians openly hobnobbed with each other and the tools and attitudes of organised crime came to permeate the system as a whole.

Meanwhile, the Russian underworld was wracked by an almost-decade-long struggle between gangs and their allies and patrons for turf, precedence and resources. Indeed, the *bandity* ('bandits') as often fought amongst themselves. To give just one example, the Shkabara–Labotski–Gnezdich gang was established by two ex-Spetsnaz (special forces) commandos in Novokuznetsk in 1992, but having become dominant in that city decided to expand to exploit the bigger opportunities of Moscow. When they did this, they were challenged by the Lyubertsy group, at the time one of the city's largest, but the newcomers faced them down with a show of firepower. However, the group soon began to tear itself apart. One gang leader felt that one of his lieutenants had ambitions on his position: he tried to kill his underling with a bomb, but instead was injured in the blast and shot by his understandably disgruntled subordinate. Meanwhile, a new gang was rising in Novokuznetsk, but when three gunmen were sent to murder its head they failed. Two of the three were killed by their own godfather as punishment and the third sent back out to kill the rival, this time successfully. Nonetheless, members of the gang began to be known even amongst themselves as the 'disposables' for their rate of attrition, and a mix of fear, vendetta and greed led to a series of fratricidal killings that had effectively destroyed the group by 1995.[11] This case illustrates three key features of that time: gangs rose and fell depending on firepower but also cohesion, with the former far easier to accumulate; this was a time of anarchy in the underworld, with no meaningful internal or external limits on the gangsters' actions; and the situation was ultimately unsustainable.

The protection market and its understandings

The most important business decision I can make is knowing whose roof to shelter under . . . If I get that right, everything else should fall into place.

Russian entrepreneur, 1997[12]

As the state declined and organised crime ascended, for a while business people ended up coming to treat gangs simply as alternative service providers, different sources of the *krysha* – 'roof', slang for protection – so crucial to any venture in such uncertain times: 'The harder the rain, the tighter the roof has to be.'[13] Vadim Volkov wrote of 'violent entrepreneurship . . . the way in which groups and organizations that specialize in the use of force make money,'[14] and Federico Varese applied to Russia the model developed by Diego Gambetta, of a mafia as 'a particular type of organized crime that specializes in one particular criminal commodity . . . the supply of *protection*'.[15] Either way, the essence is that credible and deployable violence and threat can be monetised, in a market in which numerous suppliers compete on price, effectiveness, perceived reliability and brand name. In this context, protection meant more than just not being shaken down; it also meant not being cheated. The courts were corrupt, and, even if one could get a judgment in one's favour, enforcing it would be problematic. Besides, this could take years and the best the courts could often do was order repayment of any outstanding debts or damages at the original rate. Given that, even after inflation had subsided from the crippling levels of the early 1990s, it remained high (in 1999 it was still running at 37 per cent), in that time the real value of the financial loss would have shrunk dramatically. As a result, businesses were often willing to turn to organised crime to adjudicate disputes and enforce judgments, as they could do so promptly, even if the cost could be as high as 50 per cent of the total sum in question.[16]

In the words of Vladimir Vyshenkov, once a police investigator and then a crime journalist, 'a market is born, and it has to be regulated. What does it mean to regulate? "You're right, you're wrong. Give it to him." Who is going to do that? Suddenly athletes see a niche. They enter this market and say, "We'll decide who's right and who's wrong. But we're going to collect taxes in exchange."'[17] Amongst the first to seize this opportunity were sportsmen, typically wrestlers, boxers and martial artists, but where they led, all kinds of other groups followed, from corrupt cops to Chechens, Afghan War veterans to street gangs.

Quickly, it became institutionalised, interwoven into national and local social, economic and political structures. These 'enforcement partnerships' as Volkov called them could be one off, or else regularised and long term, typically costing 25–30 per cent of a firm's revenues.[18] As they began operating increasingly behind apparently legitimate structures, whether charities, holding companies or private security agencies, gangs were less likely to extort money from businesses with the overt threat of violence.

As will be discussed in more detail later, for this to work, the gangsters had to be, in that classic *vor* phrase, 'honest criminals'. Yes, they were law breakers, and sometimes leg breakers, but they also had to be true to their word. The early 1990s may have offered opportunities for some *bandity* to do well today without thinking of tomorrow, but even in that decade, the scope and tolerance for such *disorganised* organised crime was relatively limited. The gangs that prospered, and especially those profiled later in the book which became the major corporations of the underworld, did so because they understood the importance of the *ponyatiya*, the notion of the informal but nonetheless powerful 'understandings' defining underworld life. In Russian street gangs, as Svetlana Stephenson's field work has demonstrated, the emphasis of the *ponyatiya* is especially on issues of 'manly' values such as being tough and not backing down, as well as staying loyal to the gang.[19] This is in many ways very reminiscent of the original *vor* code.

The 'adult' organised crime structures likewise internalised some of the same macho culture, although already in the age of the gun and its hired wielder, personal physical prowess was less important than being smart and ruthless. An apocryphal story recounted by Volkov about the resolution of a dispute between a *vor* who used the name Vasia Brianski and some Azeri gangsters outside St Petersburg helps illustrate this: 'The bandit Vasia Brianski pulled out a gun, but a cool Azerbaijani displayed no fear and, pointing to his own forehead, said: "Okay, shoot me." The trick, which was intended to demonstrate to others Vasia's lack of resolve and thus win the contest, did not work. Vasia put the gun to the man's forehead and shot him.'[20]

The reason I suggest this story might be folklore more than history is that I heard similar tales about gangsters from both Moscow and Vladivostok, always told by someone who had himself heard it second- (or third-) hand. The key point is that the moral drawn was not that the Azeri had guts (which may well have been the case, and that would probably have been the lesson in the classic days of the 1930s *vory*) but that his killer both understood the challenge and didn't shirk from doing what was needed. As one of the storytellers put it, 'you do what you have to do, even if it means getting wet' – in other words, bloody – 'but you let the other guy start it.'[21]

In the violence, there was a hint of restraint, a sense that you tried to avoid wars, even if you won them when they must be fought, and a clear commitment to following through on threats and promises alike. Reflecting the role of these 'enforcement partnerships', though – and without some form of trust, how can there be a partnership in a time without enforcement mechanisms? – their *ponyatiya* also put great emphasis on being reliable in positive as well as negative terms. It was not enough simply not to make threats without being able to back them up, it was necessary to make good on one's promises, too. The old code had essentially considered promises made to *frayery*, non-criminals, as having no real weight. Now, that was bad for business and, in the form of the post-Soviet *ponyatiya*, the code once again rewrote itself to adapt to the needs of the times.

There were, of course, essentially predatory gangs, the cost of protection was a hidden tax on a new generation of entrepreneurs, and there remained all kinds of uncertainties within this market.[22] It could certainly not be considered a good thing, merely an understandable response to a bad situation. But in the main, organised criminals increasingly sought to reach understandings with their clients and with each other, offering a smooth life so long as the right officials were paid off, the right firms received contracts. Indeed, the criminals now often considered themselves as protectors and arbiters. As one put it to Nancy Ries, 'well, the traders and speculators are always cheating each other . . . We protect the businessmen from each other. We ensure the collection of debts and recover stolen goods. Our clients' partners known who is protecting them . . . A good *krysha* means good business.'[23]

In this respect, organised crime was simply another business sector, a facilitator within Russia's still-unruly business environment. In the words of one middle-ranking Moscow mobster I spoke to, 'in the early years, we fought because we had to or because we didn't know better, but by [1996–7] we could settle down and become businessmen rather than generals'.[24]

From *bandity* to *biznismeny*: the 2000s

Very often the most likely to succeed in these stormy oceans are not the picture-perfect, clean-shaved, deep-tanned, well-built, and fashionably attired yachtsmen under the immaculate white sails, but unpleasant-looking ugly skippers in command of a pirate ship. One should not be appalled. These are the laws of initial capital acquisition, applicable everywhere.

Controversial former aluminium tycoon Lev Chernoy, 2000[25]

Vladimir Putin, who succeeded Yeltsin as acting president in 1999 before a snap – and carefully managed – election in 2000, is widely credited as having tamed the *bandity*. The anarchy of the 1990s passed, and with it the indiscriminate violence and the public fear. He deserves some credit, to be sure. Unlike Yeltsin, he had a clear vision for Russia, anchored on a strong state.

There was no room in it for anything suggesting that the government was not in charge, whether opposition in parliament or gangsterism on the streets. However, Putin was as much symptom as cause: his elevation coincided with deeper political and economic pressures that permitted and indeed demanded this partial reassertion of central state authority. Putin made it clear that he would not tolerate overt or implicit challenges to the government. In the months leading up to his election, the flight of criminal capital out of Russia rose as gangsters hurriedly prepared themselves for a swift exit, in case Putin's tough law-and-order rhetoric was more than just campaign theatre. One gangster told me that, in an echo of how people lived during Stalin's time, he always kept a packed suitcase under the bed. However, whereas in the 1930s this was done so that one had essentials to take when the secret police arrived, for him it was in case he had to make a dash for the airport after one of his informants in the police tipped him off that he was going to be arrested.

This was ironic considering that, during his time as deputy mayor of St Petersburg, Putin had regularly encountered the city's underworld, and particularly the powerful Tambovskaya group.[26] Putin's official spokesman Dmitri Peskov has claimed that '[s]ome public organisations, non-governmental organisations, security services of foreign countries and certain media' have been trying to 'rock the boat in our country', and above all to 'discredit President Putin', by linking him with criminals.[27] But it has been reported widely in Russian and international media, and explored by Karen Dawisha in her book *Putin's Kleptocracy*, that Putin's job as deputy mayor had been to manage relations with a variety of powerful interests. It was important for the city administration to have a smooth relationship with the criminals, and this allowed them to expand their empire so long as they also enriched local officialdom and accepted its overall political control.[28] This was in many ways the model for Putin's national policy, and the criminals soon realised that what was available to them was an implicit social contract, their own 'little deal'. So long as they were more discreet, so long as they cut officials into part of the action, then the state would not treat them as a threat. Of course, the police would still try to catch criminals, but they did not need to fear any sustained, comprehensive crackdown. Indeed, one gangster remembers being in effect briefed on this new line by a police officer: 'They'd find reasons to bring us in or meet us at one of our usual places. Then this man, a major, told me that times had changed, but it need not be a problem. We just had to be cooler, smarter, and everything would be fine.'[29]

In many ways this paralleled Putin's taming of the oligarchs, the mega-rich businessmen who had become such a politically powerful force under Yeltsin: they were offered a quiet life so long as they didn't challenge the Kremlin. The three who were least willing to accept Putin's terms, Boris Berezovsky, Mikhail Gusinsky and Mikhail Khodorkovsky, were forced into exile in the UK or, in the last case, sent to prison, but the rest fell into line. Likewise, most gangs were happy to accept these new rules of the game, not least because the mob wars of the 1990s had already played themselves out. Turf boundaries had largely been agreed and hierarchies established, and further conflicts would be bad for business. The result was that higher-order organised crime became increasingly regularised, corporately minded and integrated with elements of the state. When gangs did turn to *razborka*, the violent settling of scores – as sometimes they inevitably did – it was in a far more precise and targeted way, the sniper's bullet supplanting the indiscriminate car bomb or drive-by shooting that had been such a bloody fixture of the 1990s.

The end of the *vorovskoi mir*?

We should recognise that our criminals are now so much more like yours. The old ways and understandings that used to define Russia's underworld are fading. I suppose this is a good thing, but there is even a part of me that wonders what will survive of Russia's traditions, even the bad ones.

Former Russian police investigator, 2016[30]

The old-style *vory v zakone*, with their prison records, garish tattoos and clannish rituals, increasingly became anachronisms. The name and the mythology would survive, but lose their strength and meaning. In their heyday, the *vory v zakone* were called on to arbitrate disputes between gangs and individual criminals and also to manage the *obshchak*, the common fund that groups would maintain to support members and their dependants. The *obshchak* was at once a pension plan and a life insurance policy, and to steal from or misuse it was one of the greatest sins in the criminals' eyes. *Vory v zakone* were thus chosen by their peers on the basis of, ironically enough, their moral standing: they were thieves and murderers, but they were trusted to resolve disputes fairly and administer the *obshchak* honestly.

Although there are now still criminals calling themselves *vory v zakone* and funds called *obshchaki*, these mean very different things. The title has become a largely empty honorific, often one bestowed as a favour or bought as a vanity perk. These faux *vory* are known by the surviving traditionalists as *apelsiny*, 'oranges'. The etymology of the term is disputed: it reflects either a view amongst Slavic gangsters – and probably an accurate one – that they are disproportionately from the Caucasus, a region they associate with fruit sellers, or else the belief that this type of poseur-criminal is the kind of vain soul who spends a lot of his time topping up his tan on the beaches of the Mediterranean, Black or Caspian seas. Either way, the overwhelming majority of the modern *vory* are such 'oranges' who use the title but have not earned it according to the old traditions, nor do they accept any accompanying limitations on their behaviour.

For example, Andranik Sogoyan, an Armenian gangster convicted in absentia in 2013 in Prague on attempted murder charges, was 'crowned' as a *vor v zakone* in 1994 according to the old rules. Following long-standing Russian usage, Sogoyan has a criminal nickname, in this case 'Zap' or 'Zaporozhets', after an ancient small Soviet car, which his face is meant to resemble. However, police reports suggest he does not maintain an *obshchak* and he arranged for a young relative to be 'crowned' in 2012 by a group of his cronies. In other words, even those who rose through the hard old ways are often happy to see the rules relaxed for their family and friends.[31]

Likewise, although there are still funds known by the term *obshchak*, they are no longer the idealised social security of old, beyond some smaller, local gangs which retain the former sense of all-for-one mutuality. Instead, they are essentially groups' operational budgets and escrow accounts, moneys held in store to pay off higher-order gangs and corrupt officials, seed-corn capital for new ventures, and profits awaiting distribution. In this way, the forms of the old underworld continue, but in a very different context. This context is the world of the new breed of gangster, the *avtoritet* ('authority'). He – and it almost always is still he – is a criminal-businessman. His portfolios of interests will typically span the legitimate and illegitimate economies but also politics, as will be discussed in the following chapters.

In many ways, the murder in Moscow of legendary *vor* Vyacheslav Ivankov ('Yaponchik') in 2009 marked the beginning of the end for the old generation and the conclusive rise of the *avtoritet* and the entrepreneur. Ivankov was as old-school a *vor v zakone* as can be, a graduate of 'The

Mongol's' gang and numerous terms behind barbed wire. When released from his most recent stretch in 1991, he was already something of an anachronism to Moscow's *avtoritety*, with little interest in the new opportunities in business and political alliances, yet enough status to become a problem. So, as will be discussed in chapter 12, he was encouraged to head to America, ostensibly as a representative of the Motherland's *vorovskoi mir*, but in reality more as an exile. True to form, he immediately became personally involved in a range of violent activities and was duly arrested in 1995. In 2004, he was deported to Russia to stand trial in a murder case, a trial which collapsed mysteriously, allowing him to walk free the next year. He at once started to resume his activities, doing what he felt a *vor v zakone* ought to do: resolving disputes, grooming the next generation of gangsters, enforcing contracts and the criminal code. Yet the days when *vory v zakone* were sacrosanct within the underworld and their word was law had long since passed. When he incautiously sought to mediate a dispute between two Georgian-born gangsters, Aslan 'Ded Khasan' Usoyan and Tariel 'Taro' Oniani (see chapter 11), Ivankov literally put himself in the firing line. On the evening of 28 July 2009, he had just finished a working dinner at a Thai restaurant in northern Moscow when, even though he was accompanied by a bodyguard, a sniper using a Dragunov SVD rifle shot him in the stomach, fatally wounding him.

His funeral at Moscow's Vagankovskoye cemetery was an exercise in gangster cliché. His tombstone is, in keeping with the usual pomposity of *vor* vernacular, a black construct with a life-sized statue of 'Yaponchik' looking uncharacteristically thoughtful, sitting in a corner between walls of crosses. Elaborate wreaths from criminals and gangs across the former Soviet Union were piled on his grave, including an especially large one from Usoyan, whose side Ivankov was expected to have taken in the dispute. Pinstriped bosses were each surrounded by their contingent of shaven-headed 'bulls', while police videographers carefully recorded the scene. Oniani, tellingly, sent no flowers. But behind the theatricality, part of the reason for the scale of the funeral was that it was putting to rest not just one *vor v zakone*, but a whole era. The *avtoritety* may have been mourning a man and the culture that once would have kept him safe – but they were also likely breathing a sigh of relief. The future truly did now belong to them.

Part Three

VARIETIES

CHAPTER 9

GANGS, NETWORKS AND BROTHERHOODS

Many friends means no friends.

Russian proverb

Konstantin Yakovlev's underworld nickname was 'Kostya Mogila', or 'Kostya the Grave', and, while he was given that *klichka* for his first job as a gravedigger, he more than earned it for the bloody path he trod through the underworld until his death in 2003. During the 1990s, he had done well in St Petersburg, and was even becoming a powerful behind-the-scenes political player, bankrolling a national meeting of the nascent Fatherland–All Russia Party in 1999 through a front company.[1] Nonetheless, much of his business was based in Moscow, and he was in effect the *smotryashchy*, or 'watcher', for its criminals in Russia's second city. In the late 1990s and early 2000s, Moscow-based gangs began to make attempts to extend their authority over St Petersburg. As is often the case, an external enemy led to a closing of ranks, and the Muscovites were rebuffed by a local alliance uniting not just the dominant Tambovskaya network, but also the smaller Kazanskaya group and other gangs. This culminated in 2003 when a *skhodka* of criminal leaders – a 'sit-down' in mafia parlance – summoned Kostya to talk. He may have been a formidable figure, but, in the face of this united front, he had no choice but to switch sides. Not that it saved him: later that year, when back in Moscow for a few days, a motorbike carrying two men pulled up next to his car in traffic and raked it with Kalashnikov fire. He died on the spot, but made one final, posthumous trip back to St Petersburg and, as befits his former calling, was interred in an especially ornate tomb in the grounds of the St Alexander Nevsky monastery.[2]

Kostya's story encapsulates many of the features of this thoroughly postmodern underworld. At first, he was a member of a gang, then later a gang leader and criminal-businessman in his own right. He was also a member of wider networks. He was initially loosely connected with a St Petersburg network and strongly tied to a Muscovite one, and then later (briefly) swapped over. Compared with other underworlds where identity is relatively fixed and allegiance determined by birth or ethnicity, Russia's criminals enjoy a protean existence in which everything can be redefined or even combined, as the needs of the moment require.

Individual gangs within Russia largely fit the same shape as those elsewhere, with one or more dominant figures, a circle of core gangsters and a wider array of loosely affiliated occasional members, 'wannabes' eager to join, and contacts who provide or receive services but are not actual members. Some are ad hoc and fluid in their structure, especially those which are little more than local street gangs. Others may adopt a more formalised structure, with ranks and specialised roles. Most, though, will not go to such lengths; within the gang, those who need to know already know who is the enforcer, who has the best contacts within the police, and so forth: they do not need titles to remind them.

Overall, the Russian underworld is defined not by hierarchical structures like the Italian mafia or Japanese yakuza but by a complex and varied underworld ecosystem. There are myriad territorially based groups, some controlling just a housing estate or a neighbourhood, others cities and regions, such as Uralmash, described below. However, there is no single nationwide hierarchy. In so far as there are major structures reaching across city limits, regional boundaries and even national borders, there are a few *gruppirovki*: loose, flexible organisations more like networks than anything else. How many? Precisely because of their loose, sometimes overlapping natures, there is no consensus.[3] I have heard figures from a very implausible three (presented by an academic at the Interior Ministry Academy in 2014, who said they were the Slavic, Chechen and Georgian networks) through to twenty-plus. It all depends on how one counts and defines them, but the consensus seems to be between six and twelve.

Personally, and this is just my own count at the time of writing, I would suggest at least eight. Some are very loose networks, defined really by common interest (Solntsevo, discussed in this chapter) or culture (the Chechens, discussed in chapter 10), but little more. Others are anchored around individuals (such as those dominated still by Tariel Oniani and once by Aslan Usoyan, covered in chapter 11). Then there are those with a clear territorial focus (St Petersburg's Tambovskaya and the Far Eastern Association of Thieves, both considered in this chapter) or very loose ones dominated by specific criminal businesses, such as those concerned with the 'Northern Route' smuggling Afghan heroin, or the interconnected 'Ukrainians', who are often not Ukrainians as such, but work across the Russian–Ukrainian border and now also seek to exploit the undeclared war in south-eastern Ukraine.

Each network will have authority figures who either give orders or, more often, have the social, physical, economic and coercive power to ensure that in the main people heed their views. Most, though, have relatively little hierarchy and no sense of wider strategy. Instead, it is the component elements – the term *brigady* ('brigades') is often used for the larger ones[4] – which will typically have some more distinct sense of structure and hierarchy.

Gangs and networks

Deal with the people you know, the ones you were in prison with.
Former mob lawyer Valery Karyshev, on *vor* attitudes[5]

These larger networks exist to provide a series of benefits for their members, whether gangs or individuals. They provide access to criminal opportunities and services and presumably reliable contacts who can help a member develop some new venture or respond to a challenge. In a rapidly evolving business climate, today's protection racketeer may want tomorrow to get involved in heroin trafficking: where to find the drugs or venture capital such an operation needs? The network thus acts as a source of proven and hopefully reliable investment and capacity.

Diego Gambetta in particular has explored the vexed question of trust in the underworld: who to rely on in a world which by definition is outside the remit of credit-rating agencies, court-enforced contracts and business directories?[6] The network provides an answer to these dilemmas: new members have presumably been vetted by existing ones, and will have needed to demonstrate their effectiveness, their security, and their ability and willingness to follow through on their undertakings. Should they fail to do so, they face the passive risks of reputational harm and being frozen out of future collaborations, as well as being judged and even penalised by other members of the network.

The network also provides mutual security, especially in the face of common threats, encroachments or bad faith from outsiders. Networks rarely seek to establish territorial monopolies: Moscow is home to three major ones (Solntsevo and the Oniani and Usoyan groups), has a strong presence from another (the Chechens) and also hosts a plethora of smaller groups such as the Mazutkinskaya, Izmailovskaya–Golyanovskaya and Lyubertsy gangs, which rise, fall and sometimes persist, perhaps loosely associated with one of the big groupings, but often with none or several. This is business as usual, but sometimes an attempt to upset the status quo in a major way will require a collective response.

Attempting to identify the main networks is harder than it may seem, not least as many of these groupings are very diffuse and others merge together. Nonetheless, it is possible to identify some on which most underworld and police sources alike agree. Of the Slavic ones, Solntsevo is the most extensive, certainly the most transnational, but in many ways a victim of its own success. It is now so large that it is too diffuse to be more than a loose array of contacts and local and personal groups. Solntsevo is based – as much as anywhere, these days – in Moscow, while St Petersburg is the home of their rival organisation once known as Tambovskaya (or just 'Tambov'), even though it is not really called by its old name any more, nor has it acquired a new one. The very fact that names matter so much less is in itself a signal that these are not conventional hierarchical organised crime structures. Moving out into the provinces, the Yekaterinburg-based network still generally known as Uralmash and the remnants of the Far Eastern Association of Thieves are the most powerful in central Siberia and the Russian Far East respectively. The Association was never as organised as its name suggests, and has become less so since the death in 2001 of founder Yevgeny Vasin ('Dzhem'). In many ways it can almost be considered the trade association of the 'Easterners,' not least in their relations with the *varyagy* ('Varangians'), the gangsters from European Russia. Within the 'highlanders' from the Caucasus, the main movers are the organisations dominated by Tariel 'Taro' Oniani and, until his death in 2013, Aslan 'Ded Khasan' Usoyan, the diffuse but notorious Chechens and a group of insurgent young bloods who cohered originally around the Azeri Rovshan Dzhaniyev. Each of these various groupings will be explored in more detail below.

The question of the actual degree of organisation in Russian organised crime is therefore obviously a vexing one, although it speaks to a wider criminological debate as to just where one draws the line between 'organised crime' and 'crime that is organised'. A useful study by the UN Office on Drugs and Crime identified five main types of organised crime grouping:

'Standard hierarchy': Single hierarchical group with strong internal systems of discipline.

'Regional hierarchy': Hierarchically structured groups, with strong internal lines of control and discipline, but with relative autonomy for regional components.

'Clustered hierarchy': A set of criminal groups which have established a system of coordination/control, ranging from weak to strong, over all their various activities.

'Core group': A relatively tightly organized but unstructured group, surrounded in some cases by a network of individuals engaged in criminal activities.

'Criminal network': A loose and fluid network of individuals, often drawing on individuals with particular skills, who constitute themselves around an ongoing series of criminal projects.[7]

In Russia, all five types are evident. However, the larger, the more important and the more geographically and functionally extensive they are, the more likely groupings are to have adopted the latter forms.

The 'standard hierarchy' and the Uralmash brigade

Uralmash is a financial group, not an organised criminal society . . . Uralmash has the most civilised and democratic style of work. Nobody stifles businessmen, many problems were resolved, and their fear of partnership disappeared.

Yekaterinburg businessman Andrei Panpurin, 1993[8]

The 'standard hierarchy' is generally found in two main kinds of gang: the very local ones involved largely in protection racketeering and the provision of illegal goods and services, and those groups which emerge within disciplined state agencies, typically the police, military and security apparatus, and which replicate their formal chain of command. Such a structure, though, struggles to embrace widely varied interests and members. It works for military-style gangs, but is less effective in managing ones which may be dominated by a mix of old-school thugs, modern criminal-businessmen and corrupt officials. This tends to make them brittle, prone to fracture under stress. This was particularly evident in the case of the Uralmash *gruppirovka*, which rose as a classic 'standard hierarchy', but has only been able to survive by reforming itself as a very different kind of gang.[9]

In February 2006 Major General Alexander Yelin, deputy head of the MVD's Organised Crime Directorate, claimed that in 2005 'a gang called Uralmash was eradicated in Sverdlovsk Region'.[10] At the time, this assertion was widely mocked, not least in Yekaterinburg, capital of the region and home of the gang. It certainly suffered body-blows in the first half of the 2000s, but even the MVD was forced later to quietly drop its proud claim: when the police arrested the *vor* 'Sukhy Novik' in 2009, they accused him of being a Uralmash kingpin, even though the gang was meant to have been destroyed four years before. However, the real impact of a decade's police pressure had been to prevent it from either evolving into a complex network like so many other groups, or emerging from the underworld altogether. Instead, it reverted to its original, closely knit form.

A city in the Urals, halfway across Russia, Yekaterinburg has a long criminal history. The Soviets renamed it Sverdlovsk and it became a transit station for convicts destined for the Gulags. When the camps were opened, the region was afflicted by mobs of rootless ex-convicts, known as 'blue gangs' because of their extensive tattoos, as we saw in chapter 6. Until the late 1980s, organised crime in Yekaterinburg was largely concerned with protection and smuggling rackets, in the hands of a succession of *vory v zakone*. But then a new generation of gangsters arose in the local sports clubs and gymnasia. A gang of two dozen such athlete-gangsters keen to turn muscle into cash emerged, including a skier, a wrestler, two boxers, a footballer and his black-marketeering brother. At first, they began shaking down stallholders at local markets and setting up illegal distilleries to profit from the anti-alcohol campaign. However, they needed space for expansion, and the collapse of the USSR in 1991 and its consequent economic crisis provided just that.

The gigantic Uralsky Mashinostroitelny Zavod (Ural Machine-Building Plant – generally just called Uralmash) was the city's headline employer; its northern working-class Ordzhonikidze neighbourhood was likewise generally known as Uralmash because it housed so many of the factory's workers, and the gang derived its name from this. Desperate for revenue, the plant's management began renting out and selling properties, and the newly moneyed gang began buying. Almost overnight, racketeers became rentiers. In the process, they also began to become significant enough to gain the attention of the 'blue' criminals who still dominated the local underworld. In 1992–3, the newly renamed Yekaterinburg was ripped apart by a gang war which in many ways replicated the 'bitch wars' of the 1950s: the 'blues' under the *vor* 'Trifon' were individually tough, but less unified and disciplined than the 'sportsmen'. The latter also benefited from the tacit support of the local political elite, whom they bribed widely and generously, acquiring a reputation as 'reasonable gangsters' (a term a former local police officer used describing them to me).

The 'blues' were broken, followed by Uralmash's other main rival, the Tsentralnaya gang. By 1993, Uralmash was dominant in Yekaterinburg. It moved quickly to establish its legitimate and illegitimate business empire and also sought political legitimacy by funding youth clubs, running charity campaigns and presenting itself as a club of concerned local businessmen. When the police arrested one of its alleged leading lights in 1993 on extortion charges, carefully orchestrated public protests followed, leading business figures extolled his charitable work, and political pressure was brought to bear. He was released within a few months.[11]

Uralmash could have gone either way. It had founded or taken over a wide range of companies, some of which were highly profitable within the essentially legitimate sector. It involved itself in local politics through regional governor Eduard Rossel – whom it had publicly supported in his 1995 election – and in 1999 it was formally registered as a political organisation, the Uralmash Social-Political Union. Perhaps because it was a provincial gang with less direct opposition, but also fewer opportunities, Uralmash retained the tight hierarchy of its inception, enforced by a so-called 'security squad' trained by former commando instructors.[12] There was a clear leadership, and an equally clear pecking order of lieutenants (known as brigadiers in old *vorovskoi mir* style). Uralmash's various enterprises managed to avoid duplication and competition, in part because of often micro-managing control from above. In many ways, the model was military in its insistence on the chain of command.

This worked for a while, but it left Uralmash vulnerable. In Putin's new era, it made the mistake of remaining too visible, too potentially powerful. Its chief at the time, Alexander Khabarov, overreached himself in both upperworld and underworld politics. He supported the muscular City Without Drugs initiative in Yekaterinburg while seeking to drive away gangs from the Caucasus. In part this was, ironically enough, a bid to control the local drug trade. He held a seat on Yekaterinburg city council between 2002 and 2005, even running for mayor in 2003. Just as alarming to Moscow, Uralmash had become involved in struggles over the region's potentially lucrative resources, something the capital wanted to be able to dispense itself. In 2001, for example, the Ural Mining and Metals Company and the Kyshtym Electrolytic Copper Plant were duelling for the Karabashsky copper-smelting works. When Kyshtym Electrolytic Copper was facing defeat, it is alleged that Uralmash got involved. Ural Mining and Metals suddenly and unexpectedly agreed to create a joint venture with its erstwhile rival. Law enforcement sources suggested to me that this decision may have been in part made because they had been contacted by Uralmash and encouraged to ponder the still-fresh memory of the fate of Oleg Belonenko, managing director of the Uralmash plant. He had been shot dead after he launched a campaign to cleanse his company of any links with the gang of the same name.

Uralmash became regarded in Moscow as a test case and the police and procuracy were tasked with making an example of it. Khabarov was arrested in 2004 and charged with racketeering. He died in prison the next year, his death apparently suicide but widely considered murder. His deputy fled the country ahead of an arrest warrant. Uralmash's hierarchical structure, once a strength, became a key weakness. The police – and criminal rivals – knew whom to target, and the operations of the system required management from above and thus regular contact between leaders and led. The plausible deniability that is often the godfather's best friend was hard to maintain when there were telephone taps and other information attesting to people's direct role in managing the gang's operations.

Uralmash seemed doomed and rival gangs began to circle. However, a new generation of leaders emerged who proved decisive and flexible. With some retrenchment, they restructured to present a less visible target and to retreat from politics. They even tried to avoid using the name Uralmash so as to downplay the extent to which their various smaller criminal enterprises were still part of a single network. Uralmash has become something more like a club of powerful criminal-businessmen, numbering between fourteen and eighteen, who closely coordinate the operations of their respective outfits, maintaining tight discipline but a low profile. It retains many of the characteristics of its earlier incarnations, including a reluctance to include non-Slavs, probably reflecting both the relatively crude nationalism of its founders and their continued struggle to hold their position on east–west trafficking routes against encroachments of north Caucasian gangs from the south-west and Central Asians from the south-east. Its evolution demonstrates both that many local gangs within Russia will tend to adopt more basic and traditional forms, and also that these models have distinct limitations when the organisations acquire greater economic and political ambitions. As Uralmash demonstrated, when those contradictions bite, the group can either diffuse into a network or retrench back onto its core criminal activities. In many places, we see the former, but Uralmash decided on the latter, simpler course.

The 'regional hierarchy' and the Far Eastern Association of Thieves

This is my district, and I want order here!
          Vor v zakone Yevgeny Vasin, in a TV interview, 2000[13]

In 1890, Anton Chekhov wrote to a friend regarding the Russian Far East, 'What crying poverty! The poverty, ignorance and pettiness are enough to drive you to despair. For every honest man there are ninety-nine thieves, who are a disgrace to the Russian people.'[14] Sadly, he would probably have recognised the region a century later. From its distinctive state emerged a relatively unusual form of organised thuggery and exploitation.

'Regional hierarchies' are relatively rare, and the Russian experience would seem to suggest they are generally only encountered in circumstances in which an artificial degree of centralisation is required by some kind of external pressure. This could be a political leadership that insists on dealing with a single counterpart and in turn demands that this interlocutor be able to discipline his subordinates as the price for continued survival. Or else it could be an external threat that forces otherwise hostile gangs to create a common structure in the face of a greater foe. The rise (and fall) of the Far Eastern Association of Thieves demonstrates both.

Even by the unruly standards of the 1990s, the Russian Far East – sparsely populated, far from Moscow, characterised by sources of valuable natural resources and widespread poverty – witnessed violent struggles between gangs. Many were over relative pittances. Others, though, were about, or else could impact on, the massive potential profits to be made from the region's extractive and fishing industries. In general terms, the functional near-collapse of the state apparatus gave regional bosses across Russia much freedom of manoeuvre to engage in or sanction criminal deals, but the relative isolation of the Far East (and its seeming irrelevance to politics in Moscow) made for even greater scope for the predatory exploitation of the region's resources.

The underworld of the Russian Far East was thus relatively primitive. Many settlements could not sustain more than one, quite small local gang, typically working with the administration. Cities such as Vladivostok, capital of the Maritime Region, had more, but even then had nothing like the complexity of the criminal ecosystems of a Moscow or a St Petersburg. The paucity of resources and a lack of mutually beneficial interactions between these gangs, along with weaknesses in local law enforcement, tended to make competition more common and more bloody. The *strelka* ('little arrow'), a meeting held between competing gangs to resolve their differences, increasingly became little more than an excuse for a firefight. Turf wars were common, with conflicts in 1995–6 and 1997–8 almost seamlessly merging.[15] The 1997–8 war, triggered by struggles over the fishing industry and the December 1997 regional parliamentary elections (and the subsequent redistribution of spoils and sinecures) led to a particular bloodletting.[16] Several gang bosses were killed, including Anatoly 'Koval' Kovalev and Igor 'Karp' Karpov; two entrepreneurs were tortured and buried alive; the CEOs of several local companies were gunned down; a hitman from St Petersburg, Artur Altynov, was murdered, probably to conceal the identity of his employer. Allegations were made that elements of the local military and security apparatus were involved and even that one murder was sanctioned at a high ranking official level.

However, there were also forces pressing for an end to these hostilities. First of all, the political and economic leadership, cohering around the administration of Maritime Region governor Yevgeny Nazdratenko – a survivor, he remained in office from 1993 until 2001 – became increasingly alarmed that these conflicts impeded their ability to exploit the region's resources to their own advantage and might even induce Moscow to take a hand. (Indeed, this was to happen under Putin.) Secondly, the arrival of representatives of gangs from European Russia – so-called *varyagy* ('Varangians') in local criminal parlance – demanding tribute or obedience also focused the minds of the *vostoki* ('easterners'). Believing, like Milton's Satan, that it was 'better to reign in Hell, than serve in Heaven', they looked to ways of resisting the encroachments of their richer, more numerous and politically better connected brothers from over the Urals.

The outcome was the rise of the Far Eastern Association of Thieves, whose grandiose title belies its ramshackle nature. This was closer to a trade association or guild for criminals of the Russian Far East, presided over by senior *vor v zakone* Yevgeny Vasin ('Dzhem') until his death (by natural causes) in 2001. Under Vasin, who was based in Komsomolsk-na-Amure, the Association became a confederation of local gangs (most of the 'standard hierarchy' variety and many quite antediluvian, still clinging to the *obsh-chak* and the old ways of the *voroskoi mir*). They had considerable autonomy within their agreed territories and businesses, but had to accept the rulings of Vasin and the Association's inner council in disputes. This did not prevent turf wars, by any means, but it did ensure that they did not spread as far as they might and would always take second place to the strategic interests of the collective. When, for example, a group of *varyagy* – themselves having just been driven out of their core business in Krasnoyarsk – tried to take over a haulage firm servicing the eastern stations on the Trans-Siberian Railway, feuding gangs in Khabarovsk called a truce to repel the outsiders (after which, they returned to their war).

As well as uniting the region's gangs, Vasin had an additional card to play against the *varyagy*, which became a third factor for unity in its own right: the Chinese. The Russian Far East quickly became an area of interest for Chinese criminals, even before the legitimate investment that is now reshaping the region.[17] Chinese merchants established shuttle-trading networks across the border to sell cheap, stolen and counterfeit goods. These traders were prey to protection racketeers on both sides of the border. Russo-Chinese joint ventures proved particular targets: in 1994, the deputy director of one was killed in Nakhodka; in 1995 the Khabarovsk offices of another were gutted by grenades; in 1996, Chinese gangsters tried to kidnap three Chinese business people in Vladivostok. However, these commercial contacts also brought with them interested potential collaborators from the Chinese underworld. Drugs, weapons, illegal migrants and then eventually timber, raw materials, rare wildlife and other more recondite commodities began to be traded, and the Russians also became launderers for a growing share of Chinese criminal cash. As it became clear that the potential profits were immense, gangs in such gateway cities as Vladivostok, Blagoveshchensk and Khabarovsk fought over these connections. However, the Chinese criminal market was just too big for any one or two gangs to service, the local political authorities wanted to ensure no one scared off this gold-egg-laying goose, and the *varyag* threat loomed.

As a result, Vasin drew on the Chinese to help fight off the European Russians – not with men or guns, but with money – and also used them to consolidate the position of the Association. If you wanted to be able to get a cut of the Chinese action, you needed to be a member in good standing. Despite all the jostling and sporadic violence which marked the under-world of the Russian Far East, this combination of carrot and stick helped keep the Association together through the 1990s. These were unusual circumstances, though, and Vasin, in fairness, was an unusual man, a *vor* of the old school who managed to combine ruthlessness, authority and diplomacy. Power-broker and elder statesman, he was in effect also the Association's ambassador, able to deal with his counterparts in Moscow, the Urals and St Petersburg in its name. Even before his death, though, the Association was breaking apart. Connections with China and its under-world had become increasingly deep, dense – and destabilising. In places such as Blagoveshchensk and along the river Amur, gangs from south of the border had become virtually dominant thanks to the influx of Chinese legal and illegal migrants and, more often, Chinese money. Elsewhere, such as in Vladivostok, there was greater parity: Chinese partners tended to have the economic strength, Russians the political cover. However, as always, it was over the division of spoils that the criminals fell out. Gangs along the southern coast or border could tap into these new profits and saw little reason to share the proceeds with those from the interior.

Furthermore, the new-model *varyagy* were less interested in the region, and its political elite, while no less rapacious, was less able to maintain a cosy condominium with the gangsters. The overall political situation changed after Nazdratenko resigned in 2001 (ostensibly after a heart attack although persistent rumours suggest it was at the Kremlin's behest) and the Maritime Region came under closer scrutiny from Moscow. With Vasin's death that same year, the Far Eastern Association of Thieves was also fatally wounded, even if it would take a few years for it to realise this. No successor of comparable stature emerged and the Chinese are now happy to establish their own bilateral relationships rather than work through the Association. After all, the importance of the Chinese connection is only growing. Everything from fish to timber is smuggled out of Russia and finished goods and illegal migrants are smuggled in. Perhaps $1 billion of the $8 billion-plus Chinese heroin market now comes from Afghan drugs smuggled across Russia and Central Asia,[18] but that pales before the tallies of these other products. Even illegally logged Russian timber for the Chinese construction market is a massive industry, worth perhaps $620 million.[19]

Although from time to time the Association is still mentioned, in practice it faded from existence around 2005, leaving a patchwork of gangs based around territories, ethnicity, leaders and specialities, caught – like a metaphor of the Russian Far East as a whole – between a receding European Russia and a rising China. Indeed, according to Bertil Lintner, Vasin was succeeded by his main Chinese contact, the enigmatic Lao Da ('Elder Brother'), as 'the main organised crime figure in Vladivostok'.[20] This is something of an overstatement, not least given that between 2004 and 2008 the city's mayor was Vladimir Nikolayev, the kickboxer and convicted gang leader known by the unlikely nickname 'Vinni-Pukh' ('Winnie-the-Pooh').[21] Nonetheless, the very fact that some believed a Chinese gangster could have risen to such heights demonstrates the extent to which the Association may have ultimately done no more than delay the incorporation of Russian Far Eastern crime into wider, more powerful regional criminal economies.

The 'clustered hierarchy' and the Northern Route

Afghan drug traffic is like a tsunami constantly breaking over Russia – we are sinking in it.
         Viktor Ivanov, head of the Federal Anti-Narcotics Service, 2013[22]

Gangs which seem to fit the 'clustered hierarchy' model – in other words, constellations of individual, semi-autonomous groups which nonetheless have to work together extensively – tend to be confined to those primarily involved in a single, specific activity which requires such cooperation. The classic fields are drug and people trafficking. In Russia, this is especially associated with the heroin-trafficking structures servicing the so-called Northern Route from Afghanistan. This is actually a constantly changing array of routes, with streams of drugs merging, separating and paralleling each other as they writhe west and east. It stretches from Central Asia into and through Russia (also satisfying the domestic market) to Europe, China and even beyond. Some shipments travel all the way to South America (where it is typically swapped for cocaine), North America and Africa. The Northern Route accounts for up to 30 per cent of the total global heroin flow, and the proportion is rising.[23]

This is a trade largely carried out by a sequence of criminal organisations: according to the United Nations, 80 per cent of the opiate trafficked through Central Asia is controlled by organised groups using long-term routes.[24] Afghan criminal networks, local warlords and insurgents dominate production and processing in-country and bring the drugs to, or just over, the country's borders. At that point they are typically sold on to Central Asian gangs – small, based around family, clan or neighbourhood – and then perhaps from gang to gang. For example, a typical arrangement for Turkmen gangs is that they sell on to Uzbeks who, in turn, sell on to Russians in Tashkent or Samarkand. Occasionally, Russian networks seek (to use the jargon of business) to bring vertical integration into their supply chains and procure heroin directly, but this depends on contacts and the protection and sanction of local criminal and political elites (in so far as there is a difference between the two).

From Turkmenistan, drugs move to the port of Turkmenbashi for trafficking across the Caspian Sea to Baku, or else by land into Uzbekistan and thence Kazakhstan. From Tajikistan they flow into Uzbekistan or Kyrgyzstan, then north into Kazakhstan and then Russia, or else east from Kyrgyzstan into China. Some of this trafficking is by car or even mule or horse, but the aim is to feed it into the region's transport infrastructure, so road, rail and air hubs such as Dushanbe, Tashkent, Samarkand and Almaty are key interim destinations.[25] The Russian leg of this Northern Route is largely dominated by ethnic Russian and Russian-based gangs (including Georgian and Chechen *gruppirovki*), with a small proportion handled by Central Asian criminals, often using the diaspora of migrant labourers in Russia, and largely selling to and through those expatriates.

Of the route's total flow, more than a third stays in Russia. According to official figures, almost 6 per cent of the country's population, some 8.5 million people, are drug addicts or regular users.[26] The key challenge is the growing proportion of users becoming addicts and the use of harder and more dangerous narcotics. Some 90 per cent of drug addicts use heroin at least part of the time, making Russia the world's leading heroin-using nation per capita; highly dangerous drugs such as *krokodil* (desomorphine), which rots away users' flesh, are also making considerable headway, with the consequent impact on mortality. Russians consume some 20 per cent of global heroin production.[27] The remainder heads west into Europe or east and south into China, where it is largely sold in wholesale quantities to local gangs for resale.[28]

Unsurprisingly, access to and control over this lucrative and growing business has become a source of considerable rivalry between gangs (and corrupt officials). Some major groupings have tried to build their own structures as far along the supply chain as makes sense, which generally means to Kazakhstan, and managing the shipment westward. Networks including Solntsevo and Tambovskaya, the Oniani group and the Chechens, for example, have been known to move large, consolidated shipments by road, rail or air along the primary transport arteries: the Trans-Siberian and Baikal–Amur railway lines, the federal highways and air links. In the process, they may subcontract aspects of the work to local gangs but tend instead to deal with corrupt officials and business people able to expedite their trafficking. A very crude estimate I was given by a Russian police officer in 2011 suggested that such wholesale transfers account for more than half the total throughput of the Northern Route. However, a few large drug seizures at the time probably coloured his view; my personal and unscientific guesstimate would put the total share handled in this way at a quarter, if that.

At the other end of the scale, 15–20 per cent is handled by individual criminal-entrepreneurs who buy the drugs in or close to Central Asia. These are often people whose regular work fits this pattern, such as shuttle traders, airline staff and commercial truckers, or else foreign gangs, predominantly Central Asians. However, these traffickers often operate at the sufferance of the larger and more politically protected Russian groups and thus typically pay tribute – in the form of a share of the drugs or a cut of the profits – to local gangs.

The bulk of the route's drug trafficking is in the hands of collectives of local gangs, which over time may assume the characteristics of a 'clustered hierarchy' as their relationships become settled and they come to depend on the heroin business, which entails everyone carrying out their role within the enterprise. The shipments handled in this way tend to be individually smaller but more numerous than those of the major networks, and are generally transported by couriers and in cars or trucks. The component gangs usually take their fee in a share of the heroin, to be sold locally for profit and to defray operational costs, or even passed on to gang members as compensation for their work. Thus, this form of trafficking disproportionately contributes to the domestic heroin market. This is also the main way trafficking to China is handled, not least as the major networks have not yet reached an agreement over access. Gangs therefore tend to move drugs to border cities and then sell on to Chinese counterparts operating under the cover of import–export businesses or shuttle traders.

One particular operation active in 2012 helps illustrate these relationships.[29] A heroin shipment worth around $1.2 million when finally sold on the street was assembled from consignments of opium bought from several Afghan suppliers by 'Behruz', an Uzbek criminal-entrepreneur directly related to a senior figure within the customs service. Behruz paid the Afghans in cash and goods and passed a fee on to his relative in order to ensure he remained safe and unhindered. He managed a processing facility outside Andizhan in eastern Uzbekistan, where the opium was converted into heroin. Then, he gathered the shipment in Tashkent, having agreed to sell it to a Kazakh gang.

Managing such long-range games of pass-the-parcel is a complex and delicate business, especially given that the aim is always to establish links with the European market, where the prices are highest. There has to be considerable trust that upstream groups are not short-changing their partners, and that downstream groups are not stealing from the shipment. A typical response, evident in this case, is for a trusted third party to confirm both the initial size of the shipment and – considering that heroin can be (and is, before consumption) 'cut' or adulterated– its purity. In this case, the shipment in Tashkent was inspected and inventoried by 'Parovoz' ('Locomotive'), a Russian *vor v zakone* largely retired from active crime, but who maintains a side-line precisely in such work, trading on his reputation as an 'honest thief'.

The Kazakhs took control of the heroin in Tashkent, broke the shipment into a few consignments and loaded them onto commercial trucks bound for Shymkent, just over the border. From there, it was flown to Almaty in the north. The Kazakhs were a relatively small and southern-based gang with few contacts and protectors in Almaty, so they were eager to monetise their heroin quickly and have it off their hands. They retained a portion of the drugs to sell on their home turf and handed the rest over to a Russian gang whose representatives were waiting. From Almaty, the heroin was flown to Samara in southern Russia, the buyers' home city.

Again, the Russian gang took a portion of the shipment to sell locally and handed the rest on to 'Yura Serbskoi' ('Serbian Yura'), a trusted lieutenant of a Moscow-based Georgian gangster, 'Khveli'. The Samara gang was not paid, though; this transaction was actually making good on a debt accrued the year before when a similar shipment was seized by the police. The drugs moved by train to Moscow, under 'Yura's' supervision. 'Khveli' was actually working with two partners: 'Seryozha', a gangster from Kaluga, and 'Mikhail Taksista' ('Mikhail the Taxi Driver'). At this point, 'Parovoz' re-entered the scene, checking the purity of the remainder of the heroin and assessing whether as much was left as there should be. The partners divided what they had. 'Seryozha' took his portion back to Kaluga for his gang to sell direct or to trade with other local gangs, while 'Khveli' and 'Mikhail' decided to try to reach the European market. They lacked direct contacts, so 'Parovoz' – again for a consideration – put them in touch with another gangster in Moscow, 'Vadik', who had a partner in Warsaw with whom he trafficked drugs regularly.

Throughout such a process, there has to be operational security against rival gangs, law enforcement and gang members. There has to be close coordination to manage the handovers and limit how long the drugs are in the pipeline, time in which they are vulnerable and unprofitable. In this case, the journey from Tashkent to Moscow took just nine days. Furthermore, given that the main profit is downstream, where the drugs are sold close to the retail dealers, and the main costs upstream, where they are initially bought, there has to be faith in an equitable distribution of revenues. Successfully and profitably navigating this complex process thus encourages long-term relationships. There is a huge potential profit to be made, but the time and risks involved in establishing the relationships in the first place are considerable. Having done so, the incentive is to maintain those sequential relationships, something which will often require the subordination of gangs' individual autonomy to the collective venture. Over time, there has been a tendency for the most durable and effective operations to become increasingly integrated and, in particular, for a common set of rules and procedures to be established. These rules will be enforced by some coordinating body, made up sometimes of trusted third parties paid for their role (this is a classic job for *vory v zakone*) or, more often, a council of representatives of all the stakeholding gangs. In this case, 'Khveli', 'Mikhail Taksista' and 'Behruz' formed the unofficial governing council. They paid 'Parovoz' for his role directly out of their share as they had a common interest in keeping the process 'honest'. After all, they had sunk considerable time, money and social capital into establishing this route and they wanted it to last.

The 'core group' and the Tambovskaya

Petersburg – the criminal capital of Russia.
Slogan used by opponents of St Petersburg governor Vladimir
Yakovlev in his 2000 re-election campaign[30]

The 'core group' and the 'criminal network' are the main models for the largest and most significant Russian structures. Both are similar, the key distinction being whether or not they have a dominant constituent group that does not seek to manage every aspect of day-to-day operations by the structure's members but does expect obedience when it chooses to assert it. This leadership role is a difficult and often dangerous one to claim and maintain, though. In 1994, for instance, Georgian godfather Otari Kvantrishvili tried to leverage his undoubted status as the most powerful individual kingpin in Moscow into dominance within his network, with fatal results.

'Core group' networks are thus quite rare. At the time of writing, Tariel Oniani's predominantly Georgian group would seem the be the best exemplar of this model, and it is discussed in chapter 11. However, especially in its heyday, St Petersburg's Tambov (or Tambovskaya) group offered a particularly good example of such an organisation, as well as the shift away from the *bandity* and towards the criminal-business elite.[31] It was established in 1988 by 'Valery the Baboon' and Vladimir Kumarin (later also known as Barsukov, when he took his mother's maiden name), both hailing from the Tambov region, around 500 kilometres south-east of Moscow, but living and working in St Petersburg (then still called Leningrad). 'The Baboon' was a boxer and he attracted a following of like-minded thugs and martial artists as the initial core of the gang, but Kumarin provided direction and business sense. Thanks to him, they moved quickly from racketeering, organised theft and drug trafficking into the growing private business of Gorbachev's cooperative era. As a result, from the very first the group developed as both a seemingly legitimate and overtly criminal structure. Ironically enough, it was also an unintended beneficiary of Gorbachev's relaxation of censorship. Local television journalist Alexander Nevzorov ran sensationalist exposés of the 'Tambov boys' that perversely made their name, establishing their reputation for ruthlessness and effectiveness.[32] These are two powerful assets in the underworld. As a result, the group grew quickly. It survived an early turf war with the rival and more traditional Malyshevskaya gang. It would later mount what in business terms would be a leveraged takeover of this group, but its real challenge was managing its success and consequent rapid expansion. It grew so quickly and incorporated so many disparate and often competing members that conflict was almost inevitable. By 1993, an internal struggle for power had broken out, which lasted two years but led to the consolidation of the organisation under Kumarin, even though he lost his right arm in an assassination attempt in 1994. His aim was to bring renewed discipline and cohesion to the network and push it away from its roots in street crime.

By the end of the 1990s, the organisation had become the city's dominant group. Whereas once protection racketeering had essentially been regarded simply as a means of extorting payments from local businesses (typically demanding 20–30 per cent of targets' profits), now it became a weapon to take over a controlling interest in them instead. Increasingly the Tambovskaya looked to partnerships, either setting up new businesses or investing in existing ones. These companies not only served as fronts for criminal rackets, they also operated within the legitimate sector. For example, the group's private security firms employed Tambovskaya enforcers, who were thus given an excuse legally to carry weapons, but they also provided genuine protection services for clients. Indeed, according to one former customer, they actually proved very cost effective: 'You paid more than the market rate for the fat ex-cop they sent, but in practice everyone knew that you were as a result under the "roof" of the Tambov, so no one would try and rob you.'[33] In this way, the Tambovskaya was at the forefront of a general trend within Russia as power within the underworld shifted from the *vory* to the *avtoritety*.

In particular, the organisation entrenched itself within the local energy and transport sectors, including, it was alleged, the Petersburg Fuel Company (PTK), apparently unopposed by the local administration.[34] In 2001, Interior Minister Boris Gryzlov claimed that the Tambovskaya controlled up to 100 industrial enterprises in St Petersburg, as well as key interests relating to the four main sea ports of north-western Russia: St Petersburg itself, plus Arkhangelsk, Kaliningrad and Murmansk.[35] However, like the expansion of the mid-1990s, this proved a mixed blessing. The more legitimate business interests the Tambovskaya leaders acquired, the more they were forced to operate to legitimate standards and the wider the gulf grew between the *avtoritety* and the rank-and-file *bandity*. Just as the leaders of the Tambovskaya were gaining in legitimacy and political power in the upperworld – Kumarin/Barsukov even gained the nickname of the 'night governor', as the shadow administrator of the city – they were losing it in the underworld.

The result was another gang war. In 1999, local politician – and Tambovskaya protector – Viktor Novoselov was killed when someone slapped a mine on the roof of his official car, decapitating him in the blast. Another ally, nightclub owner Sergei Shevchenko, who stood for election proudly and publicly admitting 'Of course I'm backed by criminal money, I'm a bandit!',[36] was arrested and charged with extortion. He was subsequently murdered in an apparent contract killing in Cyprus in 2004. Facing claims that St Petersburg was becoming a focus for organised crime – claims which both deterred investors and were embarrassing to the new Russian prime minister and soon-to-be president, local boy Vladimir Putin – the St Petersburg authorities began to impose a degree of order. PTK, which had been a closed joint-stock company, was made an open joint-stock holding, and a process was begun to cleanse it of Tambovskaya influence.[37] Kumarin/Barsukov was unexpectedly arrested in 2007 and convicted two years later on fraud and money-laundering charges, bearing a fourteen-year sentence.[38]

The business-minded *avtoritety* remained dominant within the organisation, but they had to accept that they lacked the ability to run the gang like a single integrated business and also that they could not move wholly away from their street crime roots. They could also not afford to appear to be challenging the state. As a result, the name Tambovskaya is now little heard in St Petersburg, even though the network remains a key player not just in the city and the surrounding Leningrad region but throughout the Russian north-west. Its operations stretch over 1,000 kilometres north to Murmansk, over 700 kilometres north-east to Arkhangelsk and almost 1,000 kilometres south-west to Kaliningrad. It has largely devolved to numerous smaller outfits and operators and moved into new businesses such as methamphetamines and counterfeit goods. The role of the core appears now primarily be to resolve disputes, protect the network as a whole (especially against incursions by 'highlanders' from the north Caucasus) and to manage international flows of goods – drugs, people, stolen cars, counterfeit wares – and money.

Indeed, in many ways the primary role of the core is to operate abroad. Many of the leaders of the Tambovskaya (or Tambovskaya–Malyshevskaya[39]) have ended up operating in Spain, and others are to be found in Germany, the Baltic states and further afield. It is not that violence and coercion are no longer factors, but the core retains its influence over this loose network (one that has diffused to the point where it does not even have much of a distinctive identity) by controlling access to the money, opportunities and lifestyle to be found abroad. The *bandity* may be powerful at home, but, in the words of a Spanish police officer, 'if they want to play a full part in Tambovskaya's activities abroad, they need to stay in favour with the *avtoritety*'.[40]

Nonetheless, if they lose this position as gatekeepers, the *avtoritety* will maintain control at home only so long as they have the money to corrupt officials and pay off the *bandity*. With officials facing an anti-corruption campaign from Moscow, the profits of white-collar crime under pressure, and the *bandity* feeling stronger, the Tambovskaya network may shift back towards more violent and overt criminal businesses, especially drug and people trafficking. However, while it will hope to draw on the contacts, business assets and skills built up during the years in which the *avtoritety* held sway, its days may be numbered. It could well fracture, or be replaced by other, newer structures. The Tambovskaya may be an organisation already fading.

The 'criminal network' and Solntsevo

The most powerful Russian crime syndicate in terms of wealth, influence, and financial control ... [whose] leadership, structure, and operations exemplify the new breed of Russian criminals that emerged with the breakup of the Soviet system.

US government's *International Crime Threat Assessment*, 2000[41]

What happens when your organisation is so successful, it grows too big to manage? The natural tendency has been for structures instead to drift towards the true 'criminal network', and this is best exemplified by the infamous Solntsevo or Solntsevskaya network. Named after the south-western suburb of Moscow in which it originally emerged, it has steadily grown – but in the process has arguably lost much of its focus and identity. It began as a 'core group' but has devolved into a looser structure in which there are stronger and weaker members, but no one asserts true control.[42]

Solntsevo was founded in the mid-1980s by two relatively young gangsters going by the underworld nicknames of 'Mikhas' and 'Avera'. Neither, tellingly enough, were *vory v zakone*. Instead, they were forerunners of the modern Russian *avtoritety*, criminal businessmen interested in keeping a low profile while maximising their profits. They were fortunate enough to be able to draw on the city's criminal roots, though, not least by recruiting former members of the gang of Gennady Karkov, 'The Mongol'. Karkov had been one of Moscow's underworld kingpins, possibly even its foremost, until his arrest and conviction on charges of extortion with violence in 1972. His gang continued to operate while he was in prison, though, and represented a formidable asset for 'Mikhas' and 'Avera' in their rise to power, allowing them to trade on existing underworld reputations and muscle.

First of all, they were able to attract Vyacheslav 'Yaponchik' Ivankov, the notorious *vor v zakone* of the old school. A former boxer, Ivankov was arrested and sentenced to fourteen years' hard labour in 1982, and while in prison was formally 'crowned' a *vor v zakone* by his peers. Meanwhile, Solntsevo also formed an alliance with Sergei 'Silvestr' Timofeyev and his Orekhovo gang, another rising power. Founded in 1988, the core members of Orekhovo (or Orekhovskaya) were young sportsmen and military veterans. What they lacked in business acumen they made up for in their ability to deploy violence with enthusiastic overkill. As such, they represented the ideal

1. The Khitrovka in Moscow, pictured here in the 1900s, was perhaps the worst of the *yamy*, the slums of Russia, a place where life and death were equally cheap. This is where the lost, dispossessed and rootless of the city ended up, both as predators and prey. This is thus also where the *vorovskoi mir*, the 'thieves' world', truly took shape.

2. The tsarist police record for Joseph Vissarionovich Dzhugashvili, known by the revolutionary codename 'Koba' and, later, rather more so as Stalin. While no bank robber or highwayman himself, Stalin played a crucial role in working with the *vory* to raise funds for the Bolsheviks. This early willingness to find common cause with the underworld would later be applied to his management of the Gulags.

3. The revolutionary state had trouble creating a new police force. Here, the entrance to the offices of the 'Workers' and Peasants' Militia' in Petrograd (later Leningrad, then St Petersburg) in 1924 is guarded by two officers who had probably received virtually no training, and might not even have been literate.

4. 'Work in the USSR is a matter of honour, conscience, valour and heroism' reads the slogan over the gates to Vorkuta labour camp in 1945. This was likely little comfort to the convicts who laboured, starved and often died mining coal in the Vorkutlag, north of the Arctic Circle. In 1953, Vorkuta would be rocked by strikes which, while eventually put down by force, nonetheless helped make the case that the age of the Gulags was over.

5. To the *vory*, epaulettes represented the military and a willingness to serve the state – yet when tattooed on skin, perversely expressed a rejection of this life. This became especially significant during the 'bitches' war', when the traditionalists not only sought to demonstrate their independence, but also to mock and exclude the *voyenshchina*, the 'soldiery', as former soldiers in the camps were known.

6. 'Fight against hooliganism!' With the *vory* among the first to be freed as the Gulags were opened, the Soviet Union suffered a massive crime wave, not least as *suki* clashed with traditionalists. Much of this was officially deemed 'hooliganism' – a useful catch-all term for unruly and violent behaviour – and, as this 1956 poster shows, it became the focus of a nationwide crackdown, which would help drive the *vory* into the shadows.

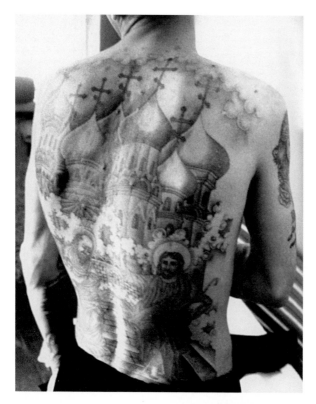

7. While many *vor* tattoos are crude in execution and meaning, some demonstrate considerable artistry. This full-back tattoo featuring religious symbolism may reflect a genuine faith or else its mockery, but it also has a very specific meaning: each onion-domed cupola on the church marks a term spent in a prison camp, and sadly there is still room for more.

8. Two Soviet air-assault troops in Gardez during the ten-year occupation of Afghanistan. Soviet forces would be withdrawn in 1989, but the long-term impacts would endure for decades. In the 1990s, the veterans, the *afgantsy*, would number amongst the 'violent entrepreneurs' quite literally muscling their way into protection rackets, while the flow of Afghan heroin into and through Russia would only grow, reaching one-third of the total global trade by the middle of the 2010s.

9. Dzhokar Dudayev, the man who declared Chechnya independent, not only dressed like a 1930s American gangster, he presided over the wholesale criminalisation of this southern republic of the Russian Federation.

10. One of the last of the true, old-school *vory v zakone*, Vyacheslav 'Yaponchik' Ivankov was a violent and brutal man, an uncomfortable partner for the new generation of criminals interested in money rather than machismo. His murder in Moscow in 2009 came as a relief to many, but such is underworld etiquette that his ostentatious grave in Vagankovskoye cemetery portrays a distinguished and even meditative figure. Those who suffered from his reigns of terror in both Moscow and, for a while, New York's Brighton Beach, might not remember quite the same 'Yaponchik'.

11. One of the more notorious Russian prisons, the Butyrka in Moscow dates back to the seventeenth century and was used as a transit facility and holding station for political prisoners under tsars and Soviets alike. Its roll of inmates is thus a virtual who's who of the dangerous, the troublesome and the independent.

12. Modern Russian criminals have access to assault weapons and a willingness to use them, so the law enforcers have evolved to match. Here, a team of special forces from the Federal Narcotics Control Service swoop on a drug gang in Kaluga in 2004. The balaclavas are to hide the officers' identities to avoid reprisals against their families.

13. It is an irony that a criminal culture which once revelled in its sacrilegiousness has in recent years become increasingly respectful of the Russian Orthodox Church. Epiphany is the January day when hardy believers plunge into icy waters, symbolically washing away their sins. Here, a man with a brace of criminal tattoos – including a *vor v zakone*'s star on his left shoulder – immerses himself in the Irtysh river in Tobolsk, Siberia. Whether this is enough to cleanse him of all sin is between the man and his God.

14. The *mafiya* in the Med. As Russian organised crime went international, different nations responded with varying levels of concern. After a decade of relative quiescence, in the mid-2000s Spain became alarmed at the extent of Russian, Georgian and other organised criminality, especially on its resort coasts. Here, the senior *vor* Gennady Petrov is being arrested in 2008 as part of 'Operation Troika', a wider crackdown on his Tambovskaya–Malyshevskaya network. Petrov was subsequently paroled to Russia for medical treatment but never returned and Moscow has made no moves to compel him to face trial.

15. In post-Soviet Russia, the private security sector is so pervasive that even the police got into the business. FGUP Okhrana, the Interior Ministry's own in-house company (later transferred to the jurisdiction of the National Guard), hired out armoured vans and moonlighting police, such as this submachine-gun-toting officer.

16. The borders between the state and the underworld are blurred in Putin's Russia. The Night Wolves motorcycle gang has been accused of criminal activities, but enjoys the patronage of the Kremlin. Here, the leader of the Night Wolves, Alexander Zaldostanov, known as 'the Surgeon', addresses a rally in the Chechen capital Grozny in 2016, in front of a massive portrait of Chechen leader Ramzan Kadyrov.

complement to Solntsevo's increasingly extensive business empire, built on the back of Gorbachev's reforms.

At this time, a conflict was raging in Moscow's underworld between Slavs and 'highlanders' from the Caucasus. Solntsevo, especially once it was linked with Orekhovo, assumed an increasingly influential role as de facto coordinator of the Russian gangs. Their ability to combine the business and diplomatic skills of the *avtoritety* with the ruthlessness and brutality of the *vory* became most evident once Ivankov was released early in 1991. He led the counter-attack against the 'highlanders', using his authority within the *vorovskoi mir* to gather support from gangs across the country. By the end of the year, an uneasy peace of sorts had been concluded between the two sides.[43]

Even after the 'highlander' threat had receded, most Slav gangs in Moscow accepted Solntsevo's role as first amongst equals. Solntsevo directly controlled underworld operations in the south-west of the city and parts of the centre, but Orekhovo split away as Timofeyev chafed at the more low-key approach favoured by 'Mikhas'. For a while, Orekhovo became notorious for its violence and its willingness to flout the law and underworld convention alike, but in 1994 Timofeyev was killed and the gang fragmented. Most of these splinters were incorporated into Solntsevo, especially after the murder of Timofeyev's successor, Igor 'Max' Maximov, in 1995.

It was clear that the city's unruly gangs would accept no single overlord. Georgian godfather Otari Kvantrishvili had been assassinated in 1994 largely because of his empire-building ambitions in Moscow. On the other hand, the profits to be made in an orderly underworld economy – as well as the need to maintain the balance between Slavs and 'highlanders' – meant that some form of arbitrating body would be useful. This was the role Solntsevo was able to assume. By the mid-1990s, it had become the dominant grouping in Moscow, alongside the more local and hierarchical Izmailovskaya–Golyanovskaya combine and Chechen-dominated groupings, such as the Tsentralnaya, Avtomobilnaya and Ostankinskaya gangs.

More to the point, Solntsevo expanded its network of contacts and members across Russia. It was an early and enthusiastic exploiter of the opportunities opened by Yeltsin's clumsy and underregulated adoption of a market economy. It moved into banking and finance. The business ethic fostered by the network's founders certainly did not preclude Solntsevo's involvement in violent extortion and protection racketeering, but it did mean that in many cases this *krysha* was more than just a levy demanded by force and threat. Solntsevo established a role as a pseudo-state agency for the enforcement of contracts. Given that the Russian *arbitrazh* courts responsible for commercial cases were in the 1990s inefficient, backlogged and corrupt, retrieving unpaid debts or winning damages for broken contracts could be a lengthy and uncertain process. Solntsevo, on the other hand, could offer to resolve such disputes in its own way for a cut of the sum in question (typically a market-beating 20 per cent), discreetly and far more quickly. In this way, Solntsevo not only profited from the inefficiencies of the Russian state, it turned an essentially parasitic process into an active partnership with the very companies it was extorting.

Nothing succeeds like success, and Solntsevo continued to grow, especially thanks to the 1998 ruble crash, which forced many local gangs into near-bankruptcy and sent them looking for more powerful and solvent partners to bail them out. By the 2000s, while Solntsevo was largely based in Moscow and the surrounding regions, including the Tver, Ryazan, Samara and Tula districts, it also had particular concentrations of constituent groups in Nizhny Novgorod, Kazan and Perm. Further afield, it was present in Ukraine (notably Crimea and the ethnically Russian Donetsk region), Lithuania and ethnically Russian northern Kazakhstan, as well as Europe, Israel and the United States.

However, this very expansion itself made the *gruppirovka* increasingly diffuse. Its boundaries became permeable, with gangs affiliating themselves with it while maintaining links, even owing primary allegiance, to other underworld combines. For example, one European-based member was overheard in a wiretapped conversation expressing uncertainty as to how to get in touch with network members back in Moscow when his main contact changed his mobile phone provider and in the process his telephone number.[44] It had no common *obshchak*, even if some of its component gangs and *brigady* did, because of the problems both in administering such a fund and in collecting dues from members strung out across the country – and world – for whom Solntsevo could well not be their primary allegiance.

Instead, Solntsevo became a true network, of smaller gangs, criminalised enterprises and individuals largely concerned with their own operations and whose interaction with the rest of the network may be minimal much of the time. Such networks can in a sense best be conceptualised as clubs: membership tends to be informal, bestowed through connections and the sponsorship of key individuals. Some of these individuals are the heads of more powerful *brigady* within the organisation, but others are simply rich, connected or charismatic enough to have authority. The links may be ongoing or occasional, strong or weak, tense or harmonious. They can easily be based on sentiment: while the Orekhovo gang is no more, there is still a perceptible core of criminals who used to work for Sergei Timofeyev and retain close connections, for old times' sake as much as anything else. The fundamental point, though, is that for at least a decade it has been impossible to talk of Solntsevo, as an organisation, actually *doing* anything. There is no central control, no real discipline to do more than expel or punish those who break the informal rules of the network. Solntsevo has become so successful it has transcended criminal organisation.

Whatever else one may say, then, Russia has a rich, intricate criminal ecosystem. From street gangs and small-scale *brigady* up to transnational networks, its organised crime has expanded to fill voids and seize opportunities not just in Russia but along the chains of trade, investment, migration and even cultural communication that now lead across the globe. Furthermore, it includes within it specialised subcultures, characterised by professional and ethnic roots, and it is to those that we next turn.

CHAPTER 10

THE CHECHEN
The gangster's gangster

It never troubles the wolf how many the sheep may be.

Russian proverb

Borz (not his real name, for fairly obvious reasons) was in many ways the stock image of the wily Chechen of a certain age: a spry man in his indefinable sixties, with the weathered skin and deep wrinkles that spoke of a hard life and an outdoors one, at that. But he had a cheerful smile, a sparkling eye and an energy to his speech and his movements that transformed him into someone younger, vital, unstoppable. He was also one of the most skilful and expensive contract killers in Moscow.

I met him, of all places, in a café in Sheremetyevo airport, which was still half shrouded in tarpaulins as it went through a much-needed *remont* or remodelling, in line with Moscow's desire to slough off its dowdy Soviet image and look like a glittering Western capital. Earlier that day, a contact I knew well enough – and trusted – had rung me up and told me there was someone I just had to meet. Who? A Chechen, a professional assassin, who was thinking of retiring and happy to talk. An invitation to have a chat with a killer for hire is something that I find almost irresistible, but, on the other hand, my recondite area of research had taught me the value of being cautious to the point of paranoia. The airport café seemed the ideal venue for a meeting, somewhere not only very public, but also behind a screen of metal detectors and humourless security guards, watched over by cameras and prowled by sniffer dogs and their handlers.

As it was, Borz was the soul of congeniality. I was immediately reminded that, while most Chechens are Muslims, they typically bear their faith lightly and flexibly as he produced a bottle of vodka and insisted that we toast not only friendship and health, but also Muhammad, may the peace and blessings of Allah be upon him. He proved delighted to talk, even as he deflected certain specific questions, and was a natural storyteller. In many ways, his tales outlined the very trajectory of the Chechens in recent decades and the ways whereby they became the most feared (and mythologised) players in the Russian underworld, not least the effects of Russian oppression: as he put it, 'the Russians taught me to want to kill, and then they taught me how to do it well'.[1] His stories were also polished from ample retelling and more than faintly hard to believe, so a few days later when I had the opportunity to mention his name and some of his claims to an officer from the Moscow police's Main Criminal Investigations Division, I was half expecting to be told that he was some Caucasus Walter Mitty canny enough to spin tales to keep a gullible Westerner buying drinks. The officer gave me a grave look. 'Oh no, that's all true. If anything, he probably didn't spill the really big stories. He's serious, a very serious man.'[2]

Born of blood

We will not break, we will not weep; we will never forget.
Inscription on a memorial to the victims of deportation, Grozny

The Chechens, a people whose national animal is the wolf, take a perverse pride in the hardships they have endured, with some reason, given that they have survived, unbroken and untamed. While the 1990s saw the resumption of their on-and-off struggle for independence, it also saw the extraordinary rise of the Chechen *bratva* ('brotherhood') within the Russian underworld.

Conquered by the Russian Empire in the nineteenth century, as it spread south into the mountainous Caucasus region, the Chechens have periodically rebelled when they have felt their masters seemed weakened or distracted. The Russians have brutally repressed them each time, crushing the forms of resistance but never managing to extinguish the desire. Stalin, true to form, adopted the most murderously comprehensive response in 1944 when the Chechens took advantage of the Nazi invasion of the USSR to launch another series of risings. On 23 February – coincidentally Red Army Day in the Soviet calendar – the entire Chechen population, along with their ethnic cousins the Ingushetians, were ordered to report to local Party centres. This was the start of 'Operation Lentil', the forced deportation of two entire nations – men, women and children – a brutal and violent process in which anything from a quarter to a half of the total population died. Stalin had them scattered across Siberia and Central Asia, and amongst the human flotsam were the newborn Borz and his family. The Chechens would not be allowed to return home until after Stalin's death.

Borz's sister died in the crowded but freezing railway carriage on the way. Guards simply hurled her body off the train when they stopped for the day's count. The rest of the family made it to Bratsk in south-western Siberia, where they were told to stay, on pain of a twenty-five-year stretch in the Gulag. Borz, his older brother and their parents scarcely made it through to the summer – a sticky, sweaty, mosquito-ridden summer – because there was no housing allocated to them, and their ration cards were often not accepted.

But they did survive, whatever it took. They took over a deserted and tumbledown hut, and hunted and foraged outside the city for food. In 1947, Borz's father managed to find work building the new Angarlag labour camp nearby. Ironically enough, the year his family's exile was lifted, 1957, Borz volunteered to join the Soviet army, a decision he explained away with a shrug and a reference to it being 'a man's job'. If nothing else, I imagine it was more rewarding than a hardscrabble life in Bratsk and less frustrating than the extensive campaign his family had to wage – which started with court cases and petitions to the local Party and ended with threats and a burned-out car – to drive out the Russian family which had taken over their farm back home. Borz became a sniper and scout, and after ten years in the ranks and with a sergeant's stripes, returned home. He became a wheeler-dealer, an enforcer, graduating up to the local crime syndicate in Shali, Chechnya's second city. As he put it, 'once I had found my family again, my brothers, we looked after each other. We fought, lived and rose together.'

And they made the big time, in their own small way. He hand-waved his way over his intervening career, but, by the time I met him, he had moved from the local underworld on the far southern borderland through to becoming one of the most feared hitmen in Moscow. The deaths to his name were not as many as other figures such as Alexander Solonik, profiled in chapter 13, but as he himself stated with quiet pride, he was no *torpedo*, as a common hitman is called. Instead, he specialised in high-risk, high-value targets: organised-crime figures, and usually senior ones at that. How much did someone have to pay him to have an enemy 'ordered', as the jargon has it? Borz wouldn't say, but by my count he lived well on maybe one or two hits a year. The policeman who expressed such grudging awe of this 'serious man' had rattled off a list of hits possibly attributable to Borz. Later rumour, though, suggested that some of them were actually carried out by his younger relatives, up-and-comers working his 'franchise'. His career thus exemplifies how the Chechens rose, united by the fierce loyalties of a dispossessed and persecuted minority, and characterised by tremendous hardiness and skill in the tradecraft of violence, such that they ended up preying not so much on ordinary Russians as on other gangs. Given how fiercely the Chechens would fight, those gangs would often rather pay them off than resist.

The highlanders

Our real problem is with the [people from the north Caucasus]; our [Russian] criminals are becoming legitimate, but these guys never change.
Russian police officer, 2012[3]

When talking to Russian law enforcers, one of the constants is their determination to discuss Georgians, Chechens and others whose origins are in the Caucasus region: one could almost believe that they are to blame for most organised crime in Russia. Admittedly, as of 2004, ethnic Georgians reportedly comprised 35 per cent of the *vory v zakone* across the former USSR, and only 2 per cent of the population.[4] Dina Siegel notes from a study of known *vory v zakone* in 2011 that fully half have Georgian names and 'according to the Russian Ministry of Internal Affairs, over a half or more than 1,200 *vory v zakone* are immigrants from Georgia.'[5] But does this mean much? At a time when the value of the title '*vor v zakone*' has been markedly debased, Russian criminals are less concerned about it but Georgians – and other criminals from the Caucasus, especially Armenians – eagerly claim or buy it still. The actual number of these so-called *apelsiny* ('oranges'), as the faux *vory* are called, matters relatively little.

That said, considering the relative proportions of such populations as Chechens (fewer than 1.5 million) and Georgians (fewer than 1 million) in a country of 143 million, it is clear that there is something distinctive about the 'highlander' or 'mountaineer' (*gorets*) peoples from the Caucasus. The Chechens represent something of a force apart. If nothing else, this is visible in the fact that, whereas the Georgians and others can boast an abundance of *vory v zakone*, only one Chechen, 'Sultan Balashikhinsky', is said to have ever joined their ranks, back when it meant something.[6] It is hardly that the Chechens were not criminal enough, tough enough or disciplined enough to merit 'coronation'. Rather, the *vorovskoi mir* was never their way.

Beyond them the 'highlanders' form a wide range of gangs, with the largest players at the time of writing being two main networks – the (erstwhile) Usoyan and Oniani *gruppirovki* – and a third, a mixed-ethnicity gang formed by the Azeri gangster Rovshan Dzhaniyev ('Rovshan Lenkoransky' or 'Rovshan from Lenkoran') that sought to challenge the status quo. To a greater or lesser extent, they all draw on a combination of clannish social organisation, a culture of banditry and vendetta, and a fierce sense of loyalty to kin rather than country. That they came from homelands where the state was often weak, alien or both only helped them emerge and prosper. Much like the Sicilians – a parallel Federico Varese and others have drawn – the 'highlanders' have for generations relied on parallel pseudo-state structures for protection and dispute resolution rather than a government they did not trust, and from this has grown a pervasive and pernicious criminal tradition.[7] While the next chapter will discuss the other 'highlanders', the Chechens need to be considered as a special case.

If the Slavic gangs have predominance in political and probably economic power within the Russian underworld and the Georgians the most *vory* – though not most members as a whole – then what is the distinctive asset for the 'highlanders' of the north Caucasus, and particularly the Chechens? The answer would appear to be cohesion and reputation.[8] The Chechen criminals, often described as the *Chechenskaya bratva* or 'Chechen brotherhood' (and occasionally *Chechenskaya obshchina*, 'Chechen commune'), have no formal structure in common. They do represent a distinctive criminal subculture, though, holding itself apart from the mainstream Russian underworld. A characteristic mix of modern 'branding' and bandit tradition means that they have such a powerful place in the Russian criminal imaginary that now they are even a 'franchise'. Local gangs not made up of Chechens compete – and pay – to be able to act as their local representatives.

Banditry and resistance are deeply ingrained within the Chechen national identity, not least in the traditional figure of the *abreg* (also rendered as *abrek*), the honourable outlaw whose banditry is driven by righteous vendetta or a refusal to knuckle under before the crimes of the powerful.[9] The *abreg* is a self-sufficient and wily figure, a Caucasus Robin Hood, who often gathers a gang of like-minded daredevils around him, raiding the rich, feeding the poor, protecting the weak and dismaying the corrupt. While essentially mythological, the figure of the *abreg* still provides a degree of legitimacy to the modern gangster.

A tradition of resistance

When shall blood cease to flow in the mountains? When sugar cane grows in the snow.

Caucasus proverb[10]

Chechens and encroaching Cossack soldier-settlers clashed and raided each other from the seventeenth century. In the nineteenth century, the Russian Empire brought the Caucasus region under its control, by conquest, punitive massacre and deportation, culminating in Stalin's act of near-genocide. Genuine tragedies make for powerful national folklore, and onto the *abreg*'s role as bandit was overlaid that of national freedom fighter. His may be an ultimately futile battle, as the state, whether tsarist, Soviet or post-Soviet, has always had overwhelming force on its side, but the *abreg* way is precisely to fight the good fight regardless. Khasukha Magomadov, the so-called 'last *abreg*', who fought the Soviets during the Second World War, was eventually killed in 1976, at the age of seventy-one, when his hideout was stormed by a combined KGB and police team. He was shot, a TT pistol still in his hand.

This became again relevant with the collapse of the USSR. In local presidential elections in 1991, Chechens overwhelmingly supported Dzhokar Dudayev, an air force officer turned nationalist politician. The Chechens declared independence, but Moscow proved unwilling to accept. Clumsy attempts to pressurise the Chechens back into the Russian Federation only served to rally them behind Dudayev, culminating in two wars: the first,

1994–6, in which the Chechens in effect fought Moscow into accepting partial autonomy, and then the second, from 1999, which saw them forced back into the fold. While Rebecca Gould quite rightly notes that none of the leaders of the anti-Russian resistance, whether nationalists or Islamists, explicitly described themselves as *abregs*,[11] nonetheless even just from personal experience I can say that Chechens – notably in Moscow, perhaps seeking to reconnect with cultural traditions or demonstrate that they have not lost that Chechen identity – sometimes used the term for maverick rebel leaders such as Shamil Basayev and Salman Raduyev.

Back in tsarist times, the Chechens' skill and ferocity had been proverbial in Russian circles. General Alexei Yermolov, imperial viceroy of the Caucasus, was especially exercised by this 'bold and dangerous people' and one of his staff officers admitted that 'amidst their forests and mountains, no troops in the world could afford to despise them' for they were 'good shots, fiercely brave [and] intelligent in military affairs'.[12] Their ability to hold their own against modern Russian firepower and numbers only burnished their image.

Meanwhile, the 'bandits' were also becoming a powerful force within the wider Russian underworld, albeit neither as omnipotent nor as omnipresent as their myth suggested. Under Dudayev, Chechnya became a virtual criminal fiefdom. Favouritism, corruption, nepotism, clientelism and localism all flourished. The Chechen police force suddenly grew from the 3,000 officers it inherited from the Soviet period to fourteen separate forces, accounting for some 17,000 armed officers, as hitmen and clan gunmen were sworn in as 'police'.[13] Likewise, the Chechen State Bank became a counterfeiter's, fraudster's and money launderer's dream. In 1992 alone, at least 60 billion rubles (then $700 million) were siphoned from the Russian Central Bank through the use of the *avizo*. This was a proof-of-funds document used to manage transactions between branches of the Russian banking system. Corrupt managers at the Chechen bank would issue some of these documents, which an accomplice would then take to Moscow and on that basis withdraw money there. When Moscow then sought to redeem the *avizo* from their Chechen counterparts, there would mysteriously turn out to be no record of them or, indeed, the customer.[14] The continued pretence that Chechnya was part of the Russian Federation was costing Moscow dear.

After Dudayev's death in 1996, his successor, Aslan Maskhadov, made some efforts to combat the more overt forms of banditry. However, these attempts were hamstrung by a lack of resources and authority and made irrelevant by the 1999 invasion. Today's pro-Russian regime under Ramzan Kadyrov, even though it claims to have the lowest crime rate of any Russian region,[15] is likewise bedevilled by credible accounts of lawlessness, banditry and corruption, and, as is discussed below, can in many ways be seen to have simply taken over the rackets of Chechnya to form a single criminal–state syndicate.

The two Chechnyas

Criminals were coming to Chechnya from all over the world – they did not have a place in their own countries. But they could live perfectly well in Chechnya.

Akhmad Kadyrov, former Kremlin-backed
Chechen president, 2004[16]

Especially during the First Chechen War, Moscow claimed that it was fighting a gangster regime in Grozny that was connected to a wider Chechen criminal diaspora throughout Russia. In 1996, for example, Interior Minister Anatoly Kulikov asserted that rebel leaders planned to send fighters to Moscow to take over banks and businesses and thus precipitate a new round of turf wars: 'The goal of the looming gangster wars is the complete destabilisation of Russia.'[17] Although the Dudayev regime was undoubtedly criminalised, in fact there emerged a striking division between the networks operating in Chechnya and those outside the republic. Nikolai Suleimanov, the powerful Chechen gangster known as 'Khoza', described this as the 'two Chechnyas'.[18] There were connections between the two, largely through kinship, with deals being struck and personnel moving from one world to the other. However, these relations were essentially prag-matic; Russian-based Chechen gangs were very keen to downplay their connections with the homeland. In part this was out of fear of being targeted by the authorities as potential fifth columnists, and in part it reflected a genuine and widening cultural divide between those Chechens who were wheeling and dealing in a larger, predominantly Russian context and those who stayed locked within the tighter and smaller world of tradition and kin back home. In 1995, Dudayev requested that *bratva* godfathers help bank-roll his regime; not only did they refuse, but at a subsequent gathering in Moscow they banned direct transfers of money, men or weapons to the rebels.[19] The former head of Dudayev's Presidential Guard, Ruslan Labazanov, had a fierce falling out with the Chechen leader in 1993 and became for a while a godfather of Chechen gangs in Moscow with the Russian government's quiet connivance, precisely because he stood in the way of any support for Dudayev.[20]

This division only grew under Putin and during the Second Chechen War, when it was made very clear to the Chechen *bratva* that any hint of support for the rebels in Chechnya would bring savage reprisal. Furthermore, the rise of Islamist radicalism within Chechnya and the rebel movement left the *bratva* unimpressed. Although Chechens are a Muslim people, theirs has tended to be a relatively moderate form of Islam, as Borz demonstrated. The gangsters' pursuit of money, power and a high-rolling lifestyle did not fit with the jihadists' puritan ideals – and, more to the point, with an open challenge to the Russian state and the repressions that would trigger. As a result, for example, when Al-Qaeda sought to procure weapons for its allies in 2000, Chechen gangs again refused to cooperate, and the jihadists ended up paying ethnic Russian criminal gangs, who smuggled the weapons into Chechnya using military supply convoys.[21]

Within Chechnya, many rebel warlords also maintained profitable side-lines in kidnap, banditry and drug smuggling. Arbi Barayev, for example, was a wilful combination of rebel warlord and bandit chieftain, who claimed allegiance to Dudayev but largely used his private army to make millions through oil smuggling, kidnapping and contract killing. Maskhadov later tried to have him arrested, earning Barayev the distinction of being wanted by both sides. As a result, he not only concentrated on his directly criminal activities, but also offered them to Islamists on a mercenary basis. He was reportedly promised, if not paid, $30 million from Al-Qaeda for kidnap-ping and subsequently beheading three British and one New Zealand tele-communications workers in 1998.[22] Barayev was eventually killed by Russian forces in 2001, but in an interesting example of the way that the confluence of war and crime often makes for strange alliances, his killers may have been drawing on local knowledge provided through back chan-nels by Maskhadov's forces.

Bratva in Russia

The Chechens are the most serious organised crime threat we face. They are motivated by a bitter resentment against Russia, they have a pre-modern sense of common loyalty, and they have the most modern weapons and means of operation.

Report from a senior Russian police officer, 1997[23]

Although Russian police officers love to talk up the 'Chechen threat', not only are the Chechens relatively few in number – they represent less than 1 per cent of the total Russian population, and most are in Chechnya – but their *bratva* remains a network that is culturally more cohesive, but structurally much looser than its Slavic counterparts. It is looser in that constituent gangs guard their autonomy even more fiercely, and any leaders who rise in such a culture tend to be able to command only their own personal gangs – over the rest of the *bratva* they merely exert the moral authority of a successful *abreg*. It is more cohesive, on the other hand, thanks to a shared sense of fierce national identity: while capable of very violent internecine conflicts, the sense of being surrounded by enemies, and Russian enemies at that, means that the *bratva* retains an unusually high degree of solidarity. Disputes are typically resolved through negotiation and the intervention of respected elder figures.

In many ways, Chechen organised crime draws on the patterns of Chechen society. Andrei Konstantinov noted that 'to survive, the Chechen people were forced to develop their internal organisations to the highest level of all the peoples of the Caucasus'.[24] They are typically either small gangs built around one or a few charismatic or effective leaders or else larger collections of such groups. Their characteristic structure is not a hierarchical pyramid so much as a snowflake, semi-independent groups around a coordinating council of elders.[25] In many ways, these correspond to the building blocks of Chechen society: the *nekye* or extended family, and the *teip*, the clan, made up of multiple families. This parallel also extends to personnel and recruitment. The smaller gangs tend to be based initially around direct kinship or other personal ties. For example, the Moscow-based group run by the gangster known as 'Malik' comprised twenty-two core members, of whom seven were his direct kin and nine more came from his *teip*, the Yalkhoi.[26] Larger groupings tend in turn to bring together a variety of these smaller gangs, united either by the area in which they operate or else the *teips* from which their leaders trace back their origins. 'Malik' and his gang were within the larger Ostankinskaya network, a gang which in the 1990s and early 2000s dominated the north-eastern Moscow neighbourhood of the same name, and which was run by members of the Yalkhoi clan. This concentration on both kinship and personal loyalties also helps explain the fierce loyalties within Chechen crime groups and the difficulties the authorities have in penetrating them and recruiting informants.

Although long known in the cities of southern Russia, the Chechens really began to become players in Moscow's underworld in the late 1980s. The Ostankino Hotel became the headquarters of a gang run by one 'Magomet the Big'. The rather larger Lazanskaya gang under Movladi Altangeriyev ('Ruslan') and Khozh-Akhmed Nukhayev, later simply known as Tsentralnaya ('Central'), ran protection and vice rackets in a collection of hotels and restaurants and the Rizhsky market. The smaller but more aggressive Yuzhnoportovaya ('South Port') gang under Nikolai Suleimanov ('Khoza') and Lechi Altimirov (variously known as 'Lecho the Bald' and 'Lecho the Beard') operated along the banks of the Moskva in the southern Pechatniki district.[27]

Generally, the Chechens were involved largely in protection racketeering and some prostitution, but several, including Altangeriyev and Nukhayev, were rumoured to maintain good links with the KGB. In particular, the security agencies would turn a blind eye to their foreign currency dealing, in return for useful information about the tourists and travellers they encountered. By the beginning of the 1990s, a fourth gang, Avtomobilnaya, emerged, but in 1991 Suleimanov, Altangeriyev and Altimirov were all arrested, fragmenting the Chechen *bratva* just at the time when the turf wars were truly hotting up. Over time, they would largely be eclipsed by Slavic gangs (most notably the Solntsevo, Orekhovo, Lyubertsy and Balashikha groupings) and also the wider 'highlander' networks of Tariel Oniani and Aslan Usoyan, discussed in the next chapter. The Chechens were simply too few, and taking them on even became a mark of machismo for Slav gangsters.

In November 1993, for example, 'Roma the Claw', a leader of the Orekhovo group, clashed with Chechen gangsters in Tsaritsyno Park in southern Moscow, as part of an escalating conflict dating back to 1991.[28]

When a sit-down went bad, the ensuing shoot-out left five Chechens dead. This bad blood led to months of skirmishes which actually made the Chechens disengage from south-western Moscow, and 'Silvestr', head of Orekhovo, gained considerable authority amongst the Slav gangs as willing to go nose to nose with the Chechens at a time when Solntsevo was still honouring a non-aggression pact with them.[29]

In part, the erosion of the Chechens' position in Moscow came about also because of pressure from the police; as noted above, especially after the outbreak of hostilities in Chechnya, these gangs were considered a particular threat. Apparently, a 1993 MVD report predicted: 'Despite the current disunity of the Chechen groups, one should not underestimate the force of Chechen tradition to unite and act together under emergency conditions, that is, we have to conclude that the Chechen groups will act as an integral whole in the largest operations and conflicts.'[30]

In hindsight, this was an alarmist assessment, but an understandable one. Concerned lest it trigger precisely the kind of 'rally round the flag' response that could turn gangsters into insurgents, Moscow held off until 1995. Then, following the mass hostage-taking in the southern Russian town of Budyonnovsk, a combined police and Federal Security Service task force launched Operation *Vikhr* (Whirlwind). The aim was to eliminate or expel any gangs in the capital suspected of ties to the Chechen regime. While most groups survived, the operation played a crucial role in weakening the Chechens in Moscow.[31] In many ways, St Petersburg became their new Russian capital, and perhaps as a response, there they became especially pricklish with respect to their independence and quick to violence; in Konstantinov's words, 'for cruelty, daring, efficiency and decisiveness, the "Chechens" of Petersburg can be compared only with the "Tambov" association.'[32]

The protection racketeers' protection racketeer

We Chechens have our ways, and everyone understands that. We are honourable: what we say we will do, we will do. And that also means we will avenge ourselves on any who wrong us. People understand that, and it helps them do business with us, and with those we work with.

'Borz', 2009[33]

However, the Chechens' failure to prosper in the same way as the other major networks also reflects their clear and conscious determination to buck the trend of diversification into business and politics. Some Chechens have certainly accumulated businesses and property and followed the *avtoritet* route. The aforementioned Nikolai Suleimanov made most of his money through fraud and was looking to shift into privatised businesses until his murder in 1994. However, many other Chechen gangs have tended not to evolve beyond their core speciality: the use and threat of violence. Perhaps remaining true to their bandit roots, they continue to be heavily involved in extortion and protection racketeering. However, in many cases they have become in effect the 'protection racketeers' protection racketeer', acquiring networks of client gangs (from any ethnic background) from whom they simply demand tribute on pain of gang warfare.

This might, actually, also help explain why the Russian police are always eager to talk up the Chechen threat: they represent competition. According to former interior minister Boris Gryzlov, the police's Main Directorate for Combating Organised Crime (GUBOP) also ended up often being the '*krysha*'s *krysha*'.[34] Indeed, GUBOP was sometimes known in Moscow in gangster style as the 'Shabolovskaya *brigada*' because of its headquarters on Shabolovka Street. GUBOP was formally dissolved in 2001 but essentially lived on in a new Directorate for Fighting Organised Crime and Terrorism (DBOPT). This went the same way in 2008, but its old customs continued in new structures.

The police have guns and badges, but the Chechens have something far more terrifying at their disposal: guns and folklore. Russians are, in a way, victims of their own literature. Nineteenth-century works such as Tolstoy's *Hadji Murat* and Pushkin's *Prisoner of the Caucasus* imparted a sometimes admiring, sometimes horrified picture of the Chechen as a fierce primitive who would never shirk from a fight, an impression only solidified by their performance during the Chechen wars. As a result, there is a general assumption that, to quote one gang hanger-on, 'you don't mess with the Chechens. If you challenge them, even if they know they will lose, they will fight, and they'll summon their brothers and their cousins and their uncles and keep fighting. Even if they are going to lose, they'll fight just to bring you down, too. They are maniacs.'[35]

There is a perverse bonus for the Chechens in being considered implacable, indomitable maniacs: it makes sense to cut a deal with them, even if the logic of force and connections would seem not to be to their advantage. This actually has made Chechen-related gang violence less common since the mid-1990s, for the very reason that people are disinclined to challenge them. While this has denied them some of the scope for expansion enjoyed by their counterparts, it does mean that the Chechens have managed to dominate their chosen niche. This is evident in the way that the authorities ascribe them such a disproportionately powerful role within the Russian underworld. It would be easy to discount this as a by-product of the way the Chechens have been demonised by state and public alike, and there is some truth in this. Certainly, ethnic Russians seeing criminals of Caucasus appearance will often simply assume they are Chechen when they could just as easily be Ingushetian, Ossetian or from one of the numerous other regional nationalities.

However, there is more to it than that: the efficiency and ruthlessness of the Chechens has given them a powerful 'brand name'. So too has their perceived honour. As one of their victims put it:

A lot of people are afraid of the Chechens, but they are very good people when you get to know them. They are loyal. They don't double-cross you, and they are honest people . . . They can do anything. If I needed a driver's licence, tomorrow they would bring me a new licence. If I needed legal help, or someone to fix a problem with my apartment, they can help out too. They are really serious people.[36]

Honest, serious, loyal, able to do anything: what's not to love? Since the late 1990s, this image has increasingly been 'franchised' to other gangs, many of which contain no Chechens and may even be entirely made up of Slavs. In conversation with Misha Glenny, I called this a 'McMafia'.[37] By being able to claim that they 'work with the Chechens' (this is the usual expression) and thus can, if necessary, call on their support, gangs acquire considerable additional authority. Victims who might otherwise consider resisting their extortion are more likely to pay; rival gangs are less likely to encroach on their turf; and even law enforcers might think twice about taking them on. In return, the gang pays a cut of its proceeds and subordinates itself to the nearest influential Chechen godfather, who may call on it for services in the future. In this respect, the Chechens, for all their traditionalism, have truly embraced the modern market.

Kadyrov's empire

*A good Muslim would never commit a crime ... I am an official
person. I am not a bandit.*

Ramzan Kadyrov, 2006[38]

The Russians won their war in Chechnya with extravagant brutality, overwhelming firepower – and Chechens. The Second Chechen War, which
began in 1999 and formally ended in 2009 when Moscow announced the
euphemistic end of 'anti-terrorist operations', was launched by Russian
troops but largely concluded through the use of Chechen militias. Many
were former rebels, able to take on the insurgents in the hills and villages on
their own terms. Several figures were instrumental to this 'Chechenisation',
but the most important were Akhmad Kadyrov and his son Ramzan. A
former rebel leader, Akhmad Kadyrov had fallen out with Dzhokar Dudayev
and threw in his lot with Moscow. His reward was to be appointed interim
head of occupied Chechnya in 2000 and then president in 2003. When he
was assassinated by a rebel bomb in 2004, his son Ramzan was still too
young legally to succeed him, although that was clearly Moscow's intent.
He quickly cycled through the positions of Chechen interior minister,
prime minister and then, in 2007, when he was finally thirty and thus
eligible under the constitution, president.

Chechnya is relatively peaceful now, but it is a cowed peace. For all that
it is technically a constituent republic of the Russian Federation, it is evident
that Kadyrov holds it in an iron-mailed fist as if it were his personal fiefdom.
The local security forces are known as *Kadyrovtsy*, 'Kadyrovites', for the
personal oath they swear to him. Even the usual institutions of central
control such as the republican police and Federal Security Service (FSB)
have been tamed, placed under men loyal to Kadyrov. When, back in 2007,
the local FSB blocked a group of armed *Kadyrovtsy* from marching into
their headquarters in Grozny, Kadyrov's forces essentially besieged the
building, and had all its entrances and exits welded shut. FSB Director
Nikolai Patrushev had personally to intervene to end the standoff, but from
then on it was clear: in Chechnya, even the FSB answered to Kadyrov.[39]

The irony is that Chechnya is arguably now more independent in practice than at any time since it was conquered under the tsars – and what is
more, it gets the Russians to pay for it. More than 80 per cent of the Chechen
republican budget is made up of subsidies from Moscow, as the Kremlin is

desperate to avoid another bloody and unpopular war in the south. Not that ordinary Chechens get to benefit from much of this. Even back in 2006, a US diplomatic cable spoke of 'massive corruption and state-sponsored banditry in Chechnya ... Presidential Advisor Aslakhanov told us last December that Kadyrov expropriates for himself one-third off the top of all [federal] assistance.'[40] Money has gone on extravagant vanity projects, such as the construction of a shiny commercial centre to which nobody goes, and a huge mosque dedicated to Akhmad Kadyrov.

Somehow, a luxurious lifestyle is achieved for Ramzan Kadyrov.[41] While his official income is around 5 million rubles ($78,000),[42] he has a personal zoo, and a stable of luxury cars including a Lamborghini Reventón, one of only twenty ever made and costing $1.25 million. It seems money also goes to keeping his family and subordinates – the two are often one and the same, such as cousin and parliamentarian Adam Delimkhanov – happy and loyal.[43] Meanwhile, Kadyrov has been accused by the US Treasury of overseeing 'an administration involved in disappearances and extrajudicial killings'; according to a Reuters report quoting a senior US State Department official, 'one or more of Kadyrov's political opponents were killed at his direction' – an allegation that Kadyrov implied was a smear, but did not deny, defiantly stating on social media that 'I can be proud that I'm out of favor with the special services of the USA ... the USA cannot forgive me for dedicating my whole life to the fight against foreign terrorists.'[44] Ordinary Chechens who display any lack of enthusiasm for his regime also disappear.[45]

There are thus still 'two Chechnyas'. One, the mother country itself, features sometimes on trafficking routes, including heroin from Afghanistan and women into the Middle East. However, it is really best considered a single criminal–feudal operation, where the primary business is diverting and embezzling state funds.[46] So long as Kadyrov controls the government – and the 20,000 or so *Kadyrovtsy* – and Moscow feels it cannot afford to move against him, this situation is likely to continue. The other Chechnya, the Chechen criminal diaspora, has developed its own distinctive niche else-where in Russia, one largely built on its reputation for timeworn gangster virtues of honour and implacable vendetta. Are these old-style gangsters in a new underworld? Or, given the emergence of the 'Chechen franchise' and their capacity to prey on the predators, are they in fact very modern, simply leveraging a traditional (and sometimes mythologised) image to build them-selves a formidable brand?

CHAPTER 11

THE GEORGIAN
The expatriate *vor*

My homeland is wherever I live well.

Russian proverb

Summer 2003 saw all the pomp and pageantry of the Georgian Orthodox Church and state on display at the funeral of Dzhaba Ioseliani. The burial took place in the graveyard of the thirteenth-century Sioni Cathedral of the Dormition in Tbilisi, where patriarchs of the church are laid to rest, and was presided over by the current one. The mourners represented the cream of Georgian society, led by President Eduard Shevardnadze himself.[1] No one seemed disturbed that Ioseliani had been one of the most notorious organised-crime figures in the country, a man who had run not just an underworld empire but his own private army. Now, he was being honoured by President Shevardnadze, a man whose career had really taken off in Soviet times when he became known as Georgia's 'hammer of the mafia', the interior minister who seemed to be the first in that position to want to do something about his small republic's reputation for freewheeling corruption and criminality. It has long been clear that time can turn gangsters into icons; Ioseliani's case made it evident just how short that time may be. Indeed, it had happened long before his death. The Georgian bestselling author Nodar Dumbadze admitted he had modelled a key character in his book *White Flags* – the 'honest *vor*' – on his childhood friend Ioseliani. He was himself honoured by the Georgian State Institute of

Theatre and Cinema, from which he received a doctorate, for his own books and plays.[2]

It is fair to say that Ioseliani, who once said that in Soviet times 'there were only two ways: prison or the Young Communist League. I chose the first one',[3] was not your typical gangster, but then again, even by the standards of the 'mountaineers' of the Caucasus, Georgia has been something of a special case. The Armenians and the Azeris have their criminal diaspora in Russia, to say nothing of the other north Caucasus peoples of the Russian Federation, from Dagestanis to Ingush. But certainly through the 2000s and into the 2010s, there was a common belief, even within the Russian underworld, that Georgians played a disproportionate role, at the Russians' expense. According to an article in *Izvestiya*, in 2006, Georgian godfathers comprised almost a third of the underworld leaders in Moscow, and more than half across the country as a whole. The Slavs often claim that it is because they maintain their stranglehold by force; as one 'source familiar with the criminal milieu' put it, 'those of our guys who have tried to rise up against this have been killed . . . They don't let our guys rise up.'[4] This may help them feel better, but actually bears little resemblance to the truth.

The *lavrushniki* ('bay leaves'), as Slavic gangsters often call the Georgians, have long played an important role in Russia's underworld. However, their strength has rested not on violence and threat so much as entrepreneurialism and their talents for deal making. New pressures and opportunities, though, are driving them and the other 'highlanders' in three different directions. Three specific godfathers perhaps best illustrate these trajectories: Tariel Oniani the empire builder, Aslan Usoyan the network weaver, and Rovshan Dzhaniyev the insurgent.

Bay leaves: the Georgians in Russia

I remember my father's friend's wife, a very dignified woman . . . coming and asking me, 'Do you know any thieves in law? I have a problem I need sorting out.' She didn't have any idea what she was asking for, just that she had heard the thieves in law can help you.

Georgian academic, 2009[5]

Perhaps it is no surprise that Georgia's gangsters retained a positive reputation for so long, as the republic itself has long enjoyed – or suffered from –

its own reputation as a land of good wine, easy living, long dinners and gangster bosses. Even back in tsarist times, Georgian criminals crossed the boundaries between rural banditry and urban gangsterism, and that most (in)famous Georgian, Stalin himself, blurred the lines between revolution and plunder, as discussed in chapter 3. Under Soviet rule, the scale of criminality in the republic was infamous: it was known for corruption 'second to none . . . carried out on an unparalleled scale and with unrivalled scope and daring'.[6] The Soviet Union's slide into institutionalised corruption in the 1960s and 1970s meant that, despite overt campaigns against 'speculation', bribe taking, embezzlement and theft, there emerged 'organised criminal clans of a new type which brought together professional criminals, black marketeers – the clients of whom existed amongst bureaucrats at the highest level – and corrupt law enforcement officials'.[7] The role of the *vory v zakone*, known in Georgian as *kanonieri qurdi*, was as elsewhere often to be the connector between these various worlds. Furthermore, they were active and numerous: according to Soviet police data, as of the end of the USSR, one in three of all *vory v zakone* were Georgians, even though they made up only one in fifty of the total population.[8]

Alexander Gurov, the Soviet police criminologist who arguably did the most to bring the problem of organised crime to the fore, is sure that, even back in the 1970s, Georgia's gangsters already had a place at the table and in the system. He recounted that a local Party boss, whenever the crime figures looked embarrassingly excessive or there was the risk of an inquiry from higher up, 'would summon to a meeting the [local police] chief, the [local KGB] chief, and the local crime boss, and say, "How can you have allowed there to be such a rise in crime?" He would address this first and foremost to the crime boss. Who would at once start "taking steps to reduce the crime rate".[9]

In keeping with their nation's lively traditions of black marketeering and corrupt politics, the Georgian *vory* were the first and most enthusiastic to involve themselves in politics and then take full advantage of Gorbachev's reforms of the 1980s. To a considerable extent, this was down to the authority and initiative of Dzhaba Ioseliani. A *vor v zakone*, convicted bank robber and killer, in 1982 he convened a *skhodka* in Tbilisi at which he advocated, largely with success, that the criminals actively seek to infiltrate and control local political institutions. Even by this time, the Georgian *vory* felt much less strictly bound by the traditional codes of the *vorovskoi mir*, establishing gangs based around family and kin and handing power from father to son in a dynastic manner technically proscribed by the rules of the underworld. This meant, however, that they were able to mesh much more closely and directly with Georgia's kin-based politics, and thus they had a head-start on their criminal counterparts elsewhere in burrowing into the political elite.

Ioseliani would continue to play a pivotal role in Georgian politics, and one in which his background as, in his own words, 'a known thief and an unknown artist' (he had distinct creative pretensions, writing books and plays) seemed little obstacle.[10] He proved to be as effective a politician and warlord as a gangster, and in 1989 founded a nationalist paramilitary movement, the Mkhedrioni ('Knights'), which was as much a criminal venture, involved in protection racketeering, drug dealing, kidnapping and organised robbery, as a political one. (Ioseliani embraced this with typical panache, calling it 'a patriotic organisation, but based on the thieves' tradition.[11]) At the forefront of persecuting Abkhaz and Ossetian minorities (and engaging in some looting on the side), the Mkhedrioni also became the stormtroopers of rising nationalist demagogue Zviad Gamsakhurdia. As is so often the way, the two ambitious men fell out: after Gamsakhurdia became independent Georgia's first president, he had Ioseliani arrested and imprisoned. Such a figure makes a dangerous enemy and prisoner, though. A few months later, he was freed in a coup that would force Gamsakhurdia to flee and, for the next few years, he played a powerful role in the new government, before being again arrested, then pardoned. Eventually Ioseliani died of a heart attack in 2003.

Georgia's criminals were thus heirs to an exceptionally entrepreneurial tradition and engaged in illicit business years before the *avtoritety*. They also benefited from an early shift towards seeking to subvert and control political institutions. Although Ioseliani's career may have ended in prison and disgrace, it also saw a *vor* occupying the roles of kingmaker and parliamentarian: a powerful example, even if the very unruliness of the Mkhedrioni undermined some of the folklore of the 'good gangster'. Many Georgian criminals chose to operate in Russia during the 1990s and 2000s, especially after Ioseliani's fall, because of the opportunities there or because their roots were in the Georgian expatriate community. Otari Kvantrishvili, profiled in chapter 8, was just one of many.

However, Georgian politics also provides a much more direct reason for the numbers of *lavrushniki* in contemporary Russia's underworld. Following the 2003 'Rose Revolution', which toppled President Shevardnadze after disputed elections, new president Mikheil Saakashvili's government embarked on a serious campaign against the *vory*, one that drew on lessons from the Italian struggle against the mafia. Mere membership of the *qurduli samkaro* – 'thieves' world' in Georgian – was criminalised. The property of *vory v zakone* could be seized and they would be held in a special maximum-security prison, where they could be segregated from the other prisoners. Meanwhile, a massive purge of the law enforcement apparatus was launched in a notably effective campaign against corruption, while a public education programme sought to combat widespread attitudes that condoned bribe-taking and glorified the gangsters.[12] Faced with the threat of arrest, harsh detention and the confiscation of their assets, Georgia's *vory* upped and left.

Tariel Oniani and the Georgian 'iron'

Oniani knows how it's done, how to build an organisation, how to use it; the Georgian iron slid over everything.

Russian criminologist, 2014[13]

In the sometimes opaque slang of the Russian underworld, the phrase 'to iron the firm' (*utyuzhit firmu*) emerged in the 1980s as a term for ripping off ('ironing') foreigners ('the firm'). In the 2000s, it became used more broadly for exploiting any bunch of outsiders, whether from a different city, gang, ethnic group or country. By the 2010s, when I heard it at all, it had begun to acquire a more aggressive sense, 'straightening out' in the sense of making people pay up whether they liked it or not, through direct intimidation and extortion. It is a fitting way of describing the trajectory of Tariel Oniani ('Taro'), a Georgian crime boss who has become perhaps one of the most dangerous and destabilising forces within the modern Russian underworld, precisely because he is careless of the customs, understandings and balances which have, in the main, kept the peace there for years.

In 2006 Georgia's general prosecutor, Zurab Adeishvili, asserted that there was not a single *vor v zakone* left in the country; he was slightly exaggerating the case but not by much.[14] In essence, their power had been broken, even if this is a long way short of saying that the country had no more criminals or organised crime. Of course, these exiles had to go somewhere, and for many the destination was Russia. One of the greatest beneficiaries was Oniani. In some ways, though, the rise of this particular Georgian godfather has been at the expense of the old ways of Georgian organised crime. He largely abandoned the old habits of sticking to kin and focusing on the deal, or rather subordinated them to the ruthless pursuit of control within his organisation, and power within the wider underworld. This is not a man who makes allies, when he can make subjects.

Oniani's career was made on the run. A *vor v zakone* and lifelong criminal – his first conviction was for armed robbery at the age of seventeen – Oniani fled Georgia in 2004, moving first to France, then Spain. In 2005, he was forced to flee again, ahead of a Spanish arrest warrant. He already had substantial assets and allies in Russia, so he moved there under the short-lived alias 'Tariel Mulukhov', aggressively building his operations and wooing his fellow Georgian exiles. An outsider, he demonstrated no qualms about moving into others' turfs and businesses and ignoring established mechanisms for resolving intergang disputes.

He rose rapidly, but gained enemies with equal celerity. In particular, he began an increasingly overt campaign against Kurdish-Georgian gang leader Aslan Usoyan. There were previous grounds for a feud, although it is also likely that Oniani simply felt that Usoyan, as the highest-profile Georgian-born gangster operating in Russia, was the man to beat. In 2006, senior Georgian crime boss Zakhar Kalashov ('Shakhro the Younger'), an ally of Usoyan's, had been arrested in Spain. Usoyan appointed the *vor* 'Lasha Rustavsky' to be the guardian of 'Shakhro's' assets and the group's *obshchak*, but Oniani claimed that he was owed a share of it from joint money-laundering and illegal-immigrant-smuggling operations. With 'Shakhro' sentenced to seven and a half years in prison, a general squabble began within the Georgian criminal diaspora about these funds. Oniani was able to exploit this to his advantage, not least winning over the violent gang leader 'Merab Sukhumsky' and his brother Levon, a noted contract killer, with promises of a share of the *obshchak*.

Exploiting and exacerbating the rivalries and suspicions inevitable in an underworld proved one of Oniani's particular strengths. At a time when most senior criminal figures were eager to maintain the peace and concentrate on business rather than war, Oniani could leverage his intransigence and his apparent willingness to bring the whole structure crashing down to his advantage. By 2007, his feud with Usoyan was leading to tit-for-tat killings that threatened to spark a wider war. In 2008, it fell to Russian gangsters, of all people, to try to broker a peace between them. A *skhodka* was arranged on Oniani's yacht, but it was raided by the police: thirty-seven *vory v zakone* were briefly detained and subjected to the embarrassment of being paraded on TV, even though none were eventually charged. This was a bad start to the negotiations (Oniani may have tipped the police off, precisely for that reason), but in any case, they foundered on Oniani's refusal to compromise, even after one of his right-hand men, Gela Tsertsvadze, was murdered. Faced with the threat that the Russians would side with Usoyan, Oniani then agreed to allow veteran *vor* Vyacheslav 'Yaponchik' Ivankov to try and arbitrate their dispute so as to appear willing to cooperate. However, as covered in chapter 8, Ivankov was then murdered; recurring reports have suggested that 'Yaponchik' – who knew Usoyan – was on the verge of ruling against Oniani, who silenced him first.

In July 2010, Oniani was sentenced to ten years in a maximum-security prison for his role in the kidnap in Moscow in 2009 of fellow Georgian businessman 'Johnny' Manadze, for whose release he was demanding a $500,000 ransom.[15] That he was arrested is perhaps unsurprising considering that he was one of the highest-profile gangsters in Russia, and was also wanted on an Interpol red notice international arrest warrant. More surprising was that he was held (and refused bail, even when his lawyers offered 15 million rubles, equivalent to $480,000), tried and awarded a serious sentence.[16] There has been suspicion that the government was trying to defuse a mob war by taking him out of circulation, or else that the conviction was 'ordered' – bought and paid for – by Oniani's enemies.

However, imprisonment does not seem to have interfered with Oniani's ability to manage his criminal empire. A flow of visitors – and even Skype calls from his cell – seem to be allowing him to continue to set policy and visit vengeance upon his enemies. After all, his is a much more overtly hierarchical and rigidly and ruthlessly disciplined organisation than is the norm for larger criminal combines in Russia, essentially following the model of the 'core group'. Oniani showed himself willing to allow many of his associates considerable autonomy, but he expected them to kick a share of their proceeds up to him. Ironically enough, this was often described as the *obshchak*, although what was once envisioned as a common kitty to help ordinary members in distress had become the boss's personal slush fund. More to the point, this autonomy was regarded as a privilege rather than a right, and members of the group were expected to show absolute obedience when called upon by Oniani or one of his inner circle, all Georgians. These are drawn largely from the Kutaisi clan, the largest Georgian crime group in Russia, with some fifty *vory v zakone* and numerous other gangsters in its numbers, and which also operates across Europe.[17] The Kutaisi clan's chief, Merab Dzhangveladze ('Dzhango'), appears to have been Oniani's right-hand man; indeed, this led to Usoyan trying to have him stripped of his status as a *vor* in 2008, although this means little in today's more diffuse and opportunistic underworld. This combination of size, discipline and audacity made – and at the time of writing still makes – Oniani's organisation, while not the largest in the Russian underworld, probably the most dangerous, dynamic and destabilising.

Grandfather Hassan's boys

We are peaceful people and don't bother anybody . . . We are for peace, in order to prevent lawlessness.

Aslan Usoyan, 2008[18]

If Oniani's gang represents one model of 'highlander' organised crime – disciplined, centralised, dominated by a single leader and a single ethnicity – then that of the criminal godfather Aslan Usoyan ('Ded Khasan', 'Grandfather Hassan'), murdered in 2013, represents another. His organisation, sometimes known as the Tbilisi clan, became characterised by relatively loose affiliations and, above all, an avowedly multi-ethnic character, but this came only in the final stage of Usoyan's complex career.[19] In this respect, it represented a traditional Georgian model – essentially, the gang as a cooperative underworld business enterprise linked by kinship and charisma – updated to the modern era. It remains to be seen how long it will survive its founder.

Perversely, it is thus worth starting Usoyan's story near, albeit not quite at, its end. Negotiating succession is one of the riskiest times for godfathers and gangs alike, especially for those with relatively informal internal rules and no clear, strong and legitimate hierarchy. External rivals and the police may seek to take advantage of temporary disunity and mistrust; internal power struggles sharpen; losers bear grudges or fear reprisals; winners seek to promote their cronies and harbour suspicions of their rivals. In 2011, it looked as if Usoyan might be able to navigate these rocky waters. He had risen to become one of the dominant figures within Russia's complex multi-ethnic underworld. A member of Georgia's small Yezidi Kurdish minority, he was one of the few *vory v zakone* who had managed to adapt to the world of the *avtoritety*. He had survived near-elimination at the hands of his rivals in the late 1990s (and multiple assassination attempts) to emerge as a consummate dealmaker, able to reach accommodations with the state, ethnic Russian gangs, Georgians and Chechens alike.

In January 2013, though, he was stepping out of Moscow's Stary Faeton, the restaurant at which he would habitually combine dining with meeting allies, clients and petitioners. As he walked across the interior courtyard shared by a trio of such establishments, an unknown assassin who had been waiting at an upstairs window across the street opened fire with an AS-Val, a specially built silenced rifle only issued to Russian commandos. His first shot hit Usoyan in the neck. The gunman made a clean getaway; Usoyan died in hospital shortly after.[20] Ultimately, Russia still awaits a pioneer able to show the way to an honourable retirement and smooth transition within the top echelons of the underworld.

Born in Tbilisi in 1937, Usoyan opened his criminal record with a sentence for pickpocketing while just an adolescent. After an early criminal career in Georgia, he lived and worked across Russia and in Uzbekistan. In that time, his star rose within the underworld, and he acquired the rank of *vor v zakone* and a reputation as a shrewd operator. By the late 1980s, he was preying on black marketeers, earning him the muscle, connections and wealth to prosper in the post-Soviet era. At a time when many other criminal organisations were adopting a more networked structure, though, Usoyan's – like those of many other Caucasian criminals – was a more conventional gang of the 'core group' variety, built around kinship, personal connections and hierarchy.

His operations extended across central and southern Russia and he forged connections with key figures within Moscow – including 'Yaponchik' and Alexei 'Petrik' Petrov, head of the Mazutkinskaya group[21] – as well as a whole string of local kingpins in cities such as Nizhny Tagil, Yekaterinburg and Perm. Interestingly, Usoyan very specifically made it clear that while he was *from* the 'highlander' regions, he was not one *of* them. Indeed, figures such as 'Yaponchik' and 'Yakutyonok', his kingpin in Perm, warmed to him for that very reason.[22]

In the process, Usoyan became one of the holders of a common *obshchak* still existing at the time, in effect an underworld banker. A high point of his influence in that time came in 1995, ironically when he was arrested in a police raid on a gathering he was hosting in Sochi. Some 350 senior criminals had assembled, ostensibly to pay their respects to murdered *vor v zakone* Rantik 'Synok' Safaryan. In practice, though, this was a pretext for a regular *skhodka*.[23] All the attendees were released for lack of evidence of any crime, but the public recognition that Usoyan was hosting such an event consolidated his standing within the underworld. The next year, the newspaper *Nezavisimaya gazeta* published a league table of Russia's gangs – such were the wild 1990s that organised crime almost seemed to have become a national sport, and certainly a national fascination – that put Usoyan's combine third, after only Solntsevo and the Far Eastern Association of Thieves.[24]

However, with visibility comes vulnerability. In 1997 Usoyan was arrested again, charged with the murder of rival kingpin Amiran Pyatigorsky. He was acquitted, but Pyatigorsky's death was just part of a wider war with 'Rudik', an Armenian gang leader eager to loosen Usoyan's grip on the Caucasus region of Mineralnye Vody.[25] 'Rudik' continued to apply direct methods – Usoyan survived his next assassination attempt in 1998 – but realised that the most dangerous attacks are often oblique ones. He began to question Usoyan's stewardship of the *obshchak*, accusing him of embezzlement and mismanagement. Usoyan's misfortune was that the 1998 financial crisis saw the ruble devalued dramatically, and with it the once seemingly safe government bonds in which much of the *obshchak* was held. His former allies turned on him, especially as rumours and suspicions still encircled him about the fate of 'Shakhro the Younger's' *obshchak*. For a while, even Usoyan's status as a *vor v zakone* may have been revoked.

No one befriends a gangster who seems to be on the way down. More of Usoyan's lieutenants were killed or defected and an old feud flared up again. In the early 1990s, although based in Moscow, Usoyan had been made a *smotryashchy* (overseer) responsible for monitoring the activities of the gangs in St Petersburg and resolving disputes. This was very much a feature of the older days of the *vorovskoi mir*, in which a senior *vor v zakone* could operate as local arbiter. The post-Soviet underworld is rather different, though, and by 1994 Vladimir Kumarin, head of the Tambovskaya network, had begun to believe that Usoyan was trying to use this role to assert his personal authority over the city. Usoyan thus became the latest manifestation of a traditional St Petersburg bugbear: the bumptious upstart from Moscow who thinks he can throw his weight around in the 'second city'. Once his position began to be weakened elsewhere, Usoyan quickly found his authority in St Petersburg disappear and his local allies with it.

In some ways, though, these perils were the making of Usoyan. The prospect of a widening mob war that could tear the Russian underworld apart worried many senior criminals and they began trying to broker some accord. Furthermore, Usoyan himself realised he needed allies and adopted a new strategy. Where once he had looked for subordinates, now he looked for allies and partners. By the end of 1999, he had agreed a ceasefire with 'Rudik'. In order to rebuild his empire on more cooperative, networked lines, Usoyan needed also to find some cohering principle that could hold it together, to replace personal loyalty to him. He did so by charting a middle course between the three main ethnic groups dominating the Eurasian underworld: the Slavs, the Chechens and the Georgians.

While connected with Georgian crime groups in Tbilisi, for almost three decades, Usoyan's operations had been based in Moscow and the north Caucasus. He did not really fit within the Georgians, especially as they had become increasingly dominated by Tariel Oniani. However, he was able to understand and work with them, just as he could with the Russians and the Chechens. Likewise, although a product of the old order of the *vory*, Usoyan was also a canny and successful entrepreneur and dealmaker, able to treat with the *avtoritety*. He was thus able to reinvent himself to exploit a gap in the market. He could appeal not only to the other 'highlanders', but also to criminals of every race, region and specialism. The leaders of this new network ranged from Usoyan's kin (including his nephews, the *vory v zakone* 'Yura Lazarovsky' and Dmitry 'Miron' Chanturia), through Georgians, to Russians, Armenians, Azeris and even some Central Asians.[26] He also formed a close alliance with Moscow's Slavic Slavyansky gang.[27]

The network had considerable geographic scope. Its heartlands were Moscow (particularly its northern and eastern districts) and the surrounding area, and the Yaroslavl, Ural, Krasnoyarsk, Irkutsk, Krasnodar and North

Caucasus regions. Outside Russia, it operated in Ukraine, Moldova, Belarus, Armenia and Georgia, but relatively little any further afield. In this respect an old-school gangster, Usoyan had almost no interests in North America and very few in Europe, although there was some investment in Spain, Greece and the Balkans, especially in hotels and similar property. Even so, these were not platforms for future operations so much as rainy-day investments.[28]

In September 2010, Usoyan was shot in the stomach in central Moscow.[29] He survived, but refused to name publicly whom he suspected of ordering the attack. Privately, he blamed Oniani. The traditional options would be a counter-attack or an attempt to buy off his enemy, but the seventy-three-year-old Usoyan again changed the rules. He began to divest himself of his main criminal assets and duties. At first it was assumed this was a ploy, but it became clear that in fact he was genuinely trying to manage the complex and unusual process of an orderly restructuring of his criminal empire and the distribution of its assets into associated but autonomous business units.[30] 'Yura Lazarovsky' and 'Miron' Chanturia assumed day-to-day control of most operations within Russia: 'Yura' took over Usoyan's businesses in the North Caucasus and southern Russia, especially the Krasnodar region, while Chanturia handled activities in Moscow, central Russia and the Yaroslavl region and became Usoyan's spokesman and nego-tiator within the Moscow underworld.[31]

It is possible that this could have worked. Both Usoyan's heirs, while young (then twenty-nine and thirty-one, respectively), were relatively well regarded. Most importantly, they were backed actively by Usoyan himself and also his confidant and consigliere, the *vor v zakone* 'Edik Osetrina'. However, Usoyan's murder in 2013 and the subsequent transfer of full authority to Chanturia left his plans in crisis. While the Usoyan *gruppirovka* leadership formally recognised Chanturia as their new chieftain, it did not look as if he had the authority, skills and credibility to step into his uncle's shoes. One detective involved in the case expressed his doubts, noting that Usoyan's strength was in his powerful network of connections, 'someone he did a favour for twenty years ago, someone on whom he has incriminating evidence . . . With his death, that authority is lost. No one will listen to Miron.'[32] As of 2017, Usoyan's project to manage an orderly transfer of power seems to have come to fruition in a posthumous way, but his network is quietly falling apart.

The rise of the youngsters

Rovshan is not the kind of a guy to do that; he lives by the rules and would not have ordered [a hit] on a thief.
                    Cousin of Rovshan Dzhaniyev, 2013[33]

Beyond Tariel Oniani, the other main suspect for organising Usoyan's death was Rovshan Dzhaniyev, a relatively young Azeri gangster whose rise demonstrates one of the problematic by-products of the relative stability of the 2000s underworld: a decline in social mobility. In the 1990s, ambitious younger gangsters could expect rapid promotion thanks either to the exploitation of new opportunities (often seized from other gangs) or the murders of their seniors. However, as turf boundaries hardened, killings declined and new opportunities became scarcer, promotions came more slowly and rarely. Dzhaniyev, profiled in chapter 14, emerged as an outsider, looking to shake up the existing order, and as a result, became a magnet for other disgruntled younger criminals and a symbol of a worrying generational tension.

If Chechens and Georgians dominate the 'highlander' communities within the Russian underworld, it is important not to ignore other ethnicities such as the Armenians and Azeris. Armenian organised crime remains generally a low-level phenomenon in Russia and even such kingpins as the *vor* 'Khromoi', arrested in Moscow on drug charges in 2009, cooperate rather than compete with their Russian counterparts. This may help explain why Russian and Armenian criminals abroad also seem especially able and willing to work together. They have to, really: since the death of the senior Armenian gangster Rafik Bagdasaryan ('Rafik Svo') in 1993, they have never managed to maintain the kind of unity needed to be major players.[34] Azeris, though, form a more distinct community, one which has been able to rely both on kinship ties and on its members' ability to move back and forth between Russia and Azerbaijan, to avoid arrest and smuggle goods. Thus, in many cities from Moscow to Yekaterinburg to Vladivostok, relatively small but tightly knit Azeri communities spawned their own gangs.

Rovshan Dzhaniyev, 'Rovshan Lenkoransky' ('Rovshan of Lenkoran'), hailed from southern Azerbaijan. With a criminal career spanning prison terms in both Azerbaijan and Ukraine, he built himself a power base in Abkhazia, a region of Georgia now under Russian control, from which he appears to have had aspirations to form a 'highlander' network of his own.

He certainly did not lack for confidence and ambition, and his criminal organisation developed connections in Azerbaijan, Ukraine and Moscow. In particular, he seemed to want to usurp Usoyan's role in the 'highlander' community. The fact that many of the older-generation Azeri godfathers in Russia seemed willing to work with Usoyan perhaps made this inevitable.[35]

This was a formidable ambition. Dzhaniyev was in many ways a classic gangster, one who from the first believed in action over planning, a shoot-first kind of criminal, with a string of killings to his name. Ironically enough, in some ways this lack of nuance actually contributed to his appeal to footsoldiers in other groups, impatient and often frustrated with their criminal-businessman superiors. He was able to craft his personal myth as the daring bandit-chief – in some ways an *abreg* – harking back to an older, simpler and more exciting day.

As a result, he managed to attract a multi-ethnic collection of younger criminals, not only Georgians, including his right-hand man, Dzhemo Mikeladze, and Abkhazians, but also Dagestanis, Armenians and even Russians, including Alexander Bor ('Timokha'), a former cohort of 'Yaponchik's'. The common denominator was that they were unhappy with the status quo. Sometimes they were simply stranded in a criminal no-man's land. 'Timokha', for example, was a new-model white-collar gangster in many ways, having run 'Yaponchik's' business operations in the USA, including stock manipulations in partnership with the Gambino mafia family.[36] However, in Moscow he found himself exposed and friendless and needed to find new allies and protectors in a hurry. More often, though, Dzhaniyev's followers were simply not well suited to the underworld of Putin's Russia, where the slick and the smart entrepreneur called the shots and the old-style gangster was stuck in middle management.

According to some reports, Dzhaniyev was blamed by Usoyan for his attempted murder in 2010, although this may well have simply been a way for the latter to avert opening hostilities with Oniani (at whom he had first pointed the finger).[37] Dzhaniyev continued to be a force in the underworld, even while regularly dropping out of sight, before his assassination in Turkey in 2016. His demise was perhaps unsurprising, not just because of his possible role in Usoyan's death, but also because he had openly challenged the status quo.

Although his gang proved short lived, Dzhaniyev's rise was a symptom rather than a cause of a generational struggle in the making and of the tensions between criminal organisations that are essentially mono-ethnic, and those which are more inclusive. Up to the end of the Soviet Union and even into the 1990s, organised crime in Russia tended to be ethnically structured. As elsewhere, modernity, social and physical mobility, and the greater interpenetration of societies has broken down these old divisions. Just as the 'Italian mafia' in prohibition-era America included such distinctly un-Mediterranean figures as 'Dutch' Schultz and Meyer Lansky, of German-Jewish and Polish-Jewish stock respectively, so too did business and the search for capable allies break down the old solidarities in Russia.

In their own ways, Oniani, Usoyan and Dzhaniyev all offered different answers to the questions of how to create something that could fit the new times without completely abandoning the old ways and the loyalties they continued to embody. Usoyan offered a federation of semi-autonomous but mutually supportive groups, in many ways a 'highlander' equivalent of the networks that had come to dominate Slavic organised crime. Dzhaniyev gathered an alliance of the disgruntled, ambitious and frustrated, for whom a common desire to shake up the existing order transcended ethnic origins. Neither proved successful. Rather, it is Oniani's ruthless and centralised model that is currently prevailing. It is hard to believe this will last for long, though. The habitually networked Georgians are coming to be dominated by Oniani's ruthless machine, but given that it is doubtful he will seek to elevate a successor, much less manage the process with grace and effect, his empire will likely also break apart on his death, if not before. As one of Moscow's criminal investigation officers observed in 2015, 'the Georgians [gangsters] will take a while to discover that their day has already gone'.[38]

The distinctiveness of the Georgians may reflect certain cultural characteristics but it was, ultimately, more than anything else the product of specific environmental factors: the strength of the local informal economy in Soviet times, the struggles for power in post-1991 Georgia, the expulsion of the *vory*, the characters of Oniani and Usoyan.[39] It is therefore hard not to see the struggles between these models as a desperate and brutal last gasp before the 'highlanders' too are assimilated into the multi-ethnic, multi-commodity, crime–business–politics networks of the modern Eurasian underworld. Resistance is futile.

CHAPTER 12

THE GANGSTER-INTERNATIONALIST

Uninvited to the feast, but going anyway.

Russian proverb

The 1990s were times of hype and horror as 'the Russian mafia' – often regarded as a single, monolithic conspiracy – emerged as a suitable bugbear to replace the Soviet threat. FBI Director Louis Freeh thought that 'Russian organized crime presents the greatest long-term threat to the security of the United States . . . The United States is presented with a well-organized, well-funded, sophisticated and brutal conspiracy'.[1] To US Representative Henry Hyde from Illinois, 'this international enemy, the Russian mafia, is as deadly a threat as there could be and it comes from within as well as without their country'.[2] In 1993, David Veness, then deputy assistant commissioner of the British Metropolitan Police, warned that 'in five years' time there is no doubt that the major threat confronting the inner cities of the United Kingdom will come from central, eastern European and Russian countries'.[3]

It is certainly true that one of the most striking characteristics of Russian organised crime is how quickly and effectively it has become a truly global phenomenon, even a brand. Its networked, post-modernist model not only allows these criminals to respond quickly to new opportunities, it permits the incorporation of new members regardless of ethnicity, so long as they can work within the Russians' rules. The first wave of expansion into Europe was largely by *vory* moving to areas with sizeable Russian communities or, as in the case with many former Warsaw Pact or Soviet states, where they had existing contacts with local criminals and corrupt officials. The Baltic States, Poland and Hungary were all early targets, soon followed by a drift into Austria and Germany (where they were able to capitalise on existing contacts in the east). Similar early targets were Israel (where many used real or fake Jewish ethnicity to ensure immigration rights) and the USA.

But the world was changing. The heavy-handed criminal expansion of the early 1990s provoked a backlash from states and criminals alike, and the *vory* were often arrested, deported or simply forced to flee. As ever, though, they adapted. The transformation had already begun at home from thuggish street *vor* to entrepreneurial *vor*-broker, and this became all the more important for their entry into the global criminal market. The ensuing two decades have demonstrated that this poses a much more serious, if at the same time less dramatic, threat. The modern Russian *vory* are not interested in challenging or undermining the West, but in enjoying the opportunities it provides. They have certainly not moved, mob-handed, into the inner cities of America, Britain or the Continent.

Mafias do not, on the whole, migrate. As Federico Varese has meticulously demonstrated in his *Mafias on the Move*, the myth of a globalised, universal criminal class able to migrate to wherever a new opportunity seems to be emerging is just that – a myth. Generally, when 'mafiosi find themselves in the new locale [it is] not of their own volition; they have been forced to move there by court orders, to escape justice or mafia infighting and wars. They are not seeking new markets or new products but are instead just making the most of bad luck.'[4] Even when they do move, the odds are they will fail in their efforts to establish their criminal enterprises in a new land, where they lack local contacts, often even the local language. Instead, Varese's findings are that for this transplantation to be successful, there are two requirements:

> First, no other mafia group (or state apparati offering illegal protection) must be present. It is too much of an uphill struggle for an incoming mafia to set up shop in the presence of a powerful local competitor. Second, a mafia group is most likely to succeed in transplanting when its presence coincides with the sudden emergence of new markets.[5]

The presence of a market without an existing occupier is a rare and generally temporary phenomenon. Organised crime from Russia is undoubtedly a significant feature of the global underworld, but usually in the form of facilitators rather than street-level thugs. These *vory* are the business partners of local groups: selling them heroin from Afghanistan, laundering their money through Russia's still-murky financial system, providing weapons and occasionally someone who knows how to use them. In this way, even if the Russian *mafiya* (as it is sometimes called) is not a direct problem in a country, it can have a serious impact by providing existing gangs with access to expertise, services and criminal products to which normally they could never aspire.

Hence the question must be: what form does Russian and Eurasian organised crime take when it moves abroad? Is it a wolf, working alone or in a pack, a restless predator roaming from one kill to the next? An octopus, sending its questing tentacles in search of food from a safe haven? Or a virus, lacking any plan or central mind, simply infecting those hosts which offer the right conditions and which lack antibodies sufficient to hold the disease at bay? However unflattering it may sound, and although one can point to some cases of effective and strategic 'conquest', in the main the viral analogy holds good. This is an entrepreneurial, diffuse form of criminality which allows it quickly to exploit vulnerabilities but which is often as easily pushed back. Yet it can then reappear when a new opportunity arises, having lain dormant until society's resilience diminishes.

On definitions

Who are they? The mafia is like the government, except that it works. Seriously, the mafia is, well, whatever it wants to be.

                              Kolya, Russian student, 1996[6]

There is also the fundamental question of what is actually meant by 'Russian organised crime'. This is an important point, as it is often crudely interpreted by analogy: parallels are drawn between the Russian gangs' engagement with business and the Japanese yakuza's, or between the rules of the *vory* and the Sicilian mafia's code of silence. This even applies to law enforcers in Russia and, especially, beyond, who seek to force these criminal groupings into the traditional pyramidal model, with a godfather at the top, lieutenants beneath him, and footsoldiers at the base, simply because this is the kind of structure with which they are familiar and comfortable.

From personal experience, I recall a painful afternoon spent with a team of smart, enthusiastic European police analysts in the late 2000s, who were trying to understand how a particular Russian group operated. Time and again, a pyramid would appear on the whiteboard, only to be erased as the complexities of this organisation's structure and operations became clear. Eventually, one threw up his hands and said, 'It's not a gang, it's a bunch of Facebook friends!' (I'll spare everyone's blushes by not naming the country in question.)

There is more than a little truth in this. Instead of the classic hierarchical gang, often drawn from a single ethnicity, home region or kin group, this is a flexible, networked criminal phenomenon that embraces a wide range of businesses (both licit and illicit), practices and even nationalities, but nonetheless has certain distinctive ways of operating. Indeed, 'Russian organised crime' may not necessarily be Russian, is often not especially organised, and does rather more than just crime.

The modes of organisation and the extent to which these criminals engage in non-criminal business are best explored later, but it is worth dwelling here on the 'Russianness' of these gangs. In the West, other terms are often used, especially by official agencies, notably 'Eurasian organised crime' (the FBI's term of choice) or 'Russian-speaking organised crime' (more generally found in Europe). Both have their merits, over and above the political correctness of not singling out a specific ethnic as well as national group. However, 'Russian-speaking organised crime' is problematic in that it is sometimes simply wrong; while Russian is certainly the lingua franca within this criminal world, an Armenian gangster is more likely to speak Armenian to his cousin and co-conspirator, while gangs operating in the USA often use English, especially as they induct second- or third-generation migrants or other locals. As for 'Eurasian organised crime', while it undoubtedly has far greater descriptive value, it also carries with it the implication that a St Petersburg *avtoritet*, a South Ossetian gangster-warlord and a Central Asian drug kingpin operate, organise and think the same way. It is probably the most capacious and useful such term, but, for the sake of this book, the commonplace 'Russian organised crime' is used for not just Russian gangs but also Slavic groups resident in the rest of the world, as well as for those which may not be predominantly Slavic, but which broadly share the same cultural and operational characteristics, while also having some direct relationship with Russia itself. I do not pretend to offer a detailed exploration of the underworlds of all the post-Soviet states in themselves, on which, fortunately, there is an increasingly robust scholarship.[7]

Bad neighbours: organised crime in post-Soviet Eurasia

The Russians think they own our country. They don't but unfortunately there are many here, businessmen, political figures, criminals, who are willing to sell it to them.

Moldovan police officer, 2006[8]

Russian organised crime gangs operate throughout what Moscow from time to time calls the 'Near Abroad' – the other post-Soviet states, with the exception of the Baltics. Sometimes they are locally based, sometimes they are offshoots of home groups and sometimes they work in partnership with indigenous gangs. This is a two-way process, even if usually skewed in favour of the Russians. Some Ukrainian and even Belarusian gangs and criminals operate autonomously in Russia, for example, along with groups from the Caucasus. In most cases, the Russians operate locally in partnership with or with the approval of local criminal interests, whether running their own operations or, more often, providing a transnational connection to local rackets which would benefit from this.

Sometimes, this is because there is already a thriving indigenous underworld. Ukraine is a good example, a country in which all the main Russian combines have interests, operations, partners and people, and where even the culture of the *vory* is still present. Solntsevo has a long-standing relationship with the criminal–political 'Donetsk clan', which was the power base for former president Viktor Yanukovych, for example. In the early 1990s, the Russian gangs often had relatively free rein, but the local underworld matured, facilitated by the extensive corruption of the local and national political elite. Taras Kuzio has suggested that Ukraine prior to the 2013–14 'Maidan Revolution' became a 'neo-Soviet mafia state'.[9] As with the similar claim made by British journalist Luke Harding about Russia,[10] this is a neat phrase that obscures more than it explains. Nonetheless, there is certainly extensive corruption and in many ways pre-Maidan Ukraine, by a rather roundabout route, came to resemble Russia, with its 'raiding' of businesses and circles of corruption. Its organised crime structures are still broadly similar to Russia's, albeit rather smaller and less concerned with the outside world, but equally linked to corrupt elites and oligarchic control of the economy.[11]

When Moscow annexed Ukraine's Crimean peninsula in 2014, though, it did so – as will be discussed later – with the active support of local *vory*, and it then used and empowered others in the south-eastern Donbas region to fight and therefore excuse its subsequent proxy war with Kiev.[12] Since then, Ukraine has been going through a painful and uncertain attempt to attain the dream of the Maidan, of a democratic, liberal, law-based state, while Moscow and Kiev are locked into an undeclared, low-intensity war that, at the time of writing, shows no sign of abating. Yet, for all this, the gangsters are truly internationalist in their opportunism. Ukraine and Russia may be at virtual war, but their criminals continue to cooperate as before. One officer from the SBU, Ukraine's security service, ruefully told me that 'the flow of drugs through Donbas, into Ukraine, and then into Europe simply has not shrunk by a single percentage point, even while bullets are flying back and forth across the front line'.[13]

This is one model where the Russians are more powerful in overall terms, but encounter a sufficiently entrenched domestic underworld that there are no opportunities for direct transplantation or domination. This is evident in many other parts of the former Soviet Union too, although more often the reason is that an authoritarian regime is jealously guarding its monopoly of coercive force and informal influence and thus commands a majority share in its local underworld. In Belarus, for example, President Alexander Lukashenka's downright neo-Soviet regime keeps the under-world under its thumb in a manner reminiscent – as in so much else – of the USSR in the 1970s. In oil-rich and rights-poor Azerbaijan, key groups need to be connected with (and pay off) the Aliyev regime to survive.[14] Further east, in Central Asia, a succession of more-or-less authoritarian regimes resting on exploitative elites run Tajikistan, Turkmenistan, Kazakhstan and Uzbekistan. Beyond low-level street gangs, which are often suppressed by security forces unconcerned with legal niceties, the main crime organisa-tions will invariably either be run by elements of the elite apparatus or be heavily dependent on them. Their role is often to act as agents diverting profits from corruption and embezzlement of state assets to the elite, or else to manage key illegal businesses for them, especially drug trafficking. Here, the gangsters are often little more than deniable agents of the corrupt elites.

A second model, visible in Moldova, Armenia and Kyrgyzstan, is where the local underworld is weak or fragmented, but so too is the state. In Kyrgyzstan, for example, gangsters put gunmen on the streets to help bring down President Askar Akayev in the 2005 'Tulip Revolution', in the process demonstrating that the state was unable to maintain a monopoly of armed force.[15] However, in such countries, the criminals are essentially only relatively large fish in distinctly small pools. The Russian-based networks are able to cherry-pick their opportunities, but still find it convenient to work with and through local criminals much of the time. It might be possible for the Russians to assume a more dominant role if they had to, but local gangs are typically keen to work with them, obviating the need.

Georgia offers a model all its own. Although the *vory v zakone* may have been expelled, with an undoubted impact on the underworld, that has not magically dispelled organised crime, but has simply transferred power to a new generation. There remain considerable interactions between criminals in Georgia and those in Georgian and other 'highlander' gangs in Russia and beyond. However, the state of relations between Tbilisi and Moscow since Russia's invasion in 2008 is such that there has been little scope for substantial penetration by Russian networks. The rise in 2012 of the Georgian Dream party, founded by Bidzina Ivanishvili, a billionaire with considerable interests in Russia, led to a more emollient policy towards Moscow. However, there are again no unclaimed business opportunities for the Russians quickly or easily to exploit.

Finally, there are the unrecognised pseudo-states of Transnistria (in Moldova), South Ossetia and Abkhazia (in Georgia), and perhaps Donbas soon enough. These all exist on Moscow's sufferance and while they have local underworlds – generally closely linked with the political leaderships – these are small-time players and unable meaningfully to challenge the larger Russian combines. As a result, these regions have become and remain free economic zones for the Russian criminal networks. However, their utility is limited by their relative isolation, small size and notoriety. Although the case has been made that Transnistria, for example, is turning itself into a working de facto state,[16] the enclave once infamously described in a European Parliament report as 'a black hole in which the illegal trade in arms, the trafficking in human beings and the laundering of criminal finance' all thrive,[17] continues to depend to a considerable extent on criminal and informal activities, from money laundering to smuggling.[18]

The rise and fall of the first wave

*Sure, doing business abroad was about money – but it was also about
security. Back in the 1990s, you didn't know what was going to happen
at home, so you needed a bit of stability in your life.*

Russian-Ukrainian gangster, 2006[19]

Regardless of their progress within post-Soviet Eurasia, the successes of the
vory in central and eastern Europe and beyond in the 1990s seemed at the
time to buck Varese's assertions about the difficulty and rarity of external
expansion. They appeared to have not just the appetite for empire building
but also the capacity. Russian and Chechen gangs clashed for supremacy
over the underworld of the Baltic states: for example, 'during the "bloody
autumn" of 1994, about a hundred murders related to organized crime were
committed' in Estonia, a country of just 1.5 million people.[20] Prague was for
a while home to representatives of all the main networks such as Solntsevo,
Tambovskaya and the Chechens, as well as Semyon Mogilevich, the mobster
banker. In 1996, the Israeli police identified thirty-five senior Russian *vory*
operating in Israel, some twenty of whom were members of Solntsevo or
closely linked with the network.[21] They emerged as key players within the
Israeli underworld after a brutal struggle in 1996–8 that left many of the
country's indigenous gang leaders dead, while the country became a key
money laundry for the Russians.[22]

What all this reflected was a temporary advantage caused by the
disproportion between the relative resources of the Russian and Eurasian
gangs at the time and the local institutions, law enforcement structures
and criminal rivals they were facing. In some ways, one could draw a
parallel with the Soviet invasion of Afghanistan in 1979: seizing the main
cities and communications routes of this divided and impoverished country
was no great feat. Actually holding and pacifying it would take greater
political and military resources than the Soviets were able or willing to
expend, especially as their very presence galvanised opposition. After ten
years, the Soviets withdrew from Afghanistan not because they had been
beaten, but simply because the dwindling benefits of occupation were so
clearly outweighed by its costs, and there was no prospect of victory on the
horizon. This was defeat on the balance sheet rather than on the
battlefield.

Likewise, in the early 1990s, there were numerous easy initial opportunities for the *vory*. The new democracies of central Europe, not yet cradled within the European Union, were impoverished and had inherited discredited police forces and anachronistic legal codes akin to Russia's. Further afield, police were unprepared for the new challenge and there were specific market opportunities. In Israel, the Law of Return – which grants an automatic right of immigration to those able to demonstrate Jewish ancestry – proved an appealing loophole for *vory* who either met this criterion or, more often, paid to have the necessary documents produced in Russia. In the United States, the presence of indigenous, entrepreneurial criminal enterprises, especially in New York's Brighton Beach, seemed also to offer a beachhead for quick expansion. In those days, you could be a tattooed thug and still get a visa, and you didn't need to be too smart when local police forces still hadn't adapted to this new challenge, often not even having Russian-speaking officers.

Furthermore, Russia's criminals had particular reasons to want to internationalise their operations as quickly as possible. There was a pervasive (if misguided) belief that there could be a hard-line Communist revival or even some kind of nationalist–authoritarian coup. This helps explain the extreme measures taken – with Western acquiescence – to rig the 1996 presidential elections to ensure Boris Yeltsin beat his Communist rival.[23] It also helps explain the gangsters' enthusiasm for hedging themselves against trouble at home. By internationalising, they could secure revenue streams in alternative currencies (to protect them from the collapse of the ruble), prepare fall-back options if they were suddenly denied access to their main sources of income, and perhaps gain the right to live abroad through citizenship, investment or strategic marriage. That way, they could escape the Motherland if things suddenly began to look dangerous.

To this end – and at the time this was something that escaped the attention of scholars, law enforcers and other observers alike, myself included – for many Russian *vory* in the 1990s, developing operations abroad was not so much a source of revenue, but a drain: a loss-leader or investment in personal security. It was also a matter of prestige, a form of consumption as conspicuous as the shiny imported limousine and the equally shiny domestic arm-candy. Where it could, Russian organised crime did what most ethnic migrant gangs do: preyed on its own people, exploiting immigrants who lacked their own resources, their own support structures and, often, faith in local law enforcement. (After all, a recent arrival from Russia or the USSR was likely to see authority figures in uniform as more dangerous than reassuring.)

However, many of these new opportunities were only temporary. The economies and law enforcement structures of central Europe largely stabilised and developed through the 1990s and domestic gangs soon sought to contest control of these markets. While they were typically smaller than the aggregates of the Russian structures against which they were matched, the real arithmetic is concerned with resources available in theatre. In other words, just as the Afghan rebels did not have to face off against the whole Red Army, only the 100,000–150,000 men of the so-called Limited Contingent of Forces in Afghanistan, so too the total size of the crime network was less relevant than the actual commitment in, say, Tallinn or Tel Aviv.

This is where the distinctive characteristics of the network become especially significant. A traditional, hierarchical structure can – in theory – quickly throw more resources into a conflict. Unless there is some compelling, existential challenge involved which is common to all parties, then in a network securing additional resources is a vastly more complex and difficult process. Other members, individual and collective, need to be persuaded to join the conflict, which requires the expenditure of social capital, or credible prospects of a solid return. It is relatively easy to persuade others to join ventures which have a proven profitable track record and promise a continued return. The Afghan heroin trade is a good case in point. On the other hand, how do you persuade independent entrepreneurs in the underworld to join what seems to be a losing or at least uncertain struggle? The answer, as Varese suggests, is that people will only do so when they feel they have no alternative.

Furthermore, the indigenous gangs' home turf advantage in central Europe in particular often manifested itself in the tacit or even active support of local police and security structures, which had also come to terms with the 'invasion' they faced. The debate about the intrusion of Russian organised crime often quickly acquired a clearly nationalist tone, with talk of 'colonisation' and 'imperialism', and became securitised. The presence of Russian gangs began to be considered – not without reason – also in terms of the presence of potential Russian spies, saboteurs and agents of influence. As one Estonian Security Police (Kapo) officer put it to me, 'in the late 1990s, and again after 2007 [when Moscow launched a cyberattack on Estonia], dealing with Russian gangs was not just a police issue, but a vital security one'.[24] Thus, especially in central Europe and the Baltic states, a moral panic about the Russians led to a particular focus on combating them, even at the expense of addressing indigenous threats. As a result, by the end of the 1990s, the first expansionist wave of Russian and Eurasian *vory* had largely been cut down to size. They had been either forced to withdraw or brought down to becoming just one more player in their respective foreign underworlds.

Samosval and Yaponchik: empire builders or exiles?

It's wonderful that the Iron Curtain has gone, but it was a shield for the West. Now we've opened the gates and this is very dangerous for the world.

Russian investigator Boris Urov, 1993[25]

One of the recurring debates about the expansion of European empires in the nineteenth century has been how far one can ascribe imperialism to the Machiavellian strategies of metropolitan governments and how far one should instead look to the self-interest, values, ambitions and interactions of the men on the ground, from soldiers to merchants, who often shaped or simply ignored policy from the centre. So, too, it is essential to realise in this context that what from the outside may look like grand strategy may well in fact be the result of a confluence of intent, chance and personal interest. In November 1993, for example, Solntsevo's leadership decided that they wanted a representative in Italy, not least because of their existing collaborations with Italian criminals and a sense that it offered a permissive environment for their activities.[26] Reportedly Monya Elson, a Russian gangster who had fled New York to Italy, said, 'Here you can do whatever you want, it is not Europe.'[27]

The initiative was eventually entrusted to Yury Yesin ('Yura Samosval'), a senior Solntsevo figure and *vor v zakone*, but it is hard to know for sure how far this reflected instruction from above or initiative from below. Yesin had been close to Sergei 'Silvestr' Timofeyev, the one-time Orekhovo chieftain whose violent ways led to his murder in September 1994, and it was

assumed that all the *Silvestrovskie*, his associates, were targets. In a telephone conversation tapped by the Italian police, one of Yesin's accomplices
said, 'Even the police say that only after all the *Silvestrovskie* are killed, will
there be peace.'[28] This was not an unreasonable belief: fellow *Silvestrovets*
Sergei 'Boroda' Kruglov, a man of similar criminal status to Yesin, was also
killed alongside Timofeyev. Yesin already had some assets in Italy, he had
associates who knew Italy (including an Italian with a Russian wife) and,
more to the point, he was looking for a bolthole. The prospect of heading to
Italy was ideal, and within a month of Timofeyev's death, Yesin and his
crew were there.

So did Yesin start trying to muscle into existing criminal businesses and
generally act as the representative of a colonial power? Not at all: as Varese
has demonstrated, if anything, he and his crew went out of their way to
keep a low profile. He had sacrificed a considerable degree of authority and
influence in Moscow for security and his new role largely consisted of
investing in the legal sector, laundering money and sometimes being the
link man in wider connections. Most of the money made was spent in Italy
and on maintaining the group and their lifestyles. In other words, this was
neither a profit centre for Solntsevo as a whole, nor an aggressive operation.
Rather, it emerged from the confluence of the network grandees' desire to
have an 'honorary consul' in Rome in case of need, and an individual's
desire to leave Moscow to signal that he was not seeking to avenge his
former patron, and to put some distance between himself and the war in
which Timofeyev had died. Even so, by 1996 Yesin had come to the Italian
police's attention and he was arrested the next year. Although he was eventually released on a technicality relating to the admissibility of wiretap
evidence, he was expelled from the country and this little Solntsevo cell was
no more.[29]

A similar pattern is visible in efforts to infiltrate the United States
through New York's Brighton Beach neighbourhood. When crime organisations do manage to expand, they tend not to move physically from their
home base but instead establish local offshoots, especially within diaspora
and migrant communities. They are a migratory resource, facilitating the
inflow of criminals through invitation, work opportunity (real or otherwise) or even marriage (again, real or otherwise). They are a business
resource, not least in brokering contacts for the gangsters. The largest
concentration of Russians outside post-Soviet Eurasia is in the USA.

According to the 2010 American Community Survey, there were then just under three million Americans identifying themselves as of Russian origin, although most are assimilated and speak no Russian. This is a granular diaspora, made up of different waves with their own defining characteristics. If one considers simply foreign-born native Russian speakers in the USA, a steadily growing cohort (up from just over 700,000 in 2000, according to the census, to over 850,000 in 2007[30]), then New York remains a key centre for them, even if the appeal of Brighton Beach, their traditional haven, is becoming less marked than that of Manhattan and other parts of the city.

There are undoubtedly organised crime gangs based within the ethnic Russian communities in the United States. But efforts to turn them into outposts of some global crime empire failed and, as with Yesin's abortive endeavour, as much as anything else reflected underworld politics back at home. Before 1991, violent organised crime had been a local problem in Brighton Beach, but it was relatively primordial. For the previous two decades, groups had risen and fallen which preyed upon their own community. The 'Potato Bag Gang' in the 1970s (which defrauded new immigrants, selling them bags of potatoes they thought were antique gold coins) gave way to groups run by figures such as Yevsei Agron (who favoured using an electric cattle-prod on his enemies), Marat Balagula (who pioneered a shift towards white-collar crimes) and Monya Elson (who built a close working relationship with the New York mafia).[31]

In 1992, though, Russian *vor v zakone* and Solntsevo associate Vyacheslav 'Yaponchik' Ivankov came to New York. A gathering of gangster leaders in Moscow had charged Ivankov with bringing Brighton Beach's gangs into the fold.[32] He duly began asserting his authority in the neighbourhood and also making himself some money on the side. Old school enough not to be afraid of getting his hands dirty, it was perhaps inevitable that he would be caught. In 1995 the FBI arrested him on extortion charges. He served nine years in a US prison before being deported home. Officially, this was to face charges of murdering two Turks in Moscow in 1992, but in practice that case quickly and conveniently collapsed as police witnesses contradicted their statements and said they had never seen him. Ivankov walked free.[33]

During his brief reign of terror in so-called 'Little Odessa', Ivankov did appear to be in charge and successfully began reconnecting Brighton Beach with some kind of Russian gangster international; FBI and NYPD alike reported a spike in money transfers to and from the Motherland, for example. However, after he was no longer there, these connections were revealed for what they really were: either based on simple pragmatism – each party had something to gain – or else essentially artificial, established and maintained through the expenditure of funds, social capital and coercion, all resources prone to depletion. In effect, 'Yaponchik' was paying out of his own pocket to make himself look successful.

But perhaps this should not come as a surprise, as in hindsight his dispatch to New York seems to have been motivated less by a serious belief that he could be some new criminal Columbus finding a new world for the Russians to exploit but rather the answer to a perennially vexing problem: what to do with a warrior when the war is over? Ivankov had been the marshal of the Solntsevo-led struggle against the 'highlanders' in Moscow, a mob war he had prosecuted with vigorous savagery. His presence in the capital represented a continued risk to the new status quo. The Chechen and other leaders resented him. Given the importance of the vendetta amongst many 'highlander' communities, there was the constant risk that some hothead would try to avenge a relative and in the process destabilise the tense peace. Besides which, the tattooed Gulag veteran was an uncomfortable peacetime comrade for the new generation of *avtoritety*, one with a dangerously strong reputation especially amongst the more thuggish criminal element. Finding some pretext to get Ivankov out of Moscow for a while, but one which would seem to him like an honour rather than exclusion, became a priority. 'Little Odessa' seemed the ideal solution. Once again, then, 'expansion' actually meant 'exile', a continuation of underworld politics by other means, and proved a fragile and short-lived adventure.

In the 1990s, then, the dramatic accounts of the Russian mafia's outward expansion, whether wolves in the fold, tentacular predators or viral exploiters of Western weakness, were understandable but overblown. The Russians certainly had strengths, and new, uncontrolled markets beckoned. More to the point, they had reasons to expand their operations abroad, even sometimes when they were not cost effective. Soon enough, though, local providers would move into those markets, local law enforcement would respond to the challenge and, as with all empires, the cost would force retreat. But rather than marking the end of Russian criminal engagement with the world, this simply led to its metamorphosis into new and more effective forms.

From conquistadores to merchant-adventurers

Listen, last time, our gangsters thought they could just bully their way in. This time they will be much smarter.

Russian police official, 2011[34]

The Czech police, Interior Ministry and Security Information Service (BIS) all periodically warn that Russian organised crime represents a serious challenge to the country.[35] There are certainly many Russians there – walk through the spa town of Karlovy Vary and you hear more Russian spoken than Czech – as well as Russian money in real estate and business. But actual evidence on the ground of Russian crime since the 1990s is minimal. Instead, it is usually Czech gangsters who are brought to justice, or criminals from the local Vietnamese gangs, which are increasingly responsible for trafficking marijuana and methamphetamines.[36] Are the official warnings just a ritual excoriation of a mistrusted former occupier? There certainly seems to be a hint of moral panic about it. Two shootings in 2008, for example, led BIS sources to raise the spectre of a gang war between Russian-speaking groups in Prague. It never happened.

Yet that does not mean that the Russians are not there. Over the 1990s, many were forced out of the country and a number of their operations closed down. They withdrew from much street-level activity (though some Ukrainian gangs still victimise the Ukrainian community in Moravia[37]). But they maintained contacts, all of which could be built on afresh. Their role in the Czech Republic's underworld by the 2010s was best summed up by one police officer as 'the criminals behind the criminals, not controlling them, but selling them everything they need'.[38] They have instead concentrated on working as illegal wholesalers, criminal coordinators and underworld investors in businesses of every kind.

After all, even if it does not constitute the merciless and irresistible conspiracy of alarmist myth, there is no doubt that Russian and Russian-linked organised crime can be found across the globe. It is defrauding millions out of the US Medicare and Medicaid programmes, swapping heroin for cocaine with Latin American drug gangs, laundering money around the Mediterranean, selling guns in Africa, trafficking women into the Middle East and raw materials into East Asia, and buying up real estate in Australia. Antarctica appears the only continent – so far – untouched.

But the Russians are on the whole not trying to supplant or subjugate local gangs. If anything, the opposite is true. Although there are exceptions, in the main Russian networks do not just coexist with their local counterparts, they actively seek partnerships.

Having failed to force their way into markets against local opposition, the real path to a global presence for the Russians has been serving those markets and meeting real or perceived needs. If the unsuccessful 1990s model was the conquistador, the swaggering and swashbuckling imperialist, then his modern counterpart is the merchant-adventurer. This model demonstrates four main characteristics. First of all, just like Soviet citizens during the 1980s anti-alcohol campaign, the Russians enter the market as providers of commodities for which there is a genuine demand. These could be illicit goods, whether narcotics, counterfeit DVDs and cigarettes for Europe, trafficked women for the Middle East, or cheap, poached or smuggled raw materials for the Chinese market. At least as often, the commodity is expertise. Even back in the 1990s it was the Russians who introduced the New York Cosa Nostra to the heady, white-collar profits from fuel excise scams, and these days 60 per cent of the Russian or Eurasian organised crime operations investigated by the FBI across the USA relate to frauds of one kind of another.[39]

Second, they are able to fulfil these demands 'honestly', in the sense that they are able provide them more easily, cheaply or efficiently than alternative sources, rather than relying on artificial advantages such as the use of violence to drive out the competition or uneconomic subsidies. A classic example is their role providing financial services to the global underworld. Any criminal needs the ability to move and above all launder their profits so that they can use the money they make safely, without law enforcement being able to prove connection to a crime. The Russians have been able to develop a wide range of laundries, often through their own financial system, but also by exploiting less scrupulous or demanding jurisdictions abroad. Typically, the money is first 'prewashed' within the former Soviet region, such as through Ukraine or Moldova, knowing that, while this does not provide particular respectability, it does at least add an extra layer of legal and technical complexity for police investigators or diligent bank officers seeking to identify the source of the funds. Then it will move through countries such as Cyprus, Israel and Latvia, where the Russians have established relationships and front companies, before moving on to increasingly highly regarded jurisdictions, not least the City of London, in order to 'wash' it thoroughly.

Having established these laundries, though, and embedded themselves in the financial systems of other countries, the Russians have assiduously marketed them to other criminals. A particular example is the Bank of New York (BNY) case, part of the international laundering ring broken by the Italian-led Operation Spiderweb investigation in 2002, originally hunting Sicilian mafia funds.[40] Via a ring organised by two Russian émigrés, BNY was used to launder $7 billion coming out of and through Moscow from a variety of sources: corrupt Russian officials, businesses looking to evade tax and currency transfer controls, Solntsevo and even foreign gangs such as the Sicilians. The BNY case was a massive operation, but hardly unique except in scale,[41] and epitomises the way the Russians create criminal service industries and then offer them to wider circles of clients, winning business by being relatively cheap, efficient and secure.

Third, the Russians are willing to deal with other criminals of near enough any type, ethnicity or structure. It is an irony that gangsters from a society in which racist, even xenophobic, attitudes are still quite common are the new internationalists, eager to cut deals with anyone and happy to recruit not just agents but partners outside their community. A genuine credit card fraud case helps illustrate the extent to which Russians have seamlessly integrated themselves into multinational enterprises. A Vietnamese shopkeeper in California would covertly duplicate a customer's credit card information, which was then transmitted to Chinese criminals in Hong Kong and thence to Malaysia. There the data was embossed onto false credit cards. These were couriered by air to Milan, where Neapolitan gangsters from the Camorra sold them to a Russian group in the Czech Republic. The cards were flown to Prague and distributed to agents who fanned out to the major cities of Europe where they almost – but not quite – maxed out their cards buying luxury goods. These goods were then flown back to Moscow for sale in retail outlets.[42] What could be a better example of today's global supply chains?

A final characteristic is a particularly sharp awareness of the under-world and upperworld political contexts in which they operate. Their ability to prosper at home has, after all, been dependent upon these skills. Arguably, the failure of the first wave of overseas expansion was often precisely because the Russians did not adequately consider the bigger picture of how their intrusions into other countries would play with their rivals on the street and with the authorities. As a result, the Russian gangs abroad now tend to avoid overt displays of their criminal status, hiding behind indigenous allies, anonymous front corporations and legitimate Russian expat and business communities. They are also especially prone to seek to woo and buy local protectors within the political community.

This model reflects the mix of pressures, opportunities and resources at the Russians' disposal. Perhaps their greatest asset is Russia itself. Its underworld is a rich, diverse and dynamic source of goods and services of every kind, as is its often-compromised financial system. Furthermore, Russia's institutions often work to the criminals' advantage. The constitution's Article 61 explicitly bans the extradition of Russian citizens, offering a haven to such internationally wanted figures as the aforementioned Semyon Mogilevich. The close intertwining of business, crime, politics and the security apparatus also means that the gangsters can often rely on access to official resources, and even advance warning of foreign investigations. Beyond this, the Russian diaspora, while not a suitable foundation for empire building, does provide a convenient array of contacts and representatives; they work best for the criminals when thought of as bridges rather than bases.

Even small concentrations can prove important. The arrival of Russian tourists, retirees and sun worshippers on the coast of Spain since 1994, for example, has led to local gang outposts forming, largely in Valencia and on the Costa del Sol and the Costa Brava.[43] Here they established large-scale money-laundering operations, on the back of running tourism and real estate ventures, blending legitimate business – as, after all, many Russians want to travel to Spain and even buy property – with the illicit. Initially largely in the hands of individual criminal-entrepreneurs, these operations became dominated by the Tambovskaya or its former rival, the Malyshevskaya gang, essentially because the greatest profits were to be earned by working to launder funds for these bigger players. In other words, the initiative to join the network came at least as much from the Spanish-based entrepreneurs as from the centre, often following social contacts with network members holidaying in or retiring to Spain. A very similar pattern obtains in Cyprus, where Russian tourists and Russian business have established a safe and welcoming haven for Russian crime, especially money laundering.[44]

A tale of two underworlds

The Russians we actually arrest here tend to be pretty unimpressive:
pimps, smugglers, shoplifters. I don't see this 'Russian mafia', honestly.
British police officer, 2015[45]

This should not suggest that every Russian or Eurasian gangster expat is a smooth-operating criminal service provider. While within Russia itself there has often been a confluence of 'blue collar' and 'white collar' organised crime structures – tattooed *vory* and suited *avtoritety* alike – outside, there is a sharper differentiation between the two. The networks of the *avtoritety* connect with a wide range of criminal markets and counterparts, but will typically do so behind the scenes, interacting with their clients; these are not strategic alliances so much as the workings of the global marketplace.

There are Russian and Eurasian gangs involved in direct, street-level criminal activity, but these tend to be rather different. Many have little to do with Russia today. Often when the police or the press talk of 'Russian organised crime' in the West, they are actually talking about Georgians, Armenians and the like, who are disproportionately involved in the street-level activities of post-Soviet crime abroad. Indeed, these groups are also increasingly multi-ethnic – Russian-speaking more than simply Russian, if even that – and in the process less distinctively 'Russian' in organisation and modus operandi. For example, in the United States the cases worked by the FBI's Eurasian task forces are increasingly multi-ethnic ventures. In states such as Florida and California, Armenians are as commonly encountered in these organisations as Russians. The California-based Armenian Power grouping, for example, was at the heart of Operation Power Outage, which led to the indictment of 102 people in 2011 on a range of charges largely relating to multimillion-dollar frauds. While the detainees from Los Angeles, Miami and Denver were predominantly Armenians, they included Russians, Georgians and Anglo-Saxons – and they were also linked to Mexican gangs.[46] The use of Russian as a lingua franca for these gangs is declining and increasingly they speak English within their own ranks or in their negotiations with others. Ethnic and gang solidarity, once regarded as a key strength of the Russian gangs, is a thing of the past, with members as willing as any other criminals to cut a deal with the authorities in their own interests.[47]

These groups in the USA have especially acquired a reputation for complex and lucrative frauds of private and government medical insurance schemes. Overall, by 2011, an estimated $60–90 billion was being stolen a year from the Medicare and Medicaid budgets.[48] Russian and Eurasian gangs appear to be the largest players in this business, but even so they do not account for an absolute majority of losses. In 2010, the Armenian Mirzoyan–Terdjanian Organisation was charged with stealing $100 million from Medicare, for example.[49] Breaking the records, though, was a Ukrainian and Russian operation in Brighton Beach that involved nine clinics and allegedly conspired to defraud private medical insurance companies of $279 million over five years, until it was broken in 2012.[50] Both cases were largely proven in the courts, and their masterminds received sentences of three and twenty-five years in prison, respectively.

If the networks of high-level kingpins (often still connected with Russia) and the low-level émigré gangs represent two separate strands, they none-theless still sometimes connect. The latter often rely on surviving *vory v zakone* and *avtoritety* to provide them with the credibility, connections and even protection they might otherwise lack. The Mirzoyan–Terdjanian Organisation, for example, was under the protection of Armen Kazarian ('Pzo'), an Armenian-born *vor*.[51] Likewise, according to the authorities, an illegal gambling and money-laundering ring uncovered in New York in 2013 paid semi-retired *vor v zakone* Alimzhan 'Taivanchik' Tokhtakhounov $10 million simply for the right to use his name to reassure potential part-ners of their bona fides and scare off predators.[52] Europol has also noted the presence of such 'so-called retired leaders who do not seem to be anymore directly linked to a criminal organisation but in fact still exercise control and influence over its activities both in the EU and in the Russian Federation'.[53]

'Pax Mafiosa' or global economy?

One day, two guys are trying to kill each other, and the next day they are doing a dope deal together.
                    US Drug Enforcement Agency officer, on the Russians[54]

Claire Sterling, in her book *Crime Without Frontiers*, suggested that the world was being carved up by a global consortium of crime groups in a 'Pax Mafiosa'.[55] Likewise, former US Secretary of State John Kerry wrote in 1997 of a 'global criminal axis' composed of the 'Big Five' (Italian, Russian, Chinese, Japanese and Colombian organised crime) in league with a host of lesser powers, from Nigerians to Poles.[56] This certainly sounds fun, conjuring images of the SPECTRE organisation in James Bond films, of shadowy lords of the underworld meeting around a polished mahogany table, ideally in an extinct volcano. Sadly, or fortunately, it is far from the truth. Instead of some global criminal condominium, in the real world we see a global criminal marketplace. The very difficulty of expansion into new territories means that there is little incentive for major criminal combines to compete on anything but a local and specific level; at worst, they simply do not interact. Given that 'Russian organised crime' is no more monolithic than any other variety, particular local conflicts need not and generally do not interfere with other opportunities for mutually benefi-cial business.

Italian-based gangs were probably the first to actively reach out to their Russian counterparts in the early 1990s, seeing new scope for trading goods and favours and, in particular, the chance to launder money through a chaotic, uncontrolled and criminalised banking system. Originally this just involved the Sicilian mafia but soon they were joined by the Calabrian 'Ndrangheta, the Neapolitan Camorra and the Apulian Sacra Corona Unita. Since then, other particular partners have been the Chinese in the Russian Far East and Latin American drug gangs (from whom the Russians buy cocaine or swap it for heroin).[57]

However, this process works both ways and the very characteristics which make Russia such a congenial breeding ground for its own criminals have also sometimes made it appealing to foreign gangs. As discussed in chapter 9, in the Russian Far East, the imbalance of power between Russian and Chinese crime – in many ways a by-product of their respective economies – is increasingly evident. While the former still have consider-able street muscle as well as corrupt links with local authorities and law enforcers, their main asset is increasingly as the local agents and repre-sentatives of the Chinese gangs or dealers in the goods they seek or can offer, something only exacerbated in the post-2008 economic slowdown.

One particular bone of potential contention as of writing is the new Ussuri Bay casino–tourism resort outside Vladivostok. Intended to tap into the massive Pacific Rim gambling industry (worth $34.3 billion in 2010 and continuing to grow[58]), Ussuri Bay is explicitly being developed to compete with Macao, currently the highest-volume gambling resort in the world. (It is also worth noting that any attempt by Russian gangs to muscle into Macao are fiercely beaten back by the Triads, who dominate the city's underworld.[59]) This development has divided the Chinese themselves; those gangs – primarily mainland ones – with existing connections in Russia hope to benefit, while the expatriate Triads who see instead a threat to their Macao revenues are unenthused. It remains to be seen whether these tensions lead to conflict and whether that spills into Russia.

The Chinese case is, however, the exception; in the main foreign gangs do not seek directly to intrude onto the turfs of local Russian ones. For example, Russo-Japanese gang connections are strong and evolving, with the former providing a range of criminal goods and services for their yakuza counterparts, even though this has also been affected by the state of the world economy. As well as prostitutes and methamphetamines, for example, the Russians sell the yakuza stolen cars. According to the Japanese National Police Agency, at their peak Russian gangs shipped 63,000 stolen cars to Japan in a year.[60] However, with money being tighter in Russia since 2008 and yet luxury cars still being in demand, there has since arisen a reverse flow of new Japanese vehicles being stolen for smuggling into Vladivostok. Meanwhile, yakuza money has drifted strategically into businesses in Russia that they think would be profitable and useful. In particular, this has meant local financial institutions and companies involved in shipping (invaluable for smuggling), fishing (both for illegal fishing and also smuggling) and gambling (especially useful as money laundries).

More generally, as already discussed, Russia's still undercontrolled ports, airports and land routes make it a favoured hub for smugglers. As well as the Afghan heroin Northern Route, Russia accounts for a share of Latin American cocaine smuggling, especially as the European market becomes more important, as well as both a source and turntable for synthetic drugs. Likewise, Russia is an important route for people traffickers and smugglers, especially those operating from China. These criminals, usually linked to but not part of the mainland or Triad gangs, work through both indigenous gangs and representatives in local ethnic Chinese communities. In Moscow, for example, they largely work with Russians, because they have better contacts with local law enforcement and a lower profile. At the same time, they increasingly also use contacts in the city's ethnic Chinese community, to meet and safehouse illegal migrants before delivering them to airports or railway stations for the next stage of their travels. In short, the globalisation of the underworld has also forced the Russians to begin to share their own markets with competitors and partners from around the world.

Truly exploring the extent and forms of Russian and Russian-based criminal operations in the rest of the world, and their cooperation with other underworld players, could take up a book in its own right. Nonetheless, what is clear is that this is not a story of conquest. In 2000, journalist Robert Friedman excitedly claimed that 'the mob dominates Russia and Eastern Europe in a bear hug. It is also turning Western Europe into its financial satrapy' and went on to quote an FBI source as saying, 'In a few years . . . the Russian mob will be bigger than La Cosa Nostra in America. And perhaps GE, and Microsoft, too.'[61] Instead, what has happened is that global capitalism has embraced the Russian underworld in its 'bear hug'. The logics of market penetration, of competitive advantage and of joint ventures have shaped this post-modern criminal expansion. There were few profitable niches up for grabs within local underworlds, but the Russians discovered new ones in the global criminal service market, providing funds, services and goods for national gangs. However much the Medicare fraudsters of the USA may make, their profits pale into insignificance compared with the estimated $13 billion a year the Russian Northern Route for Afghan heroin is worth, for example,[62] or the counterfeit and untaxed cigarette trade. As one Russian police officer put it, with every appearance of pride, 'our *vory* are the best capitalists in the world'.[63]

Part Four

FUTURE

CHAPTER 13

NEW TIMES, NEW *VORY*

Be patient, Cossack, and a chieftain you'll be.

Russian proverb

There certainly has been change in Russia since Putin's accession to power in 1999–2000, even what might look like progress. Consider the case of Sergei 'Osya' Butorin, the man who arranged the death of several of the gangsters already profiled in this book, including Otari Kvantrishvili, the man who thought himself Moscow's boss of bosses, and the notorious contract killer Alexander Solonik. Butorin's past is as dark and gory as any, as he repeatedly demonstrated that he was the kind of man perfectly willing to get his own hands dirty in 'wet work': bloodshed, a piece of both KGB and gangster jargon. A former security guard and small-time thug, he gravitated towards violent protection racketeering in the late 1980s. He became the head of Moscow's Orekhovo gang in 1994, a group that specialised in extortion and violence.[1] Orekhovo was part of a wider organisation dominated by Sergei 'Silvestr' Timofeyev, but when a radio-controlled bomb scattered him and his Mercedes along a hundred-metre stretch of Moscow's Tverskaya-Yamskaya Street in 1994, 'Osya' moved quickly to grab power by the means he knew best.[2] He gathered around himself a team of sportsmen and heavies, including his left-hand man, Alexei Sherstobitov ('Lyosha the Soldier'), a former Spetsnaz special forces officer. His style was effective, if unsubtle, as befitted those gory times. On one warm summer's day later that year, for example, rival gang leader Alexander Bidzhamo ('Assyrian Alek') was sitting in a Moscow street café with three of his bodyguards when they were mowed down with machine gun fire.[3]

This was not a modus operandi bound to win friends. By 1999, Butorin's enemies had become too strong, too numerous, too determined to take him down. So, he faked his own death, even arranging his own funeral, his 'ashes' being laid to rest in a modest niche in the Nicholas-Archangel Cemetery. Meanwhile, he had cosmetic surgery to alter his appearance and fled to Spain. This was no retirement, though, and Butorin continued his criminal activities there until his arrest in 2001. He spent eight years in prison, then was extradited to Russia (despite an attempt to claim political asylum). In the past, gangsters ending up in a Russian court tended to walk, as witnesses failed to show and judges ruled unexpected mistrials. However, after a serious, meticulously run trial, Butorin was found guilty in 2011 of no fewer than twenty-nine murders and sentenced to life.[4]

So things are changing, little by little. There is a slow process taking place which is likely to see the country's 'exceptionality' diminishing. The Russian underworld's very distinctiveness reflected the unique circumstances in which it arose. As Russia acquires branches of HSBC and Starbucks, as Russians watch The Simpsons and The Sopranos, as Russians travel and study abroad, as their financial systems become more interconnected with others' and as the legacies of Soviet rule recede, then bit by bit their criminals will likewise increasingly come to resemble ours. Globalisation will some day homogenise us all. According to Alimzhan 'Taivanchik' Tokhtakhounov, wanted in the USA on multiple warrants and accused of being a vor v zakone, the change has been dramatic: 'There is no organised crime in Russia. None . . . There are hooligans, there are some lightweight bandits, there are drunks who come together to get up to something. But organised, concrete crime nowadays does not exist.'[5]

Tokhtakhounov is, perhaps, not the most dispassionate of observers, but certainly the Russian underworld of the twenty-first century does not have vory as understood in the terms of the 1970s, nor the 1950s, nor the 1930s. But the very fact that one can talk about these three iterations of the same concept immediately tells us something about the mutability of the term.

To the *blatnye*, after all, the *suki* were a complete betrayal of everything for which the *vorovskoi mir* stood, and yet by the 1960s a *vor* meant someone who internalised the values of the 'bitches'. The 'good old days' always have a particular allure, but while today's criminals may not have as formalised a code as the old *vory*, they do have their 'understandings', and their own folkways. If the successors to the *vory* truly had no code, it is hard to see how they could have done so well in such business sectors as protection, in which long-term efficiency is won through reliability and 'brand name' rather than muscle, or at least muscle alone.

Instead, in an age of market economics and pseudo-democratic politics, where power is largely disconnected from any real ideology beyond an inchoate blend of nationalisms, arguably it is rather that the *vory* have diversified, and perhaps even colonised the wider Russian elites. There are racketeers, drug traffickers, people smugglers and gunrunners – but there is also a deepening connection with the worlds of politics and business. Today's *avtoritety* are exploiting the opportunities of Russia's cannibalistic capitalism, and likewise the state itself, or at least its agents, are exploiting their own criminal opportunities in an increasingly organised way. In 2016, for example, the police raided the apartment of one of their own senior officers, Colonel Dmitry Zakharchenko, ironically enough the acting head of a department within its anti-corruption division. There they found \$123 million: so much money that the investigators had to pause the search while they found a container large enough to hold all that cash.[6] He denies any wrongdoing and as of writing the case is ongoing, but a widespread assumption is that it was not all his, but rather that he was the holder of the common fund, the *obshchak*, of a gang of 'werewolves'. Werewolves? Organised crime groups within the police forces are enough of a problem that its members even have their own nickname in common parlance: *oboroten*, 'werewolf'.

The word *vor* may be in disuse, terms such as *obshchak* may have new meanings, the very codes and behavioural patterns of the criminals may have again adapted, but in many ways this reflects not the disappearance of the *vorovskoi mir*, so much as renewed adaptation, a fading of the boundaries between that 'thieves' world' and everybody else's. The *vory* and their values have moved to the heart of the state, in the culmination of a process begun in the first half of the twentieth century.

Deep crime and the deep state

Grinda cited a 'thesis' by Alexander Litvinenko, the former Russian intel-
ligence official who worked on [organised crime] issues before he died in
late 2006 in London from poisoning under mysterious circumstances,
that the Russian intelligence and security services – Grinda cited the
Federal Security Service (FSB), the Foreign Intelligence Service (SVR),
and military intelligence (GRU) – control [organised crime] in Russia.
Grinda stated that he believes this thesis is accurate . . . Grinda said that
he believes the FSB is 'absorbing' the Russian mafia . . .

US diplomatic cable, 8 February 2010[7]

Spanish national court prosecutor José 'Pepe' Grinda González, a particular
scourge of Russian gangs in his country, infamously dubbed Russia a 'mafia
state', not least in this leaked cable. It is certainly a catchy epithet, but what
does it actually mean? To Grinda, rather than being under the control of
the criminals, the Kremlin (or at least the security apparatus) is a shadowy
puppeteer making the gangs dance on its strings. In practice, the truth is
rather that the relationship between organised crime and the state at local
and national levels is complex, nuanced and often strikingly cooperative. It
is as simplistic to suggest that organised crime outright controls the Kremlin
as that it is controlled by it. Rather, it prospers under Putin because it can
go with the grain of his system.

There is, needless to say, a very high level of corruption, which provides a
very conducive environment for organised crime. Even President Putin has
acknowledged the problem and vowed to 'eliminate the root causes of corruption and punish particular officials', adding, 'We defeated oligarchy. We will
surely defeat corruption.'[8] However, there is little evidence he truly intends –
or at least, has so far intended – more than a public show of resolution and a
periodic purge of officials sufficiently junior and far outside his personal
circle to be disposable scapegoats. The relationship between the elite and the
gangsters is not just one of buyer and bought, but typically of symbiosis or
deeply rooted and mutually profitable relationships, which are often long
term. In the 1995 elections for governor of the Ural region, for example, the
Uralmash crime group openly supported the successful candidate, Eduard
Rossel. He is then said to have asserted that its members no longer engaged in
crime – reportedly contrary to the views of his own police.[9] Did Rossel 'run'
Uralmash, or did Uralmash 'own' Rossel? The answer, of course, is that neither

was the case. Instead, expert observers believe it could have been something from which both sides expected to benefit and which lasted precisely so long as those expectations endured. Meanwhile in Moscow, persistent gossip has linked Mayor Yury Luzhkov with the capital's crime syndicates, notably Solntsevo. He has always denied any such connections and has never been charged or convicted of any criminal offence. Although unproven, these rumours were were reflected in a classified US diplomatic cable:

> Luzhkov used criminal money to support his rise to power and has been involved with bribes and deals regarding lucrative construction contracts throughout Moscow. XXXXXXXXXXXX told us that Luzhkov's friends and associates (including recently deceased crime boss Vyacheslav Ivankov) ... are 'bandits' ... the Moscow government has links to many different criminal groups and it regularly takes cash bribes from businesses. The people under Luzhkov maintain these criminal connections.[10]

Luzhkov was forced to step down in 2010, though, and the day of the autonomous political–criminal fiefdom has largely passed. St Petersburg, for example, had been the cradle of the powerful Tambovskaya group described earlier in the book, whose boss, Vladimir Kumarin, who also goes by the name Vladimir Barsukov, became known as the 'night governor'. In his days as deputy mayor in the 1990s, Vladimir Putin had reportedly liaised with the Tambovskaya and Barsukov had since then built a business empire through the city and region.[11] However, the very public power of a gangster in Putin's home city was an abiding embarrassment and vulnerability for the president and in 2007 some 300 police commandos were deployed to arrest him. Prosecutor General Yury Chaika feared leaks so much that he kept the St Petersburg police largely in the dark, flew in special forces from Moscow on Emergencies Ministry aircraft – not even ones from the Ministry of Internal Affairs – and later said that 'if we had acted differently, [Barsukov] would have been warned' because 'we have discovered leaks in the prosecutor general's office and city government, as well as the police and security agencies'.[12] In 2009, Barsukov was convicted of fraud and money laundering and sentenced to fourteen years in prison.[13]

Perhaps the last remaining fiefdom outside Chechnya was far to St Petersburg's south, in Makhachkala, capital city of the North Caucasus republic of Dagestan.[14] Since 1998, it had been run and all but owned by

Said Amirov. It took a special man to control what was arguably the most unruly city in Dagestan, itself in many ways the most unruly republic in the Russian Federation. Amirov appeared virtually indestructible in every sense of the word. He survived at least a dozen assassination attempts (some say fifteen), including one in 1993 that left him in a wheelchair, with a bullet lodged in his spine, and a rocket attack on his offices in 1998. Just as important, he appeared politically unassailable. Despite continued allegations of brutality, corruption and crime links, he saw out four Dagestani leaders and three Russian presidencies.

No wonder that, as well as 'Roosevelt' – because of his wheelchair – he was known as 'Said the Undying', after Koshchei the Undying, an immortal villain from Russian folklore. When Moscow finally decided to move against him, in 2013, it had to consider the strength of his local power base. This included not only his own private army of bodyguards but also considerable influence in the Dagestani police and, allegedly, a drug-trafficking gang known as the Kolkhozniki ('Collective Farmers'). As a result, his arrest was closer to a raid in hostile territory, spearheaded by FSB special forces brought in from outside the republic, backed with armoured vehicles and helicopter gunships. Such was the concern about his sway over the local authorities, Amirov was immediately airlifted to Moscow, along with his nephew and nine other suspects.

If Moscow had been happy enough to let him build his fiefdom for fifteen years, why did it turn against him? Part of the reason appears to have been that he fell foul of the powerful Investigatory Committee, owing to his involvement in the 2011 murder of one of its regional heads, Arsen Gadzhibekov. Likewise, although Amirov was convicted on the basis of a different case, his plot to use a surface-to-air missile to shoot down a plane carrying Sagid Murtazaliyev, head of the Dagestan Pension Fund, started the process rolling. Amirov was sentenced to ten years in a maximum security prison colony – the prosecution asked for thirteen – and the loss of his state awards (including some, ironically enough, given him by the FSB). This was unprecedented for one of the Kremlin's former local strongmen, and a cautionary tale for other local kleptocrats.

But even the Investigatory Committee could not reach in and pluck someone like Amirov from his fortress-home and deposit him in Lefortovo prison without a political decision having been made in the Kremlin. The very attributes which once seemed to make Amirov such an admirable local proxy – his skill at managing the complex ethnic and factional politics of Dagestan, his ruthlessness, his network spanning both the underworld and the upperworld, his industrial-scale corruption, his acquisitive ambition for himself and his family – all had become liabilities.

The modern Russian state is a much stronger force than in the 1990s, and jealous of its political authority. The gangs which prosper in modern Russia tend to do so by working with rather than against the state, and a new political generation has risen to power dependent for their futures on the Kremlin's patronage rather than local underworld contacts. In this respect, if Russia is truly ruled by a 'deep state' – the term comes from the way Turkey for so long seemed to be run by an inner elite within an elite, controlling politics behind the scenes[15] – then there are also 'deep crime' structures. An inventive study by Michael Rochlitz of the Higher School of Economics in Moscow, for example, found an apparently clear correlation between local government officials using illegal methods to take over businesses and their success in bringing out the vote for Putin.[16] In other words, do well by the Kremlin, and the Kremlin will turn a blind eye. Connecting political figures, government officials, business leaders and criminal kingpins, these loose networks of patronage and mutual interest are very difficult to plot – Luzhkov's alleged links, for example, are a matter of rumour and conjecture – but they undoubtedly exist and play a role in shaping Russian policy. But only when they remember that perennial truism: the state is the biggest gang in town.

'It's all business'

From wild, barbaric methods [organised crime] moves to civilised ones, becomes a part of the state machine and to a certain extent contributes to the country's prosperity.

Criminologist Alexander Gurov, 1996[17]

I remember once talking to a Russian entrepreneur whose business seemed mainly to involve unloading poorly made counterfeit CDs onto the market on behalf of some Ukrainian gangsters out of Donetsk. When asked about how he felt about working with organised crime, he airily waved the suggestion away: 'It's all business, just business.' A key characteristic of today's Russian organised crime is the scale and depth of its interpenetration with the (sometimes only seemingly) legitimate economy. It is impossible to deny that this is a considerable problem, with criminals controlling financial, commercial and industrial enterprises, exerting influence over government contracts and simply stealing businesses and assets. However, it is equally impossible to put any kind of meaningful figure on it. An apocryphal claim that organised crime controlled '40 per cent of the Russian economy' in the 1990s continues to do the rounds, but largely only because there is no authoritative data to replace it.[18] This is a question both epistemological and ontological: what does 'controlled by organised crime' mean and how can we determine this anyway? If a million dollars was earned through embezzlement, then reinvested in legitimate business, would the revenue that accrued be dirty money? And what about the money made by reinvesting those profits? When does 'dirt' fade? Unpicking dirty from clean money in Russia is a hopeless task, not least given that in the 1990s it was next to impossible to make serious amounts of money without engaging in practices that in the West would be questionable at best, downright illegal at worst. For instance, during 1994, every day an average of 104 enterprises were privatised – and 107 privatisation-related crimes committed.[19]

Since then, though, the overt role of gangsterism in most of the economy has undoubtedly, if unevenly, been declining. 'Raiding' – the seizure of assets and companies through physical or legal coercion – remains a serious problem,[20] but it is increasingly conducted through the courts or state apparatus instead of by means of violence or its threat. A British-based businessman told me that he had twice had to fly to Moscow at a moment's notice in 2009 because of attempts to steal a property of his. The first time, thugs appeared at the door and bulled past the single security guard. The businessman had to call in favours from the local police to have them expelled. The second time, though, the raiders came in the form of lawyers and bailiffs, bearing documents alleging that the property had been signed into their possession to discharge a (non-existent) debt. Whereas getting rid of the thugs took a few hours and, I suspect, a moderate bribe to the police chief, dealing with the legal challenge took weeks and much more paid out in legal fees and illegal inducements alike. At least until the 2014 economic slowdown, whose effects are covered in the next chapter, business people had been reporting that overt protection racketeering was largely a declining threat except in certain specific cases: the more backward provinces, the most vulnerable enterprises, and those which teeter on the margins of illegality such as kiosk and market vendors and stores selling counterfeit or untaxed goods. Overall, the use of the law instead of extrajudicial methods to resolve business disputes increased from the late 2000s.[21]

'Regular' financial crime is a growing problem, though. The 2007 PricewaterhouseCoopers Global Economic Crime Survey reported that 59 per cent of the Russian companies surveyed had suffered from economic crimes in the past two years, 10 per cent up from 2005, with the average reporting direct financial damage at $12.8 million, suggesting that the total direct cost of economic crime in Russia had more than quadrupled in the period 2005–7.[22] Perversely, though, this is in some sense reassuring as these crimes were overwhelmingly 'civil': contracts were secured by bribes, employees fiddled the books, and business partners padded invoices. Direct evidence of organised crime, whether violence, intimidation or signs of criminal conspiracies, was strikingly absent.

However, the interpenetration of upperworld and underworld in Russia is still worryingly evident and problematic within the business realm. Most senior *avtoritety* – and even many more junior figures – maintain a portfolio of interests ranging from the essentially legitimate, through the 'grey' (for example, legal storefronts also selling untaxed goods, or a legal factory using smuggled raw materials or trafficked and indentured labour) to the wholly illicit. They are, after all, interested in money, power and security and are willing to turn their hand to whatever maximises them. This means that they usually have public roles within the legitimate economy and will shift their attention and funds between business interests as whim and opportunity dictate.

'Ironing the firm'

The Magnitsky case is . . . the clearest case study of how the whole system has been criminalised in Russia, of how officials steal from their own country, how they then murder people who stand in their way, and then how the whole system protects them when they get caught.

Bill Browder, Western businessman, 2011[23]

Under Putin, corrupt officials have continued their ascent back to the commanding heights they occupied in Soviet times. A particularly heinous case has become known as the Magnitsky affair after its greatest victim, but it really involved a British businessman of American descent, Bill Browder, and his Hermitage Capital Management fund.[24] Established in 1996 to take advantage of new business opportunities in Russia, it did very well for itself and its principal. Between 1996 and 2006, it was one of the biggest foreign investment funds operating in Russia and Browder himself was making hundreds of millions of dollars.

Since the 1980s, when tourists began to become more common in Moscow and Leningrad, Russian gangsters have used the phrase 'ironing the firm' to mean stealing or extorting money out of foreigners. It was perhaps inevitable that, with so much money in play, Hermitage Capital Management (HCM) fell due for an 'ironing'. Although Browder had been an outspoken fan of Putin's in the past, his business model often depended on a form of shareholder activism on steroids, challenging the corrupt and inefficient management of many of the biggest players in the Russian economy. Given the degree to which his targets were clients of even bigger players within the political system, Browder began to be viewed as an irritant, and in 2006 he was barred entry from Russia as a 'security threat'. That left HCM vulnerable and in 2007 police raided its offices and carried away documents, computers and the all-important company seals. These seals were then used to falsify evidence of fraud, even while officially being held as evidence themselves. On the basis of fines levied as a result, claims were made fraudulently on HCM's behalf for a tax refund of 5.4 billion rubles ($230 million) that was, with suspicious speed (given everyone else's experience with the Russian tax office), disbursed to three phantom companies that were used to funnel the money to the conspiracy's masterminds.

Browder's tax specialist, the Russian Sergei Magnitsky, reported the fraud and began investigating it with dogged perseverance. For his pains, he was arrested and imprisoned, and subjected to a regime of beatings, psychological pressure and denial of medical care that led to his death in prison in 2009. Meanwhile, two small-time criminals, a robber and a sawmill worker who had once been convicted of manslaughter, were arrested and convicted of somehow managing to mastermind this colossal and complex fraud. Both pleaded guilty and were handed the minimum sentences of five years. No trace of the money was found in their bank accounts, and the police then claimed that as all relevant documents had been destroyed in a mysterious truck crash, it would be impossible to track the money.

As of writing, Browder is enthusiastically pursuing the case through courts and the media outside Russia, but, however murderously egregious, it is by no means unique, except in Browder's ability and willingness to make it such a public cause. Instead, it demonstrates the interpenetration of corruption, organised crime, business and politics. Foreigners – 'the firm' – once had a special status, the geese which could lay golden eggs and who thus could be stolen from but not scared away. As foreign investment flowed into Russia, and Russian money flowed out, as companies merged and expats and Russians formed a new interstitial class of cosmopolitan managers and business people, 'the firm's' old sense of distinctiveness began to disappear. What the HCM case truly demonstrates, then, is the degree to which, just as the Russian language has become colonised by many borrowings from criminal slang, so too have regular Russian business practices become suffused with underworld habits and methods.

The gangsterisation of business

The saying 'the mafia is immortal' seems relevant for our country to this day. The wild 90s have gone into history, with their characteristics. Many legends of the criminal world, whom I knew personally, are now in the ground. Contract murders have become fewer, although there are still shoot-outs, even in the centre of the capital. The racket has disappeared in its hard form, although there are kickbacks and raids. The 'arrows' [sit-downs] have been transformed into quite decent negotiations with the participation of financiers and lawyers. Disputes with gunfights are a thing of the past. Now business does not solve its conflicts with the help of bandits and red-hot irons, but in courts . . . hence the high level of corruption.

Valery Karyshev, 2017[25]

In the late 1990s, murder was a depressingly common way of resolving business disputes.[26] The notorious 'aluminium wars' of the early 1990s, for example, saw thugs occupying factories, a string of murders, and lurid accounts of organised-crime links across the metals industries.[27] Contract killings remained frequent – according to Professor Leonid Kondratyuk of the MVD's Scientific Research Institute, even in the early Putin years they were 'seeing somewhere between 500 and 700 such killings annually . . . But those are just the murders we know for sure were contract killings. In reality, it's probably two to three times higher.'[28] Despite that, though, there has been a steady development in Russian business culture. A growing proportion, especially of younger business people and entrepreneurs, are eager to escape the old ways. Out of conviction, a desire for a safer and more predictable business climate, or to 'rejoin the West', as they see it, they eschew these methods when they can. However, cultural change takes time, and while murder is much less a feature of the business scene than it was – though still not unknown – corporate espionage, the use of political influence to swing contracts and stymie rivals, and bribery remain commonplace and continue to connect the worlds of crime and business. Likewise, the new generation crime boss is more likely than ever also to be active within the realms of legitimate and 'grey' business.

All this makes it extraordinarily difficult to distinguish between the genuine business person and the gangster-entrepreneur when one moves beyond the thugs at the bottom of the food chain. It also makes it especially hard to identify the sources of funds given the scope for considerable 'internal laundering' between businesses. Many of these gangster-entrepreneurs are happy to use the court system to resolve their disputes, not least given the extent to which money rather than justice often determines judgments. They are also frequently unwilling to turn to more coercive methods for fear of escalating conflicts and also attracting unfortunate attention (including from the West: many enjoy the opportunity to travel, shop and invest abroad).

This does not make them convinced champions of the rule of law. They appreciate a degree of predictability within the system, as well as – now that they are rich – a state apparatus dedicated to preserving property rights. However, they are also well aware that an honest and well-functioning police force and a dedicated and incorruptible judiciary would be a serious threat to them. As a result, they have a strong interest in preserving the status quo and their ability to use violence or corruption as and when their circumstances dictate. This collective commitment to the status quo preserves their power, but it also sets rules and boundaries, as do the very economics of the market. Additionally, it means that when times get harder or when the legal institutions look less able to play their part, gangster habits can revive themselves. As will be discussed in the following chapters, since Putin's return to the Kremlin in 2012, after a four-year interregnum while his puppet-president Dmitry Medvedev kept his chair warm for him, things have changed.[29] A combination of economic pressures, the breakdown in relations with the West after the 2014 annexation of Crimea and invasion of south-eastern Ukraine, and the impact of consequent Western sanctions, has meant that at the time of writing many of the bad old ways are slowly reasserting themselves.

'Everything and everyone is for sale'

In Russia, I can buy whoever and whatever I want.

'Roman', Russian *avtoritet*, 2012[30]

The economics of the market are also visible in organised crime's ability to move beyond simple corruption and into hiring or acquiring the people, skills and assets it needs for its operations. After all, the underworld is an economy in its own right. One as extensive as Russia's inevitably develops a complex array of service industries and market niches. The first and most obvious need was for people who were able credibly, willingly and effectively to use violence and there remains a strong supply of would-be thugs and leg breakers. For more sophisticated purposes, organised crime looked to sportsmen and martial artists – many of the first gangs came from sports clubs, such as the weightlifters and wrestlers who formed Moscow's Lyubertsy gang – or to current and former police and military personnel. The notorious Alexander Solonik ('Alexander the Great' or 'Superkiller') was a former soldier and OMON riot policeman who became a killer for hire, specialising in assassinating well-guarded gangsters. He later confessed to three such murders: Viktor 'Kalina' Nikiforov, Valery 'Globus' Dlugach and Vladislav 'Bobon' Vinner. He also became something of a legend, thanks to feats such as being able to shoot two-handedly (earning himself the additional nickname 'Sasha the Macedonian', as that is known as shooting 'Macedonian style' for reasons unclear); fighting his way out of a police station in 1994, killing seven security officers before finally being overpowered; and being one of the very few people ever to break out of Moscow's Matrosskaya Tishina ('Sailor's Silence') prison in 1995.[31]

While he retained links to the Orekhovo gang, of which he had once been a member, and thus the Solntsevo network into which it was assimilated, Solonik worked for a wide range of other groups, including their main rivals, the Chechens and the Izmailovskaya. This was not considered to be a problem, just a reflection of the free market of the Russian underworld. However, when he escaped prison to Greece and began to set up as a gang leader in his own right, he became a player rather than a service provider. He lost his neutral status and it fell to his former patrons, the remnants of the Orekhovskaya–Medvedkovskaya gang (one of the fragments of the Orekhovo) to eliminate him, which they did in 1997.[32]

Solonik knew full well what he was doing, but in modern Russia it is sometimes difficult even to know if you are working for the gangsters. The assassination of organised-crime boss Vasily Naumov in 1997 came as a particular embarrassment to the St Petersburg police when it emerged that his bodyguards were members of Saturn, one of their elite rapid-response squads, moonlighting and apparently engaged legitimately through a front company.[33]

This represents just one of the many ways the criminals are able to buy services from state agencies. At least it was legal, unlike a case in 2002 in which it came to light that special executive jets run by the air force for senior Defence Ministry officials were instead being chartered illegally by members of the Izmailovo–Golyanovskaya gang.[34] Services routinely engaged by the criminals range from the serious, such as wiretapping by the security agencies, through to the near-trivial, such as paying off an official for the right to place a flashing blue emergency-services light on your car. These *migalki*, a bone of contention for many Russian motorists, are widely abused by officials, business people – and gangsters – to allow them to run red lights and generally evade the traffic rules. Recently curtailed, they nonetheless epitomise a culture in which cash and connections can buy a degree of impunity from the rules, something the criminals eagerly exploit.

Some of the computer specialists – cybercriminals and cybersecurity experts alike – the gangs employ also work for the government, but most do not, forming part of a wider hacker world, with an estimated 10,000–20,000 people working in this underground sector.[35] Hackers themselves rarely fit the model of organised crime: their 'structures' are generally collectives and little more than markets.[36] Instead of becoming members of gangs, they tend instead to be outside consultants, brought in as and when needed for specific jobs, as will be discussed later.

Beyond that, the increasing sophistication of criminal operations, especially their shift towards white-collar crime, has meant a need for financial specialists, to manage both their own funds and also their economic crimes. The most infamous remains Semyon Mogilevich, who has established for himself a distinctive role as the mobster's money manager of choice. One of the FBI's most wanted fugitives and the subject of an Interpol red notice international arrest warrant, Mogilevich has been indicted on money-laundering and fraud charges but is living comfortably and openly in Moscow. As a Russian citizen, he is safe from extradition. (He is also a citizen of Ukraine, Greece and Israel.) His twenty-year career laundering and moving money for numerous organised crime groups – in the process making himself indispensable to many – provides perhaps even greater security. Indeed, when Moscow police arrested him by accident in 2008 (because he was at the time going under the name Sergei Shnaider), I heard from several police officers that the commander in question received a ferocious dressing down for landing the government with an embarrassing dilemma: how to release him without looking weak or foolish? He was eventually arraigned in a closed court, and the case was dismissed for lack of evidence.[37]

However, despite overblown descriptions as 'the most dangerous mobster in the world'[38] – his FBI wanted notice says he should be 'considered armed and dangerous' – Mogilevich is not so much a gangster in his own right, although he has been accused of very substantial frauds, as first and foremost the man gangsters turn to when they need someone to handle their money. In this respect, he is akin to such figures as Lucy Edwards, the former Bank of New York vice president who, with her husband (both naturalised Russian émigrés), was convicted of laundering some $7 billion from Russia between 1996 and 1999.[39] These are the specialists who facilitate global criminal operations.

When is a *vor* no longer a *vor*?

'*The* vory *are gone, and with them their laws, their culture.*'
'*Today's criminals are just criminals, they don't have the same rules as the old* vory.*'
'*Whether or not the* vory *really were anything like the image we have in the media, with their code and their language, that's all in the past now.*'
Conversations with three Muscovites[40]

Of the conversations quoted above, the first was with a serving police officer, the second with a long-since-retired hanger-on of the criminal world, and the third with a journalist. Yet they all share a strikingly similar perspective. Interestingly, while there are still people who call themselves *vory v zakone*, especially the *apelsiny*, the term *vor* itself has fallen into disuse. How can there be a *vorovskoi mir* only of chieftains and leaders, without footsoldiers?

That Russian organised crime has spawned such a complex service economy says much about its scale, sophistication and stability. In the process, the old *vory v zakone* are dying out, at least in their own terms. Once, if you wore a criminal tattoo to which they felt you were not entitled, you ran the risk of having that patch of skin forcibly removed with a knife – if you were lucky; now you just pay to get such a tattoo. As they made money and were freed from the shadow of the Gulag, the *vory v zakone* lost their old culture and cohesion. Crime once was something that defined people, that set them off from the rest of society. Now, it is just another route to power and prosperity.

Yet the *vory* should not be written off quite so quickly. Beyond street-level gangsterism, there is no longer the same space for the old ways, admittedly. The jump from *blatnoi* to *suka* was in many ways less dramatic, certainly less visible, than the transition of the marginal 1970s gangster or even the emerging 1980s wheeler-dealer and protection racketeer into the modern criminal businessman. But there are carry-overs, and the progression has been a relatively direct one: from preying on the black market, to engagement with it, through to involvement in all aspects of the economy, formal and informal. No longer a confined and beleaguered minority dependent on cohesion and violence for their survival, they do not need the same means of forming and maintaining their own community. The code lives on, faintly, in the form of the 'understandings' dominant within the underworld, not least the sense that an 'honest thief' should still be true to his word. The custom of *skhodki* sit-downs survives, but, interestingly enough, I have heard the phrase used by seemingly legitimate business people in the context of meeting rival companies, with no hint of irony or macho posture.

A *vor* I once spoke to bitterly complained that 'we have been infected by the rest of you and we are dying', but the infection has passed both ways. Many of the organising and operating principles of upperworld Russia follow the lead of the underworld. The concept of *krysha* ('protection') is central in business and politics, especially given the prevalence of 'raiding'. The law in such situations means nothing, the power of your *krysha* everything. There is the sense that one's word means more than a written contract, the belief that, ultimately, 'man is wolf to man' and that winning is more important than following the spirit or letter of the law. Maybe, as the closing chapters of this book will explore, it is not that the *vory* have disappeared so much as that everyone is now a *vor*, and the *vorovskoi mir* ultimately won.

CHAPTER 14

MAFIYA EVOLUTIONS

When it thunders, even the thief crosses himself.

Russian proverb

Known above all for his insurgent status within the *vorovskoi mir* (see chapter 11), the career of Azeri gangster Rovshan Dzhaniyev demonstrates the impact of some of the shocks and forces which have been shaping the Russian underworld in recent years. This is ironic since in many ways he seems to have been unaware of them, believing his destiny was entirely his to make, but this probably reflects his decisive, not to say impulsive, manner and a belief, which several who met him noted, that the world was his for the taking. In 1992, when he was just seventeen, his father – ironically enough, a police officer – was murdered by a local gangster. When the killer was apprehended in 1996, Dzhaniyev smuggled a gun to the courtroom and shot him there and then. With a twitch of his trigger finger, he established his credentials as a fearless man of action and one who understands traditions of honour and revenge. Released from prison in Azerbaijan after a lenient two years, reflecting the court's view of his mental state at the time (and perhaps also some sympathy for what he had done), he drifted into organised crime. In 2000, he shot a rival godfather on the street in Baku; again, he spent only a short time in prison, ostensibly on account of his mental health.

The impatient young gun rose on the backs of a series of convenient and mysterious (or maybe not so mysterious) murders as he moved from

Azerbaijan to Ukraine and then Russia: of his patron Mir Seymur in 2003, of Azeri kingpin Elchin Aliyev ('Elchin Yevlakh') in St Petersburg, then of Hikmet Mukhtarov and Chingiz Ahundov, key figures in Moscow's narcotics trade, who also controlled the city's fruit and vegetable markets. These, incidentally, have since 1991 been lucrative targets, fought over regularly by the Caucasus gangsters in particular, given how much of the produce comes from their regions. In 1992, Azeris controlled the three main markets – Cheryomushky, Severny and Tsaritskinsky[1] – and, while the geography of the city's wholesalers has changed over time, bloody wars for them have raged periodically ever since.[2] It is worth remembering that the Cosa Nostra made millions from their control of New York's Fulton Street Fish Market through most of the twentieth century.[3] Control of access to any commodity is valuable, and the markets are also great distribution hubs for all kinds of illegal commodities, from drugs to counterfeit goods.

By 2006, Dzhaniyev had a substantial stake in Moscow as well as Azerbaijan. However, his interests were almost exclusively in the criminal realm; he never made the jump out of pure gangsterdom into the worlds of politics and business. His gang was, as noted before, multi-ethnic, but united both by Dzhaniyev's own charisma and also by a collective impatience with the underworld status quo. These were relatively young men in a hurry, who were tired of waiting for their turn at the top, or those who otherwise had found their careers becalmed.

In 2008, the global financial crisis had knock-on effects throughout the underworld, and in Russia it forced many of the smaller gangs and those less diversified in their economic interests into retreat. Competition for assets sharpened, and those groups without powerful political connections lost out. Dzhaniyev had never bothered cultivating a *krysha* in Moscow, and he paid for this with a number of reversals, such as the closure of the Cherkizovo market in eastern Moscow in 2009. Dzhaniyev largely dominated this massive and ramshackle bazaar, using it to sell illegal goods and services and demanding tribute from traders. This was a time when the city was looking to clean up its image, though, and he lacked the political connections to be able to prevent Moscow City Council from shutting the market down, taking a substantial economic hit in the process.

Dzhaniyev was still looking for shortcuts into the big league, though, and seems to have decided that taking down Aslan 'Ded Khasan' Usoyan was the way to do this. His expectation seems to have been that this would shatter Usoyan's network and allow him to take over many of its members and businesses. He may have been behind the 2010 assassination attempt on Usoyan, but certainly this became an increasingly bitter struggle. When Dzhaniyev and his lieutenant Dzhemo Mikeladze sponsored men to be crowned as *vory v zakone* at a *skhodka* in Dubai in December 2012 – part of a ceremony at which sixteen were elevated – Usoyan repudiated this as not in accordance with the rules of the *vorovskoi mir*.[4] (Technically true, but it is doubtful if anyone cares much these days.) Presumably from the perspective that an enemy's enemy is, if not a friend, at least useful, Usoyan's blood foe Tariel Oniani then backed the coronations, even though earlier that year he had wrested control of the Pokrovsky vegetable warehouses – one of Moscow's main produce centres – from Dzhaniyev.[5]

Usoyan probably had the firepower to take on Dzhaniyev, had he been willing to escalate, but his vulnerability was precisely that he had so much more to lose. Such a war would likely have forced the state to respond, and also left him vulnerable to Oniani, a much greater threat. Instead, he had to rely on underworld politics, such as the following missive distributed in 2013:

By the Thief's Custom, the Thief's Way is forever spread! Peace, prosperity and prosperity for the Thieves and Our Home from the Lord God! We greet you as respectable people who sincerely support the course of Thieves and the life of Thieves. By this message, we Thieves warn you prisoners that Rovshan 'Lenkoran' and Gia Uglav 'Takhi' are whores, seducing people in our house and spreading disorder amongst our people. Arrestees, take into account that those who help them and their evil spirits, both in their deeds and in their image, are essentially the same, they too are whores, and so everyone who considers themselves a decent prisoner should act accordingly. We will limit ourselves to this, wishing you all the best from the Lord God, protection and unity, let Our House prosper.[6]

Dzhaniyev, much more a *vor* of the old school, had less to lose, cared less about the implications of his actions, and didn't see as far into the future. Although it is unlikely he was behind Usoyan's actual death in 2013, he certainly did not at first try and quash the idea, and, in the short term, it did nothing to weaken his reputation. For a criminal with a relatively small network and resources, notoriety can be a crucial asset, as it means that he is taken more seriously by his peers. This encourages more disgruntled criminals to join with him, creating something of a self-fulfilling prophecy. Nonetheless, it is also a dangerous thing to be an insurgent. Whether he had a hand in Usoyan's death or not, Dzhaniyev made a trebly convenient scapegoat: plausible, inconvenient and not so strong that moving against him could trigger some wider mob war.[7] Shortly after, one of Dzhaniyev's closest allies in Abkhazia was gunned down in Sukhumi,[8] and another was murdered in Moscow.[9] Dzhaniyev went to ground; according to rumour he was variously killed in Turkey, arrested in Azerbaijan, and alive and well in Dubai.[10]

Then, in 2014, Russia's annexation of Crimea and the subsequent rapid worsening of its relations with the West led to a sudden economic crisis. Again, gangs without allies, political cover and deep pockets were vulnerable. Amongst the criminals who had defected to Dzhaniyev were a number involved in the heroin trade, a key potential revenue stream Dzhaniyev considered trying to tap, but he was impatient with the complex logistics involved. Such ideas came to nothing, and so Dzhaniyev was suddenly not only a pariah but, even more seriously, an impoverished one. In such circumstances, there seems to be very little honour amongst thieves. People began to redefect away from his gang, and some of them knew his whereabouts and his plans. The end was near.

He had actually been moving between Azerbaijan and Turkey, but rumours of his earlier murder in Istanbul proved prescient: in August 2016, he was being driven through the centre of the city when, while stopped at a traffic light, his Range Rover was riddled with bullets from a silenced assault rifle.[11] But in any case, the day he dropped out of sight, his enemies, with the usual piranha sensitivities of organised crime, scented blood and began settling old scores and seizing assets. For example, Mikeladze was arrested shortly after Usoyan's death and sent to prison on drug charges; his other henchman, 'Timokha', fled back to his native Belarus but was shot and killed there in 2014.[12] By the end of 2016, Dzhaniyev's gang was essentially dead.

Obviously Dzhaniyev's own nature pretty much ensured that this was going to be a short and bloody tale. But it is also striking how far its trajectory was shaped by some key external developments, blows taken and chances missed. Organised crime in Russia and Eurasia is still powerful, of course, even if in many places transformed from its 'bandit' roots. However, such progress as has been made – and the final chapter will try to reach some conclusions about that – depends to a considerable extent on continued stability within the underworld, and how it continues to adapt to new pressures and new opportunities.

The first big shock: 2008

Until 2008, we thought that so long as we paid off the cops and the officials, everything was going to go great, that the money would keep coming in, that the future was safe.

Son of an *avtoritet*, 2014[13]

As of writing, in late 2017, the Russian underworld is at once relatively calm – the odd assassination notwithstanding – and under growing pressure. It is by no means certain that a new round of major criminal conflicts is coming and, even if it does erupt, it will not reach the same pitch or be as indiscriminate as those of the 1990s. Yet such a prospect is closer than at any time since then. One could draw a parallel with Europe on the eve of the First World War. There are ambitious, rising powers with little stake in the status quo, eager to win their 'place in the sun'; there are others desperate to maintain that status quo, but fearing a war that would be at best expensive, at worst ruinous. After all, some – let's call them the Ottoman Empires of the underworld – now no longer have the practical strength to match their status and possessions. Meanwhile, international rivalries are sublimated and fought out by proxy in the imperial struggle for colonies. There are limits to the explanatory power of that analogy, but it is certainly the case that the current underworld status quo is under threat, in part because of revanchist or insurgent groups such as the late, unlamented Dzhaniyev's, in part because of the imperial aspirations of figures such as Tariel Oniani, in part because once-mighty combines such as the Far Eastern Association of Thieves are in decline, and in part because of the scramble over new criminal opportunities.

The durability of the post-1990s underworld situation, and the division of spoils it embodied, depended on the extent to which it accurately reflected the relative strength of various gangs. As one Russian police officer told me, 'so long as there was a balance between guns and *krysha* on the one hand and revenue on the other, all went well'.[14] The world turns, though, and all empires decay; the status quo was inevitably going to become anachronistic, even under ideal circumstances. The lack of social mobility, epitomised by the rise of the Azeri upstart Dzhaniyev, is just one example of what Marxists might consider the inherent contradictions of this criminal order. In any case, these were not to be ideal circumstances, as the Russian underworld would be reshaped by a series of challenges, most notably the 2008 global economic slowdown and the 2014 Russian economic crisis, and the emergence of new opportunities.

The global financial crisis in 2008 had a serious impact on Russia, especially given the dependence of its economy on oil and gas exports.[15] The ruble tumbled in value (despite the government burning through more than $130 billion of its foreign exchange reserves to prop it up) and real incomes fell almost 7 per cent in just twelve months. After years of impressive growth, Russia fell into recession, with serious impacts on the underworld. Many gangs suddenly found themselves in trouble: there was far less scope for protection racketeering and, as government contracts were suspended or scaled down, opportunities for embezzlement likewise declined. However, others benefited from the situation. Sometimes this was because their main assets were in foreign currencies (which now were worth more rubles) or they had control of still-valuable physical assets. At other times it was because their main businesses were suited to the new environment: dealing in counterfeit or smuggled goods, for example, as people looked to cheaper ways of maintaining their lifestyles, or loan-sharking. The result was a flurry of small-scale conflicts and consolidations. Some smaller gangs were forced to integrate into larger, more prosperous networks, often simply so that their chieftains could continue to afford to pay off the police and their own henchmen alike.

So the (criminal) market contractions of 2008 spelled doom for some, but created great opportunities for others. The larger, more diversified groups cherry-picked those underworld assets they wanted and snapped them up at fire-sale prices. Gangs able to tap into state resources, whether government funds or the ability to flash a badge or grant or withhold a permit, did best. In other words, the 2008 crisis further strengthened the incestuous links between corrupt officials, the state machine and the underworld, especially at the local level.

The second big shock: 2014

The sanctions will serve to drive more Russian gangs into Europe, in my opinion; with the domestic economy in crisis and the euro worth that much more against the ruble, why wouldn't they?

Europol analyst, 2015[16]

Much the same is true of the shallower but longer financial slowdown created by low oil prices and the imposition of sanctions on Russia after its 2014 annexation of Crimea and intervention in Ukraine. Three examples from Moscow help illustrate the impact.[17] For some, desperation demands diversification, and for desperation one would be hard pressed to come up with a better place than Kapotnya, in south-eastern Moscow. Jammed uncomfortably up against the multi-lane MKAD ring road, Kapotnya is hardly an appealing place at the best of times; its traffic-clogged streets (no metro here) are lined with ugly late-Soviet brick low-rises, shrouded by the fumes from the massive Moscow Oil Refinery. One of the poorest of Moscow's neighbourhoods, Kapotnya is known as a haven for the homeless, the hopeless – and some of the city's cheapest and most disreputable brothels. As times get harder for ordinary Russians, the impoverished souls who once would go to local houses of ill repute now gravitate towards the even cheaper and more desperate individual prostitutes of the streets. Facing a fall in their revenues, the brothel owners in part have diversified to selling narcotics, their premises becoming modern-day equivalents of the old opium den. There users can buy and take cheap and destructive opiates and methamphetamines, even the infamous *krokodil*, a highly addictive and dangerous street drug that gets its name from the way users' skin can become scaly and green-tinged. To move into drug dealing, the brothel keepers typically have to get deeper into debt with the gangsters who previously just took a cut in return for leaving them free to ply their trade.

The trouble is that this kind of gangster, the small-scale local hoodlum, also feels the pinch. Typical is 'Dvornik' ('Doorman'), a thug-made-moderately-good who was arrested in 2015. His problem was that not only did he have a lifestyle to maintain that involved high-stakes gambling and imported – and thus especially expensive considering the ruble's depreciation – whisky, but he had a crew who expected to be paid and he

also owed tribute to a bigger-time gangster in return for the right to practise his rackets. As one police officer involved in the case put it, 'he had
assumed that everything was going to go like before, or even better. He
hadn't saved or made plans in case the spring ran dry.'[18]

A gang leader who can't pay his crew has no gang; a gangster who can't
pay his debts has no future. As a result, 'Dvornik' had no option but to lean
more heavily on the businesses on his turf, not least pushing those brothel
keepers all the harder. And he was not the only one, as the local cops who
also expected their regular payments in order to turn a blind eye were
feeling the pinch and increasing their own demands accordingly. This is
what led to his downfall; when one of his victims said he was unable to pay,
'Dvornik' personally delivered a savage beating so as to deter others from
pleading poverty. His victim, though, ended up in hospital; the police had
no choice but to investigate and, between forensic evidence and witness
statements, 'Dvornik' was soon behind bars. The fact that, because of the
pressure on his income, he had started to skimp on his bribes to the local
police may also have had a bearing on the case.

Some brothel keepers simply could not cope in these conditions, and
their businesses folded. Those who survived, though, generally did so by
diversifying into even more dangerous ventures, such as narcotics, and this
in turn meant that they fell further into the control of organised crime. In
many cases, they accumulated more debt. The local gangsters, themselves
under pressure, often simply sold their debts on to the larger, richer gangs
in the city, those whose activities were already sufficiently diversified that
they could ride out the present storm.

Many of the businesses on 'Dvornik's' turf came under the sway of the
vor known as 'Rak' ('Crayfish'), the local representative of Tariel Oniani's
network. If 'Dvornik' was essentially a thug, a predator extorting what he
could, 'Rak' was a professional, a criminal businessman, whose abilities
lay in maximising the value of those assets that came into his hands. He
earned his *klichka*, his nickname, because of a crayfish's willingness to eat
pretty much anything and this applied to his criminal enterprises, too.
He found new uses for the brothels which came under his sway, not least
as places to launder and move counterfeit money, or he reduced their
running costs by staffing them with trafficked sex slaves from Central
Asia. The depressing fact is that this actually got the approval of corrupt
local police officers: the higher the turnover of the business, and the more

serious the crimes involved, then the heftier the bribes they could expect. In this way, in Kapotnya at least, Russia's economic crisis meant hard times for consumers and small businesses, and the petty gangsters and corrupt officials preying on both.

Of course, one cannot extrapolate too much from a single neighbourhood, especially not one which is an impoverished and squalid outlier by Moscow's standards. (Although one could retort that Moscow itself is a wealthy and opulent outlier by Russia's standards.) Nonetheless, new opportunities arose for those individuals and groups able to seize them in the midst of crisis. The devaluation of the ruble again meant that those gangs whose businesses earned dollars, euros or other harder currencies had disproportionate domestic spending power. One of the most significant of these is the drug trade, but those gangs able to offer foreign criminals money-laundering services, for example, also expect their fees in kind. Hacking is also not a ruble business, for instance, nor is the international trade in women or weapons.

The day of the cheeserunners

Russia declares war on cheese, cracks down on 'dairy mafia'
CNN headline, 2015[19]

Thus, the greatest opportunities fell to those gangsters able to operate across Russia's borders. However, for many this meant having to develop new connections and alliances, which in turn brought complications. For example, one 'Pyotr Banana' built up a lucrative niche criminal enterprise after the 2008 financial slowdown on the back of a small Moscow-based trucking company he took over from his older brother after the latter died in a road accident that some think was actually a *razborka*, a gangland settling of scores. Initially he stuck with the existing formula of using spare space on shipments to move contraband and counterfeit goods, but he soon realised that there was serious money to be made smuggling heroin. By 2012, he was running monthly shipments into Belarus, for sale to a local gang which would then move it into Lithuania, and these represented his main source of income. After 2014, though, heroin was increasingly complemented with a new commodity being smuggled back into Russia: cheese.

As 'Pyotr Banana' discovered, Belarus had long been a turntable for all kinds of smuggling to and from Europe, with counterfeit cigarettes and heroin heading west, stolen cars and untaxed luxury goods passing east.[20] When the Kremlin slapped counter-sanctions on Western foodstuffs in 2014, consumers seeking their Italian salami and French cheeses had to turn to the black market, and Belarus became one of the key suppliers. Ironically, Moscow's efforts to prevent such sanctions busting through the 'grey market' – legitimate companies trying to bypass the control regime – only handed a greater market share to the outright criminal smugglers, who had the years of experience and corrupt contacts to move shipments across the border. Lest this sound trivial, consider than a single 'cheese-runner' gang broken up in 2015 was accused of earning two billion roubles (some $34 million) in just six months.[21]

'Pyotr Banana', though, had little personal experience in either acquiring or dealing in these commodities. In order to be able to break into this unexpected realm of what some call the *sery gastronom*, the 'grey delicatessen', he had to acquire a variety of new partners. One was a Belarusian official connected with an *agrokombinat* or food and agriculture corporation, who handled the importation, recruited through a brother-in-law who was a member of the gang which bought 'Pyotr Banana's' heroin. Then there was an official at Rosselkhoznadzor, Russia's Federal Service for Veterinary and Phytosanitary Surveillance, who somehow got the shipments duly certified for sale. Finally, although some of the cheese then ended up in Moscow's supermarkets, most was moved through *produkty* corner shops, and this required 'Pyotr Banana' also to partner with a Dagestani gang that controlled a string of them.

On one level, this is a classic example of the kind of on-the-fly entrepreneurialism that has long been a Russian strength, selling heroin for euros and banned groceries for rubles. In the process, though, 'Pyotr Banana' became dependent on corrupt officials over whom he had relatively little leverage and a gang from the North Caucasus with distinctly prickly relations with the Slav and Georgian groups dominating Moscow's underworld. This may prove an uncomfortable position for him in the future, but he, like many other lower- and middle-ranking criminal-entrepreneurs, has had to take whatever opportunities came his way.

New opportunities

On the one hand, times are hard, but on the other hand, there are all kinds of great new ways to make money, from buying guns from the Donbas to smuggling embargoed goods into the country. What's sure is that nothing will stand still – and that means . . . more pressure on the current order.

Interpol analyst, 2015[22]

Successive economic squeezes have made the struggle for control of key revenue streams – especially new ones – all the more important. The Afghan heroin Northern Route was and is the most lucrative, of course, but also the hardest to break into. Nonetheless, it has meant that gangs along the main arteries, able either to participate directly or simply to demand tribute for safe passage, have become increasingly wealthy. With wealth, gangs can corrupt officials, bankroll further opportunities, keep leaders and 'soldiers' happy and attract new recruits, including disaffected members of other gangs.

The upsurge in criminal connections with Belarus has likewise been a bonanza for the gangs of nearby Russian cities such as Bryansk and especially – because of its location on the Moscow–Minsk road – Smolensk. These gangs were, to be blunt, hardly glittering prizes in the Russian underworld. Before 2014, they were very much the impoverished country cousins of the powerful Moscow and St Petersburg networks. However, they then began prospering unexpectedly because of their ability to 'tax' the through-flow of smuggled goods. This gave them the extra resources to be able to attract more members, bribe officials and invest in new criminal businesses.

In the longer term, though, China offers greater opportunities, even if they are distinctly harder for Russian gangs to tap and may indeed require a willingness to accept a subordinate position. The decay of the Far Eastern Association of Thieves after Yevgeny Vasin's death in 2001 and the failure of a *skhodka* held in 2012 to try and resolve disputes between the 'easterners' has left this market very much up for grabs, as discussed in chapter 9. Conflicts between interior and coastal and border gangs look set to intensify, with Chinese and other Asian gangs (including some yakuza and Koreans) eager to capitalise on the outcome.

As Vladimir Putin increasingly legitimises his rule – and pays off his closest allies – with various prestige projects, this too creates all kinds of new opportunities, large and small. The 2014 Sochi Winter Olympics was a particularly infamous honeypot, and one which may have contributed to Aslan Usoyan's assassination in 2013. The whole project cost an estimated $55 billion, making it the most expensive winter Games on record.[23] In part, this reflects the challenges of mounting winter games in a subtropical venue, but it is also a product of staggering levels of waste and theft. According to the international NGO Transparency International, corruption added fully 50 per cent to the construction costs, suggesting perhaps $15 billion was up for grabs.[24] Usoyan was the first of the major players to identify the potential profits to be made following the 2007 decision to award the games to Sochi, which was one of his power bases. He moved quickly into the local construction and hospitality industries, although in fairness it appears to have been corrupt officials and business people who stole the greatest sums. Nonetheless, Usoyan's local preponderance (he 'was like a governor here, but from the criminal world . . . It's like a second government'[25]) was resented sufficiently that his network suffered a regular toll of local agents and lieutenants murdered by his rivals. In 2009, local *vor* Alik 'Sochinsky' Minalyan was killed in Moscow, possibly while visiting Usoyan.[26] In 2010, two of Usoyan's men were gunned down in Sochi itself, with one – property speculator Eduard Kokosyan ('Karas') – killed.[27] Of course, the real money was made by the oligarchs granted the major contracts worth billions, but even through subcontracted work such as providing labour-ganged workers (often virtually trafficked from Central Asia and forcibly returned once the job was done), the major criminal players could also benefit from the actual construction.

The government's decision in 2009 to ban all organised gambling and instead develop four (later six) Las Vegas-style casino tourism hubs is also having an inevitable impact on the underworld.[28] Of course, in reality this is proving every bit as effective as prohibition in the United States and Gorbachev's anti-alcohol campaign, driving habitual gamblers into underground, unregulated games and casinos run by organised crime. Beyond competition over these games, the new mega-sites, all at border locations meant also to cater for overseas markets, offer inviting new business prospects for the criminals. The planned sites are at Vladivostok (for the Pacific market), Kaliningrad (for Europe), Azov City in the south-western Rostov region (for the Middle East) and a remote spot in the Altai region in southern Siberia (for central and western Asia), to which were later added Yalta, in Crimea, and Sochi. Priority was given to Vladivostok's Ussuri Bay Resort, which opened in 2015, and gangs (and corrupt local officials) inevitably sought to snap up strategic real estate and construction companies and secure padded contracts for businesses under their control.[29] The potential profit from these new ventures is again a powerful force attracting opportunists and distorting the status quo.

The *khaker*: the virtual *vor*

Everyone knows that Russians are good at maths. Our software writers are the best in the world, that's why our hackers are the best in the world.
Lt. Gen. Boris Miroshnikov,
MVD Department K (cybercrimes), 2005[30]

Elsewhere in the Russian underworld, one of the more striking transformations has been happening in virtual rather than real space. The country has long been a rich source of licit computer programmers and hackers alike, for a variety of reasons. In the 1990s, when hacking was in its infancy, a combination of a tradition of advanced mathematical training, primitive hardware (which encouraged programmers to learn raw code rather than relying on software) and a lack of decent legal opportunities all contributed to the rise of the *khaker*. Today there are far more jobs available, at home and abroad, not least in such world-class Russian companies as the Kaspersky Labs computer security corporation. However, as a legacy of those early years, there is still a strong hacker culture – both 'white hats', devoted to the pleasure of the art, and more destructive 'black hats' – and also a strong appreciation of the criminal opportunities.

According to industry analyses, in 2011 Russia accounted for about 35 per cent of global cybercrime revenue, or between $2.5 and $3.7 billion.[31] This is wildly out of proportion with the country's share of the global information technology market, which at the time was around 1 per cent. Even though China and the USA are still in the lead, it is striking just how many key players and operations in global cybercrime are Russian. As of 2017, the five FBI 'most wanted' cybercriminals are four Russians (one a Latvian Russian) and a cell of Iranian hackers.[32] An operation which stole around $1 billion from some 100 financial institutions around the world in 2015 using the so-called Anunak malware (malicious software) was tracked back to Russia. In addition, the man who has been dubbed 'King of Spam' (although cited only as a mere number 7 on Spamhaus's alleged 'Top Ten Worst' list) is a Russian, Pyotr Levashov, arrested in Spain in April 2017.[33]

Furthermore, just as Russian gangs have become service providers in other criminal sectors, many computer criminals around the world have taken advantage of programs and tools created in Russia and sold by Russians, or else the secure servers provided by such enterprises as the infamous Russian Business Network (RBN). This was a source of services including secure 'bullet-proof hosting' for everyone from hackers to paedophiles, as well as spamming and identity theft. Described by the internet security company VeriSign as 'the baddest of the bad . . . a for-hire service catering to large-scale criminal operations',[34] RBN was at one time reportedly linked to around 60 per cent of all cybercrime.[35] It grew out of computer crime operations in St Petersburg in the late 1990s, although it only formally registered as an internet site in 2006. It seemed impenetrable to government efforts to hack into or locate it. Persistent rumours suggested it had a powerful *krysha* thanks both to its willingness to help Russia's intelligence services conduct some operations, not least a massive attack on Estonia's information infrastructure in 2007, and the fact that 'Flyman', its organiser, was related to a powerful St Petersburg politician.[36] Later in 2007, though, it seemingly disappeared but may well have simply migrated to servers in other jurisdictions and be operating under new names.[37]

At home, the hackers generally appear not to be part of the existing criminal networks. Instead, much like professional assassins, forgers or money launderers, they are specialists for hire, engaged for a particular operation. More often, they form their own virtual groups and networks, increasingly cross-border and multi-ethnic ones, to commit crimes either for themselves or for hire to other gangs. They were, for example, reportedly the technical experts who cracked police databases for the Japanese yakuza in the 1990s,[38] transferred stolen money abroad for Australian gangsters in the 2000s,[39] and obtained credit card details for the Italians in the 2010s.[40]

War or peace?

There will be no new criminal revolution in Russia . . . We can state: the epoch of criminal wars is in the past.

Interior Minister Rashid Nurgaliyev, 2009[41]

I have never met a police officer with a good word to say for Rashid Nurgaliyev, a former KGB veteran who spent nine years heading the Ministry of Internal Affairs (until 2012), during which time, according to one of his erstwhile subordinates, he 'saw his job as being to keep the country quiet, nothing more'.[42] Certainly one cannot regard him as being especially percipient, as the result of all the new challenges and opportunites discussed above is that the Russian underworld and the wider Russian-focused crime diaspora are both undergoing a new round of transformations. It may not mean war, but it certainly will mean some kind of revolution.

However great the strains on the Russian underworld, there are many within it who want to maintain the status quo and avoid any wider conflicts. Even Rovshan Dzhaniyev was really looking for a place at the top table more than the demolition of the whole structure. All the country's criminal kingpins appreciate that a nationwide turf war would not only put them, their organisations and their fortunes in jeopardy from their rivals, but would likely also force the government to crack down with greater rigour and vigour. In the words of Lieutenant General Igor Zinoviev, head of MUR, Moscow's criminal intelligence division, 'you have to consider yet another fact. All the leaders of the criminal world of the 1990s are already elderly people. Most of them have long gone legitimate – heading some fund or being part of the management of some commercial structure . . . A return of the '90s is unprofitable for everyone.'[43]

Furthermore, the authorities themselves seem to be eager to head off any major conflict. Shortly after Aslan Usoyan's murder, for example, the police took the unusual step of raiding a meeting of Tariel Oniani's senior lieutenants, who had gathered to ponder its implications.[44] They were all detained overnight before being released, a warning that the police knew who they were and where they could be found. Nonetheless, this will for the foreseeable future remain a tense and dangerous situation and it is hard to predict the outcome.[45] Even the criminals are uncertain, hoping for peace, but fearing war:

Representatives of the criminal world are of the same opinion: the bloody skirmishes will not return, there are other methods to solving problems: fraud, corruption, blackmail. Yesterday's thugs have matured and become serious people who do honest business. But, apparently, not all problems are solved without the use of weapons, and in some cases the surest method is that 'no person means no problem'.[46]

Several main factors are likely to determine the trajectory of the Russian underworld in the next few years: whether the majority Slavic gangs remain united and out of the conflicts within the 'highlander' community; whether the Chechens, who have a strength and reputation disproportionate to their numbers, are dragged into them; the personal agendas of key figures; and the intentions and interests of the state. Four main potential scenarios emerge. The first is of peace through superior firepower, whereby a wider conflict and any substantive reordering of the underworld is avoided as the Slavic gangs and the Chechens remain relatively united and able credibly to threaten retaliation against parties deemed to be troublemakers, probably with the tacit and maybe even the active approval of the state.

If the coalition supporting the status quo is forced instead to accede to a limited underworld reshuffle, the result could be apocalypse postponed. By buying off some insurgent elements and eliminating or facing down others, they would hope to bleed off enough pressure to avert a wider conflict without the need for comprehensive changes. However, partial reorganisation is in many ways harder to manage than a flat opposition to any change, and the chances are that this would trigger at the very least local conflicts.

It is possible, though, that the conflict could continue to smoulder or even escalate, but remain confined to the 'highlanders'. In many ways, this is the present default outcome. The result could be a single, unified 'highlander' organisation, but more probably they would be fragmented and weakened, allowing the Slavs and perhaps also Chechens to take over many of their operations outside their regional strongholds.

The last likely outcome is that, even if none of the principal actors want this, some incident sparks the present combustible mix of generational, ethnic, economic and personal rivalries. Although such a broader mob conflict would not last the best part of a decade, as during the 1990s, a major and bloody redefinition of the underworld balance of power would lead to greater violence on the streets and also have wider political implications. Elements of the local and security elites linked to organised crime would be dragged into the fray. More to the point, the Kremlin could not sit back and see the days of *bespredel*, disorder, return.

It is, of course, impossible to predict which scenario will prevail. These pressures have so far not only been worsening relations between gangs, but also undermining their internal cohesion. In 2008, for example, two Tambovskaya members were assassinated outside St Petersburg. Both were part of the group controlled by the gangster known as 'Basil Khimichev' ('Basil the Chemist'), who in turn owed allegiance to 'Khokol' (a slang term for a Ukrainian), a senior Tambovskaya figure now living in exile.[47] The killings seem to have been related to a struggle within the Tambovskaya itself over the growing drug-trafficking business. Likewise, the arrest in 2016 of 'Shakhro the Younger' (see chapter 11) raised questions about the partition of his criminal empire that were at least temporarily shelved when, in February 2017, he sent a message to his gang starting with the unambiguous words 'I'm not dead yet' and warning against any such moves.[48] Although the authorities went through a pro forma inquiry as to how his message could have been smuggled out of the high-security Lefortovo prison, several informed observers of the scene have told me that they permitted it, precisely to try and prevent any cannibalisation of his network, which would almost certainly have led to violence.

Vladimir Putin's state-building project entailed a tacit understanding with the criminals, who avoided any large-scale crackdown by acknowledging the primacy of the regime and abandoning the indiscriminate street violence of the 1990s. The balance of power shifted back to the political elites, much as in Soviet times. The state is once again the biggest gang in town, and local and national political/administrative figures are stronger than their criminal counterparts. However, it is not an especially unified 'gang' and as Putin's grip on the elite appears to weaken, especially as speculation grows about a possible succession after the 2018 presidential elections, there are dangers. While the movers and shakers of central government have little reason to fear or need the criminals – even if they do often move within common social circles – at a local level, the opportunities for deeper cooperation nationally between political and criminal are much more evident and the relationship not quite so one sided. One by-product of this is that even if the national government does ever get serious about fighting corruption and organised crime, this may be resisted and side-lined on the ground by the gangsters' allies, clients and patrons. Besides which, any conflict will undermine a central element of President Putin's legitimating mythology: that he was the one man who could finally restore order to Russia.

CHAPTER 15

THE CRIMINAL WARS

Not everyone who carries a knife is a cook.

Russian proverb

Can the *vory* themselves be weaponised? In September 2014, Estonian Kapo (security police) officer Eston Kohver was about to meet an informant in a secluded wood near the village of Miikse, close to the border with Russia. He had back-up close to hand, but nonetheless no one was expecting what actually happened: an armed FSB snatch squad crossed the border, jamming his radio and hurling stun grenades to disrupt any attempt to prevent them from seizing him. It was clearly a set-up.[1] Kohver was taken first to Pskov and then Moscow. There, he was accused of having been on the Russian side of the frontier (despite the fact that Russian border troops had signed a protocol confirming that the attack happened inside Estonia[2]) and convicted on trumped-up espionage charges. Even his service radio and pistol were paraded as 'proof' of his status as a spy. Although sentenced to fifteen years in prison, a year after his kidnap he was traded for a Russian agent, but this does not seem to have been the primary reason for this brazen raid. It was not even about making a point of Russia's capacity and willingness to intrude.

Rather, the intent seems to have been to derail Kohver's ongoing investigation. Yet the investigation was not about anything that would seem to warrant causing such a diplomatic incident, merely illegal cross-border cigarette trafficking. The evidence, backed up by conversations with Estonian and other security officers, suggests that the FSB was facilitating the smuggling activity in return for a cut of the profits. This was not for the enrichment of the officers concerned, but to raise operational funds for active political measures in Europe that had no Russian 'fingerprints' on them. As Estonia's then-president, Toomas Hendrik Ilves, tweeted at the time, 'Kapo, like FBI in US, deals both with counterintelligence *and* organized crime. Just in some places they turn out to be same.' In this, he was reminding us of something former CIA Director James Woolsey had said in 1999: 'If you should chance to strike up a conversation with an articulate, English-speaking Russian . . . wearing a $3,000 suit and a pair of Gucci loafers, and he tells you that he is an executive of a Russian trading company . . . then there are four possibilities.' These were that he was a businessman, a spy, a gangster, or 'he may be all three and that none of those three institutions have any problem with the arrangement.'[3]

Useful idiots and dangerous opportunists

[In Russia] the nexus among organized crime, some state officials, the intelligence services, and business blurs the distinction between state policy and private gain.
James Clapper, US director of national intelligence, 2013.[4]

At the time of writing, the United States is still wracked by claim and counter-claim about Russian efforts to suborn people close to President Donald Trump, and also his links with alleged and suspected Russian and other gangsters. Whatever the truth about such allegations, this does point to a very real issue. Russia's organised crime has played an important role in the opening hostilities of what has been called the 'new Cold War' – or the 'Hot Peace'[5] – that truly took shape in 2014 with the seizure of Crimea. All intelligence services sometimes make use of criminals (the mafia helped open doors for US agents in Sicily in the Second World War, for instance, although the extent to which they did this has been overstated[6]). However, when intelligence agencies work with or through criminals, they typically seek to maintain clear boundaries (ideally the gangsters should never know with whom they may be working). In the Russian case, these boundaries are too often blurred, permeable – and often the *vory* turn out to be the ultimate beneficiaries.

A particular 'spook–gangster nexus' has emerged. On the one hand, the security agencies have long used the *vory* and their criminal networks as occasional tools for leverage and intelligence gathering. Spanish prosecutor José Grinda González reportedly said that, in his view, the Kremlin's 'strategy is to use [organised crime] groups to do whatever the [government of Russia] cannot acceptably do as a government'.[7] Gangsters are not just paid but offered immunity in return for carrying out covert missions. Grinda claimed, for example, that *vor v zakone* Zakhar Kalashov sold guns to Kurdish terrorists to destabilise Turkey under orders from the GRU, Russian military intelligence. Likewise in Latvia, a country increasingly important to Moscow as a financial bridgehead into the European Union, Russia's foreign intelligence service, the SVR, has not only been unmasked seeking to fund sympathetic politicians, it has also been connected with local ethnic Russian gangsters, encouraging them also to offer their support.[8]

A quintessential example is Viktor Bout, a man whose career spanned the worlds of crime, business and intelligence work – and often all three at the same time – and which has now led him to a prison in the USA. As an intelligence officer, probably from the GRU, he set up an air freight business specialising in shipping to dangerous destinations. Alongside delivering aid, he was also implicated in sanctions busting and arms dealing. It is unclear whether his offer in 2008 to sell 700 Russian Igla surface-to-air missiles to Colombian FARC narco-rebels was on Moscow's behalf (although the volume of the missiles he could acquire suggests so), but as he was used from time to time as a deniable front by the government, yet in the process granted freedom to break the law with impunity, it is hard to tell.[9]

Likewise, one Western businessman of my acquaintance setting up a venture in Murmansk found himself in 2011 being pressurised by local gangsters; when he turned to the police, they brought in the local FSB, who suggested that he might want to bring in one of their former senior officers as a partner. When the businessman declined the invitation, he found financial information he had provided the FSB being used by the criminals. Where, ultimately, was the line between the spooks and the crooks?

Clearly, the presence of Russian and Eurasian organised crime has subtle, as well as obvious effects. Europol's *2008 Russian Organised Crime Assessment*, for example, concluded that it had a 'medium level direct impact' on the European Union, mainly felt through their trafficking operations, but a:

high level indirect impact on the EU. This is experienced through money laundering and investments. These activities distort and may even destroy legal competition; raise prices and inflation in the property and other similar markets; increase corruption of business practices and culture; create concrete losses to legal business and national economies in the EU; increase the lucrativeness and social acceptance of criminal activities; facilitate OC-penetration and integration into legal structures; legalise the proceeds of crime, the criminals and their activities and in turn also seriously damage many legal elements of the EU societies.[10]

Since then, though, the concern has clearly sharpened, as the impact of Russian criminal penetration is increasingly seen not simply as a law enforcement issue, but as something much more serious. Although in the main, gangsters are gangsters, sometimes they can be state assets, too.

The first criminal war: taking Crimea

Is Crimea the first conquest in history conducted by gangsters working for a state?
A question I was asked at a NATO workshop, 2015

The answer to the above question, as is so often the case when academics are asked seemingly simple questions, is complex. It is hardly novel for gangsters to be used in times of war, but, unusually in this case, the criminals were combatants, not just collaborators, and they were not merely unleashed against an enemy like eighteenth-century privateers – pirates given sanction so long as they attacked the other side – but integrated into the invader's forces. When Russia invaded Ukraine, it did so not only with its infamous 'little green men' – special forces without any insignia – but also with criminals. To the gangsters, this was not about geopolitics, less yet about redressing what Putin called the 'outrageous historical injustice'[11] that occurred when the Crimean peninsula was transferred from Russia to Ukraine in 1954, it was about business opportunities.[12]

From the first, Moscow's campaign to wrest Crimea from Kiev depended on an alliance with local underworld interests. Sergei Aksyonov, the premier of the new Crimean region, is alleged to have had a *vor* past, having gone by the nickname of 'Goblin' back when he was a member of the Salem organised crime group in the 1990s.[13] Aksyonov rejects all claims of such links as being part of a slander campaign initiated by political opponents, but the one time he brought a defamation action against someone who made these allegations, the Appeals Court dismissed the case as groundless.[14]

Nonetheless, the respective trajectories of both Aksyonov and the Salem tell us something about Crimea's own development, and the role the *vory* could play in Russia's near-bloodless seizure of the peninsula. (It is hardly coincidental that the two parts of Ukraine in which Russia is, as of writing, entrenched are both areas where the old-style *vory* are equally thick on the ground.) Even before the collapse of the USSR at the end of 1991, Crimea had become a haven for smuggling, black marketeering and a lucrative array of embezzlement schemes centring on the region's health spas and holiday resorts. As independent Ukraine struggled in the early 1990s both with economic crisis and the near-collapse of its law enforcement structures, organised crime assumed an increasingly visible and violent form. Simferopol was fought over by two rival gangs, the Bashmaki ('Shoes') and the Salem (named after the Salem Café, in turn named after Simferopol's sister city).[15] They were at once entrepreneurs and predators, forcing local businesses to pay tribute and sell their goods on pain of arson, beatings and worse. A retired (he says) criminal-entrepreneur recalled one ferry trip to Kerch, at the eastern tip of the peninsula, in which he was accompanied by a courier carrying a suitcase stuffed with cans of cheap whitefish roe, which Salem would force restaurateurs to buy as expensive 'beluga caviar'; a gaggle of prostitutes recruited for brothels in Yalta; and a pair of hungover and heavily tattooed 'bulls' – mob enforcers – returning from a party in Novorossiysk. As he put it, 'all Crimean crime was on that boat'.[16]

This was an inherently unstable situation: not only was there pressure from political and business elites for the police to reassert their authority, but the gang war was beginning to prevent either side from actually turning a profit. The conflict escalated until a paroxysm of murder and violence in 1996 left both gangs on their knees. It also opened a window of opportunity for Gennady Moskal, the Crimean police chief between 1997 and 2000, to launch a crackdown on overt gangsterism. Crimea became a more peaceful place, but claims that the gangs were finally broken were a convenient fiction. 'Alfrid', a grizzled Tatar veteran of the 1990s turf wars, claimed that 'the punks just grew up, they realised wars were bad for business and there was a lot more money to be made in business. Moskal just helped them make the jump.'[17] The more senior and less blatantly thuggish leaders – including one *brigadir*, known as 'Goblin' – instead took their money and their connections and went (semi-)legitimate, in business and politics. Indeed, usually they were involved in both, leveraging their continued, although less overt, criminal alliances to further their political and economic ends.[18] In this respect, Crimea's *vory* followed much the same pattern as in Russia.

By the 2000s, these gangster-businessmen were increasingly dominant within Crimea. Kiev appeared to have little interest in bringing good governance and economic prosperity to this peninsula of ethnic Russians, and this gave the local elites both free rein and also a perverse legitimacy. Crimea regarded itself as neglected by, and separate from, the political mainstream. In this political, economic and social vacuum, the new mafia–business–political empires could thrive. As one US embassy cable in 2006 put it, these 'Crimean criminals were fundamentally different than in the 1990s: then, they were sportsuit-wearing, pistol-wielding "bandits" who gave Crimea a reputation as the "Ukrainian Sicily" and ended up in jail, shot, or going to ground; now they had moved into mainly above-board businesses, as well as local government.' It added that 'dozens of figures with known criminal backgrounds were elected to local office in the March 26 elections'.[19] Viktor Shemchuk, former chief prosecutor of the region, recalled that 'every government level of Crimea was criminalised. It was far from unusual that a parliamentary session in Crimea would start with a minute of silence honouring one of their murdered "brothers".[20]

The key commodities were control of businesses and, increasingly, land. Some of the former leaders of the Bashmaki, for example, were accused of trying to take over SC Tavriya Simferopol, Crimea's main football club, largely for the properties it owned.[21] More generally, as prices rose – especially as Tatars, displaced from their Crimean homelands under the Soviets, began to return home – the gangster-businessmen and their allies within the corrupt local bureaucracy sought to snap up real estate and construction projects to take advantage of this market.

Although Crimea was part of Ukraine, many of the most lucrative criminal businesses, such as trafficking narcotics and counterfeit or untaxed cigarettes, depended on relationships with the Russian criminal networks. It helped that Russia's Black Sea Fleet still had its base at Sevastopol in Crimea under a treaty with Kiev, and that so many navy veterans had retired locally: there was common civilian and military traffic back and forth. When the Ukrainian state began to totter as President Yanukovych struggled with the Maidan protesters, Moscow was able to begin to reach out to potential allies in Crimea through underworld channels. According to a conversation with a Russian police officer, representatives from Solntsevo had visited Crimea for talks with local *vory* even before 4 February 2014, when Crimea's presidium, or governing council, considered a referendum on its status. The Muscovites came not just to feel out the scope for further criminal business, but also to gauge the mood of the local underworld.

Aksyonov, head of the Russian Unity party, seemed an ideal choice as a Kremlin figurehead. Even though he had been elected to the regional parliament in 2010 with just 4 per cent of the vote, he was ambitious, ruthless and alleged to be closely connected with both political and criminal power-brokers on the peninsula.[22] When Moscow moved to seize Crimea on the morning of 27 February, it deployed the 'little green men', some local police who solidly supported the coup, and also thugs in mismatched fatigues and red armbands, nonetheless often clutching brand new assault rifles. These 'self-defence forces' spent as much time occupying businesses – including a car dealership owned by a partner of Ukraine's next president, Petro Poroshenko[23] – and throwing their weight around on street corners as they did actually securing strategic locations. While some were veterans and volunteers, many were the footsoldiers of the peninsula's crime gangs, who had temporarily put their rivalries aside to pull Crimea out of Ukraine.

The new elite is thus a triumvirate of Moscow appointees, local politicians and gangsters made good. And they did indeed make good, quickly moving to skim funds from the sums Moscow provided to start developing the peninsula, and simply expropriating properties owned by the Ukrainian government and its allies. In theory, these properties were sold at auction to raise more development funds, but often in practice the 'auctions' were clearly rigged sweetheart deals.[24] 'Alfrid', for example, made no bones about the fact that he was taking many of his liquid assets, and using the cash to snap up properties. 'This is like privatisation in the 1990s,' he said, 'one of those chances in life when you can make a fortune if you move fast and know what you're doing.' For 'Alfrid', in his sixties, this was his 'pension plan.'[25]

Meanwhile, Sevastopol could begin to challenge the Ukrainian port of Odessa as a smuggling hub. Historically, Odessa had handled the lion's share of not just Ukrainian but also Russian smuggling across (and very occasionally beneath) the Black Sea. Whether or not Sevastopol ever could emerge as a credible rival, especially in light of Western sanctions, is in a way irrelevant: the very possibility that it might do so forced Odessa's godfathers to lower the 'tax' they levy on criminal traffic through the port, an example of black-market economics at its most basic.

The second criminal war: burning the Donbas

The beneficiaries are the politicians, the oligarchs and the gangsters. Coal, gold, petrol and tobacco. That is what they are fighting for in eastern Ukraine.

Russian journalist Yuliya Polukhina, 2016[26]

Perverse incentives are the bane of many a seemingly well-thought-through plan. If Moscow is offering to replace your car any time it gets stolen or written off, then why bother driving safely or locking it at night? Indeed, why not say it was stolen and sell it on? Sadly, the same is true when applied to munitions promised to militia groups in the Donbas region of south-eastern Ukraine. Recruit criminals and adventurers, arm them, put them in a messy, fluid conflict sitting across established smuggling routes, and pledge to make good on expenditures in battle, and one should hardly be surprised when skirmishes against Ukrainian government forces are started for no reason beyond providing an excuse to burn off, say, 10,000 rounds of ammunition, while claiming to have used twice as much. When the replace-ment 20,000 rounds appear from depots deeper in the Donbas, the excess can neatly be dumped onto the black market for a profit.[27]

Moscow presumably thought that by relying heavily on local militias it could fight its undeclared war against Kiev deniably and on the cheap, but in practice it created a situation in which it was often scarcely in control of its notional proxies. Indeed, from the first it was being embezzled by them, and soon began to pay the price in terms of an upturn in violent crime and illegal arms dealing back home. In Rostov-on-Don, the southern Russian city acting as a logistical support hub for the war, there was a growing problem. In 2015, the Rostov region was the ninth most criminal in all Russia, but by 2016 it had become the seventh, and the city itself had become, according to some measures, the most dangerous in Europe – having not even been in the top ten before.[28]

At the time the Donbas operation must have seemed a great idea. Crimea had been easy, and, as if carried forward by the momentum of their success, the Russians then became even more ambitious. The idea was not to annex the grimy, smokestack Donbas, despite its relatively large ethnically and linguistically Russian population. Instead, it was to generate a pseudo-revolt there to put pressure on Kiev. Ukraine would, the Russians reasoned, have to acknowledge Moscow's regional hegemony, something they assumed would be quick and inevitable. Thus, if in Crimea the aim was to create a new order, in the Donbas it was as much as anything else to create chaos, even if a controlled, weaponised chaos.

To this end, the Russians set out to engineer a local insurrection by Russian-speakers alarmed at the new regime in Kiev. They tried to stir up trouble in various cities in the region, most of which was either put down or never really took off in the first place. In Donetsk and Lugansk, though, initial successes allowed Moscow to set up proxy regimes, the so-called Donetsk and Lugansk People's Republics. The Russian army remained the final backstop for these pseudo-states, but Moscow wanted to make this look like a genuinely popular movement. It encouraged nationalists, adventurers, mercenaries and Cossacks from Russia to join local forces. There arose as a result a bewildering array of militias, often-ramshackle collections of genuine volunteers, defectors from the government and local gangsters.

For the *vory*, this was a priceless opportunity to turn their street muscle into a form of legal power. Although post-Soviet Ukraine had had at best partial success in building a working law-based state (if anything, by 2014 corruption was an even greater problem there than in Russia[29]), the east had been especially problematic, in the grip of a seemingly unbreakable cabal of business oligarchs and corrupt political managers. In short, 'Donbas's magnates – some criminals already under Soviet law – prevented the rule of law from emerging in the Donbas and severely limited the formation of a civil society'.[30] Combine that with a heavy concentration of local prisons, and a faltering local economy that encouraged street gangs, and it is perhaps no surprise that it was commonly said that 'every third man in the Donetsk region is in prison, has been in prison, or will be in prison'.[31]

Once the Russians had separated part of the Donbas from government control, the region's criminal leaders held a *skhodka* in December 2014, to decide how to respond.[32] They opted to take full advantage of the new situation and, indeed, to encourage *vory* from government-held areas of the

Donbas to head into the rebel territory.[33] Meanwhile, the illegal production of counterfeit alcohol and tobacco and its export to Russia, Ukraine and Europe increased, now that the criminals were essentially in charge.[34]

It is perhaps interesting that the commanders of the 'rebellion' went largely by call-sign names such as 'Motorola', 'Batman', 'Strelkov' ('Shooter') and 'Givi', as if in homage to gangster *klichki*. Most of the headline figures were enthusiastic adventurers or veterans of the military and security worlds. However, second-rank militias and many junior commanders came from the underworld. With them came a culture of intimidation, violence and theft. One Russian volunteer, who had gone to fight genuinely believing Moscow's propaganda that Ukrainian 'fascists' were out to persecute the Russians, had a rude awakening when he actually joined a militia: 'When you get there, from the very first minutes you realise that this is not a military unit – it is a real gang.'[35]

The rebels certainly can create, and have created, chaos, and as of writing in 2017 no end to this miserable conflict seems in sight. But then, when it comes to 'weaponisation', chaos is easier to generate than control. Several commanders have been assassinated, probably by Russian special forces precisely because they became too wilful and too dangerous. Much of the smaller-scale fighting appears uncontrolled, as often as not triggered by boredom or the opportunity to make money. Meanwhile, Rostov-on-Don has seen its murder rate soar (up 19 per cent in 2016) and the supply of illegal weapons expand dramatically as Kalashnikovs and even heavier weapons trickle back onto the Russian black market.[36] Whether or not the Kremlin considers all this to be a success, there is little question that the Donbas is a criminal war, and not just in terms of international law.

The third criminal war: Crimintern

Now a kind of 'nationalisation of the mafia' is taking place: the mafia structures are actually being replaced by the real authorities.
Police Lt. Gen. (retired) Vladimir Ovchinsky, 2016[37]

Since Putin's return to the presidency after his brief period as puppeteer-premier in 2008–12, Russia has increasingly become a mobilisation state.[38] In practice, if not in law, the regime reserves to itself the right to call on any individual or organisation, from a company to a media outlet, to advance the Kremlin's agenda. This could range from donating funds to a cause it wants deniably to support, through to providing a handy cover identity for a spy. In essence, this is nothing new. In the early 2000s a huge palace was built at Gelendzhik on the Black Sea, alleged to be for Putin's use and funded by money provided by oligarchs as a 'levy' intended to go towards improving the health infrastructure. That has been denied, but whatever the truth it is known as 'Putin's Palace'.[39] In recent years, though, Putin's Russia has, psychologically at least, been put on a war footing, especially as the new geopolitical conflict has emerged. Increasingly, dissent has been framed as treason, and the interests of the current regime presented as the interests of Russia as a whole.

Combine this with the long-standing connections between the underworld and the upperworld, through the security agencies in particular, and the scope for a distinct type of mobilisation has emerged. In the past, the state had used those connections essentially negatively: to assert the new rules of the game after Putin's rise to power, for example, or to warn Chechen gangs off supporting the rebels back home. Since then, though, just as the Soviet state used *vory* as instruments, whether controlling political prisoners in the Gulags or compromising foreigners, so Putin's Kremlin has also put them to use.

Now, it is hardly the case that all Russian criminal operations are instruments of Kremlin influence abroad. Not every group or network can be induced to become part of what one could call Moscow's 'Crimintern', its underworld successor to the old Soviet Communist International. Those which can I have defined as 'Russian-based organised crime' (RBOC): the crucial feature is that, while operating abroad, they retain a strong stake in Russia. Maybe it means their members still have family there, or assets, or that the core of their network is in Russia. Either way, it means the Kremlin has leverage. As a Western counter-intelligence officer inelegantly but evocatively put it to me about one RBOC *vor*, 'so long as his balls were in Moscow, the Russians could always squeeze'.[40] This is not necessarily about ethnicity, nor language, but exposure. Some of the ethnically Russian gangster expats in Spain, for example, have essentially migrated, moving their families and assets out of their homeland. Others, though, retain strong personal and professional connections back home. Likewise, key figures within the Georgian gangs operating in France, Italy, Greece and the Low Countries maintain significant links with Russia. Artur Yuzbashev, arrested in France in 2013 for his role in an international burglary ring and convicted in 2017, not only had a Chechen bodyguard, but had been arrested in Moscow in 2006.[41] He served just two months in prison on drug possession charges, but, in that time, he established links with a Russian-based crime group that reportedly continued after he arrived in France in 2010. Conversely, the sizeable organised crime network of Georgian and Armenian gangsters charged in 2012 on counts of burglary and theft across France and Belgium had no direct contact with Russia, and therefore did not constitute RBOC.[42]

Nonetheless, RBOC is occasionally but increasingly used to play a variety of roles in Moscow's 'political war' to divide, distract and demoralise the West, especially Europe, albeit only when Russia's intelligence services have no alternative.[43] Although its security agencies are increasingly developing their own in-house hacking capabilities, for example, Moscow still depends on recruiting cybercriminals or simply calling on them from time to time, in return for their continued freedom. In particular, they provide 'surge capacity' for major operations such as the attacks on Estonia in 2007 and Georgia in 2008 as well as ongoing cyber-disruption in Ukraine. These hacks are often intended to support political subversion, and this requires money. As the Kohver case demonstrated, RBOC groups can also be tapped for *chornaya kassa* ('black account') funds, which can be used for mischief abroad more easily than directly moving money out of Russia, and without as clear a risk of the payments being tracked back to Moscow.

On a more tactical level, professionals adept at moving people and goods across borders are valuable to intelligence operations. In 2010, for example, eleven deep-cover SVR spies in the USA were unmasked in the FBI-led Operation Ghost Stories.[44] Arguably the most able of them went by the name Christopher Metsos, and he managed to flee to Cyprus. He was arrested but then released on bail, at which point he promptly disappeared, despite all efforts to keep him under surveillance. Several US counter-intelligence officers expressed the opinion to me that RBOC people traffickers deployed their knowledge and connections to covertly send Metsos back to Russia or into another jurisdiction where regular Russian intelligence officers could finalise his return.

At the most muscular end of the spectrum, some assassinations ascribed to Russian intelligence appear to have been subcontracted to RBOC, such as those of several supporters of Chechen and other North Caucasus militants in Istanbul. Nadim Ayupov, whom the Turkish authorities accuse of murdering three alleged Chechen terrorists on behalf of the FSB, was a member of a Moscow-based organised crime group which had until then specialised in car theft.[45] Likewise, RBOC groups may be behind the covert support of Russian-linked paramilitary organisations such as the Hungarian National Front, and notably the agitators who took part in the Moscow-backed attempted coup in Montenegro in 2016 in a bid to prevent it from joining NATO.[46]

The fourth criminal war: blowback

'We honestly don't know sometimes if these guys are spies or criminals. But the thing is, even if they're doing operation [intelligence] work here in Germany, they're embezzling, stealing and raiding companies back in Russia.'

I ask whether they do the Kremlin more harm than good.

'Ah . . . If I were Putin, I'd be more worried about what they're doing at home.'

Conversation with German intelligence officer, 2016[47]

However, there are serious risks for Moscow in this kind of state–crime collusion. It is easy to understand the temptations for Vladimir Putin. Russia is not in the best position to claim great-power status and challenge the West. Its military is smaller than the combined forces of European NATO, even without counting Canada and the USA. Its economy is smaller than that of New York state.[48] However, it is an authoritarian regime able to focus its resources on its goals; Putin does not have to worry unduly about democratic accountability; and he has the combination of pragmatism and ruthlessness to exploit whatever advantages he can find. Russia's under-world may be a serious drain on the country's social, political and economic development, but it also can be and is being mobilised as a tool of foreign policy, in arguably the world's first criminal–political war.

Has the Kremlin properly calculated the risks, though? Not just in terms of Russia's plummeting global standing (though that is undeniable), but also in terms of the way that contact with the *vory* further corrupts the state security officers, whom erstwhile FSB Director Nikolai Patrushev called the 'new nobility' of Russia.[49] Their privileged status, lack of effective oversight and use of extralegal methods in their day jobs have all contributed to making them incubators of criminal networks and circles. As journalists Andrei Soldatov and Irina Borogan, the best independent Russian observers of these spooks, put it:

> In Soviet times, the members of the KGB were part of an elite. But when the Soviet Union collapsed and Russia plunged into the new capitalism, few KGB officers emerged as business leaders. They were outflanked by younger, fleeter hustlers: a new breed of oligarchs. Instead, KGB veterans found their calling in second and third tiers of the new business structures, running the security departments of the tycoons' empires. No longer masters of the universe, they now served the new rich.[50]

Who are the 'new rich' of Russia, then? Consider Sergei (for obvious reasons this is not his real name), a colonel in the FSB whom I have met a few times in Moscow. He is a smart and impressive man, focused and educated. He remembers the 1990s as a 'time of troubles' and more than once expressed with apparent sincerity his belief that 'Putin was sent by God to save Russia'. I also have no doubts at all that he is as corrupt as they come. He comes from working-class stock, went to university, then for reasons never quite clear served a tour as a junior army officer before joining the KGB and transitioning to its successor service after 1991. He doesn't seem to have inherited, and his wife doesn't work, but nonetheless he owns a massive house on the outskirts of the capital with all the trappings of the Muscovite nouveau riche, from the three-car garage (Range Rover for him, BMW for her, Renault for the live-in housekeeper) to the imported marble countertops, massive flat-screen TVs on seemingly every wall, and a pool house in the garden.

Sergei, I understand, is a service provider. His position within the FSB allows him to access the wealth of information that the security services in an authoritarian state hold. If you need to know exactly how much money a target has before shaking them down, if you want to know who really owns that company you've got your eye on, or if you would simply like to have someone's private mobile phone number, and that of his mistress, then Sergei's your man. It presumably does not prevent him from also doing his job well, but at the same time the access and assets of his position are available for hire. Most of his clients appear to be 'business', but in modern Russia, where the worlds of business, crime and politics intersect so freely, this means nothing.

The more the security services use criminals as assets, whether hackers or killers, the more they have contact with them, the greater the risk of compromise, so that the handler can become the hireling. In 2012, for example, Jeffrey DeLisle, a sublieutenant in the Canadian navy, was arrested for being a spy for the GRU. He worked at HMCS *Trinity*, an intelligence fusion centre responsible for collating materials not just from Canadian services but also its allies in the UK, the USA, Australia and New Zealand. As such, he had access to a phenomenal array of secrets, but as the investigation proceeded it became clear that the tasks he was set included finding out what the Royal Canadian Mounted Police knew about suspected Russian gangsters in the country.[51] Speaking to Canadian security officers, it is clear that they do not have any sense of quite why the GRU would want to know this. It seems more likely that someone somewhere in the chain of command simply realised that, given DeLisle's position, he could effortlessly access information that could quickly be monetised and sold to the criminals in question. The history of the *vory* is of criminals who found ways to work within a powerful regime and to twist it to their ends. From the labour camps to the black market, they adapted and thrived by understanding how to exploit their environment to their advantage. It would be dangerous and foolish to assume that today's successors to the Soviet *vory* are any less capable.

CHAPTER 16

BANDIT RUSSIA
The theft of a nation?

A thief's country is any place where he can steal.

Russian proverb

'What is the difference,' a Russian policeman once sourly joked to me, 'between a mafioso and a politician?' The punchline turned out to be 'I don't know either.'[1] Many national leaders around the world like to talk tough on national security, but it is hard to see many being willing to use criminal slang at a press conference. In 1999, though, Vladimir Putin memorably said of Chechen terrorists, 'If we find them in the toilet, we'll whack them, even in the outhouse.' He used the word *mochit*, which literally means 'to wet', and comes from criminal slang recorded as far back as the 1920s. In a term that ended up being adopted even by the KGB political police, *mokroye delo*, a 'wet job', was a killing, wet because blood was shed. When Putin – at the time still prime minister, but President Boris Yeltsin's heir apparent – used a term like this, it not only consolidated his status as a leader with a touch of the bad-boy street hoodlum, it also sanctioned the spread of such language throughout official society.[2]

There had been a transfer of *vor* phrases, even customs, before. Within the Soviet Spetsnaz special forces, for example, a test for new recruits was to place a clean, white towel inside the barracks door: whoever casually makes himself at home and wipes his dirty boots on it shows himself to be in the know, not a clueless greenhorn.[3] This custom was originally one of the ways *blatnye* in the labour camps recognised one of their own.[4] Yet this was so much more deliberate and mainstream. Suddenly, politicians and commentators alike were talking about *razborki* (violent score-settling) and *skhodki* (meetings), about who was under whose 'roof' and who had 'ordered' (in the sense of taking out a contract killing) whom, and how many *limonki* ('little lemons', a million rubles) that might have cost. Like gangsters, after all, Russians must live *po-ponyatiyam*, 'according to the understandings' – in other words, acknowledging the unwritten codes and hierarchies, not just the formal ones.

In some ways, this is the final irony. *Fenya*, once a token of deliberate separation from the rest of society, has become enthusiastically incorporated by that same society. The thieves' language has been tamed, adopted and commodified in what may seem a final victory of sorts by the mainstream. Of course, there had always been a bleed out of criminal expressions into youth and counter-culture slang, but these tended to be transitory phenomena, as today's cool becomes tomorrow's embarrassing anachronism. Terms like *pakhan* (gang leader) for father and *dokhodyaga* (a *zek* on the verge of starvation) for a skinny guy came and went out of fashion without leaving a mark, unlike the way this more recent adoption of criminal language has reached the mainstream.

No country for old thieves?

Nowadays we don't really have any real thieves. Everything is sold for a price and decided by money.

Yevgeny, career criminal[5]

The question is, how far has this affected truly Russian public and political culture? Of course, the process goes two ways. Mainstream society has adopted criminal slang not just because it was exciting to break such taboos after years of stultifying and po-faced Soviet jargon, nor yet simply to follow Putin's example. It also reflected a fundamental process of criminalisation of politics and daily life, a way of describing the *byt*, the experiences of the day to day, communicating a world in which clan loyalty, ruthless competition and naked exploitation were the order of the day.[6] Yet words make worlds, and the spread of this idiom must surely also have contributed to this process. Linguist Mikhail Grachev has said, 'Thieves' terms denote a lexicon of aggression [and] when they cross over into common usage, they gradually influence our psyche for the worst.'[7] Viktor Erofeyev, a writer himself no stranger to the margins of acceptable language, likewise presented the way Russia has evolved as being both cause and effect: 'A whole new vocabulary was needed to reflect the emerging bandit-capitalist reality; and on the vacant lot of Soviet newspeak neologisms culled from the jargon of prison life and drug culture sprouted like bamboo. Those words transformed Russian into a language of desire, irony, coercion, and pragmatism.'[8]

As the Russian underworld loses its old myths and codes, as the title of *vor v zakone* becomes commodified and turned into an empty vanity, as the senior criminals set up corporations and charities and seek to blend into mainstream society, and as politicians start talking like gangsters, who is taming and teaching whom? Somewhere around the turn of the twenty-first century, state-building thieves and criminalised statesmen met in the middle. The Russian-American journalist Paul Klebnikov – himself killed in a mob hit in Moscow in 2004 – quoted Konstantin Borovoi, chair of the Russian Commodity Exchange, as saying, 'The mafia is an attempt to imitate the government. It has its own tax system, its own security service, and its own administrative system. Any entrepreneur, in addition to paying taxes to the government, has to pay taxes to this shadow government.'[9]

In the 1990s, the state was in crisis, not failed but failing. Since then, it has recovered, in part by not simply taming but absorbing the underworld, or at least those more far-sighted elements who were trying to 'imitate the government'. It is too simplistic simply to call this a 'mafia state'. Under Putin, while people at the heart of the regime are undoubtedly interested in enriching themselves, there is also an ideological mission dear to his heart. Putin's appeals to Russian patriotism, his self-declared mission of restoring to Russia its 'sovereignty' and its status in the world – making Russia great again – appear to be more than just self-justificatory rhetoric. Likewise, when the interests of the Kremlin and the underworld collide, it is the latter which accommodates the former. As the arrests of figures such as St Petersburg's criminal 'night governor' Vladimir Barsukov/ Kumarin demonstrate (see chapter 13), this is not a regime which ignores challenges.

Instead, two processes have taken place. One could be called the – limited – 'nationalisation' of the underworld. Some of its members have been rolled into the state elite, whether in the form of *avtoritet* businessmen or gangsters turned politicians. At the same time, there is a clear consensus that the licence the criminals have received is contingent on their living *po-ponyatiyam*, with the state periodically defining these understandings, whether it means not supporting the Chechen rebels or doing the intelligence services an occasional favour.

The second process is the 'gangsterisation' of the formal sectors, one which long predates Putin, but whose parameters have again become more clearly defined under him. In politics, the state will rule by presidential decree and legislative process when it can, but will use behind-the-scenes deals and deniable violence when it must. In the process, it creates a climate of impunity and permissiveness that encourages its agents and allies to act extralegally, whether in the case of the murder of opposition figure Boris Nemtsov in 2015, widely assumed to have been carried out by men answerable to Ramzan Kadyrov,[10] or the attacks splashing caustic chemicals into the face of opposition leader Alexei Navalny in 2017.[11] In effect, this is a state still torn between a legalising impulse and a habitual lawlessness.

Likewise, business contracts are now generally enforced by courts, not killers,[12] but when times are hard, old habits quickly reassert themselves. 'Raiding' others' assets, stealing them with false documents or through spurious legal cases, diminished sharply in the 2000s and early 2010s, but the post-2014 pressures on the economy quickly led to a resurgence.[13] When the economy is under pressure, business once again ducks into the shadows. In 2016, according to Rosstat, the Federal Service for State Statistics, 21.2 per cent of working Russians were employed in the informal sector, a rise of 0.7 percentage points on the year before and the highest level since 2006 when the current formulation was introduced. Meanwhile, according to a study from the Russian Presidential Academy of National Economy and Public Administration, more than thirty million people were in the 'shadow labour market', equating to over 40 per cent of the economically active population.[14] In business, as in politics, there is an urge to reform, to move away from past practices where influence, corruption and violence trumped the logics of competition and the market, and the security of the law. However, the way in which capitalism came to Russia, the way in which from the beginning individual and regime self-interest saw the market uncoupled from the institutions meant to buttress and sustain it, the way the legitimate sector swallowed the criminals, their dirty money and their dirtier methods – all this has meant that certain instincts still run deep. It is perhaps no wonder – if unfair – that one Western economic attaché in Moscow paused in a description of his travels in Russia and said, 'But the trouble is that we pretend to treat them like a real, working economy. It's not: it's all a film set. Just we think we're shooting a commercial, and they're still trying to work out which Godfather movie they're in.'[15]

Headstones and blockbusters: representations of gangsterism

'Are you gangsters?'
'No, we're Russians.'

Exchange from the film *Brat 2*, 2000

What would a gangster movie be without a funeral scene? Near the entrance of Vagankovskoye cemetery in west-central Moscow is a telling juxtaposition. On the one hand there is a contemplative stone angel, the grave of Vlad Listyev, the principled and popular TV anchor and journalist, whose murder in 1995 has never been solved, but was likely because of a struggle for the Ostankino TV network. Almost opposite is the massive and pompous grave of brothers Amiran and Otari Kvantrishvili, godfathers killed around the same time. Another angel, but haloed and with wings outstretched, stands before a tall stone cross, hands on the shiny, gold-lettered headstones of the two gangsters. The contrast between the physical representations of respect and reverence between the two is striking.

Perhaps it ought to have been a clue that he was not really dead that, when 'Osya' Butorin decided to fake his end in 1999, he had his ashes placed in a modest little niche in a quiet ceremony, rather than posthumously throwing the kind of lavish ritual gang leaders regarded as their due in those days. The mobster funeral, a staple of the 'wild 1990s' and almost a loved cliché since, was not just a chance to say farewell to a colleague (or rival), an opportunity to do business, and a display of wealth and adherence to underworld etiquette. It was much more. It was a case of 'practising gangsterdom', not least as much of the pomp was self-consciously modelled on the cinematic displays in films from the West. It was also a demonstration of power: for this moment, that slice of ground belonged not to society, not to the state, but to the *vory*.

Such displays matter, especially when given permanence through gravestones and similar monuments. Looking at the criminal graves of Moscow and Yekaterinburg, Olga Matich deconstructed the photorealistic tombstone imagery that on the one hand sought to erase the violence of the gangsters' lives (and often deaths) while at the same time highlighting virtues of the milieu: physical strength, family and wealth.[16] Many deceased gangsters, after all, were shown in sports clothes and displaying symbols of their success, from BMW car keys to chunky jewellery. Unsubtle, to be sure; tasteless, absolutely. But fitting memorials of the values of the 1990s thieves' world. From personal observation of the cemeteries of Moscow, by the 2000s styles were changing. The indulgence of brash statuary for the mightiest gangsters was still the norm, but these were more likely to be representations of the criminal looking contemplative, with nary a thick gold chain in sight, or of angels and similar features of Orthodox iconography. Aslan 'Ded Khasan' Usoyan's grave, for example, dwarfs even that of the Kvantrishvilis, but it is ambiguous: a life-sized statue of the man, standing besuited between two tall obelisks. He could as easily have been an oligarch or a theatre director as a godfather. The intent, one might speculate, is to downplay the criminal and above all the outsider.

A similar metamorphosis has taken place in popular culture. Remember that the eighteenth-century gangster Vanka Kain, profiled in chapter 1, was perhaps the first (anti-)hero of popular Russian literature, inspiration for a whole series of tall tales originally recounted in the tavern or around the stove before making it to the page.[17] His myth became encrusted with all kinds of romantic and over-the-top story-lines, from the exaggerated (robbing imperial palaces) to the redemptive (Kain was willing to give up his life of crime to marry a good woman). Ultimately, though, he was an 'honest thief' but not an honest man, a bad man whose only virtue was that the people trying to catch him were no better, underlining the essential moral bankruptcy of much of the rest of society.

The gangster has been normalised in post-Soviet Russia. Although there is now a much more vibrant and popular vein of cop and spook drama in literature, and on film and TV, the gangster is still very much a staple. Fictional tales and 'true crime' accounts still fill the bookshops, and organised crime is regularly on the screen. It may no longer be possible to talk of the 'near-total criminalization of post-Soviet popular culture, the preoccupation with crime as a subject matter in virtually every narrative genre.'[18]

On the other hand, as representations of the police have also become more popular (and more positive), perhaps 'criminalisation' has simply given way to 'law-and-ordering'. Either way, the lurid, ultra-violent and implicitly enthusiastic representations of the 1990s have at least partially given way to something more nuanced.

Consider, for example, the trajectory from the films *Brat* ('Brother') and *Brat 2*, through the TV series *Brigada* to the more recent *Fizruk* ('PE Teacher'). The first *Brat* movie (1997) was a small-budget production following Danila Bagrov, recently demobilised from his national service, as he drifts through a gangster-ridden and run-down St Petersburg, more interested than anything else in the latest CDs from Nautilus Pompilius, a Russian rock group. Nonetheless, not least thanks to his feckless brother Viktor, he finds himself drawn into a series of gangster clashes in which – despite his frequent claims that he just did paperwork in the military – he demonstrates an unruffled and lethal competency. Sometimes he is a knight in shabby armour, sometimes a killer for hire, but either way this film, which became a cult hit, portrays the underworld as something seedy, amoral, but also inescapable and beyond the control of legitimate means. To become a vigilante, a 'good law breaker', is the only effective response.

The success of the first film led to the quick release of *Brat 2* in 2000, which has a rather different, nationalist undertone. A series of misadventures brings Danila to Chicago, where he and his brother end up cutting a swathe through American and Ukrainian gangsters alike. Viktor stays in the USA, but Danila returns home with the girl, with the money, and with his Russian pride intact, and the chance to deliver a keynote address exalting the spirituality of Russian values over American materialism:

American, what's your power? Is it really money? My brother says it's money. You've got lots of money – so what? Truth is a real power. Whoever is right is strong. You cheated on a man and took away his money. Did it make you stronger? No, it did not, 'cause you are not right, and the person you cheated on is. That means he's stronger.

This glossier iteration was clearly written and filmed with a much sharper sense of its message, at a time when – as Yeltsin handed over power to Putin – the supposed 'revival' of Russia was suddenly on the national agenda. The

USA is portrayed as, if not evil, then certainly deeply flawed, but perhaps most interestingly perverse was Russians' evident pride in their thugs. They may have gangsters, but at least their gangsters are tougher than anyone else's.

Once, Russia's fictional criminals were wheeler-dealers. Isaac Babel's 1920s *Odessa Tales*, for example, relate picaresque anecdotes about Benya Krik, larger-than-life Jewish godfather of Odessa's Moldavanka ghetto before and during the Revolution. His thuggish criminality is balanced with an amiable cunning and pragmatism: he will fight off the police when he must, but would rather reach some implicit truce when he can. In this respect, he lived up to the popular conception of the Odessan: 'experienced, shrewd, a trickster, a manipulator, a maneuverer, a man of ingenuity, a screamer, an exaggerator, a speculator'.[19] Likewise Ostap Bender, the whimsical conman in Ilya Ilf and Evgeny Petrov's *The Twelve Chairs* (1928) and *The Golden Calf* (1931) – and possibly also an Odessan, like his creators[20] – considers himself 'the great combinator' and relies on luck, wits, charm and a glib tongue in his efforts to amass a fortune and take it to live a new life in Rio de Janeiro. He preys on underground millionaires, profiteers and stupid Communist Party hacks alike, and in the process also demonstrates a keen awareness of the political environment in which he must operate.

In his fascinating study of the worst of 1990s Russian popular culture, though, Eliot Borenstein unpicks how the darkly pessimistic naturalism of the 1980s gave way to a gaudy, gory genre of sex and violence, pulp fiction on methamphetamine.[21] While the cerebral *detektiv* (detective) whodunit survived, it was for a while drowned out by the visceral *boyevik* (fighter) action story. This is a genre of almost characterless hard men (and some women) of violence, who often lack even names, being referred to simply by such soubriquets as *Yary* ('Savage') or *Beshenaya* ('Rabid Girl').[22] It provided 'a symbolic vocabulary for the expression of fundamental anxieties about national pride, cultural collapse, and the frightening new moral landscape of Yeltsin's Russia', albeit often a very crude and simple vocabulary.[23] Danila Bagrov in the *Brat* movies is a *boyevik* given a third dimension: he has a name, a backstory, some motivation, but in essence he too is a response to a time of *bespredel* (disorder), the hope that someone – someone else – will stand up and fight.

As Vanessa Rampton put it, 'such a bleak portrait of Russian reality paradoxically allow[ed] Russians to simultaneously glorify having lived through this unique period.'[24] However, Danila the innocent-eyed vigilante was less in keeping with the 2000s. As organised crime once again began to recede from direct public view, it became less terrifying, more open to being shown in soft focus. The TV miniseries *Brigada*, the first episode of which aired in 2002, could perhaps be described as three parts *The Sopranos*, one part soap opera. It depicted the lives of four friends involved in organised crime from 1989 through to 2000, starting with petty racketeering in the street markets of Gorbachev's USSR, through to politics and revenge as the underworld turned. There are umpteen ins and outs, but the mutual (if not always guaranteed) loyalty of the *brigada* is juxtaposed with the plots of corrupt policeman Vladimir Kaverin, the recurring villain, who even sells guns to the Chechen rebels. Furthermore, the gangster-heroes, while undoubtedly flawed, often enjoy a good life, as well as the fraternity of the group.

In a perceptive analysis, Serguei Oushakine suggests that a core theme of *Brigada* is a depiction of the 'renegotiation of new social positions' in a time of sudden social and economic change.[25] However, most crucial is precisely the way that the series charts the movement of crime from the margins to the heart of the system: 'In *Brigada* the "law" of bandits and the "law" of the state are not merely coexisting or even competing with each other. Instead, it is their supplementarity, the unwilling but inescapable codependency of the (civilized) criminal and the (corrupt) official that makes profitable economic and political exchanges possible.'[26]

From violent outsiders in a world which cannot avoid them, through consummate insiders nonetheless more honest than the people with badges and suits, the final stage in what one could be considered the normalisation of the gangsters is epitomised by the popular TV comedy series *Fizruk*. As of writing it is in its fourth season, having started in 2013–14. The protagonist – 'hero' might be putting it a little strongly – is Foma, a gangster of the old school who had been the head of security to Mamai, an *avtoritet* of the new. Having moved across into the realms of legitimate(ish) business, Mamai sacks Foma at the start of the series for his 'outdated' ways. In an age of suits and brunches, leather-jacketed Foma, boorish and *vorish*, no longer fits. In a bid to regain his position, Foma decides to try and get close to Mamai's rebellious daughter Sanya, and to do that he bribes his way into a position as gym teacher at her school.

What follows are all kinds of fish-out-of-water and schoolyard antics, as well as a sometimes touching connection between Foma and Sanya, and the inevitable chalk-and-cheese romance with a prim fellow teacher. But for the purposes of this analysis what is most interesting is that Foma's gangster aspect is not in itself the heart of the series. It is not underplayed, and were this a Western programme arguably some of the violence and gutter language would be excised, and a redemptive arc to Foma's story introduced much more quickly and clearly. But what matters is not so much that Foma is a gangster – accentuated by his friend and sidekick 'Psikh' ('Psycho'), who is still more clearly in the criminal world – but that he is not a teacher. He could as easily be a cop, a soldier, a journalist or a spy and the same motif would apply. In other words, the implication from *Fizruk* is that gangsters are people, too: not innocent Robin Hoods, not vicious predators, neither paragons to idolise not parasites to condemn, just ordinary folk like the rest of us.

Of course, these are just a few examples from a massive body of written and visual representations of the underworld since 1991. Today the lurid *boyevik* genre is still popular and to be found in many a bookshop. There are even websites such as PrimeCrime, which since 2006 has not only accumulated thousands of pages chronicling the deeds of *vory* great and small, but even has comment sections where criminals, wannabes and fanboys exchange news and views on their favourite gangsters.[27] Nonetheless, the central message is of confluence, as the gangsters seek to normalise their own status, and society embraces or at least accepts them, no longer the feared outsider but just another facet of life.

Mainstreaming mobster music: *russky shanson*

Russian chanson is like a pornographic magazine. Everyone reads it, everyone listens to it, but they're afraid to admit it.
DJ from Radio Petrograd Russky Shanson[28]

This process has been especially evident in music. In the past, Gulag songs inevitably travelled out into popular culture, and some of the *fenya* in youth slang can be explained by its use by counter-culture jazz musicians in the 1970s.[29] But this was very much an underground phenomenon; even the great singer-songwriters of the day such as Vladimir Vysotsky, who blended elements of *blatnye pesny* ('criminal songs') with romantic ballad traditions, largely owed their fame to unofficial 'apartment concerts' and clandestine tape recordings, the so-called *magnetizdat*. When Mikhail Gorbachev began his *glasnost* programme, loosening many of the restraints of censorship and orthodoxy, prison and criminal themes and language – along with those of other hitherto taboo subcultures and topics, such as the Afghan War and drug abuse – quickly moved closer to the mainstream.

The result was the popular *russky shanson* musical genre (a term only apparently coined in the 1980s), frequently cloyingly romantic, sometimes shockingly dark, but often referencing criminal and prison experiences or using the language of the underworld. Back in Soviet times, the milder forms which avoided overtly criminal or rebellious themes – often called *dvorovye romansy*, 'courtyard romances' – were tolerated, while true *blatnye pesny* survived outside the official media. Since then, though, both have thrived – anyone who has taken a gypsy cab in Moscow has probably heard a radio tuned to Radio Shanson – and spawned a whole array of subgenres. There is the jollier vein of ballads about dumb cops and cunning robbers, often set in – where else? – Odessa; there are plaintive tales of love lost through imprisonment and dreams of return; there are gritty accounts of scores settled and traitors executed.

One of the first real stars of *shanson* in its criminal form was Mikhail Krug, whose first three albums were released unofficially but nonetheless copied and circulated widely. He openly socialised with gangsters in his home town of Tver and even wrote one of his songs, 'Vladimir Tsentral', to honour local kingpin 'Sasha Sever', who had served time in the prison of that name. Krug was killed during a break-in to his home in 2002, and, when one of the robbers realised whom they had shot, he killed his accomplice in the hope of preventing not the authorities but the gangsters from identifying him.[30] (He failed.) More circumspectly, another of the big names of *shanson*, Alexander Rozenbaum, is the co-owner of the 'Tolsty Frayer' chain of pubs, essentially the 'Fat Non-Criminal' in *fenya*.

As well as traditional balladeers accompanied by their guitars, there are now those who mix in rock elements such as Grigory Leps, blacklisted by the US Treasury Department in 2013 on the basis of claims that he handled moneys for a criminal.[31] Claims against Leps aside, the association of organised crime and music is hardly unique to him. For example, the veteran Georgian-born singer and politician Iosif Kobzon is frequently called 'Russia's Sinatra', a judgement based on his alleged criminal associations as much as his crooning style. Kobzon – who is also barred from the USA –

has reportedly interceded for criminals (he was rumoured to have been behind the early release from prison of Vyacheslav 'Yaponchik' Ivankov in 1991[32]).

The significance of the *shanson* genre is that, unlike gangster rap or the even more explicitly criminal Latin American *narcocorridos* ('drug ballads'),[33] it was never the edgy music of a disenfranchised and rebellious ethnic group or youth cohort. Rap and hip-hop may now be widely heard, but their roots are still in the projects and the ghettos of the United States, not the suburbs. Conversely, *shanson* is much more centrally located in the Russian cultural world. Radio Shanson has the fifth largest audience in Russia[34] and, even amongst young people, the genre is the third most popular (after Western pop and rock music).[35] However, the experience of the Gulags was a universal one, affecting Bolshevik theoreticians, army officers, teachers and peasants alike, and when the songs of the camps came with the returning *zeki*, they likewise suffused all strata of Soviet society from the first. Thus, the significance of the recurring themes of the genre ought to be considered as expressions of mainstream, not marginal culture. These are, even in their more whimsical moments, distinctly toxic ones. Consider, for example, Villi Tokarev, an émigré to New York's Brighton Beach Russian community whose *shanson* music made it back to the Motherland before he did. His 'Vory-Gumanisty' ('Humanist Thieves') makes it clear that there is no prospect of a decent life lived honestly, even for the 'professor, writer and . . . poet' in the gang, because 'he who does not steal lives like a beggar'.[36]

In the end, *shansons* are essentially fatalistic – life is hard and unfair, and it forces you down roads you might otherwise have avoided – and yet also vibrant. They lack, in the main, the overt violence and macho swagger of gangster rap; when the songs refer to violence, it is often couched in euphemism. Even in the more explicit lyrics, slang slightly softens the effect. For example, the popular 'Gop-Stop' (a mugging, 'gop' referring to a *gopnik*, a disparaging term for someone who in Britain might be called a 'chav' and in the USA 'white trash') is about an attack on a 'treacherous bitch' who spurned the singer. 'Semyon' is enjoined to 'take this feather . . . and slice her under the rib', using a prison term for a knife. In the main, though, *shanson* seems to navigate between melancholia and a whistling-in-the-dark zest for life that precisely draws its vigour from the knowledge that prison, death and betrayal are likely just around the corner.

What is to be done?

The question of the effectiveness of the ongoing fight against criminali-
sation is the question of whether Russia will exist in ten years' time.
Valery Zorkin, chair of the Constitutional Court, 2010[37]

They may enjoy watching films about gangsters and even listen to *Radio Shanson*, but there is no evidence that ordinary Russians are happy with the present corrupt and criminalised situation. Admittedly, their main problem is corruption, because that directly and visibly affects their daily lives, while the gangsters have receded into the shadows. Ironically enough, even many within the elite, however much they have enriched themselves under the present order, appear to feel it is time to move on. From a purely anecdotal perspective, I am struck by how often I encounter a sense from the new rich (and especially their pampered but well-travelled offspring) that, to quote one, 'Russia needs to be a regular country, a European one, and that means an end to the time of stealing.'[38] If nothing else, ending the 'time of stealing' would, to them, mean not a meticulous restitution of their riches to all those from whom they had been stolen, so much as the creation of a rule-of-law state in which their wealth was now both legitimate and protected. After all, under Putin the real currency is not the ruble, but political power, and mere money and property are at best something held in trust until the day the state or some predator with a higher *krysha* and sharper teeth comes and takes it from you.

Back in the 1990s, the veteran geostrategist Edward Luttwak asked, 'Does the Russian mafia deserve the Nobel Prize for economics?' He went on to argue that 'in purely economic terms the conventional wisdom is all wrong' as modern and broadly humane advanced economies evolved from 'lean and hungry wolves that . . . originally accumulated capital, by seizing profitable market opportunities – often by killing off competitors in ways that today's anti-monopoly commissions would not tolerate – and by cutting costs in every way possible, not excluding all the tax avoidance they could get away with.'[39] He was at once right on the nail, and dangerously wrong: right in that it was indeed from previous generations of robber barons, slavers and exploiters of every stripe that today's Western elites emerged; wrong to suggest that it was some inevitable and irreversible process, such that one could and should just sit back and wait for it to happen. From the democratic rollbacks currently witnessed in central

Europe (and perhaps even the USA), to the two-steps-forward, one-and-a-half-back fight against organised crime in Italy, it is clear that, just as there are natural processes driving societies towards law and regularisation, so too there are destructive ones. When there has been any kind of meaningful progress in cutting organised crime down to size – nowhere has it been wholly eliminated – then it has been through a combination of three basic necessities: effective laws and the presence of judicial and police structures able and willing to uphold them; political elites willing or forced to allow those structures to function; and a mobilised and vigilant public eager and determined to ensure that the work is done.

Russia's laws and institutions largely meet the necessary criteria on paper but are thoroughly undermined in practice. Despite attempts at reform,[40] any attempt to bring genuine legality to this society faces the serious problems of corruption, a lack of resources for police and courts alike and, in particular, the blatant manipulation of the law by the political elite. Despite Vladimir Ovchinsky's downbeat assertion that 'MVD anti-mafia units constantly turn into mafia minions',[41] though, there are forces for change. Many within the judiciary, especially within the junior ranks, genuinely believe in the rule of law. I have met good Russian cops – even ones willing to take a petty bribe but essentially committed to taking down the bad guys – who would like to do their job. Since the chaos of the 1990s, there has been a distinct change, especially amongst the new generation of younger police officer. It is not that corruption has become anathema. Indeed, if anything my unscientific sense tallies with the rather more methodologically robust analysis by Alexis Belianin and Leonid Kosals of Moscow's Higher School of Economics that finds there is a strong commitment to retaining a degree of corruption.[42] Rather, there has been a distinct shift in the limits of 'acceptable corruption'. One officer rationalised it in terms of substitution: 'If the guy would anyway get a fine, then why not take a bribe to let him go? He's still out of pocket, and anyway, he'd probably just bribe the judge or prosecutor instead. But he still pays for his crime.'[43] However, for the kind of offence that would merit a custodial sentence, he definitely felt only a 'bad cop' – he actually used the *fenya* term *musor*, 'trash', akin to the British 'filth' – would take a bribe to overlook it. The specific example he gave was speeding and causing an accident in which no one was hurt and insurance would cover the damage, compared with a situation in which a victim was hurt or killed. Furthermore, all the examples given involved turning a blind eye: actively engaging in criminal acts (beyond taking the bribe) had become 'bad cop' territory.

To be sure, at present the police operate within a system in which most of the senior criminals are untouchable – the superiors of the unlucky officer who arrested underworld banker Semyon Mogilevich left him in no doubt about that – but they generally do what they can, and often wish it were more. Although there are no institutions which could wholly be said to be on the side of reform, there are clear factions within the Justice Ministry, the Ministry of Internal Affairs, the Ministry of Finance, the Audit Commission and the General Prosecutor's Office who are. However, the Kremlin still appears to believe that reform should be limited to the minimum necessary to maintain the legitimacy and effectiveness of the system.

But what elite, unprompted, reforms a system that grants it the opportunity to steal with impunity? There is little evidence of any serious will on the part of the Russian elite to do anything, especially as power becomes more and more tightly held by Vladimir Putin and a shrinking circle of like-minded (and generally highly acquisitive) allies. In the 1990s, it was still possible for people to draw fanciful parallels with the 'robber barons' of the nineteenth-century United States and consider organised crime a passing phase out of which the country would naturally grow, or even a necessary step in the building of capitalism. Gavriil Popov, former mayor of Moscow, said that 'the mafia is necessary given the current situation in Russia . . . it fulfils the role of Robin Hood, distributing wealth'.[44] Of course, this was nonsense: organised crime was and is closer to the sheriff of Nottingham, eagerly acquiring the power to plunder and then exploiting it as much and for as long as it can. There appear to be no such illusions now; Russians of every class seem fully aware of the rapacious and self-serving nature of the corruption–gangster nexus.

For all that Russia has its elections and campaigns, it is at best a 'hybrid democracy', an authoritarianism hiding behind the façade of the process. Nonetheless, even in such regimes, the opinion of the people is not entirely irrelevant. While the state dominates TV, there is still scope for serious investigation and discussion in the print and online media, and a relatively internet-savvy population has many ways it can find out what is going on. The problem appears to be a lack of faith that anything can be done about it, that change is even possible. This is something with which anti-corruption campaigner and opposition leader Alexei Navalny is struggling as I write. The first step in fighting organised crime and corruption is, after all, to have hope.

This is likely to be a generational process. Italy after the Second World War was a democracy, and its soap-opera politics were characterised by regular elections, ridiculously frequent changes in government and a vibrant media. It had good laws, courts and well-funded police forces. However, behind all that, for more than four decades it was essentially a corrupt one-party state: somehow the dominant Christian Democrat Party was always at the heart of government, and it was the primary 'roof' for organised crime. In return, the mafia paid up in cash and by delivering the southern vote for the *Democristiana*, time and again. It took the shocking murders in 1992 of two dedicated investigative magistrates, Paolo Borsellino and Giovanni Falcone, to galvanise a public that was increasingly sick of the situation. Facing electoral decimation, the Italian elite grudgingly unleashed the magistrates and the police, and the start of a serious campaign against the mafia began.[45] Twenty-five years on, there has been real progress, but also steps back and steps missed, and all in the context of an existing working, democratic state.

Post-Soviet Russia has only part of the institutional framework, and fewer than three decades' experience. It seems unlikely that Putin will reinvent himself in any meaningful way as a 'hammer of the mafia', and his immediate successor may well turn out to be a pragmatic kleptocrat happy to rebuild fences with the West, but not challenge the power of organised crime and the acquisitive instincts of the elite at home. Italy still isn't there; Japan, which started its real fight against the yakuza at the same time, is in much the same place as Italy. Russia will get there, but not tomorrow.

A helping hand?

I don't know what the fuss in the West is about the Russian 'mafia'.
We've always been this way. It's just that you're finally finding out.
            Yuri Melnikov, head of Russia's Interpol bureau, 1994[46]

Nor is there much that the outside world can do, especially given that in the current geopolitical environment any efforts to bring about change inside Russia will be viewed as hypocritical at best, hostile interference and an attempt at 'soft regime change' at worst. But 'not much' is not nothing. A key step would be to attack criminals' assets abroad more vigorously and, perhaps most importantly, address a common temptation to turn a blind eye to money that is slightly grubby in the name of business. Even before the 1998 crisis sent financial institutions scrambling for business, it was an open secret that many would gladly accept dirty money so long as it had been 'prewashed' enough that the bankers could claim to be 'shocked, shocked' if it was proven to be dirty. Many of the world's financial capitals, from Dubai and Nicosia to London and Hong Kong, still tend to be more concerned about preventing the influx of dirty money in the abstract than in practice. As John Kampfner wrote, with passion but also sense, 'if the price of making the City [of London] a haven for low-tax oligarchs and other assorted spivs is to turn London into a mobsters' paradise, then that is our lookout'.[47] This is a classic case of short-term gains with serious long-term costs, and Cyprus, whose 2013 financial bailout was jeopardised by the presence of dirty Russian money in its system, offers a cautionary tale, but it is one few are heeding.

Part of the reason why the *vory* of the new age avoid tattoos, no longer speak *blatnaya muzyka* (or at least no more than everyone else) and generally seek to blend in with the mainstream is in part precisely so as not to be excluded from the benefits of globalisation. And in the main, so long as they do not practice their violent entrepreneurship in our countries, so long as they are high-rolling guests, investors, shoppers and tourists, we are happy to let them.

One Russian once asked me, 'Why do you in Britain hate our mafia in Russia but love them at home?'[48] He had a point. Many countries have proven as willing to accept the 'right' (in other words, wealthy) kind of people with criminal links as they have been to accept inward investment of questionable origins. After the Magnitsky affair, the US passed the 'Magnitsky Act' in 2012, a measure targeting Russians believed to be connected with that criminal case for sanctions. The anger and dismay this generated in Russia demonstrates the power of 'naming and shaming' as well as excluding criminals and their protectors from desirable ports of call. There are costs both practical and political for the West, but it might be a small inducement for many of the powerful figures in the criminal-business world to 'clean' themselves if their underworld activities seem to prevent them from holidaying on the Riviera or their children from attending foreign universities.

Ultimately, though, the Russian people are the first and worst victims of today's iteration of the *vorovskoi mir* and it will be for them to tame it, as eventually I believe they will. There is always the Orientalising temptation to somehow suggest that certain peoples, from Italians to Russians, are naturally prone to corruption and gangsterism. And it is true that there is historical 'form'. George Dobson, the *Times* correspondent in Russia in the late nineteenth century, dourly observed:

> The two features of the Russian character which struck me most when first I went to Russia were their great hospitality . . . and their lawlessness. By this, I mean their absolute contempt for laws of all sorts . . .
>
> If a law exists, someone seems to consider it his bounden duty either to flatly refuse to acknowledge it or, more generally, to see how he or she can manage to get round it.[49]

However, perhaps the last word ought to go to one of the Afghan War veterans I introduced at the very start of this book. In 1993, I briefly reconnected with Vadim, the police officer. As one of the OMON special police, he and his team were increasingly often being sent in to arrest gangsters and break up armed incidents. They had been issued heavy, uncomfortable, old-fashioned, army-surplus body armour that no one really trusted. They were using a battered old UAZ van that needed to be jump-started on a cold morning, and often had no more than a quarter of a tank of petrol. They were risking their lives, while being paid the same as the women who sat in booths at the base of the long escalators in the metro stations, watching that no one fell, and occasionally shouting at people to stay in line. He had acquired a one-year-old child, a scar from a ricochet and quite a drinking habit. And yet for all that he was unconscionably, unreasonably, unfathomably optimistic. 'These are mad times,' he admitted, 'but they won't last. We'll survive. We will learn how to be European, how to be civilised. It just may take a while.'[50] He probably did not mean quite this long, but all the same, I think he is right.

GLOSSARY OF COMMONLY USED TERMS

49ers	Non-political prisoners convicted under Article 49 of the Soviet Criminal Code
58ers	Political prisoners convicted under Article 58 of the Soviet Criminal Code
apelsin	'Orange', modern term for *vor v zakone* (see below) assumed to have bought his title
artel	Tsarist-era artisans' cooperative
avtoritet	'Authority', new-generation crime boss
besprizornik	Homeless child
blat	Favours, pull
blatar	See *blatnoi*
blatnaya muzyka	'Thieves' music', criminal slang
blatnoi	Traditionalist thief, also *urka*, *blatar*, *urkagan*
bratva	Brotherhood
brigada	'Brigade', organised crime group
brigadir	'Brigadier', local lieutenant of a gang boss
byk	'Bull', a heavy
bytovik	'Everyday-lifer', petty criminal generally forced into crime by need
Chekist	Slang for a political police officer (from the Cheka, the first Bolshevik force)
chestnyaga	'The honest', unconverted, traditionalist thief

etap	Prisoner transfer between camps
fartsovshchik	Black marketeer
fenya	Criminal slang, also *ofenya*, *blatnaya muzyka*
frayer	Outsider, non-criminal
FSB	Federal Security Service
gruppirovka	Crime group
Gulag	Labour camp (from acronym for Main Directorate of Camps)
KGB	Committee of State Security (Soviet political police)
klichka	Criminal nickname
kodlo	Early criminal gang
krysha	'Roof', protection
ksiva	Slip of paper, note
lavrushnik	'Bay leaf', disparaging Slavic criminal term for Georgians
militsiya	'Militia', Soviet police
MVD	Ministry of Internal Affairs
nalevo	'To the left', through the black market
oboroten	'Werewolf', corrupt police officer
obshchak	Common gang funds
ofenya	See *fenya*
pakhan	Senior criminal
patsan	Prospective member of the thieves
ponyatiya	'Understandings', informal gang code of behaviour
razborka	Violent settling of scores
shestyorka	'Sixer', gofer or hanger-on
skhodka	Gangster meeting, a 'sit-down'
smotryashchy	Watcher, overseer
strelka	'Arrow', gangster meeting specifically to resolve a dispute
suchya voina	'Bitches' war', Gulag struggle amongst criminals in the late 1940s and early 1950s
suka	'Bitch', criminal abandoning the traditional code
tolkach	Fixer
torpedo	'Torpedo', hit man
tsekhovik	Black-market entrepreneur
urka	See *blatnoi*

urkagan	See *blatnoi*
varyag	'Varangian' ('Viking'), term for gangsters from Moscow and European Russia used by criminals in other Russian regions
vor	Thief
vor v zakone	'Thief in law', thief within the code
vorovskoi mir	'Thieves' world', traditional criminal culture
voyenshchina	'Soldiery', Gulag prisoners who had been in the Red Army
yama	Slum
zek	Gulag prisoner

NOTES

Preface

1. Notably Valery Chalidze, in his *Criminal Russia: Essays on Crime in the Soviet Union* (New York: Random House, 1977), but it was also buried within the memoirs of many survivors of the Gulag labour camps.

Introduction

1. The details came from a retired police officer who had served in the Leningrad police but did not experience this case first hand. The best guide to the tattoos of the Soviet underworld is Danzig Baldaev's three-volume *Russian Criminal Tattoo Encyclopedia* (London: Fuel, 2006–8).
2. See Kelly Barksby, 'Constructing criminals: the creation of identity within criminal mafias', unpublished PhD dissertation, Keele University, 2013.
3. Mark Galeotti, 'Criminal histories: an introduction', *Global Crime* 9, 1–2 (2008), p. 5.
4. Attributed to John Gotti, cited in *New York Magazine*, 7 November 1994, p. 54.

1. Kain's Land

1. Conversation, Moscow, 1993. 'Graf' was a so-called *brigadir*, a gang boss's local lieutenant.
2. Explored in great depth in Barend ter Haar's *Ritual and Mythology of the Chinese Triads: Creating an Identity* (Leiden: Brill, 2000).
3. See Peter Hill, *The Japanese Mafia: Yakuza, Law, and the State* (Oxford: Oxford University Press, 2003), pp. 36–41.
4. Especially and gaudily evident in their extravagant tombstones and mausolea; see Olga Matich, 'Mobster gravestones in 1990s Russia', *Global Crime* 7, 1 (2006).
5. For accounts of this progression, see Joseph Serio and Viacheslav Razinkin, 'Thieves professing the code: the traditional role of the *vory v zakone* in Russia's criminal world and adaptations to a new social reality', *Low Intensity Conflict & Law Enforcement* 4, 1 (1995); Alena Ledeneva, 'Organized crime in Russia today', *Jamestown Foundation Prism* 4, 8 (1998); Federico Varese, *The Russian Mafia: Private Protection in a New Market Economy* (Oxford: Oxford University Press, 2001); Mark Galeotti, 'The Russian "Mafiya": consolidation and globalisation', *Global Crime* 6, 1 (2004); Joseph Serio, *Investigating the Russian Mafia* (Durham, NC: Carolina Academic Press, 2008).

6. Peter Gattrell, *The Tsarist Economy, 1850–1917* (London: Batsford, 1986), p. 32.
7. V. I. Lenin, 'On the question of national policy' (1914), in *Lenin: Collected Works* (Moscow: Progress, 1972), p. 218.
8. W. H. Parker, *An Historical Geography of Russia* (London: University of London Press, 1968), p. 312.
9. Neil Weissman, 'The regular police in tsarist Russia, 1900–1914', *Russian Review* 44, 1 (1985) p. 51.
10. Renamed the *Razboinyi prikaz*, 'Banditry Bureau', in 1571; J. L. H. Keep, 'Bandits and the law in Muscovy', *Slavonic & East European Review* 35, 84 (1956).
11. Robert Abbott, 'Police reform in the Russian province of Iaroslavl, 1856–1876', *Slavic Review* 32, 2 (1973), p. 293.
12. Respectively the 1856 *Pamyatnaya kniga politseiskikh zakonov dlya chinov gorodskoi politsii* (Memorandum Book of Police Duties for Members of the City Police) and the companion volume for rural police, the 1857 *Pamyatnaya kniga politseiskikh zakonov dlya zemskoi politsii*.
13. Donald Mackenzie Wallace, *Russia* (London: Cassell, 1905), vol. 2, p. 14.
14. This is explored further in several contributions to Stephen Lovell, Alena Ledeneva and Andrei Rogachevskii (eds), *Bribery and Blat in Russia: Negotiating Reciprocity from the Middle Ages to the 1990s* (Basingstoke: Macmillan, 2000), especially Vadim Volkov, 'Patrimonialism versus rational bureaucracy'; Janet Hartley, 'Bribery and justice in the provinces in the reign of Catherine II'; and Mark Galeotti, ' "Who's the boss, us or the law?" The corrupt art of governing Russia'.
15. Valery Chalidze, *Criminal Russia: Essays on Crime in the Soviet Union* (New York: Random House, 1977), p. 28.
16. David Christian, 'Vodka and corruption in Russia on the eve of Emancipation', *Slavic Review* 46, 3–4 (1987), p. 472.
17. Robert Abbott, 'Police reform in Russia, 1858–1878', PhD dissertation, Princeton University, 1971, p. 26.
18. Robert Thurston, 'Police and people in Moscow, 1906–1914', *Russian Review* 39, 3 (1980), p. 334.
19. *New York Times*, 31 October 1909.
20. *Vestnik politsii*, 22 September 1910.
21. Ben Eklof and Stephen Frank (eds), *The World of the Russian Peasant: Post-Emancipation Culture and Society* (Boston: Unwin Hyman, 1990), p. 147.
22. Alexander Pushkin, *The Captain's Daughter and Other Tales* (originally 1836) (New York: Vintage, 2012), p. 107.
23. Cathy Frierson, *All Russia Is Burning! A Cultural History of Fire and Arson in Late Imperial Russia* (Seattle: University of Washington Press, 2004), p. 100.
24. Daniel Brower, *The Russian City between Tradition and Modernity, 1850–1900* (Berkeley: University of California Press, 1990), p. 196.
25. Cathy Frierson, 'Crime and punishment in the Russian village: rural concepts of criminality at the end of the nineteenth century', *Slavic Review* 46, 1 (1987).
26. Chalidze, *Criminal Russia*, p. 12.
27. Frierson, 'Crime and punishment in the Russian village', p. 65.
28. Christine Worobec, 'Horse thieves and peasant justice in post-Emancipation Imperial Russia', *Journal of Social History* 21, 2 (1987), p. 284.
29. V. V. Tenishev, *Administrativnoe polozhenie russkogo krest'yanina* (St Petersburg, 1908), pp. 54–5, quoted in Neil Weissman, 'Rural crime in tsarist Russia: the question of hooliganism, 1905–1914', *Slavic Review* 37, 2 (1978), p. 236.
30. Weissman, 'Rural crime in tsarist Russia', p. 233.
31. Stephen Frank, 'Narratives within numbers: women, crime and judicial statistics in Imperial Russia, 1834–1913', *Russian Review* 55, 4 (1996), p. 552.
32. George Yaney has developed this notion of a traditional Russian duality in laws between those of the state and those from below: see George Yaney, 'Law, society and the domestic regime in Russia, in historical perspective', *American Political Science Review* 59, 2 (1965).

33. Frierson, 'Crime and punishment in the Russian village', p. 60.

34. Ibid., p. 59.

35. Marquis de Custine, *Empire of the Czar: A Journey Through Eternal Russia* (New York: Anchor, [1843] 1989) pp. 124–5.

36. *Vestnik politsii*, no. 18 (1908), quoted in Weissman, 'The regular police in tsarist Russia', p. 51.

37. Weissman, 'The regular police in tsarist Russia', p. 47.

38. *Istoricheskii ocherk obrazovaniya i razvitiya politseiskikh uchrezhdenii v Rossii*, 1913, cited in ibid., p. 49.

39. Anton Blok, 'Bandits and boundaries: robber bands and secret societies on the Dutch frontier (1730–1778)', in Blok, *Honour and Violence* (Cambridge: Polity, 2001).

40. Peter Laven, 'Banditry and lawlessness on the Venetian Terraferma in the later Cinquecento' in Trevor Dean and Kate Lowe (eds), *Crime, Society, and the Law in Renaissance Italy* (Cambridge: Cambridge University Press, 1994).

41. He became the hero of a whole series of tales, especially those serialised in the *Moskovskii listok* newspaper; see James von Geldern and Louise McReynolds, *Entertaining Tsarist Russia* (Bloomington: Indiana University Press, 1998), pp. 221–30.

42. Chalidze, *Criminal Russia*, p. 12.

43. Georgi Breitman, *Prestupniy mir* (Kiev, 1901), quoted in Stephen Frank, *Crime, Cultural Conflict, and Justice in Rural Russia, 1856–1914* (Berkeley: University of California Press, 1999), p. 128.

44. Worobec, 'Horse thieves and peasant justice', p. 283.

45. L Vesin, 'Konokradstvo, ego organizatsiya i sposoby bor'by s nim nasleniya', *Trudy Imperatorskogo vol'nogo ekonomichestogo obshchestva* 1, 3 (1885), cited in ibid., p. 283.

46. Vesin, 'Konokradstvo, ego organizatsiya i sposoby bor'by s nim nasleniya', cited in Frank, *Crime, Cultural Conflict, and Justice in Rural Russia*, p. 130.

47. Frank, *Crime, Cultural Conflict, and Justice in Rural Russia*, p. 130.

48. Worobec, 'Horse thieves and peasant justice', p. 287.

49. Frank, *Crime, Cultural Conflict, and Justice in Rural Russia*, pp. 276–8.

50. Eklof and Frank (eds), *The World of the Russian Peasant*, p. 145.

51. Worobec, 'Horse thieves and peasant justice', p. 283.

52. Orlando Figes, *Peasant Russia, Civil War: The Volga Countryside in Revolution, 1917–1921* (London: Phoenix, 2001), pp. 340–6.

53. Andrei Konstantinov and Mal'kol'm Dikselius, *Banditskaya Rossiya* (St Petersburg: Bibliopolis, 1997), pp. 58–9. See also Aleksandr Sidorov, *Zhigany, urkagany, blatari: podlinnaya istoriya vorovskogo bratstva, 1917–1940* (Moscow: Eksmo, 2005), and I. M. Matskevich, *Mify prestupnogo mira: o zhizni i smerti izvestnykh prestupnikov proshlogo i nastoyashchego* (Moscow: Prospekt, 2015), pp. 147–218.

54. Figes, *Peasant Russia, Civil War*, pp. 352–3.

55. Lynne Viola, *Peasant Rebels under Stalin: Collectivization and the Culture of Peasant Resistance* (Oxford: Oxford University Press, 1998), p. 178.

56. Sheila Fitzpatrick, *Stalin's Peasants: Resistance and Survival in the Russian Village After Collectivization* (Oxford: Oxford University Press, 1995), p. 183.

2. Eating Khitrovka soup

1. W. Bruce Lincoln, *In War's Dark Shadow: The Russians before the Great War* (Oxford: Oxford University Press, 1983), p. 128.

2. Vladimir Gilyarovskii, *Moskva i moskvichi* (Moscow: AST, 2005).

3. Roshanna Sylvester, *Tales of Old Odessa: Crime and Civility in a City of Thieves* (DeKalb: Northern Illinois University Press, 2005), p. 39.

4. L. M. Vasilevskii, *Detskaya 'prestupnost' i detskii sud* (Tver: Oktyabr', 1923) p. 38, quoted in Peter Juviler, *Revolutionary Law and Order: Politics and Social Change in the USSR* (London: Free Press, 1976), p. 8.

5. Evgenii Akel'ev, *Povsednevnaya zhizn' vorovskogo mira Moskvy vo vremena Van'ki Kaina* (Moscow: Molodaya gvardiya, 2012).

6. Peter Gattrell, *The Tsarist Economy, 1850–1917* (London: Batsford, 1986), p. 67.

7. Ibid., p. 50.

8. Nicolas Spulber, *Russia's Economic Transitions: From Late Tsarism to the New Millennium* (Cambridge: Cambridge University Press, 2003), p. 52

9. Gattrell, *The Tsarist Economy*, p. 67.

10. Robert Johnson, *Peasant and Proletarian: The Working Class of Moscow in the Late Nineteenth Century* (Leicester: Leicester University Press, 1979), p. 84

11. Reginald Zelnik, *Labor and Society in Tsarist Russia: The Factory Workers of St Petersburg* (Stanford: Stanford University Press, 1971), pp. 52–6.

12. Lincoln, *In War's Dark Shadow*, p. 118.

13. The most compelling account of the miserable life led by the urban workers is the chapter 'Life in the lower depths' in Lincoln, *In War's Dark Shadow*, pp. 103–34. A fictionalised but still effective study is Henri Troyat, *Daily Life in Russia under the Last Tsar* (Stanford: Stanford University Press, 1961) – especially relevant are chapters 5, 'Baths, traktirs and night shelters' (pp. 51–62), and 7, 'The workers' (pp. 87–107).

14. Zelnik, *Labor and Society in Tsarist Russia*, p. 250.

15. In Moscow in 1902, for example, there were only thirty-nine women aged 15–39 for every hundred men. Johnson, *Peasant and Proletarian*, p. 56.

16. See Laurie Bernstein, *Sonia's Daughters: Prostitutes and their Regulation in Imperial Russia* (Berkeley: University of California Press, 1995); Barbara Alpern Engel, *Women in Russia, 1700–2000* (Cambridge: Cambridge University Press, 2003), pp. 99–100.

17. Joan Neuberger, *Hooliganism: Crime, Culture, and Power in St Petersburg, 1900–1914* (Berkeley: University of California Press, 1993) pp. 64–5, 229.

18. Fedor Dostoevsky, *Crime and Punishment* (Cutchogue, NY: Buccaneer, [1866] 1982), pp. 14, 68.

19. Vsevolod Krestovskii, *Peterburgskie trushchoby* (1864), excerpted in James von Geldern and Louise McReynolds, *Entertaining Tsarist Russia* (Bloomington: Indiana University Press, 1998), pp. 121–8.

20. Alexander Kuprin, *Yama: The Pit* (Charleston, SC: BiblioBazaar, [1909] 2006), p. 21.

21. Maxim Gorky, *The Lower Depths* (Mineola, NY: Dover, [1902] 2000).

22. James von Geldern, 'Life in-between: migration and popular culture in late Imperial Russia', *Russian Review* 55, 3 (1996) p. 369.

23. Rachel Rubin, *Jewish Gangsters of Modern Literature* (Urbana: University of Illinois Press, 2000), p. 21.

24. Something which even some police officers admitted: see R. S. Mulukaev, *Obshcheugolovnaya politsiya dorevolutsionnoi Rossii* (Moscow: Nauka, 1979), p. 25.

25. Daniel Brower, *The Russian City between Tradition and Modernity, 1850–1900* (Berkeley: University of California Press, 1990), p. 197.

26. Lincoln, *In War's Dark Shadow*, p. 126.

27. *Peterburgskii listok*, 7 July 1906, quoted in Joan Neuberger, 'Stories of the street: hooliganism in the St Petersburg popular press', *Slavic Review* 48, 2 (1989), p. 190.

28. Aleksei Svirskii, *Peterburgskie khuligany* (1914), p. 260, quoted in Neuberger, *Hooliganism*, p. 247.

29. Fredric Zuckerman, *The Tsarist Secret Police in Russian Society, 1880–1917* (Basingstoke: Macmillan, 1996), p. 105; Iain Lauchlan, *Russian Hide-and-Seek: The Tsarist Secret Police in St Petersburg, 1906–1914* (Helsinki: SKS-FLS, 2002), p. 303.

30. Robert Thurston, 'Police and people in Moscow, 1906–1914', *Russian Review* 39, 3 (1980), p. 335.

31. The 'strengthened guard' (*usilennaya okhrana*) provisions granted officials the right to ban public gatherings, close businesses, impose various administrative penalties and have cases transferred from civilian to military courts. The tougher 'extraordinary guard' (*chrezvychainaya okhrana*) provisions also included the establishment of special military units to help the police maintain public order.

32. Theofanis Stavrou (ed.), *Russia under the Last Czar* (Minneapolis: University of Minnesota Press, 1969), pp. 97–8.
33. Best discussed in Neuberger, *Hooliganism*. For a definition of the boulevard press, see in particular pp. 15–22. For a useful digest, see her 'Stories of the street'.
34. George Dobson, *Russia* (London: A. & C. Black, 1913), p. 143.
35. *Vestnik politsii*, 31 August 1909.
36. Thurston, 'Police and people in Moscow', pp. 334, 325.
37. Neil Weissman, 'The regular police in tsarist Russia, 1900–1914', *Russian Review* 44, 1 (1985), p. 47.
38. Ibid., p. 48.
39. Ibid., p. 48.
40. Thurston, 'Police and people in Moscow', p. 326.
41. *Vestnik politsii*, 4 February 1910.
42. Vladimir Gilyarovskii, *Moscow and Muscovites* (Montpelier, VT: Russian Information Services, 2013), p. 39.
43. Brower, *The Russian City*, pp. 141–2.
44. Sylvester, *Tales of Old Odessa*, p. 40.
45. *Odesskie novosti*, 19 August 1917, quoted in Boris Briker, 'The underworld of Benia Krik and I. Babel's *Odessa Stories*', *Canadian Slavonic Papers* 36, 1–2 (1994), p. 119.
46. This is especially explored in Valery Chalidze, *Criminal Russia: Essays on Crime in the Soviet Union* (New York: Random House, 1977), pp. 37–44; and Yakov Gilinskiy and Yakov Kostjukovsky, 'From thievish *artel* to criminal corporation: the history of organised crime in Russia', in Cyrille Fijnaut and Letizia Paoli (eds), *Organised Crime in Europe: Concepts, Patterns and Control Policies in the European Union and Beyond* (Dordrecht: Springer, 2004).
47. Johnson, *Peasant and Proletarian*, pp. 91–2.
48. See Hiroaki Kuromiya, 'Workers artels and Soviet production methods', in Sheila Fitzpatrick et al. (eds), *Russia in the Era of NEP: Explorations in Soviet Society and Culture* (Bloomington: Indiana University Press, 1991)
49. Andrei Konstantinov and Mal'kol'm Dikselius, *Prestupnyi mir Rossii* (St Petersburg: Bibliopolis, 1995), p. 27.
50. D. A. Dril, 'O merakh bor'by s prestupnost'yu nesovershennoletnikh', in *Trudy sed'mogo s'ezda predstavitelei russkikh ispravitel'nykh zavedenii dlya maloletnikh, okt. 1908 goda* (Moscow, 1909), p. 18, quoted in Neuberger, *Hooliganism*, p. 182.
51. V. P. Semenov, *Bytovye usloviya zhizni mal'chikov* (St Petersburg, n.d.) p. 6, quoted in Neuberger, *Hooliganism*, p. 179.
52. Neuberger, *Hooliganism*, pp. 171–2.
53. Ibid., p. 190.
54. Lincoln, *In War's Dark Shadow*, pp. 126–7.
55. Isaac Babel, 'The King', in Babel, *Collected Stories* (Harmondsworth: Penguin, 1961), p. 181.
56. Sylvester, *Tales of Old Odessa*, p. 55.
57. Lincoln, *In War's Dark Shadow*, p. 127.
58. Neuberger, *Hooliganism*, pp. 241–2.
59. Sylvester, *Tales of Old Odessa*, p. 32.
60. Conversation, Moscow, 1989.
61. Zelnik, *Labor and Society in Tsarist Russia*, p. 21. Daniel Brower makes the point that in the closing decades of tsarism peasant workers were less likely to move as an *artel*, but even so, the institution has deep social roots, and would indeed re-emerge within the Soviet system as both part of and also a rival to the 'brigade' structure. Brower, *The Russian City*, p. 144; Stephen Kotkin, *Magnetic Mountain: Stalinism as a Civilization* (Berkeley: University of California Press, 1997), p. 89.
62. Sylvester, *Tales of Old Odessa*, p. 58.
63. Maximilien de Santerre, *Sovetskie poslevoennye kontslageri i ikh obitateli* (Munich: IPI SSSR, 1960), p. 55.
64. Sylvester, *Tales of Old Odessa*, p. 24.

65. Ibid., p. 56.

66. Brower, *The Russian City*, pp. 178–80.

67. For Mishka Yaponchik's career, see Oleg Kapchinskii, *Mishka Yaponchik i drugie: kriminal i vlast' v gody Grazhdanskoi voiny v Odesse* (Moscow: Kraft+, 2015); Fedor Razzakov, *Bandity vremen sotsializma: khronika ros. prestupnosti, 1917–1991* (Moscow: Eksmo, 1996), pp. 63–4.

3. The birth of the *vory*

1. Kirill Ashotov, 'Korsar Koba', *Versiya*, 18 January 2016.

2. David Shub, 'Kamo: the legendary Old Bolshevik of the Caucasus', *Russian Review* 19, 3 (1960).

3. Conversation, Kiev, 1991.

4. Ilya Ilf and Evgeny Petrov, *The Twelve Chairs* (1928) and *The Golden Calf* (1931).

5. Orlando Figes, *A People's Tragedy: The Russian Revolution, 1891–1924* (London: Penguin, 1998), p. 400.

6. Mark Galeotti, 'Private security and public insecurity: outsourced vigilantism in modern Russia', in David Pratten and Atreyee Sen (eds), *Global Vigilantes* (London: Hurst, 2007), pp. 267–89.

7. Robert Daniels, *Russia: The Roots of Confrontation* (Cambridge, MA: Harvard University Press, 1985), p. 111.

8. Quoted in Paul Hagenloh, *Stalin's Police: Public Order and Mass Repression in the USSR, 1926–1941* (Washington, DC: Woodrow Wilson Center Press, 2009), p. 27.

9. Joseph Douillet, *Moscow Unmasked* (London: Pilot Press, 1930), pp. 163–5.

10. Oleg Kapchinskii, *Mishka Yaponchik i drugie: kriminal i vlast' v gody Grazhdanskoi voiny v Odesse* (Moscow: Kraft+, 2015), pp. 88–255; Fedor Razzakov, *Bandity vremen sotsializma: khronika ros. prestupnosti, 1917–1991* (Moscow: Eksmo, 1996), p. 64.

11. V. I. Lenin, *Polnoe sobranie sochinenii* (Moscow: Gosizdat, 1958–65), vol. 26, p. 372, quoted in Steven Barnes, *Death and Redemption: The Gulag and the Shaping of Soviet Society* (Princeton: Princeton University Press, 2011), p. 250.

12. Quoted in *International Herald Tribune*, 15 April 1994.

13. Quoted in Peter Juviler, *Revolutionary Law and Order: Politics and Social Change in the USSR* (London: Free Press, 1976), p. 15.

14. Ibid., p. 19.

15. *Svobodnaya pressa*, 27 June 2015; *Vechernaya Moskva*, 7 December 2016.

16. *Petrovka-38*, 11 August 2015.

17. *Moskovskaya Pravda*, 27 July 2012.

18. Margaret Stolee, 'Homeless children in the USSR, 1917–1957', *Soviet Studies* 40, 1 (1988); Alan Ball, 'The roots of *besprizornost'* in Soviet Russia's first decade', *Slavic Review* 51, 2 (1992).

19. Alan Ball, *And Now My Soul Is Hardened: Abandoned Children in Soviet Russia, 1918–1930* (Berkeley: University of California Press, 1994), pp. 70–6.

20. Douillet, *Moscow Unmasked*, pp. 118–19.

21. Ball, *And Now My Soul Is Hardened*, p. 83.

22. Douillet, *Moscow Unmasked*, p. 124.

23. Conversation, Moscow, 2005.

24. Hagenloh, *Stalin's Police*, p. 37.

25. Razzakov, *Bandity vremen sotsializma*, pp. 13–16.

26. Ibid., pp. 10–11.

27. Hagenloh, *Stalin's Police*, p. 41.

28. V. P. Khaustov et al. (eds), *Lubyanka: Stalin i VChK-GPU-OGPU-NKVD, yanvar' 1922–dekabr' 1936* (Moscow: Demokratiya, 2003), p. 113.

29. Pavel Stuchka (ed.), *Entsiklopediya gosudarstva i prava* (Moscow: Izdatel'stvo kommunisticheskoi partii, 1927), vol. 3, p. 1594.

30. Hagenloh, *Stalin's Police*, p. 118.

31. Jacques Rossi, *The Gulag Handbook: An Encyclopedia Dictionary of Soviet Penitentiary Institutions and Terms Related to the Forced Labor Camps* (New York: Paragon House, 1989), p. 200.

32. For a magisterial analysis of this system, see Anne Applebaum, *Gulag: A History* (New York: Doubleday, 2003).

33. Ibid., p. 581.

34. Wilson Bell, 'Was the Gulag an archipelago? De-convoyed prisoners and porous borders in the camps of western Siberia', *Russian Review* 72, 1 (2013).

35. Quoted in ibid., p. 117.

36. Roger Brunet, 'Geography of the Gulag archipelago', *Espace géographique*, special issue (1993), p. 230.

37. Sarah Young, 'Knowing Russia's convicts: the other in narratives of imprisonment and exile of the late imperial era', *Europe-Asia Studies* 65, 9 (2013).

38. Svetlana Stephenson, *Crossing the Line: Vagrancy, Homelessness, and Social Displacement in Russia* (Aldershot: Ashgate, 2006), pp. 76–83.

39. Conversation, Moscow, 2005.

40. Quoted in Mark Vincent, 'Cult of the "urka": criminal subculture in the Gulag, 1924–1953', PhD dissertation, University of East Anglia, 2015, p. 76.

41. Aleksandr Gurov, *Professional'naya prestupnost': proshloe i sovremennost'* (Moscow: Yuridicheskaya literatura, 1990), p. 108.

42. Alexander Dolgun, *Alexander Dolgun's Story: An American in the Gulag* (New York: Alfred A. Knopf, 1975), p. 140.

43. Alexander Gorbatov, *Years of my Life: Memoirs of a General of the Soviet Army* (New York: W. W. Norton, 1964), pp. 140–1.

44. Michael Solomon, *Magadan* (Princeton: Vertex, 1971), pp. 134–5.

45. Varlam Shalamov, *Kolyma Tales* (Harmondsworth: Penguin, 1994), p. 411; Eugenia Ginzburg, *Within the Whirlwind* (New York: Harcourt Brace Jovanovich, 1981), p. 12.

46. Ginzburg, *Within the Whirlwind*, p. 400.

47. Dimitri Panin, *The Notebooks of Sologdin* (London: Hutchinson, 1976), p. 85.

4. Thieves and bitches

1. The best source of these songs appears to be Maikl Dzhekobson and Lidiya Dzhekobson, *Pesennyi fol'klor GULAGa kak istoricheskii istochnik*, 2 vols (Moscow: Sovremennyi gumanitarnyi universitet, 1998–2001), and I have drawn from references in Mark Vincent, 'Cult of the "urka": criminal subculture in the Gulag, 1924–1953', PhD dissertation, University of East Anglia, 2015.

2. Michael Solomon, *Magadan* (Princeton: Vertex, 1971), pp. 185–6.

3. Quoted in Yuri Glazov, ' "Thieves" in the USSR as a social phenomenon', in *The Russian Mind since Stalin's Death* (Dordrecht: Springer Netherlands, 1985), pp. 37–8.

4. Gustav Herling, *A World Apart* (London: William Heinemann, 1951), p. 65.

5. Solomon, *Magadan*, p. 127.

6. Galina Ivanova, *Labor Camp Socialism: the Gulag in the Soviet totalitarian system* (Abingdon: Routledge, [2000] 2015), p. 169.

7. Lev Kopelev, *To Be Preserved Forever* (Philadelphia: Lippincott, 1977), p. 234.

8. Wilson Bell, 'Was the Gulag an archipelago? De-convoyed prisoners and porous borders in the camps of western Siberia', *Russian Review* 72, 1 (2013), pp. 135–6.

9. Sergei Dovlatov, *The Zone: A Prison Camp Guard's Story* (Berkeley: Counterpoint, 2011), p. 58. Dovlatov was a prison guard in the 1960s and his book, originally published in 1982, while fictional, draws heavily on those experiences.

10. Kopelev, *To Be Preserved Forever*, p. 222.

11. Dzhekobson and Dzhekobson, *Pesennyi fol'klor GULAGa*, quoted in Vincent, 'Cult of the "urka" ', p. 66.

12. Varlam Shalamov, *Sobranie sochinenii v 4-kh tomakh* (Moscow: Khudozhestvennaya literatura, 1998), p. 63.

13. Anne Applebaum, *Gulag: A History* (New York: Doubleday, 2003), p. 446.
14. Dimitri Panin, *The Notebooks of Sologdin* (London: Hutchinson, 1976), pp. 150–1.
15. Edwin Bacon, *The Gulag at War: Stalin's Forced Labour System in the Light of the Archives* (Basingstoke: Macmillan, 1996), p. 93.
16. Vladimir Kuts, *Poedinok s sud'boi* (Moscow: RIO Uprpoligrafizdata, 1999), quoted in Applebaum, *Gulag*, p. 466.
17. Joseph Scholmer, *Vorkuta* (London: Weidenfeld & Nicolson, 1954), p. 22.
18. Applebaum, *Gulag*, p. 302.
19. Conversation, Moscow, 2009.
20. Scholmer, *Vorkuta*, p, 204.
21. Shalamov, *Sobranie sochinenii*, vol. 2, pp. 60–1.
22. Anatoly Levitin-Krasnov, *Ruk tvoikh zhar* (Tel Aviv: Krug, 1979), p. 276.
23. Quoted in Applebaum, *Gulag*, p. 470.
24. See ibid., chapters 22–4; Steven Barnes, *Death and Redemption: The Gulag and the Shaping of Soviet Society* (Princeton: Princeton University Press, 2011), chapter 5.
25. Valerii Abramkin and Valentina Chesnokova, *Ugolovnaya Rossiya: tyurmi i lagerya* (Moscow: TsSRUP, 2001), pp. 10–11.
26. Maximilien de Santerre, *Sovetskie poslevoennye kontslageri i ikh obitateli* (Munich: IPI SSSR, 1960), pp. 59–60.
27. Golfo Alexopoulos, 'A torture memo: reading violence in the Gulag', in Golfo Alexopoulos et al. (eds), *Writing the Stalin Era: Sheila Fitzpatrick and Soviet Historiography* (New York: Palgrave Macmillan, 2011), p. 166.
28. Barnes, *Death and Redemption*, p. 180.
29. Ivanova, *Labor Camp Socialism*, p. 122; Stéphane Courtois et al., *The Black Book of Communism: Crimes, Terror, Repression* (Cambridge, MA: Harvard University Press, 1999), p. 239.
30. Courtois et al., *The Black Book of Communism*, p. 239.
31. Ibid., p. 240.
32. Quoted in Applebaum, *Gulag*, p. 476.
33. Ibid., pp. 478–9.
34. Andrea Graziosi, 'The great strikes of 1953 in Soviet labor camps in the accounts of their participants: a review', *Cahiers du monde russe et soviétique* 33, 4 (1992).
35. Miriam Dobson, *Khrushchev's Cold Summer: Gulag Returnees, Crime, and the Fate of Reform after Stalin* (Ithaca, NY: Cornell University Press, 2009), p. 109.

5. Thief life

1. Conversation, Moscow, 2005.
2. Andrei Konstantinov and Mal'kol'm Dikselius, *Prestupnyi mir Rossii* (St Petersburg: Bibliopolis, 1995), p. 6.
3. Anne Applebaum, *Gulag: A History* (New York: Doubleday, 2003), pp. 283–4.
4. For the best English-language discussion of these rituals, see Federico Varese, *The Russian Mafia: Private Protection in a New Market Economy* (Oxford: Oxford University Press, 2001), pp. 147–52; Federico Varese, *Mafia Life: Love, Death and Money at the Heart of Organised Crime* (London: Profile, 2017), pp. 17–22.
5. Varlam Shalamov refers to *kombedy* in the same context, a Bolshevik contraction for their Committees of Poor Peasants, an emergency measure introduced in 1918 and used to requisition and distribute food, and consolidate Soviet power in the countryside. The term could as easily have been used ironically as not. Shalamov, *Kolyma Tales* (London: Penguin, 1994), p. 200.
6. Quoted in Herman Ermolaev, *Censorship in Soviet Literature, 1917–1991* (Lanham, MD: Rowman & Littlefield, 1997), p. 56.
7. Anne Applebaum concludes that 'there are enough similar sources, told by a wide enough range of prisoners, from camps from the early 1930s to the late 1940s, to be certain that they did take place'. Appelbaum, *Gulag*, pp. 398–9.

8. David Robson, 'Are there really 50 Eskimo words for snow?', *New Scientist*, no. 2896 (2012).

9. Viktor Berdinskikh, *Vyatlag*, quoted in Applebaum, *Gulag*, p. 286.

10. There are several good dictionaries of prison and criminal slang, including Aleksandr Sidorov, *Slovar' sovremennogo blatnogo i lagernogo zhargona* (Rostov-on-Don: Germes, 1992); and Yurii Dubyagin and A. G. Bronnikov, *Tolkovyi slovar' ugolovnykh zhargonov* (Moscow: Inter-OMNIS, 1991). Yurii Dubyagin and E. A. Teplitskii, *Kratkii anglo-russkii i russko-angliiskii slovar' ugolovnogo zhargona / Concise English-Russian and Russian-English Dictionary of the Underworld* (Moscow: Terra, 1993) is especially useful.

11. Victor Herman, *Coming Out of the Ice: An Unexpected Life* (New York: Harcourt Brace Jovanovich, 1979), p. 193.

12. *Zhigany* comes from *zhiganut'*, 'to lash', a term used in the tsarist-era penal colonies for the most pathetic and destitute convicts. Vlas Doroshevich, *Russia's Penal Colony in the Far East* (London: Anthem Press, 2011), pp. 191–4; Andrew Gentes, *Exile to Siberia, 1590–1822* (Basingstoke: Palgrave Macmillan, 2008), p. 176.

13. Caroline Humphrey, 'Dangerous words: taboos, evasions, and silence in Soviet Russia', *Forum for Anthropology and Culture*, no. 2 (2005), p. 389.

14. Serguei Cheloukhine, 'The roots of Russian organized crime: from old-fashioned professionals to the organized criminal groups of today', *Crime, Law and Social Change* 50, 4–5 (2008), p. 356.

15. Cited in Humphrey, 'Dangerous words', pp. 376–7.

16. In 1839, I. I. Sreznevskii produced the crucial *Ofensko-russki i russko-ofenskii slovar'* ('Ofenya-Russian and Russian-Ofenya Dictionary'). M. N. Priemysheva, 'I. I. Sreznevskii ob ofenskom yazyke', *Acta Linguistica Petropolitana* 3, 3 (2007), pp. 335–61.

17. Valery Chalidze, *Criminal Russia: Essays on Crime in the Soviet Union* (New York: Random House, 1977), p. 57; Leonid Finkelstein, 'The Russian lexicon, 2001', *Jamestown Foundation Prism* 7, 3 (2001).

18. Such as German/Swiss Rotwelsch and the French vagrants' and thieves' cant identified from the register of Paris's Châtelet prison.

19. It is hard to be certain, but it seems likely that this particular usage only emerged in the late 1920s (that certainly appears the earliest that it is recorded by police accounts).

20. James Davie, 'Missing presumed dead? – the *baikovyi iazyk* of the St Petersburg *mazuriki* and other pre-Soviet argots', *Slavonica* 4, 1 (1997).

21. Ibid., p. 34.

22. Peter Juviler, *Revolutionary Law and Order: Politics and Social Change in the USSR* (London: Free Press, 1976), pp. 35, 56.

23. For good studies of this, see Steven Smith, 'The social meanings of swearing: workers and bad language in late imperial and early Soviet Russia', *Past and Present*, no. 160 (1998); Manuela Kovalev, 'The function of Russian obscene language in late Soviet and post-Soviet prose', PhD dissertation, University of Manchester, 2014.

24. Paweł Mączewski, 'The visual encyclopedia of Russian jail tattoos', *Vice*, 15 October 2014, https://www.vice.com/en_uk/article/9bzvbp/russian-criminal-tattoo-fuel-damon-murray-interview–876 (accessed 6 October 2017).

25. Alexander Solzhenitsyn, *The Gulag Archipelago* (New York: Harper & Row, 1974–8), vol. 2, p. 441.

26. Alix Lambert, *Russian Prison Tattoos: Codes of Authority, Domination, and Struggle* (Atglen, PA: Schiffer, 2003), p. 19.

27. See for example Danzig Baldaev, *Russian Criminal Tattoo Encyclopedia* (London: FUEL, 2006–8); Lambert, *Russian Prison Tattoos*. It is, however, necessary to add one warning note, as much of the general discussion of tattoos depends heavily on Baldaev's illustrations, which are sometimes contradictory and hard to confirm.

28. Baldaev, *Russian Criminal Tattoo Encyclopedia*, vol. 3, pp. 33–5.

29. Thomas Sgovio, *Dear America! Why I turned against Communism* (Kenmore, NY: Partners' Press, 1979), pp. 166–9.

30. Mihajlo Mihajlov, 'Moscow Summer' (1966), quoted in Miriam Dobson, *Khrushchev's Cold Summer: Gulag Returnees, Crime, and the Fate of Reform after Stalin* (Ithaca, NY: Cornell University Press, 2009), p. 120.
31. Federico Varese, 'The society of the *vory-v-zakone*, 1930s–1950s', *Cahiers du monde russe* 39, 4 (1998), p. 523.
32. Varese, *The Russian Mafia*, pp. 147–50.
33. Quoted in ibid., p. 150.
34. For some useful ruminations on Russian gangster nicknames, see ibid., pp. 192–201.
35. Nanci Condee, 'Body graphics: tattooing the fall of communism', in Adele Marie Barker (ed.), *Consuming Russia: Popular Culture, Sex and Society since Gorbachev* (Durham, NC: Duke University Press, 1999), p. 350.
36. Anton Antonov-Ovseyenko, *The Time of Stalin: Portrait of a Tyranny* (New York: Harper and Row, 1981), p. 316.
37. Conversation, Moscow, 1990.
38. Applebaum, *Gulag*, p. 288
39. Doroshevich, *Russia's Penal Colony in the Far East*, p. 292. He uses the word *zhigany*, but from context clearly means *blatnye*.
40. Shalamov, *Kolyma Tales*, p. 7; Michael Solomon, *Magadan* (Princeton: Vertex, 1971), p. 134.
41. Maximilien de Santerre, *Sovetskie poslevoennye kontslageri i ikh obitateli* (Munich: IPI SSSR, 1960), p. 63.
42. Applebaum, *Gulag*, p. 287.
43. Dobson, *Khrushchev's Cold Summer*, p. 121.
44. Shalamov, *Kolyma Tales*, p. 427.
45. Applebaum, *Gulag*, pp. 307–17; Steven Barnes, *Death and Redemption: The Gulag and the Shaping of Soviet Society* (Princeton: Princeton University Press, 2011), pp. 99–105.
46. Shalamov, *Kolyma Tales*, p. 415.
47. Ibid., pp. 427–9.
48. Chalidze, *Criminal Russia*, p. 52.
49. Gustav Herling, *A World Apart* (London: William Heinemann, 1951), p. 31.
50. Eugenia Ginzburg, *Within the Whirlwind* (New York: Harcourt Brace Jovanovich, 1981), pp. 353–4.
51. Chalidze, *Criminal Russia*, p. 59.
52. See for example the female tattoos in Dubyagin and Teplitskii, *Kratkii anglo-russkii i russko-angliiskii slovar'*, pp. 266–77.

6. The unholy trinities

1. Fedor Razzakov, *Bandity semidesyatykh, 1970–1979* (Moscow: Eksmo, 2008), p. 30; Zdenek Šámal, *Ruské Mafie* (Prague: Ivo Železný, 2000), pp. 23–4; *Segodnya*, 18 October 1994.
2. Razzakov, *Bandity semidesyatykh*, p. 480.
3. Quoted in Miriam Dobson, *Khrushchev's Cold Summer: Gulag Returnees, Crime, and the Fate of Reform after Stalin* (Ithaca, NY: Cornell University Press, 2009), p. 125. Quite what a 'thieves' tone of voice' might have been was sadly left unexplained.
4. Lydia Rosner, *The Soviet Way of Crime: Beating the System in the Soviet Union and the USA* (Boston: Praeger, 1986), p. 29.
5. Yuli Daniel, *This is Moscow Speaking* (London: Collins Harvill, 1968), pp. 77–8.
6. Their ground-breaking chronicler was Yurii Shchekochikhin, notably in 'Predislovie k razgovoru', *Literaturnaya gazeta*, 6 June 1984; *Sotsiologicheskie issledovaniya* 1/1997; and *Allo, my vas slyshim: iz khroniki nashego vremeni* (Moscow: Molodaya gvardiya, 1987).
7. Conversation, Moscow, 1991.
8. Dobson, *Khrushchev's Cold Summer*, p. 112.
9. Conversation, Moscow, 1990.

10. Quoted in Jeffrey Hardy, ' "The camp is not a resort": the campaign against privileges in the Soviet Gulag, 1957–61', *Kritika* 13, 1 (2012), fn. 37.

11. David Remnick, *Lenin's Tomb: The Last Days of the Soviet Empire* (New York: Random House, 1994), p. 183.

12. Yuri Brokhin, *Hustling on Gorky Street: Sex and Crime in Russia Today* (New York: Dial Press, 1975), p. 111.

13. Fedor Razzakov, *Bandity vremen sotsializma* (Moscow: Eksmo, 1996), p. 68.

14. Conversation, Moscow, 1990.

15. *Ogonek* 29/1988, p. 20.

16. Best explored by Svetlana Stephenson, in her *Gangs of Russia: From the Streets to the Corridors of Power* (Ithaca, NY: Cornell University Press, 2015) and her earlier 'The Kazan Leviathan: Russian street gangs as agents of social order', *Sociological Review* 59, 2 (2011).

17. Razzakov, *Bandity vremen sotsializma*, p. 93.

18. Stephenson, *Gangs of Russia*, pp. 23–32. See also Lyubov' Ageeva, *Kazanskii fenomen: mif i real'nost'* (Kazan: Tatarskoe knizhnoe izdatel'stvo, 1991).

19. This is the exchange not of goods or services so much as obligations, often traded for future considerations, best explored by Alena Ledeneva in her *Russia's Economy of Favours: Blat, Networking and Informal Exchange* (Cambridge: Cambridge University Press, 1998).

20. James Millar, 'The Little Deal: Brezhnev's contribution to acquisitive socialism', *Slavic Review* 44, 4 (1985).

21. Reproduced in James Heinzen, *The Art of the Bribe: Corruption under Stalin, 1943–1953* (New Haven: Yale University Press, 2016), p. 148.

22. Ibid., p. 37.

23. The *tolkach*'s role was best explored by Joseph Berliner, in his *Factory and Manager in the USSR* (Cambridge, MA: Harvard University Press, 1957) and 'The informal organization of the Soviet firm', *Quarterly Journal of Economics* 66, 3 (1952).

24. Samuel Huntington, *Political Order in Changing Societies* (New Haven: Yale University Press, 1968) p. 69

25. Quoted in William Clark, *Crime and Punishment in Soviet Officialdom: Combating Corruption in the Political Elite, 1965–1990* (Armonk, NY: M. E. Sharp, 1993), p. 190.

26. Fedor Burlatskii, ' "Mirnyi zagovor" protiv N. S. Khrushcheva', in Yurii Aksyutin (ed.), *N. S. Khrushchev: materialy k biografii* (Moscow: Izdatel'stvo politicheskoi literatury, 1988), p. 211.

27. For the best description of Rokotov's career, see Brokhin, *Hustling on Gorky Street.*

28. *Sotsialisticheskaya industriya*, 9 and 10 April 1981; *Trud*, 9 April 1981.

29. CIA, *Military Compensation in the Soviet Union* (1980), p. 11.

30. William Clark, *Crime and Punishment in Soviet Officialdom*, pp. 153–7; Fedor Razzakov, *Bandity vremen sotsializma*, pp. 49–50.

31. Conversation, Moscow, 1990.

32. *Literaturnaya gazeta*, 20 July 1988; Razzakov, *Bandity semidesyatykh.*

33. Vadim Volkov, *Violent Entrepreneurs: The Use of Force in the Making of Russian Capitalism* (Ithaca, NY: Cornell University Press, 2002), p. 62.

7. Gorbachev's gangsters

1. Fedor Razzakov, *Bandity vremen sotisalizma* (Moscow: Eksmo, 1996), pp. 64–5.

2. *The Russian Primary Chronicle: Laurentian text* (Cambridge, MA: Medieval Academy of America, [1953] 2012), p. 97.

3. Sandra Anderson and Valerie Hibbs, 'Alcoholism in the Soviet Union', *International Social Work* 35, 4 (1992), p. 441.

4. N. N. Ivanets and M. I. Lukomskaya, 'The USSR's new alcohol policy', *World Health Forum* 11 (1990), pp. 250–1.

5. Arkady Vaksberg, *The Soviet Mafia* (London: Weidenfeld & Nicolson, 1991), p. 234.

6. Conversation, Moscow, 1990.
7. Well illustrated in Caroline Humphrey, ' "Icebergs", barter, and the mafia in provincial Russia', *Anthropology Today* 7, 2 (1991).
8. Federico Varese, *The Russian Mafia: Private Protection in a New Market Economy* (Oxford: Oxford University Press, 2001).
9. V. Semenov, 'Krutye parni', *Ekonomika i zhizn'*, January 1991, p. 180.
10. Anthony Jones and William Moskoff, *Ko-ops: The Rebirth of Entrepreneurship in the Soviet Union* (Bloomington: Indiana University Press, 1991), p. 80.
11. Valerii Karyshev, *Zapiski banditskogo advokata* (Moscow: Tsentrpoligraf, 1998), p. 31.
12. *Krasnaya zvezda*, 4 October 1989.
13. *Ogonek* 29/1988.
14. Varese, *The Russian Mafia*, pp. 127–8.
15. Nikolai Modestov, *Moskva banditskaya: dokumenty khronika kriminal'nogo bespredela 80–90-kh gg.* (Moscow: Tsentrpoligraf, 1996), pp. 103–5.
16. *Pravda*, 4 April 1987 (this individual, incidentally, went on to become a police commando).
17. Vadim Volkov, *Violent Entrepreneurs: The Use of Force in the Making of Russian Capitalism* (Ithaca, NY: Cornell University Press, 2002); Vadim Volkov, *Silovoe predprinimatel'stvo, XXI vek* (St Petersburg: European University of St Petersburg, 2012).
18. Andrei Konstantinov, *Banditskii Peterburg* (St Petersburg: Folio-Press, 1997), pp. 140–6.
19. Volkov, *Violent Entrepreneurs*, p. 10.
20. Dmitrii Gromov, 'Lyuberetskie ulichnye molodezhnye kompanii 1980-kh godov: subkul'tura na perepute istorii', *Etnograficheskoe obozrenie* 4/2006. See also Svetlana Stephenson, 'The violent practices of youth territorial groups in Moscow', *Europe-Asia Studies* 64, 1 (2012); Hilary Pilkington, *Russia's Youth and its Culture: A Nation's Constructors and Constructed* (London: Routledge, 1994), pp. 141–50.
21. Vladimir Yakovlev, 'Kontora "Liuberov" ', *Ogonek*, May 1987.
22. Mark Galeotti, *Afghanistan: The Soviet Union's Last War* (London: Frank Cass, 1995), pp. 45–102.
23. Personal communication, 1990.
24. *Pobratim* (SVA newspaper), no. 10 (1991).
25. *Komsomolskaya Pravda*, 29 April 1989.
26. *Krasnaya zvezda*, 4 October 1989.
27. Conversation, Kiev, 1991.
28. Karen Dawisha, *Putin's Kleptocracy: Who Owns Russia?* (New York: Simon & Schuster, 2014).
29. Kruchina left a suicide note, expressing fear for the future, but many still question whether he truly took his own life, considering how convenient his death was for so many people.
30. *Rossiiskie militseiskie vedomosti*, September 1993, October 1993.
31. *Literaturnaya gazeta*, 20 July 1988.
32. Stephen Handelman, *Comrade Criminal: Russia's New Mafiya* (London: Michael Joseph, 1994), pp. 18–20.

8. The 'Wild Nineties' and the rise of the *avtoritety*

1. Vyacheslav Razinkin and Aleksei Tarabrin, *Elita prestupnogo mira: tsvetnaya mast'* (Moscow: Veche, 1997), p. 17.
2. *New York Times*, 14 April 1994.
3. Federico Varese, *The Russian Mafia: Private Protection in a New Market Economy* (Oxford: Oxford University Press, 2001), p. 184.
4. Ibid., p. 181; *Moscow Times*, 25 April 2012; Alexander Kan, 'Profile: Iosif Kobzon: RussiancroonerandMP', BBCNews, 17 February 2015, http://www.bbc.com/news/world-europe-31497039 (accessed 3 January 2018).
5. Valeriya Bashkirova et al., *Geroi 90-kh: lyudi i den'gi – noveishaya istoriya kapitalizma v Rossii* (Moscow: Kommersant/ANF, 2012), p. 254.

6. Conversation, Moscow, 2005.
7. *Kommersant*, 30 September 2008.
8. Associated Press, 7 June 1994.
9. Ibid.
10. William Cooper, 'Russia's economic performance and policies and their implications for the United States', Library of Congress Congressional Research Service, June 2009, p. 2.
11. *Kommersant*, 2 June 1995.
12. Conversation, Cambridge, 1997.
13. Tobias Holzlehner, ' "The harder the rain, the tighter the roof": evolution of organized crime networks in the Russian Far East', *Sibirica* 6, 2 (2007), p. 56.
14. Vadim Volkov, *Violent Entrepreneurs: The Use of Force in the Making of Russian Capitalism* (Ithaca, NY: Cornell University Press, 2002), p. 27.
15. Varese, *The Russian Mafia*, p. 4 (emphasis in the original).
16. Petr Skoblikov, *Vzyskanie dolgov i kriminal* (Moscow: Yurist, 1999), pp. 76–81.
17. Carl Schreck, 'Blood sport: the rise of Russia's gangster athletes', Radio Free Europe/Radio Liberty, 8 May 2016.
18. Volkov, *Violent Entrepreneurs*, p. 51.
19. Svetlana Stephenson, *Gangs of Russia: From the Streets to the Corridors of Power* (Ithaca, NY: Cornell University Press, 2015), chapter 7, especially pp. 172–9.
20. Volkov, *Violent Entrepreneurs*, p. 71.
21. Conversation, Moscow, 1993.
22. Varese, *The Russian Mafia*, pp. 102–20.
23. Nancy Ries, ' "Honest bandits" and "warped people": Russian narratives about money, corruption, and moral decay', in Carol Greenhouse et al. (eds), *Ethnography in Unstable Places: Everyday Lives in Contexts of Dramatic Political Change* (Durham NC: Duke University Press, 2002), p. 279.
24. Conversation, Moscow, 2011.
25. *Fortune* 141, 12 (2000), p. 194.
26. This is lengthily explored in Dawisha, *Putin's Kleptocracy*, especially chapter 3. These allegations, while never proved, have been widely made and discussed both in Russia and abroad. Putin and his spokespeople have rejected these claims, but they have not been challenged in court. For a representative sample, see: 'Ot Tambovskoi OPG do massazhista Putina', *Dozhd-TV*, 6 September 2017; 'Russia: Putin's Past Becoming a Hot Internet Topic in Moscow', *EurasiaNet*, 6 January 2016; 'Vladimir Putin linked to shady property deals', *The Australian*, 31 August 2015; '"Putin involved in drug smuggling ring" says ex-KGB officer', *Newsweek*, 13 March 2015; 'Malen'kaya prachechnaya prem'er-klassa', *Nezavisimaya gazeta*, 10 April 2011; Jurgen Roth, *Die Gangster aus dem Osten* (Munich: Europe-Verlag, 2004); 'Gryaznaya zona Evropy', *Sovershenno sekretno*, 1 July 2000; 'Le nom de M. Poutine apparaît en marge des affaires de blanchiment au Liechtenstein', *Le Monde*, 26 May 2000. The court papers for the major Spanish case launched against members of Tambovskaya and associated gangs in 2015 several times mention both Putin specifically and also those close to him as patrons of people within Tambovskaya. Indeed, the US National Security Agency specifically sought to tap the telephone of Tambovskaya leader Barsukov/Kumarin to investigate whether he was in touch with Putin after the latter's rise to the presidency; see The Intercept, 16 May 2016.
27. *Guardian*, 'Kremlin accuses foreign parties of Putin smear campaign before elections', 28 March 2016, available at: https://www.theguardian.com/world/2016/mar/28/kremlin-foreign-putin-smear-campaign-election (accessed 25 January 2018).
28. Dawisha, pp. 128–41.
29. Conversation, Moscow, 2010.
30. Conversation, Moscow, 2016.
31. For more on Sogoyan, see 'Court sentences alleged member of Russian criminal group to 22 years', ČTK, 28 February 2013.

9. Gangs, networks and brotherhoods

1. *Moscow Times*, 4 June 2003.
2. Andrei Konstantinov, *Banditskii Peterburg*, rev. ed. (St Petersburg: Amfora, 2009).
3. Joseph Serio is especially acute on the ridiculous variation in numbers and the general problems with statistics in his *Investigating the Russian Mafia* (Durham, NC: Carolina University Press, 2008), chapter 4.
4. An interesting carry-over from Gulag days, when *brigady* were work details, under an appointed or elected *brigadir*.
5. Valerii Karyshev, *Zapiski banditskogo advokata* (Moscow: Tsentrpoligraf, 1998), p. 254.
6. See Diego Gambetta, *The Sicilian Mafia: The Business of Private Protection* (Cambridge, MA: Harvard University Press, 1993); Diego Gambetta, *Codes of the Underworld: How Criminals Communicate* (Princeton: Princeton University Press, 2009).
7. UN Office on Drugs and Crime, *Results of a Pilot Survey of Forty Selected Organized Criminal Groups in Sixteen Countries* (Vienna: United Nations, 2002), p. 34.
8. *Vechernyi Ekaterinburg*, 29 May 1993, quoted in Vadim Volkov, *Violent Entrepreneurs: The Use of Force in the Making of Russian Capitalism* (Ithaca, NY: Cornell University Press, 2002), p. 118.
9. This section draws on my article 'Behind the scenes: Uralmash gang retreats into the shadows', *Jane's Intelligence Review* 21, 9 (2009), used with permission. See also Andrei Konstantinov and Mal'kol'm Dikselius, *Banditskaya Rossiya* (St Petersburg: Bibliopolis, 1997), pp. 311–18; Volkov, *Violent Entrepreneurs*, pp. 116–22.
10. RIA Novosti, 7 February 2006.
11. Volkov, *Violent Entrepreneurs*, p. 118.
12. James Finckenauer and Yuri Voronin, *The Threat of Russian Organized Crime* (Washington, DC: National Institute of Justice, 2001), p. 15.
13. Quoted in *Komsomol'skaya Pravda*, 25 October 2001.
14. Simon Karlinsky (ed.), *Anton Chekhov's Life and Thought: Selected Letters and Commentary* (Evanston, IL: Northwestern University Press, [1973] 1997), p. 173.
15. Tobias Holzlehner, ' "The harder the rain, the tighter the roof": evolution of organized crime networks in the Russian Far East', *Sibirica* 6, 2 (2007).
16. V. A. Nomokonov and V. I. Shulga, 'Murder for hire as a manifestation of organized crime', *Demokratizatsiya* 6, 4 (1998).
17. Vladimir Ovchinsky, 'The 21st century mafia: made in China', *Russia in Global Affairs*, January 2007; Eric Hyer, 'Dreams and nightmares: Chinese trade and immigration in the Russian Far East', *Journal of East Asian Affairs* 10, 2 (1996).
18. UN Office on Drugs and Crime, *The Global Afghan Opium Trade: A Threat Assessment* (Vienna: United Nations, 2011).
19. Daniela Kleinschmit et al. (eds), *Illegal Logging and Related Timber Trade: Dimensions, Drivers, Impacts and Responses* (Vienna: International Union of Forest Research Organizations, 2016), p. 49; see also Tanya Wyatt, 'The Russian Far East's illegal timber trade: an organized crime?' *Crime, Law and Social Change* 61, 1 (2014).
20. Bertil Lintner, 'Chinese organised crime', *Global Crime* 6, 1 (2004), p. 93.
21. He already had a criminal record by the time of his election, when he was widely known by his nickname. *Komsomol'skaya Pravda*, 18 August 2004. He was later arrested, charged and convicted of abuse of his office in 2007. *Izvestiya*, 25 December 2007.
22. *Russia Beyond the Headlines*, 13 September 2013.
23. It was 25 per cent in 2009, according to UN Office on Drugs and Crime, *The Global Afghan Opium Trade*, p. 20.
24. UN Office on Drugs and Crime, *The Global Afghan Opium Trade*, p. 46.
25. Ibid., p. 45.
26. RIA Novosti, 17 September 2013.
27. RIA Novosti, 12 March 2013; Interfax, 11 July 2013.
28. UN Office on Drugs and Crime, *The Global Afghan Opium Trade*.
29. This is drawn from operational materials shared with me by law enforcement agencies; some details have been changed as this is at the time of writing an ongoing investigation.

30. Volkov, *Violent Entrepreneurs*, p. 115.
31. See Andrei Konstantinov, *Banditskii Peterburg* (St Petersburg: Folio-Press, 1997); Volkov, *Violent Entrepreneurs*, pp. 108–16.
32. Konstantinov, *Banditskii Peterburg*, pp. 364–6.
33. Conversation, Cambridge, 1997.
34. This is a key claim in Dawisha, *Putin's Kleptocracy*, pp. 141–5.
35. Interfax, 8 August 2001.
36. *Boston Globe*, 6 December 1998.
37. *Leningradskaya Pravda*, 23 May 2003; *Izvestiya*, 3 March 2009; *Novaya gazeta*, 1 November 2009.
38. *New York Times*, 14 May 2009.
39. The smaller Malyshevskaya group has largely been integrated into the Tambovskaya, especially outside Russia.
40. Conversation, The Hague, 2013.
41. United States Government Interagency Working Group, *International Crime Threat Assessment* (2000), p. 74.
42. This section draws on my article 'Empire of the sun: Russian organised crime's global network', *Jane's Intelligence Review* 20, 6 (2008), used with permission. See also Valerii Karyshev, *Solntsevskaya bratva: istoriya gruppirovki* (Moscow: EKSMO-Press, 1998); Konstantinov, *Banditskaya Rossiya*, pp. 73–168.
43. *Moskovskie novosti*, 26 November 1995.
44. From operational materials shared with me, 2006.

10. The Chechen

1. Conversation, Moscow, 2009.
2. Conversation, Moscow, 2009.
3. Conversation, Moscow, 2012. The actual word he used was 'blacks', a disparaging Russian slang term for people from the Caucasus.
4. Georgi Glonti and Givi Lobjanidze, *Professional'naya prestupnost' v Gruzii: vory-v-zakone* (Tbilisi: TraCCC, 2004), p. 34.
5. Dina Siegel and Henk van de Bunt (eds), *Traditional Organized Crime in the Modern World: Responses to Socioeconomic Change* (New York: Springer, 2012), pp. 35, 39.
6. *Izvestiya*, 27 January 1994.
7. Federico Varese, 'Is Sicily the future of Russia? Private protection and the rise of the Russian Mafia', *European Journal of Sociology* 35, 2 (1994).
8. This section draws on my article 'Blood brotherhood: Chechen organised crime', *Jane's Intelligence Review* 20, 9 (2008), used with permission.
9. For excellent studies of the *abreg* tradition, see Bruce Grant, *The Captive and the Gift: Cultural Histories of Sovereignty in Russia and the Caucasus* (Ithaca, NY: Cornell University Press, 2009); Rebecca Gould, 'Transgressive sanctity: the abrek in Chechen culture', *Kritika* 8, 2 (2007). For Russian studies, see Yurii Botyakov, *Abreki na Kavkaze: sotsiokul'turnyi aspekt yavleniya* (St Petersburg: Peterburgskoe vostokovedenie, 2004); V. O. Bobrovnikov, *Musul'mane Severnogo Kavkaza: obichai, pravo, nasilie* (Moscow: Vostochnaya literatura, 2002).
10. Suzanne Goldenberg, *The Pride of Small Nations: The Caucasus and Post-Soviet Disorder* (London: Zed, 1994), p. 2.
11. Gould, 'Transgressive sanctity', p. 275.
12. Memoirs of Baron Tornau, quoted in John Baddeley, *The Russian Conquest of the Caucasus* (London: Longmans, Green, 1908), p. 266.
13. Aude Merlin and Silvia Serrano (eds), *Ordres et désordres au Caucase* (Brussels: Editions universitaires de Bruxelles, 2010), pp. 134–5.
14. Sebastian Smith, *Allah's Mountains: Politics and War in the Russian Caucasus*, rev. edn (London: I. B. Tauris, 2006), p. 133.

15. In the first half of 2011, for example, there were 1.9 reported crimes per thousand residents, but where crimes did take place they were more likely to be serious ones: almost 40 per cent were classified as serious, compared with national averages in recent years of 25–30 per cent. RIA Novosti, 18 August 2011.

16. Pravda.ru, 9 May 2004.

17. ITAR-Tass news agency, 7 October 1996.

18. Jeff Myers, *The Criminal–Terror Nexus in Chechnya: A Historical, Social, and Religious Analysis* (Lanham, MD: Lexington, 2017), p. 121.

19. This was confirmed to me by one person who was at the meeting, and another who heard about it second-hand.

20. Artem Rudakov, *Chechenskaya mafiya* (Moscow: EKSMO-Press, 2002), pp. 323–4.

21. This is drawn from operational reports from Russian and other intelligence sources.

22. Yossef Bodansky, *Chechen Jihad: Al Qaeda's Training Ground and the Next Wave of Terror* (New York: Harper, 2007), p. 108.

23. Delivered to a closed meeting on organised crime, London, 1997.

24. Andrei Konstantinov, *Banditskii Peterburg* (St Petersburg: Folio-Press, 1997), p. 155.

25. Ibid., p. 158.

26. This is drawn from operational reports from Russian police sources.

27. Rudakov, *Chechenskaya mafiya*, pp. 28–9.

28. *Rossiiskie militseiskie vedomosti*, September 1993, October 1993.

29. Rudakov, *Chechenskaya mafiya*, pp. 318–20.

30. Quoted in Aleksandr Zhilin, 'The Shadow of Chechen Crime over Moscow', *Jamestown Foundation Prism* 2, 6 (1996).

31. Rudakov, *Chechenskaya mafiya*, pp. 362–7.

32. Konstantinov, *Banditskii Peterburg*, p. 160.

33. Conversation, Moscow, 2009.

34. Roustam Kaliyev, 'Can "power ministries" be transformed?', *Perspective* 13, 1 (2002); see also Library of Congress Federal Research Division, *Involvement of Russian Organized Crime Syndicates, Criminal Elements in the Russian Military, and Regional Terrorist Groups in Narcotics Trafficking in Central Asia, the Caucasus, and Chechnya* (2002), p. 27.

35. Conversation, Kiev, 1993.

36. Stephen Handelman, *Comrade Criminal: Russia's New Mafiya* (London: Michael Joseph, 1994), p. 178.

37. Misha Glenny, *McMafia: Crime without Frontiers* (London, Bodley Head, 2008), p. 77.

38. *New York Times*, 31 January 2009.

39. *Der Spiegel*, 21 June 2007; I was also told about the incident first-hand from a then-junior FSB security officer in Moscow in 2014.

40. This cable, 'Subject: Chechnya, the once and future war', 30 May 2006, was subsequently released by WikiLeaks.

41. Ilya Yashin, *Ugroza Natsional'noi bezopasnosti* (independent expert report, Moscow, 2016) available at: https://openrussia.org/post/view/12965/ (accessed 5 January 2018). Kadyrov's official spokesperson says this report is 'crude slander, insults and unfounded accusations'; see FreeNews, 14 March 2016, available at http://freenews-en.tk/2016/03/14/spokesman-kadyrov-asks-to-have-a-thing-for-yashin-because-of-the-report-about-chechnya/ (accessed 25 January 2018).

42. According to his 2015 income declaration.

43. *Moscow Times*, 25 February 2010; *Reuters*, 5 March 2011; *Meduza*, 1 February 2016; *Washington Post*, 24 May 2016.

44. Joel Schectman, 'U.S. sanctions Chechen leader, four others under Magnitsky Act', 20 December 2017, available at: https://www.reuters.com/article/us-usa-russia-sanctions/u-s-sanctions-chechen-leader-four-others-under-magnitsky-act-idUSKBN1EE260 (accessed 25 January 2018).

45. In December 2017, the US government placed sanctions on Kadyrov under the terms of the Magnitsky Law for human rights abuses and involvement in extrajudicial killings.

'Chechnya: "Disappearances" a Crime Against Humanity', *Human Rights Watch*, 20 March 2005; European Court of Human Rights judgments in *Imakayeva* v. *Russia* (2006) and *Khantiyev* v. *Russia* (2009).

46. European Union, *European Asylum Support Office Country of Origin Information Report – Russian Federation – State Actors Of Protection* (EASO, 2017); Emil Souleimanov and Jasutis Grazvydas, 'The Dynamics of Kadyrov's Regime: Between Autonomy and Dependence', *Caucasus Survey* 4, 2 (2016), pp. 115–28; Vanessa Kogan, 'Implementing the Judgments of the European Court of Human Rights from the North Caucasus: A Closing Window for Accountability or a Continuing Process of Transitional Justice?', in Natalia Szablewska and Sascha-Dominik Bachmann (eds), *Current Issues in Transitional Justice* (Cham: Springer, 2015); United Kingdom: Parliament, House of Commons All-Party Group, *Parliamentary Human Rights Group (PHRG) Report, Chechnya Fact-Finding Mission*, 10 June 2010, available at: http://www.refworld.org/docid/4cc7ed2a2. html (accessed 5 January 2018); International Helsinki Federation for Human Rights, *Chechnya: Impunity, Disappearances, Torture, and the Denial of Political Rights* (2003).

11. The Georgian

1. This was observed by American criminologist Louise Shelley. Louise Shelley et al. (eds), *Organized Crime and Corruption in Georgia* (Abingdon: Routledge, 2007), p. 54.
2. *Kommersant-vlast'*, 10 March 2003.
3. *Georgia Times*, 26 January 2012.
4. *Izvestiya*, 5 October 2006.
5. Interviewed by Gavin Slade, in his 'No country for made men: The decline of the mafia in post-Soviet Georgia', *Law & Society Review* 46, 3 (2012), p. 631.
6. George Grossman, 'The "second economy" of the USSR', *Problems of Communism* 26, 5 (1977), p. 35.
7. Georgi Glonti and Givi Lobjanidze. *Professional'naya prestupnost' v Gruzii: vory-v-zakone* (Tbilisi: TraCCC, 2004), p. 53.
8. Georgi Glonti, *Organizovannaya prestupnost' kak odin iz osnovykh istochnikov nasil'stvennoi prestupnosti i etnicheskikh konfliktov* (Tbilisi: Azri, 1998), p. 140.
9. *Moskovskii komsomolets*, 10 November 1996.
10. *Kommersant-vlast'*, 10 March 2003.
11. Quoted in Alexander Kupatadze, *Organized Crime, Political Transitions, and State Formation in Post-Soviet Eurasia* (New York: Palgrave Macmillan, 2012), p. 118.
12. Slade, 'No country for made men'.
13. Conversation, Moscow, 2014.
14. *Lenta*, 1 April 2006.
15. *Kommersant*, 15 June 2009.
16. Gazeta.ru, 13 June 2009.
17. *Komsomolskaya Pravda*, 12 October 2015.
18. Interviewed in *Vremya novostei*, quoted in *New York Times*, 30 July 2008.
19. This section draws on my article 'Retirement plans: Russian mafia boss considers his future', *Jane's Intelligence Review* 23, 1 (2011), used with permission.
20. *Moskovskii komsomolets*, 16 January 2013.
21. *Kommersant*, 7 March 1997
22. Just as 'Yaponchik' spearheaded the Slavic gangs' fight against the Chechens and other 'highlanders' in Moscow, so too 'Yakutyonok' had fought a bitter struggle against Georgian gangsters in Perm. Federico Varese, *The Russian Mafia: Private Protection in a New Market Economy* (Oxford: Oxford University Press, 2001), p. 132.
23. *Izvestiya*, 1 June 1995.
24. *Nezavisimaya gazeta*, 2 December 1996.
25. *Novaya gazeta*, 26 September 2010; *Moskovskie komsomolets*, 16 January 2013; *Lenta*, 16 February 2013.

26. *Novaya gazeta*, 26 September 2010; *Vesti*, 20 January 2013; *Rosbalt*, 2 January 2014; *Rosbalt*, 20 January 2014.
27. *Komsomol'skaya Pravda*, 17 September 2009; *Rosbalt*, 4 January 2014.
28. NEWSru.com, 27 May 2010.
29. *Novaya gazeta*, 26 September 2010.
30. *Rosbalt*, 29 October 2010.
31. *Rosbalt*, 4 January 2014; police investigator tasked with following the network's operations, Moscow, 2015.
32. *Izvestiya*, 23 January 2013.
33. *Komsomol'skaya Pravda v Ukraine*, 7 February 2013.
34. *Argumenty i fakty*, 'Moskva' supplement, March 1997.
35. *Rosbalt*, 4 January 2014.
36. *Novaya gazeta*, 4 June 2014; *Rosbalt*, 9 October 2009; BBC Russian Service, 10 June 2014; *Republic*, 29 December 2016.
37. *Moskovskii komsomolets*, 16 January 2013.
38. Comment recounted by a former colleague, Moscow, 2016.
39. Gavin Slade has usefully questioned 'the essentialist idea that there is anything specifically in "Georgian mentality" or national culture that makes the power of the mafia inevitable there'. Gavin Slade, *Reorganizing Crime: Mafia and Anti-Mafia in Post-Soviet Georgia* (Oxford: Oxford University Press, 2013), p. 172.

12. The gangster-internationalist

1. William Webster et al. (eds), *Russian Organized Crime and Corruption* (Washington DC: Center for Strategic and International Studies, 1997), p. 1.
2. House Foreign Relations Committee Hearings on International Organized Crime, 10 October 1997.
3. *Independent*, 25 May 1993.
4. Federico Varese, *Mafias on the Move: How Organized Crime Conquers New Territories* (Princeton: Princeton University Press, 2011), p. 8.
5. Ibid., p. 8
6. Conversation, London, 1996.
7. For useful studies of the Georgian underworld, see Louise Shelley et al. (eds), *Organized Crime and Corruption in Georgia* (Abingdon: Routledge, 2007); Gavin Slade, 'The threat of the thief: who has normative influence in Georgian society?', *Global Crime* 8, 2 (2007); Gavin Slade, 'No country for made men: The decline of the mafia in post-Soviet Georgia', *Law & Society Review* 46, 3 (2012). For Ukraine, see Andrei Kokotyuka and Gennadii Grebnev, *Kriminal'naya Ukraina* (Kharkov: Folio, 2004); Taras Kuzio, 'Crime, politics and business in 1990s Ukraine', *Communist and Post-Communist Studies* 47, 2 (2014); Graham Stack, 'Money laundering in Ukraine: tax evasion, embezzlement, illicit international flows and state capture', *Journal of Money Laundering Control* 18, 3 (2015); Organized Crime Observatory, *Ukraine and the EU: Overcoming Criminal Exploitation toward a Modern Democracy?* (Geneva: Organized Crime Observatory, 2015). For Central Asia, see Filippo De Danieli, 'Beyond the drug–terror nexus: drug trafficking and state–crime relations in Central Asia', *International Journal of Drug Policy* 25, 6 (2014); David Lewis, 'Crime, terror and the state in Central Asia', *Global Crime* 15, 3–4 (2014). For more general studies, see Svante Cornell and Michael Jonsson (eds), *Conflict, Crime, and the State in Postcommunist Eurasia* (Philadelphia: University of Pennsylvania Press, 2014); Alexander Kupatadze, *Organized Crime, Political Transitions and State Formation in Post-Soviet Eurasia* (New York: Palgrave Macmillan, 2012).
8. Conversation, Chisinau, 2006.
9. *Kyiv Post*, 27 December 2011.
10. In his book, Luke Harding, *Mafia State* (London: Guardian Books, 2011), published in the USA as *Expelled: A Journalist's Descent into the Russian Mafia State* (New York: Palgrave Macmillan, 2012).

11. See Sławomir Matuszak, *The Oligarchic Democracy: The Influence of Business Groups on Ukrainian Politics* (Warsaw: Ośrodek Studiów Wschodnich, 2012).

12. I explore this more in Mark Galeotti, 'Crime and Crimea: criminals as allies and agents', Radio Free Europe/Radio Liberty, 3 November 2014.

13. Conversation, Kiev, 2016.

14. OCCRP, 'The Azerbaijani Laundromat', available at: https://www.occrp.org/en/azerbaijanilaundromat/ (accessed 5 January 2018); Sarah Chayes, 'The Structure of Corruption in Azerbaijan', Carnegie Endowment for International Peace, 2016, available at: http://carnegieendowment.org/2016/06/30/structure-of-corruption-systemic-analysis-using-eurasian-cases-pub-63991 (accessed 5 January 2018); Alexander Kupatadze, 'Political corruption in Eurasia: Understanding Collusion between States, Organized Crime and Business', *Theoretical Criminology* 19, 2 (2015), pp. 198–215.

15. Erica Marat, 'Impact of drug trade and organized crime on state functioning in Kyrgyzstan and Tajikistan', *China and Eurasia Forum Quarterly*, 4, 1 (2006); Erica Marat, 'The changing dynamics of state–crime relations in Kyrgyzstan', *Central Asia–Caucasus Analyst*, 21 February 2008.

16. See for example Helge Blakkisrud and Pål Kolstø, 'From secessionist conflict toward a functioning state: processes of state- and nation-building in Transnistria', *Post-Soviet Affairs* 27, 2 (2011).

17. Jan Marinus Wiersma, 'European Parliament ad hoc delegation to Moldova 5–6 June 2002', European Parliament, July 2002.

18. See Michael Bobick, 'Profits of disorder: images of the Transnistrian Moldovan Republic', *Global Crime* 12, 4 (2011).

19. Conversation, Kiev, 2006.

20. Walter Kegö and Alexandru Molcean (eds), *Russian Organized Crime: Recent Trends in the Baltic Sea Region* (Stockholm: Institute for Security and Development Policy, 2012), p. 58.

21. AFP, 8 September 1996.

22. Mark Galeotti, 'Israel organised crime is fragmented, but growing', *Jane's Intelligence Review* 17, 7 (2005).

23. This is now something even the Russian government implicitly acknowledges. Former president Dmitry Medvedev said in 2011 that 'there is hardly any doubt who won [that race]. It was not Boris Nikolaevich Yeltsin.' *Time*, 24 February 2012.

24. Conversation, Tallinn, 2015.

25. Robert Friedman, *Red Mafiya: How the Russian Mob has Invaded America* (Boston: Little, Brown, 2000), p. xx.

26. The best analysis of this episode is in Varese, *Mafias on the Move*. The identities of some of the individuals Varese anonymises have been added.

27. Varese, *Mafias on the Move*, p. 74.

28. Servizio Centrale Operativo, *Rapporto operativo, Yesin et alii* (Rome: Polizia di Stato, 1997), p. 21, cited and translated in Varese, *Mafias on the Move*, p. 73.

29. Varese, *Mafias on the Move*, pp. 70–1, 85–6.

30. Hyon Shin and Robert Kominski, 'Language use in the United States: 2007' (Suitland, MD: US Census Bureau, 2010).

31. These transitions are best chronicled in Friedman, *Red Mafiya*.

32. James Finckenauer and Elin Waring, *The Russian Mafia in America: Immigration, Culture, and Crime* (Boston: Northeastern University Press, 1998).

33. *Vesti*, 9 October 2009.

34. Conversation, Moscow, 2011.

35. BIS, *Annual Report of the Security Information Service (BIS) of the Czech Republic for 2008* (Prague: BIS, 2008), p. 12.

36. Kelly Hignett, 'Organised crime in east central Europe: the Czech Republic, Hungary and Poland', *Global Crime* 6, 1 (2004); Miroslav Nožina, 'Crime networks in Vietnamese diasporas: the Czech Republic case', *Crime, Law and Social Change* 53, 3 (2010).

37. BIS, *Annual Report of the Security Information Service (BIS) of the Czech Republic for 2010* (Prague: BIS, 2010), pp. 11–12.

38. Conversation, Prague, 2016.
39. California Department of Justice, *Organized Crime in California 2010: annual report to the Legislature*, p. 33.
40. *Observer*, 16 June 2002; *New York Times*, 9 November 2005.
41. For example, in 2004 Garri Grigorian, a Russian national living in the USA, was convicted of helping launder more than $130 million through shell company bank accounts in Utah.
42. Jeffrey Robinson, *The Merger: The Conglomeration of International Organized Crime* (Woodstock, NY: Overlook Press, 2000), pp. 21–3.
43. Carlos Resa Nestares, 'Transnational organised crime in Spain: structural factors explaining its penetration', in Emilio Viano (ed.), *Global Organised Crime and International Security* (Aldershot: Ashgate, 1999).
44. This dates back to the mid-1990s; see *Izvestiya*, 17 September 1996.
45. Conversation, London, 2015.
46. United States Department of Justice, 'More than 100 members and associates of transnational organized crime groups charged with offenses including bank fraud, kidnapping, racketeering and health care fraud', press release, 16 February 2011.
47. *New York Times*, 19 August 2002.
48. Congressional Record, 112th Congress (2011–2012), House of Representatives, 8 March 2011, p. H1583.
49. *USA* v. *Kasarian et al.*, 2010.
50. US Attorney's Office, Southern District of New York, 'Manhattan US attorney announces charges against 36 individuals for participating in $279 million health care fraud scheme', press release, 29 February 2012.
51. *USA* v. *Kasarian et al.*, 2010. Kasarian pleaded guilty in 2011.
52. *USA* v. *Tokhtakhounov et al.*, 2013.
53. Europol, *Russian Organised Crime Threat Assessment 2008* (partially declassified version), p. 10.
54. Quoted in Friedman, *Red Mafiya*, p. 90.
55. Claire Sterling, *Crime Without Frontiers: The Worldwide Expansion of Organised Crime and the Pax Mafiosa* (London: Little, Brown, 1994).
56. John Kerry, *The New War: The Web of Crime that Threatens America's Security* (New York, Simon & Schuster, 1997), p. 21.
57. Phil Williams, 'Transnational criminal organizations: strategic alliances', *Washington Quarterly* 18, 1 (1995).
58. US Commercial Service, 'US Commercial Service to support US pavilion at major Global Gaming Expo Asia 2013 (G2E Asia 2013)', press release, 11 March 2013.
59. Bertil Lintner, 'The Russian mafia in Asia', Asia Pacific Media Services, 3 February 1996.
60. *Far Eastern Economic Review,* 30 May 2002.
61. Friedman, *Red Mafiya*, pp. 271, 284.
62. This is the estimate given by the UN Office on Drugs and Crime in 2016.
63. Conversation, London, 2004.

13. New times, new *vory*

1. Gazeta.ru, 6 September 2011.
2. *Kommersant*, 24 February 1995.
3. *Komsomol'skaya Pravda*, 9 September 2011.
4. TASS, 6 September 2011.
5. US Attorney's Office, Southern District of New York, 'Manhattan U.S. Attorney Charges 34 Members and Associates of Two Russian-American Organized Crime Enterprises with Operating International Sportsbooks That Laundered More Than $100 Million', 16 April 2013.
6. *Life News*, 10 September 2016.

7. This cable, 'Subject: Spain details its strategy to combat the Russian mafia', 8 February 2010, was subsequently released by WikiLeaks.

8. *Guardian*, 7 February 2012.

9. Vadim Volkov, *Violent Entrepreneurs: The Use of Force in the Making of Russian Capitalism* (Ithaca, NY: Cornell University Press, 2002), p. 119.

10. This cable, 'Subject: the Luzhkov dilemma', 12 February 2010, was subsequently released by WikiLeaks.

11. This is best and forensically outlined in Dawisha, *Putin's Kleptocracy*, pp. 104–62, especially 126–32, 142–5.

12. *Der Spiegel*, 3 September 2007.

13. Gazeta.ru, 18 August 2016; *Vedomosti*, 25 December 2009; RIA Novosti, 16 January 2009.

14. This section draws on my analysis of the case in the *Moscow Times*, 15 July 2014.

15. The idea that Russia has a 'deep state' has been particularly developed by Brian Whitmore of Radio Free Europe/Radio Liberty.

16. Michael Rochlitz, 'Corporate raiding and the role of the state in Russia', *Post-Soviet Affairs* 30, 2–3 (2014).

17. *Moskovskii komsomolets*, 10 November 1996.

18. See for example Stephen Handelman, 'The Russian "Mafiya" ', *Foreign Affairs*, March–April 1994; Michael Waller and Victor Yasmann, 'Russia's great criminal revolution: the role of the security services', *Journal of Contemporary Criminal Justice* 11, 4 (1995).

19. Stanislav Lunev, 'Russian organized crime spreads beyond Russia's borders, squeezing out the local competition', *Jamestown Foundation Prism* 3, 8 (1997).

20. The best summary is Thomas Firestone, 'Criminal corporate raiding in Russia', *International Law* 42 (2008).

21. This has been especially well demonstrated by Jordan Gans-Morse: see for example 'Threats to property rights in Russia: from private coercion to state aggression', *Post-Soviet Affairs* 28, 3 (2012).

22. PricewaterhouseCoopers, *Economic Crime: People, Culture and Controls – the 4th Biennial Global Economic Crime Survey: Russia* (2007), p. 3.

23. CNBC, 26 May 2011.

24. For an excellent study, see 'Following the Magnitsky money', Organized Crime and Corruption Reporting Project, 12 August 2012. Browder's own take is in his book *Red Notice: A True Story of High Finance, Murder, and One Man's Fight for Justice* (New York: Simon & Schuster, 2015).

25. Valerii Karyshev, *Russkaya Mafiya, 1991–2017: novaya khronika banditskoi Rossii* (Moscow, EKSMO-Press, 2017), p. 374.

26. V. A. Nomokonov and V. I. Shulga, 'Murder for hire as a manifestation of organized crime', *Demokratizatsiya* 6, 4 (1998) p. 677.

27. Nicely summarised in Richard Behar, 'Capitalism in a cold climate', *Fortune* 141, 12 (2000).

28. *Moscow Times*, 4 August 2004.

29. In light of the constitutional bar on three consecutive presidential terms, Putin opted to swap jobs with his former prime minister Medvedev, even while making it clear who was in charge. In the process this reset the clock, allowing him to stand again in 2012 and then, after constitutional changes extending a presidential term from four to six years, presumably again in 2018.

30. Conversation, Moscow, 2012.

31. Nikolai Modestov, *Moskva banditskaya 2: dokumenty khronika kriminal'nogo bespredela 90-kh gg.* (Moscow: Tsentrpoligraf, 1997), pp. 7–38; Valerii Karyshev, *Aleksandr Solonik: killer mafii* (Moscow: EKSMO-Press, 1998); *Moskovskii komsomolets*, 15 February 2002; *Kommersant*, 25 January 2003.

32. Pravda.ru, 24 January 2003; Valerii Karyshev, *Aleksandr Solonik: killer zhiv?!* (Moscow: EKSMO-Press, 2003).

33. *Kommersant-daily*, 13 March 1997; *Moskovskii komsomolets*, 1 June 2003.

34. Interfax news agency, 22 April 2002.

35. *The Register*, 20 April 2010.

36. Jonathan Lusthaus, 'How organised is organised cybercrime?', *Global Crime* 14, 1 (2013).

37. *Guardian*, 25 January 2008; *CNN*, 24 October 2009; *Time*, 20 January 2011; *Vedomosti*, 19 April 2011; *RFE/RL*, 11 November 2014; *Reuters*, 27 November 2014; Varese, *The Russian Mafia*, pp. 170, 172; Dawisha, *Putin's Kleptocracy*, pp. 284–5.

38. Robert Friedman, *Red Mafiya: How the Russian Mob has Invaded America* (Boston: Little, Brown, 2000), p. 113.

39. *United States* v. *Peter Berlin, Lucy Edwards et al.*, 1999; see also Thomas Ott, 'US law enforcement strategies to combat organized crime threats to financial institutions', *Journal of Financial Crime* 17, 4 (2010).

40. Conversations, Moscow, 2014 and 2015.

14. *Mafiya* evolutions

1. *Militsiya*, August 1992, pp. 11–14.

2. *Georgian Journal*, 25 September 2014.

3. For the best study of this, see James Jacobs, *Gotham Unbound: How New York City was Liberated from the Grip of Organized Crime* (New York: New York University Press, 2001), chapter 3.

4. *Rosbalt*, 4 February 2013.

5. *Georgian Journal*, 25 September 2014.

6. Secret message circulated in prison, signed by thirty-four senior *vory*. Reproduced on the PrimeCrime website: see http://www.primecrime.ru/photo/3643 (accessed 25 October 2017). (The translation is my own, and has to take some liberties to convey the sense; instead of 'seducing', for example, the text literally says 'leading people into fornication'.)

7. *Rosbalt*, 4 February 2013.

8. *Vesti*, 21 January 2013.

9. *Vesti*, 5 February 2013.

10. *Vesti*, 6 February 2013; *Komsomolskaya Pravda*, 7 February 2013.

11. Gazeta.ru, 18 August 2016.

12. *Prestupnaya Rossiya*, 2 June 2014; *Rosbalt*, 3 June 2014.

13. Conversation, Moscow, 2014.

14. Conversation, Moscow, 2014.

15. This section draws on my 'Khoroshie vremena dlya plokhikh parnei', Radio Svoboda, 13 June 2015, used with permission. This article was subsequently published in English by the Henry Jackson Society as 'Tough times for tough people: crime and Russia's economic crisis', 18 June 2015.

16. Email conversation, 2015.

17. The following examples are drawn from conversations with Russian police and investigators, and sight of operational material in Moscow, 2014–16.

18. Conversation, Moscow, 2015.

19. CNN, 20 August 2015.

20. Vadzim Smok, 'The art of smuggling in Belarus', *openDemocracy: Russia*, 2 February 2015.

21. *Daily Telegraph*, 18 August 2015.

22. Email conversation, 2015.

23. Martin Müller, 'After Sochi 2014: costs and impacts of Russia's Olympic Games', *Eurasian Geography and Economics*, 55, 6 (2014).

24. *Christian Science Monitor*, 5 February 2013.

25. *Guardian*, 4 February 2013.

26. *RBK*, 16 January 2013.

27. *Lenta*, 26 October 2010.

28. Reuters, 1 July 2009.

29. *Financial Times*, 13 September 2015.

30. ZDNet, 6 April 2005.
31. *Moscow News*, 21 November 2011.
32. CNN, 16 March 2017.
33. *Krebs on Security*, 10 April 2017; Reuters, 9 April 2017.
34. Quoted in *The Economist*, 30 August 2007.
35. *Guardian*, 15 November 2007.
36. Joseph Menn, *Fatal System Error: The Hunt for the New Crime Lords who are Bringing Down the Internet* (New York: PublicAffairs, 2010), p. 266.
37. *Newsweek*, 29 December 2009; *Guardian*, 15 November 2007.
38. *The Economist*, 26 August 1999.
39. Stephen McCombie et al., 'Cybercrime attribution: an eastern European case study', *Proceedings of the 7th Australian Digital Forensics Conference*, 2009.
40. 'Palermo: hacker russi clonavano carte di credito statunitensi', Polizia di Stato, 29 September 2015.
41. *Nezavisimaya gazeta*, 10 February 2009.
42. Conversation, Moscow, 2015.
43. *Kommersant*, 7 November 2014.
44. Interfax, 26 January 2013.
45. This section draws on my 'Return of mob rule: the resurgence of gangsterism in Russia', *Jane's Intelligence Review* 25, 4 (2013), used with permission.
46. *Komsomol'skaya Pravda*, 2 November 2009.
47. *Vremya novostei*, 18 June 2009.
48. *Life News*, 7 March 2017. Kalashov denies his guilt and as of writing the case is still in the courts.

15. The criminal wars

1. The informant whom Kohver was meant to be meeting, Maxim Gruzdev, turned out to have been suborned by the FSB, and is currently in prison in Estonia for his role. *Re:baltica*, 13 September 2017; *Postimees*, 14 September 2017.
2. *Postimees*, 10 September 2014.
3. Hearing on Russian money laundering, 21 September 1999, quoted in Edward Lucas, *Deception: spies, lies and how Russia dupes the West* (London: Bloomsbury, 2013), p. 316.
4. 'Statement for the record: worldwide threat assessment of the US intelligence community', Senate Select Committee on Intelligence, 12 March 2013.
5. Compare Edward Lucas, *The New Cold War: Putin's Russia and the Threat to the West* (New York: Palgrave Macmillan, 2008) with Mark Galeotti, 'Not a New Cold War: Great Game II', ETH Zürich, 14 April 2014.
6. Ezio Costanzo, *The Mafia and the Allies: Sicily 1943 and the Return of the Mafia* (New York: Enigma, 2007); Salvatore Lupo, 'The Allies and the mafia', *Journal of Modern Italian Studies* 2, 1 (1997).
7. US diplomatic cable, 'Subject: Spain details its strategy to combat the Russian mafia', 8 February 2010.
8. *Guardian*, 23 January 2013.
9. Bout's career is best described in Matt Potter, *Outlaws Inc.: Under the Radar and on the Black Market with the World's Most Dangerous Smugglers* (New York: Bloomsbury, 2011).
10. Europol, *Russian Organised Crime Threat Assessment 2008* (partially declassified version), p. 13.
11. 'Address by President of the Russian Federation', 18 March 2014.
12. This section draws on my 'Crime and Crimea: criminals as allies and agents', Radio Free Europe/Radio Liberty, 3 November 2014, used with permission.
13. *Ukrainskaya Pravda*, 15 March 2014; *Delovoi Peterburg*, 10 July 2015.
14. KIAnews, 10 June 2010; *Fakty*, 3 March 2014; *Ukrainskaya pravda*, 15 March 2014; *Der Spiegel*, 25 March 2014; NPR, 5 June 2014; *New York Times*, 25 March 2015; *Novaya gazeta*, 8 February 2016.

15. *Novaya gazeta*, 8 February 2016; Andrei Konstantinov and Mal'kol'm Dikselius, *Banditskaya Rossiya* (St Petersburg: Bibliopolis, 1997), pp. 465–70.
16. Conversation, Moscow, 2014.
17. Conversation, Kazan, 2016.
18. Ibid.
19. US diplomatic cable, 'Subject: Ukraine: land, power, and criminality in Crimea', 14 December 2006.
20. 'Prosecutor talks about control by crime', *Organised Crime and Corruption Reporting Project*, 18 December 2014.
21. 'Ukrainian Football's Dark Side', BBC, 1 April 2009, http://news.bbc.co.uk/2/hi/europe/7976826.stm (accessed 5 January 2018).
22. Ibid.
23. *The Economist*, 22 March 2014.
24. *Forbes*, 30 March 2015; *Lenta*, 1 June 2015; *Lenta*, 7 June 2015; *Kryminform*, 25 June 2015; *Eurasianet*, 16 July 2015; *Al-Jazeera*, 2 September 2015; *New York Times*, 30 September 2017.
25. Conversation, Kazan, 2016.
26. *Novaya gazeta*, 23 October 2016.
27. This standard scam was explained to me both by security sources in Moscow in 2016 and a Western source in 2017.
28. *Donday*, 14 December 2016; *Komsomol'skaya Pravda*, 1 February 2017.
29. Transparency International's *2014 Corruption Perceptions Index* placed Russia 136th in the world out of 175, and Ukraine 142nd.
30. *New Republic*, 5 June 2014. See also Taras Kuzio, 'Crime, politics and business in 1990s Ukraine', *Communist and Post-Communist Studies* 47, 2 (2014), and Sergei Kuzin, *Donetskaya Mafiya* (Kiev: Poligrafkniga, 2006).
31. *New Republic*, 5 June 2014.
32. *Novaya gazeta*, 23 October 2016.
33. Gustav Gressel et al., 'Donbas: an imported war', *New Eastern Europe*, 3 November 2016.
34. *Novaya gazeta*, 23 October 2016.
35. Radio Svoboda, 17 April 2015.
36. *Argumenty i fakty*, 18 November 2016.
37. NEWSru.com, 3 July 2016.
38. This section draws on my longer report 'Crimintern: how the Kremlin uses Russia's criminal networks in Europe', European Council on Foreign Relations, 18 April 2017.
39. *Washington Post*, 23 December 2010; *Snob*, 23 June 2011; Dawisha, *Putin's Kleptocracy*, pp. 88–90, 303–4.
40. Conversation, London, 2015.
41. *L'Express*, 14 January 2016; *SudOuest*, 7 December 2017.
42. 'Hard blow against Russian-speaking mafia', press release, Europol, 19 June 2013.
43. For more on this 'political war', see Mark Galeotti, *Hybrid War or Gibridnaya Voina? Getting Russia's non-linear military challenge right* (Prague: Mayak, 2016).
44. 'Operation Ghost Stories', FBI, 31 October 2011.
45. *Hürriyet*, 19 February 2014; 'Have Russian hitmen been killing with impunity in Turkey?', *BBC News Magazine*, 13 December 2016.
46. Mateusz Seroka, 'Montenegro: Russia accused of attempting to organise a coup d'état', OSW, 6 March 2017.
47. Conversation, Berlin, 2016.
48. Mark Perry, 'Putting America's ridiculously large $18T economy into perspective by comparing US state GDPs to entire countries', *AEIdeas*, 6 June 2016.
49. *Komsomol'skaya Pravda*, 20 December 2000.
50. Andrei Soldatov and Irina Borogan, *The New Nobility: The Restoration of Russia's Security State and the Enduring Legacy of the KGB* (New York: PublicAffairs, 2010), p. 27.
51. *Globe and Mail*, 22 October 2012.

16. Bandit Russia

1. Conversation, Moscow, 2010.

2. Rémi Camus, '"We'll whack them, even in the outhouse": on a phrase by V. V. Putin', *Kultura* 10/2006.

3. Viktor Suvorov, *Spetsnaz: The Story behind the Soviet SAS* (London: Grafton, 1989), pp. 52–3.

4. Yuri Glazov, '"Thieves" in the USSR as a social phenomenon', in *The Russian Mind since Stalin's Death* (Dordrecht: Springer Netherlands, 1985), pp. 39–40.

5. Alix Lambert, *Russian Prison Tattoos: Codes of Authority, Domination, and Struggle* (Atglen, PA: Schiffer, 2003), p. 123.

6. See Lara Ryazanova-Clarke, 'Criminal rhetoric in Russian political discourse', *Language Design* 6 (2004); Michael Gorham, *After Newspeak: Language Culture and Politics in Russia from Gorbachev to Putin* (Ithaca, NY: Cornell University Press, 2014).

7. *Novie izvestiya*, 8 April 2004.

8. Viktor Erofeyev, 'Dirty words: the unique power of Russia's underground language', *New Yorker*, 15 September 2003.

9. Paul Klebnikov, *Godfather of the Kremlin: Boris Berezovsky and the Looting of Russia* (New York: Harvest, 2000), p. 36.

10. Five Chechens were convicted of the murder in 2017. Although the official line is that they worked alone, it is widely believed that Kadyrov directly or indirectly ordered them to carry out the killing and Nemtsov's family have petitioned investigators to look into his alleged involvement.

11. Although Navalny was part blinded in one attack, for example, it took several days and pressure from domestic and foreign sources before the police would even open an investigation.

12. Kathryn Hendley et al., 'Law, relationships and private enforcement: transactional strategies of Russian enterprises', *Europe-Asia Studies* 52, 4 (2000).

13. Michael Rochlitz, 'Corporate raiding and the role of the state in Russia', *Post-Soviet Affairs* 30, 2–3 (2014); Philip Hanson, '*Reiderstvo*: asset-grabbing in Russia', Chatham House, March 2014; Jordan Gans-Morse, 'Threats to property rights in Russia: from private coercion to state aggression', *Post-Soviet Affairs* 28, 3 (2012).

14. RBK, 17 April 2017.

15. Conversation, Moscow, 2016.

16. Olga Matich, 'Mobster gravestones in 1990s Russia', *Global Crime* 7, 1 (2006).

17. In Matvei Komarov's *The Tale of Vanka Kain* (1779), also known by the less snappy but infinitely more delightful title *Thorough and Reliable Descriptions of the Life of the Glorious Russian Conman Vanka Kain and the French Conman Cartouche*. The latest and probably best version is *Vie de Kain, bandit russe et mouchard de la tsarine* ('The Life of Kain, Russian Bandit and Informant of the Empress'), annotated by Ecatherina Rai-Gonneau (Paris: Institut d'études slaves, 2008).

18. Eliot Borenstein, 'Band of Brothers: homoeroticism and the Russian action hero', *Kul'tura*, February 2008, p. 18.

19. Vladimir Jabotinsky, 'Memoirs by my typewriter', in Lucy Dawidowicz (ed.), *Golden Tradition: Jewish Life and Thought in Eastern Europe*, quoted in Charles King, *Odessa: Genius and Death in a City of Dreams* (New York: W. W. Norton, 2011), p. 139.

20. Certainly Odessa itself has taken him as its own, with an Ostap Bender Square featuring a sculpture of one of those twelve chairs.

21. Eliot Borenstein, *Overkill: Sex and Violence in Contemporary Russian Popular Culture* (Ithaca, NY: Cornell University Press, 2007).

22. This violent genre is best explored in Anthony Olcott, *Russian Pulp: The Detektiv and the Russian Way of Crime* (Lanham, MD: Rowman & Littlefield, 2001) and Borenstein, *Overkill*.

23. Borenstein, *Overkill*, p. 23.

24. Vanessa Rampton, ' "Are you gangsters?" "No, we're Russians': the Brother films and the question of national identity in Russia', *eSharp* special issue (2008), p. 65.

25. Serguei Oushakine, 'Aesthetics without law: cinematic bandits in post-Soviet space', *Slavic and East European Journal* 51, 2 (2007), p. 385.
26. Ibid., p. 377.
27. This unique resource is to be found at http://www.primecrime.ru/.
28. *New York Times*, 16 July 2006.
29. Frederick Patton, 'Expressive means in Russian youth slang', *Slavic and East European Journal* 24, 3 (1980), p. 274.
30. *Izvestiya*, 9 January 2013.
31. 'Treasury designates associates of key brothers' circle members', press release, US Department of the Treasury, 30 October 2013.
32. Robert Friedman, *Red Mafiya: How the Russian Mob has Invaded America* (Boston: Little, Brown, 2000), pp. 116–17.
33. See Lore Lippman, 'The Queen of the South: how a Spanish bestseller was written about Mexican narcocorridos', *Crime, Media, Culture* 1, 2 (2005); Martín Meráz García, '"Narcoballads": the psychology and recruitment process of the "narco"', *Global Crime* 7, 2 (2006); Howard Campbell, 'Narco-propaganda in the Mexican "drug war": an anthropological perspective', *Latin American Perspectives* 41, 2 (2014).
34. Anton Oleynik, review of Valerii Anisimikov, *Rossiya v zerkale ugolovnykh traditsii tyurmy* (St Petersburg: Yuridicheskii tsentr Press, 2003), *Journal of Power Institutions in Post-Soviet Societies* 6/7 (2007).
35. V. G. Mozgot, 'The musical taste of young people', *Russian Education and Society* 56, 8 (2014).
36. Author's translation.
37. *Rossiiskaya gazeta*, 20 December 2010.
38. Conversation with a graduate student at MGIMO, the Foreign Ministry's elite university, Moscow, 2015.
39. Edward Luttwak, 'Does the Russian mafia deserve the Nobel Prize for economics?', *London Review of Books*, 3 August 1995.
40. For police reforms, see Brian Taylor, 'Police reform in Russia: the policy process in a hybrid regime', *Post-Soviet Affairs* 30, 2–3 (2014); Olga Semukhina, 'From militia to police: the path of Russian law enforcement reforms', *Russian Analytical Digest* 151 (2014); Mark Galeotti, 'Purges, power and purpose: Medvedev's 2011 police reforms', *Journal of Power Institutions in Post-Soviet Societies* 13 (2012).
41. *New Times*, 27 December 2010.
42. Alexis Belianin and Leonid Kosals, 'Collusion and corruption: an experimental study of Russian police', National Research University Higher School of Economics, 2015.
43. Conversation, Moscow, 2016.
44. Comments made during a conference in Moscow, 1995, quoted in the *Guardian*, 31 July 1995.
45. This is, of course, a drastically simplified account of the process. For more on this, see John Dickie, *Cosa Nostra: A History of the Sicilian Mafia* (London: Hodder & Stoughton, 2004), chapters 10 & 11; Jane Schneider, *Reversible Destiny: Mafia, Antimafia, and the Struggle for Palermo* (Berkeley: University of California Press, 2003).
46. Joseph Serio, *Investigating the Russian Mafia* (Durham, NC: Carolina Academic Press, 2008), p. 97.
47. *Guardian*, 26 July 2007.
48. Conversation, New York, 2009.
49. George Dobson, *Russia* (London: A. & C. Black, 1913), pp. 240–1.
50. Conversation, Moscow, 1993.

BIBLIOGRAPHY

Abbott, Robert, 'Police Reform in Russia, 1858–1878', PhD dissertation, Princeton University, 1971

Abbott, Robert, 'Police reform in the Russian province of Iaroslavl, 1856–1876', *Slavic Review* 32, 2 (1973)

Abramkin, Valerii and Valentina Chesnokova, *Ugolovnaya Rossiya: tyurmi i lagerya* (Moscow: TsSRUP, 2001)

Ageeva, Lyubov', *Kazanskii fenomen: mif i real'nost'* (Kazan: Tatarskoe knizhnoe izdatel'stvo, 1991)

Akel'ev, Evgenii, *Povsednevnaya zhizn' vorovskogo mira Moskvy vo vremena Van'ki Kaina* (Moscow: Molodaya gvardiya, 2012)

Aksyutin, Yurii (ed.), *N. S. Khrushchev: materialy k biografii* (Moscow: Politizdat, 1988)

Albini, Joseph, R. E. Rogers, Victor Shabalin, Valery Kutushev, Vladimir Moiseev and Julie Anderson, 'Russian organized crime: its history, structure and function', *Journal of Contemporary Criminal Justice* 11, 4 (1995)

Alexopoulos, Golfo, 'A torture memo: reading violence in the Gulag', in Golfo Alexopoulos, Julie Hessler and Kiril Tomoff (eds), *Writing the Stalin Era: Sheila Fitzpatrick and Soviet Historiography* (New York: Palgrave Macmillan, 2011)

Anderson, Sandra and Valerie Hibbs, 'Alcoholism in the Soviet Union', *International Social Work* 35, 4 (1992)

Antonov-Ovseyenko, Anton, *The Time of Stalin: Portrait of a Tyranny* (New York: Harper & Row, 1981)

Applebaum, Anne, *Gulag: A History* (New York: Doubleday, 2003)

Arsovska, Jana, *Decoding Albanian Organized Crime: Culture, Politics, and Globalization* (Oakland: University of California Press, 2015)

Ashotov, Kirill, 'Korsar Koba', *Versiya*, 18 January 2016

Babel, Isaac, *Collected Stories* (Harmondsworth: Penguin, 1961)

Bacon, Edwin, *The Gulag at War: Stalin's Forced Labour System in the Light of the Archives* (Basingstoke: Macmillan, 1996)

Baddeley, John, *The Russian Conquest of the Caucasus* (London: Longmans, Green, 1908)

Baldaev, Danzig, *Russian Criminal Tattoo Encyclopedia*, 3 vols (London: FUEL, 2006–8)

Ball, Alan, *And Now My Soul Is Hardened: Abandoned Children in Soviet Russia, 1918–1930* (Berkeley: University of California Press, 1994)

Ball, Alan, 'The roots of *besprizornost'* in Soviet Russia's first decade', *Slavic Review* 51, 2 (1992)

Balmforth, Tom and Anastasia Kirilenko, 'For reputed crime boss known as Taiwanchik, Moscow is "Paradise" ', Radio Free Europe/Radio Liberty, 31 May 2013

Barksby, Kelly, 'Constructing criminals: the creation of identity within criminal mafias', unpublished PhD dissertation, Keele University, 2013

Barnes, Steven, *Death and Redemption: The Gulag and the Shaping of Soviet Society* (Princeton: Princeton University Press, 2011)

Bashkirova, Valeriya, Aleksandr Solov'ev and Vladislav Dorofeev, *Geroi 90-kh: lyudi i den'gi – noveishaya istoriya kapitalizma v Rossii* (Moscow: Kommersant/ANF, 2012)

Behar, Richard, 'Capitalism in a cold climate', *Fortune* 141, 12 (2000)

Belianin, Alexis and Leonid Kosals, 'Collusion and corruption: an experimental study of Russian police', National Research University Higher School of Economics, 2015

Bell, Wilson, 'Was the Gulag an archipelago? De-convoyed prisoners and porous borders in the camps of western Siberia', *Russian Review* 72, 1 (2013)

Berliner, Joseph, *Factory and Manager in the USSR* (Cambridge, MA: Harvard University Press, 1957)

Berliner, Joseph, 'The informal organization of the Soviet firm', *Quarterly Journal of Economics* 66, 3 (1952)

Bernstein, Laurie, *Sonia's Daughters: Prostitutes and their Regulation in Imperial Russia* (Berkeley: University of California Press, 1995)

BIS, *Annual Report of the Security Information Service (BIS) of the Czech Republic for 2008* (Prague: BIS, 2008)

BIS, *Annual Report of the Security Information Service (BIS) of the Czech Republic for 2010* (Prague: BIS, 2010)

BIS, *Annual Report of the Security Information Service (BIS) of the Czech Republic for 2011* (Prague: BIS, 2011)

Blakkisrud, Helge and Pål Kolstø, 'From secessionist conflict toward a functioning state: processes of state- and nation-building in Transnistria', *Post-Soviet Affairs* 27, 2 (2011)

Blok, Anton, *Honour and Violence* (Cambridge: Polity, 2001)

Bobick, Michael, 'Profits of disorder: images of the Transnistrian Moldovan Republic', *Global Crime* 12, 4 (2011)

Bobrovnikov, Vladimir, *Musul'mane Severnogo Kavkaza: obichai, pravo, nasilie* (Moscow: Vostochnaya literatura, 2002)

Bodansky, Yossef, *Chechen Jihad: Al Qaeda's Training Ground and the Next Wave of Terror* (New York: Harper, 2007)

Borenstein, Eliot, 'Band of Brothers: homoeroticism and the Russian action hero', *Kul'tura*, February 2008

Borenstein, Eliot, *Overkill: Sex and Violence in Contemporary Russian Popular Culture* (Ithaca, NY: Cornell University Press, 2007)

Botyakov, Yurii, *Abreki na Kavkaze: sotsiokul'turnyi aspekt yavleniya* (St Petersburg: Peterburgskoe vostokovedenie, 2004)

Briker, Boris, 'The Underworld of Benia Krik and I. Babel's *Odessa Stories*', *Canadian Slavonic Papers* 36, 1–2 (1994)

Brokhin, Yuri, *Hustling on Gorky Street: Sex and Crime in Russia Today* (New York: Dial Press, 1975)

Bronnikov, Arkady, *Russian Criminal Tattoo: Police Files, vol. 1* (London: FUEL, 2014)

Browder, Bill, *Red Notice: A True Story of High Finance, Murder, and one Man's Fight for Justice* (New York: Simon & Schuster, 2015)

Brower, Daniel, *The Russian City between Tradition and Modernity, 1850–1900* (Berkeley: University of California Press, 1990)

Brunet, Roger, 'Geography of the Gulag archipelago', *Espace géographique*, special issue (1993)

Burlatskii, Fedor, '"Mirnyi zagovor" protiv N. S. Khrushcheva', in Yurii Aksyutin (ed.), *N. S. Khrushchev: materialy k biografii* (Moscow: Izdatel'stvo politicheskoi literatury, 1988)

California Department of Justice, *Organized Crime in California 2010: Annual Report to the Legislature*

Campbell, Howard, 'Narco-propaganda in the Mexican 'drug war': an anthropological perspective', *Latin American Perspectives* 41, 2 (2014)

Camus, Rémi, '"We'll whack them, even in the outhouse": on a phrase by V. V. Putin', *Kultura*, October 2006

Chalidze, Valery, *Criminal Russia: Essays on Crime in the Soviet Union* (New York: Random House, 1977)

Chayes, Sarah, 'The Structure of Corruption in Azerbaijan', Carnegie Endowment for International Peace, 2016, available at: http://carnegieendowment.org/2016/06/30/structure-of-corruption-systemic-analysis-using-eurasian-cases-pub-63991 (accessed 5 January 2018)

'Chechnya, the once and future war', US embassy, Moscow, to US secretary of state, 30 May 2006, WikiLeaks

Cheloukhine, Serguei, 'The roots of Russian organized crime: from old-fashioned professionals to the organized criminal groups of today', *Crime, Law and Social Change* 50, 4–5 (2008)

Cheloukhine, Serguei and M. R. Haberfeld, *Russian Organized Crime Networks and their International Trajectories* (New York: Springer, 2011)

Christian, David, 'Vodka and corruption in Russia on the eve of Emancipation', *Slavic Review* 46, 3–4 (1987)

CIA, *Military Compensation in the Soviet Union* (1980)

Clark, William, *Crime and Punishment in Soviet Officialdom: combating corruption in the political elite, 1965–1990* (Armonck, NY: M. E. Sharpe, 1993)

Coalition for Intellectual Property Rights, 'Special 301 filing to the office of the US trade representative', 16 February 2001

Condee, Nanci, 'Body graphics: tattooing the fall of communism', in Adele Marie Barker (ed.), *Consuming Russia: Popular Culture, Sex and Society since Gorbachev* (Durham, NC: Duke University Press, 1999)

Cooper, William H., 'Russia's economic performance and policies and their implications for the United States', Library of Congress Congressional Research Service, June 2009

Cornell, Svante and Michael Jonsson (eds), *Conflict, Crime, and the State in Postcommunist Eurasia* (Philadelphia: University of Pennsylvania Press, 2014)

Costanzo, Ezio, *The Mafia and the Allies: Sicily 1943 and the Return of the Mafia* (New York: Enigma, 2007)

Courtois, Stéphane, Nicolas Werth, Jean-Louis Panné, Andrzej Paczkowski, Karel Bartošek and Jean-Louis Margolin, *The Black Book of Communism: Crimes, Terror, Repression* (Cambridge, MA: Harvard University Press, 1999)

Crowley, Robert, 'Stepping onto a moving train: the collision of illegal logging, forestry policy, and emerging free trade in the Russian Far East', *Pacific Rim Law and Policy Journal* 14 (2005)

Custine, Marquis de, *Empire of the Czar: A Journey through Eternal Russia* (New York: Anchor, [1843] 1989)

Daniel, Yuly, *This Is Moscow Speaking* (London: Collins Harvill, 1968)

Daniels, Robert, *Russia: The Roots of Confrontation* (Cambridge, MA: Harvard University Press, 1985)

Davie, James, 'Missing presumed dead? The *baikovyi iazyk* of the St Petersburg *mazuriki* and other pre-Soviet argots', *Slavonica* 4, 1 (1997)

Dawisha, Karen, *Putin's Kleptocracy: Who Owns Russia?* (New York: Simon & Schuster, 2014)

De Danieli, Filippo, 'Beyond the drug–terror nexus: drug trafficking and state–crime relations in Central Asia', *International Journal of Drug Policy* 25, 6 (2014)

DeVille, Duncan, 'Prosecuting Russian organized crime cases', *Chicago Journal of International Law* 3 (2002)

Dickie, John, *Cosa Nostra: A History of the Sicilian Mafia* (London: Hodder & Stoughton, 2004)

Dobson, George, *Russia* (London: A. & C. Black, 1913)

Dobson, Miriam, *Khrushchev's Cold Summer: Gulag Returnees, Crime, and the Fate of Reform after Stalin* (Ithaca, NY: Cornell University Press, 2009)

Dolgun, Alexander, *Alexander Dolgun's Story: An American in the Gulag* (New York: Alfred A. Knopf, 1975)

Doroshevich, Vlas, *Russia's Penal Colony in the Far East* (London: Anthem Press, 2011)

Dostoevsky, Fedor, *Crime and Punishment* (Cutchogue, NY: Buccaneer, [1866] 1982)

Douillet, Joseph, *Moscow Unmasked* (London: Pilot Press, 1930)

Dovlatov, Sergei, *The Zone: A Prison Camp Guard's Story* (Berkeley: Counterpoint, 2011)

Dubyagin, Yurii and A. G. Bronnikov (eds), *Tolkovyi slovar' ugolovnykh zhargonov* (Moscow: Inter-OMNIS, 1991)

Dubyagin, Yurii and E. A. Teplitski, *Kratkii anglo-russkii i russko-angliiskii slovar' ugolovnogo zhargona/Concise English-Russian and Russian-English Dictionary of the Underworld* (Moscow: Terra, 1993)

Duhamel, Luc, *The KGB Campaign against Corruption in Moscow, 1982–1987* (Pittsburgh: University of Pittsburgh Press, 2011)

Dyshev, Sergei, *Rossiya ugolovnaya: ot vorov v zakone do otmorozkov* (Moscow: EKSMO-Press, 1998)

Dzhekobson, Maikl and Lidiya Dzhekobson, *Pesennyi fol'klor GULAGa kak istoricheskii istochnik*, 2 vols (Moscow: Sovremennyi gumanitarnyi universitet, 1998–2001)

Eklof, Ben and Stephen Frank (eds), *The World of the Russian Peasant: Post-Emancipation Culture and Society* (Boston: Unwin Hyman, 1990)

Engel, Barbara Alpern, *Women in Russia, 1700–2000* (Cambridge: Cambridge University Press, 2003)

Ermolaev, Herman, *Censorship in Soviet Literature, 1917–1991* (Lanham, MD: Rowman & Littlefield, 1997)

Erofeyev, Victor, 'Dirty words: the unique power of Russia's underground language', *New Yorker*, 15 September 2003

European Union, *European Asylum Support Office Country of Origin Information Report – Russian Federation - State Actors of Protection* (EASO, 2017)

Europol, *Russian Organised Crime Threat Assessment 2008* (partially declassified version), (The Hague: Europol, 2008)

Favarel-Garrigues, Gilles, *Policing Economic Crime in Russia: From Soviet Planned Economy to Privatization* (New York: Columbia University Press, 2011)

FBI, 'Operation Ghost Click: international cyber ring that infected millions of computers dismantled', 9 November 2011

Feifer, Gregory and Brian Whitmore, 'The Velvet Surrender: Russia reconquers the Czechs', *New Republic*, 17 September 2010

Figes, Orlando, *Peasant Russia, Civil War: The Volga Countryside in Revolution, 1917–1921* (London: Phoenix, 2001)

Figes, Orlando, *A People's Tragedy: The Russian Revolution, 1891–1924* (London: Penguin, 1998)

Finckenauer, James and Yuri Voronin, *The Threat of Russian Organized Crime* (Washington, DC: National Institute of Justice, 2001)

Finckenauer, James and Elin Waring, *The Russian Mafia in America: Immigration, Culture, and Crime* (Boston: Northeastern University Press, 1998)

Finkelstein, Leonid, 'The Russian Lexicon, 2001', *Jamestown Foundation Prism* 7, 3 (2001)

Firestone, Thomas, 'Criminal corporate raiding in Russia', *International Law* 42 (2008)

Fitzpatrick, Sheila, *Stalin's Peasants: Resistance and Survival in the Russian Village after Collectivization* (Oxford: Oxford University Press, 1995)

Fitzpatrick, Sheila, Alexander Rabinowitch and Richard Stites (eds), *Russia in the Era of NEP: Explorations in Soviet Society and Culture* (Bloomington: Indiana University Press, 1991)

'Following the Magnitsky money', Organized Crime and Corruption Reporting Project, 12 August 2012

Frank, Stephen, *Crime, Cultural Conflict, and Justice in Rural Russia, 1856–1914* (Berkeley: University of California Press, 1999)

Frank, Stephen, 'Narratives within numbers: women, crime and judicial statistics in Imperial Russia, 1834–1913', *Russian Review* 55, 4 (1996)

Friedman, Robert, *Red Mafiya: How the Russian Mob has Invaded America* (Boston: Little, Brown, 2000)

Frierson, Cathy, *All Russia Is Burning! A Cultural History of Fire and Arson in Late Imperial Russia* (Seattle: University of Washington Press, 2004)

Frierson, Cathy, 'Crime and punishment in the Russian village: rural concepts of criminality at the end of the nineteenth century', *Slavic Review* 46, 1 (1987)

Galeotti, Mark, *Afghanistan: The Soviet Union's Last War* (London: Frank Cass, 1995)

Galeotti, Mark, 'Behind the scenes: Uralmash gang retreats into the shadows', *Jane's Intelligence Review* 21, 9 (2009)

Galeotti, Mark, 'Blood brotherhood: Chechen organised crime', *Jane's Intelligence Review* 20, 9 (2008)

Galeotti, Mark, '"Brotherhoods" and "associates": Chechen networks of crime and resistance', *Low Intensity Conflict and Law Enforcement* 11, 2–3 (2002)

Galeotti, Mark, 'Crime and Crimea: criminals as allies and agents', Radio Free Europe/Radio Liberty, 3 November 2014

Galeotti, Mark, 'Criminal histories: an introduction', *Global Crime* 9, 1–2 (2008)

Galeotti, Mark, 'The criminalisation of Russian state security', *Global Crime* 7, 3–4 (2006)

Galeotti, Mark, 'Crimintern: how the Kremlin uses Russia's criminal networks in Europe', European Council on Foreign Relations, 18 April 2017

Galeotti, Mark, 'Dons of the diaspora: Russian organized crime in the United States and the migrant experience', unpublished paper delivered to NYU Jordan Center for the Advanced Study of Russia's Diasporas Project, 2013

Galeotti, Mark, 'Empire of the sun: Russian organised crime's global network', *Jane's Intelligence Review* 20, 6 (2008)

Galeotti, Mark, *Hybrid War or Gibridnaya Voina? Getting Russia's non-linear military challenge right* (Prague: Mayak, 2016)

Galeotti, Mark, 'Israeli organised crime is fragmented, but growing', *Jane's Intelligence Review* 17, 7 (2005)

Galeotti, Mark, 'Khoroshie vremena dlya plokhikh parnei', Radio Svoboda, 13 June 2015.

Galeotti, Mark, 'Not a New Cold War: Great Game II', ETH Zürich, 14 April 2014

Galeotti, Mark, 'Private security and public insecurity: outsourced vigilantism in modern Russia', in David Pratten and Atreyee Sen (eds), *Global Vigilantes* (London: Hurst, 2007)

Galeotti, Mark, 'Purges, power and purpose: Medvedev's 2011 police reforms', *Journal of Power Institutions in Post-Soviet Societies* 13 (2012)

Galeotti, Mark, 'Retirement plans: Russian mafia boss considers his future', *Jane's Intelligence Review* 23, 1 (2011)

Galeotti, Mark, 'Return of mob rule: the resurgence of gangsterism in Russia', *Jane's Intelligence Review* 25, 4 (2013)

Galeotti, Mark, 'The Russian "Mafiya": consolidation and globalisation', *Global Crime* 6, 1 (2004)

Galeotti, Mark, 'The Transdnistrian connection: big problems from a small pseudo-state', *Global Crime* 6, 3–4 (2004)

Galeotti, Mark, ' "Who's the boss, us or the law?" The corrupt art of governing Russia', in Stephen Lovell, Alena Ledeneva and Andrei Rogachevskii (eds), *Bribery and Blat in Russia: Negotiating Reciprocity from the Middle Ages to the 1990s* (Basingstoke: Macmillan, 2000).

Galeotti, Mark, 'The world of the lower depths: crime and punishment in Russian history', *Global Crime* 9, 1–2 (2008)

Gambetta, Diego, *Codes of the Underworld: How Criminals Communicate* (Princeton: Princeton University Press, 2009)

Gambetta, Diego, *The Sicilian Mafia: The Business of Private Protection* (Cambridge, MA: Harvard University Press, 1993)

Gans-Morse, Jordan, 'Threats to property rights in Russia: from private coercion to state aggression', *Post-Soviet Affairs* 28, 3 (2012)

Gatrell, Peter, *The Tsarist Economy, 1850–1917* (London: Batsford, 1986)

Geldern, James von, 'Life in-between: migration and popular culture in late Imperial Russia', *Russian Review* 55, 3 (1996)

Geldern, James von and Louise McReynolds, *Entertaining Tsarist Russia* (Bloomington: Indiana University Press, 1998)

Gentes, Andrew, 'Beat the Devil! Prison society and anarchy in Tsarist Siberia', *Ab Imperio*, February 2009

Gentes, Andrew, *Exile to Siberia, 1590–1822* (Basingstoke: Palgrave Macmillan, 2008)

Gerber, Theodore and Sarah Mendelson, 'Public experiences of police violence and corruption in contemporary Russia: a case of predatory policing?', *Law and Society Review* 42, 1 (2008)

Gilinskiy, Yakov and Yakov Kostjukovsky, 'From thievish *artel* to criminal corporation: the history of organised crime in Russia', in Cyrille Fijnaut and Letizia Paoli (eds) *Organised Crime in Europe: Concepts, Patterns and Control Policies in the European Union and Beyond* (Dordrecht: Springer, 2004)

Gilyarovskii, Vladimir, *Moscow and Muscovites* (Montpelier, VT: Russian Information Services, 2013)

Gilyarovskii, Vladimir, *Moskva i moskvichi* (Moscow: AST, 2005)

Ginzburg, Eugenia, *Within the Whirlwind* (New York: Harcourt Brace Jovanovich, 1989)

Glazov, Yuri, ' "Thieves" in the USSR as a social phenomenon', in Yuri Glazov, *The Russian Mind since Stalin's Death* (Dordrecht: Springer Netherlands, 1985)

Glenny, Misha, *McMafia: Crime without Frontiers* (London: Bodley Head, 2008)

Glonti, Georgi, *Organizovannaya prestupnost' kak odin iz osnovykh istochnikov nasil'stvennoi prestupnosti i etnicheskikh konfliktov* (Tbilisi: Azri, 1998)

Glonti, Georgi and Givi Lobjanidze, *Professional'naya prestupnost' v Gruzii: vory-v-zakone* (Tbilisi: TraCCC, 2004)

Goldenberg, Suzanne, *The Pride of Small Nations: The Caucasus and Post-Soviet Disorder* (London: Zed, 1994)

Gorbatov, Alexander, *Years of my Life: Memoirs of a General of the Soviet Army* (New York: W. W. Norton, 1964)

Gorham, Michael, *After Newspeak: Language Culture and Politics in Russia from Gorbachev to Putin* (Ithaca, NY: Cornell University Press, 2014)

Gorky, Maxim, *The Lower Depths* (Mineola, NY: Dover, [1902] 2000)

Gould, Rebecca, 'Transgressive sanctity: the abrek in Chechen culture', *Kritika* 8, 2 (2007)

Grant, Bruce, *The Captive and the Gift: Cultural Histories of Sovereignty in Russia and the Caucasus* (Ithaca, NY: Cornell University Press, 2009)

Graziosi, Andrea, 'The great strikes of 1953 in Soviet labor camps in the accounts of their participants: a review', *Cahiers du monde russe et soviétique* 33, 4 (1992)

Gressel, Gustav, Kadri Liik and Fredrik Wesslau, 'Donbas: an imported war', *New Eastern Europe*, 3 November 2016

Gromov, Dmitrii, 'Lyuberetskie ulichnye molodezhnye kompanii 1980-kh godov: subkul'tura na pereput'e istorii', *Etnograficheskoe obozrenie* 4 (2006)

Grossman, George, 'The "second economy" of the USSR', *Problems of Communism* 26, 5 (1977)

Gurov, Aleksandr, *Krasnaya mafiya* (Moscow: Samosvet, 1995)

Gurov, Aleksandr, *Professional'naya prestupnost': proshloe i sovremennost'* (Moscow: Yuridicheskaya literatura, 1990)

Haar, Barend ter, *Ritual and Mythology of the Chinese Triads: Creating an Identity* (Leiden: Brill, 2000)

Hagenloh, Paul, *Stalin's Police: Public Order and Mass Repression in the USSR, 1926–1941* (Washington, DC: Woodrow Wilson Center Press, 2009)

Handelman, Stephen, *Comrade Criminal: Russia's New Mafiya* (London: Michael Joseph, 1994)

Handelman, Stephen, 'The Russian "Mafiya"', *Foreign Affairs*, March–April 1994

Hanson, Philip, 'Reiderstvo: asset-grabbing in Russia', Chatham House, March 2014

Harding, Luke, Mafia State (London: Guardian Books, 2011)

Hardy, Jeffrey, '"The camp is not a resort": the campaign against privileges in the Soviet Gulag, 1957–61', Kritika 13, 1 (2012)

Hartley, Janet, 'Bribery and justice in the provinces in the reign of Catherine II', in Stephen Lovell, Alena Ledeneva and Andrei Rogachevskii (eds.), Bribery and Blat in Russia: Negotiating Reciprocity from the Middle Ages to the 1990s (Basingstoke: Macmillan, 2000)

Heinzen, James, The Art of the Bribe: Corruption under Stalin, 1943–1953 (New Haven: Yale University Press, 2016)

Hendley, Kathryn, Peter Murrell and Randi Ryterman, 'Law, relationships and private enforcement: transactional strategies of Russian enterprises', Europe–Asia Studies 52, 4 (2000)

Herling, Gustav, A World Apart (London: William Heinemann, 1951)

Herman, Victor, Coming Out of the Ice: An Unexpected Life (New York: Harcourt Brace Jovanovich, 1979)

Hignett, Kelly, 'The changing face of organized crime in post-communist central and eastern Europe', Debatte 18, 1 (2010)

Hignett, Kelly, 'Organised crime in east central Europe: the Czech Republic, Hungary and Poland', Global Crime 6, 1 (2004)

Hill, Peter, The Japanese Mafia: Yakuza, Law, and the State (Oxford: Oxford University Press, 2003)

Holzlehner, Tobias, '"The harder the rain, the tighter the roof": evolution of organized crime networks in the Russian Far East', Sibirica 6, 2 (2007)

Humphrey, Caroline, 'Dangerous words: taboos, evasions, and silence in Soviet Russia', Forum for Anthropology and Culture, no. 2 (2005)

Humphrey, Caroline, '"Icebergs", barter, and the mafia in provincial Russia', Anthropology Today 7, 2 (1991)

Humphrey, Caroline, The Unmaking of Soviet Life: Everyday Economies after Socialism (Ithaca, NY: Cornell University Press, 2002)

Huntington, Samuel, Political Order in Changing Societies (New Haven: Yale University Press, 1968)

Hyer, Eric, 'Dreams and nightmares: Chinese trade and immigration in the Russian Far East', Journal of East Asian Affairs 10, 2 (1996)

Ilf, Ilya and Evgeny Petrov, The Golden Calf (Evanston, IL: Northwestern University Press, [1931] 2009)

Ilf, Ilya and Evgeny Petrov, The Twelve Chairs (Evanston, IL: Northwestern University Press, [1928] 2011)

International Helsinki Federation for Human Rights, Chechnya: Impunity, Disappearances, Torture, and the Denial of Political Rights (2003)

Ivanets, N. N. and M. I. Lukomskaya, 'The USSR's new alcohol policy', World Health Forum 11 (1990)

Ivanova, Galina, Labor Camp Socialism: The Gulag in the Soviet Totalitarian System (Abingdon: Routledge, [2000] 2015)

Jabotinsky, Vladimir, 'Memoirs by my typewriter', in Lucy Dawidowicz (ed.), Golden Tradition: Jewish Life and Thought in Eastern Europe (Syracuse, NY: Syracuse University Press, 1996)

Jacobs, James, Gotham Unbound: How New York City was Liberated from the Grip of Organized Crime (New York: New York University Press, 2001)

Johnson, Robert, Peasant and Proletarian: The Working Class of Moscow in the Late Nineteenth Century (Leicester: Leicester University Press, 1979)

Jones, Anthony and William Moskoff, Ko-ops: The Rebirth of Entrepreneurship in the Soviet Union (Bloomington: Indiana University Press, 1991)

Juviler, Peter, Revolutionary Law and Order: Politics and Social Change in the USSR (London: Free Press, 1976)

Kaliyev, Roustam, 'Can "power ministries" be transformed?', Perspective 13, 1 (2002)

Kan, Alexander, 'Profile: Iosif Kobzon, Russian crooner and MP', BBC News, 17 February 2015, http://www.bbc.com/news/world-europe-31497039 (accessed 3 January 2018)

Kapchinskii, Oleg, *Mishka Yaponchik i drugie: kriminal i vlast' v gody Grazhdanskoi voiny v Odesse* (Moscow: Kraft+, 2015)

Karlinsky, Simon (ed.), *Anton Chekhov's Life and Thought: Selected Letters and Commentary* (Evanston, IL: Northwestern University Press, [1973] 1997)

Karyshev, Valerii, *Aleksandr Solonik: killer mafii* (Moscow: EKSMO-Press, 1998)

Karyshev, Valerii, *Aleksandr Solonik: killer zhiv?* (Moscow: EKSMO-Press, 2003)

Karyshev, Valerii, *Russkaya Mafiya, 1991–2017: novaya khronika banditskoi Rossii* (Moscow, EKSMO-Press, 2017)

Karyshev, Valerii, *Solntsevskaya bratva: istoriya grupirovki* (Moscow: EKSMO-Press, 1998)

Karyshev, Valerii, *Zapiski banditskogo advokata* (Moscow: Tsentrpoligraf, 1998)

Keep, J. L. H., 'Bandits and the law in Muscovy', *Slavonic and East European Review* 35, 84 (1956)

Kegö, Walter and Alexandru Molcean (eds), *Russian Organized Crime: Recent Trends in the Baltic Sea Region* (Stockholm: Institute for Security and Development Policy, 2012)

Kegö, Walter and Alexandru Molcean, *Russian Speaking Organized Crime Groups in the EU* (Stockholm: Institute for Security and Development Policy, 2011)

Kerry, John, *The New War: The Web of Crime that Threatens America's Security* (New York: Simon & Schuster, 1997)

Khaustov, V. N., V. P. Naumov and N. S. Plotnikov (eds), *Lubyanka: Stalin i VChK-GPU-OGPU-NKVD, yanvar' 1922–dekabr' 1936* (Moscow: Demokratiya, 2003)

King, Charles, *Odessa: Genius and Death in a City of Dreams* (New York: W. W. Norton, 2011)

Kirkow, Peter, 'Regional warlordism in Russia: the case of Primorskii Krai', *Europe–Asia Studies* 47, 6 (1995)

Klebnikov, Paul, *Godfather of the Kremlin: Boris Berezovsky and the Looting of Russia* (New York: Harvest, 2000)

Kleinschmit, Daniela, Stephanie Mansourian, Christoph Wildburger and Andre Purret (eds), *Illegal Logging and Related Timber Trade: Dimensions, Drivers, Impacts and Responses* (Vienna: International Union of Forest Research Organizations, 2016)

Kliger, Sam, 'Russian Jews in America: status, identity and integration', paper presented at the 'Russian-speaking Jewry in global perspective: assimilation, integration and community-building' international conference, Bar Ilan University, Israel, 2004

Kogan, Vanessa, 'Implementing the Judgments of the European Court of Human Rights from the North Caucasus: A Closing Window for Accountability or a Continuing Process of Transitional Justice?', in Natalia Szablewska and Sascha-Dominik Bachmann (eds), *Current Issues in Transitional Justice* (Cham: Springer, 2015)

Kokotyuka, Andrei and Gennadii Grebnev, *Kriminal'naya Ukraina* (Kharkov: Folio, 2004)

Konstantinov, Andrei, *Banditskii Peterburg* (St Petersburg: Folio-Press, 1997)

Konstantinov, Andrei, *Banditskii Peterburg*, rev. edn (St Petersburg: Amfora, 2009)

Konstantinov, Andrei and Mal'kol'm Dikselius, *Banditskaya Rossiya* (St Petersburg: Bibliopolis, 1997)

Konstantinov, Andrei and Mal'kol'm Dikselius, *Prestupnyi mir Rossii* (St Petersburg: Bibliopolis, 1995)

Kopelev, Lev, *To Be Preserved Forever* (Philadelphia: Lippincott, 1977)

Kotkin, Stephen, *Magnetic Mountain: Stalinism as a Civilization* (Berkeley: University of California Press, 1997)

Kovalev, Manuela, 'The function of Russian obscene language in late Soviet and post-Soviet prose', unpublished PhD dissertation, University of Manchester, 2014

'The Kremlin's Luzhkov dilemma', US embassy, Moscow, to US secretary of state, 12 February 2010, WikiLeaks.

Kupatadze, Alexander, *Organized Crime, Political Transitions, and State Formation in Post-Soviet Eurasia* (New York: Palgrave Macmillan, 2012)

Kupatadze, Alexander, 'Political corruption in Eurasia: Understanding Collusion between States, Organized Crime and Business', *Theoretical Criminology* 19, 2 (2015)

Kuprin, Alexander, *Yama: The Pit* (Charleston, SC: BiblioBazaar, [1909] 2006)

Kuromiya, Hiroaki, 'Workers artels and Soviet production methods', in Sheila Fitzpatrick, Alexander Rabinowitch and Richard Stites (eds), *Russia in the Era of NEP: Explorations in Soviet Society and Culture* (Bloomington: Indiana University Press, 1991)

Kuzin, Sergei, *Donetskaya Mafiya* (Kiev: Poligrafkniga, 2006)

Kuzio, Taras, 'Crime, politics and business in 1990s Ukraine', *Communist and Post-Communist Studies* 47, 2 (2014)

Lambert, Alix, *Russian Prison Tattoos: Codes of Authority, Domination, and Struggle* (Atglen, PA: Schiffer, 2003)

Lauchlan, Iain, *Russian Hide-and-Seek: The Tsarist Secret Police in St Petersburg, 1906–1914* (Helsinki: SKS-FLS, 2002)

Laven, Peter, 'Banditry and lawlessness on the Venetian Terraferma in the later Cinquecento', in Trevor Dean and Kate Lowe (eds), *Crime, Society, and the Law in Renaissance Italy* (Cambridge: Cambridge University Press, 1994)

Ledeneva, Alena, 'Organized crime in Russia today', *Jamestown Foundation Prism* 4, 8 (1998)

Ledeneva, Alena, *Russia's Economy of Favours: Blat, Networking, and Informal Exchange* (Cambridge: Cambridge University Press, 1998)

Le Donne, John, 'The provincial and local police under Catherine the Great, 1775–1796', *Canadian-American Slavic Studies* 4, 3 (1970)

Lenin, V. I., 'On the question of national policy' (1914), in *Lenin: Collected Works* (Moscow: Progress, 1972)

Levitin-Krasnov, Anatoly, *Ruk tvoikh zhar* (Tel Aviv: Krug, 1979)

Lewis, David, 'Crime, terror and the state in Central Asia', *Global Crime* 15, 3–4 (2014)

Library of Congress Federal Research Division, *Involvement of Russian Organized Crime Syndicates, Criminal Elements in the Russian Military, and Regional Terrorist Groups in Narcotics Trafficking in Central Asia, the Caucasus, and Chechnya* (2002)

Library of Congress Federal Research Division, *Nations Hospitable to Organized Crime and Terrorism* (2003)

Lincoln, W. Bruce, *In War's Dark Shadow: The Russians before the Great War* (Oxford: Oxford University Press, 1983)

Lintner, Bertil, 'Chinese organised crime', *Global Crime* 6, 1 (2004)

Lintner, Bertil, 'The Russian mafia in Asia', Asia Pacific Media Services, 3 February 1996

Lippman, Lore, 'The Queen of the South: how a Spanish bestseller was written about Mexican narcocorridos', *Crime, Media, Culture* 1, 2 (2005)

Lovell, Stephen, Alena Ledeneva and Andrei Rogachevskii (eds), *Bribery and Blat in Russia: Negotiating Reciprocity from the Middle Ages to the 1990s* (Basingstoke: Macmillan, 2000)

Lucas, Edward, *Deception: Spies, Lies and how Russia Dupes the West* (London: Bloomsbury, 2012)

Lucas, Edward, *The New Cold War: Putin's Russia and the Threat to the West* (New York: Palgrave Macmillan, 2008)

Lunev, Stanislav, 'Russian organized crime spreads beyond Russia's borders, squeezing out the local competition', *Jamestown Foundation Prism* 3, 8 (1997)

Lupo, Salvatore, 'The Allies and the mafia', *Journal of Modern Italian Studies* 2, 1 (1997)

Lusthaus, Jonathan, 'How organised is organised cybercrime?', *Global Crime* 14, 1 (2013)

Luttwak, Edward, 'Does the Russian mafia deserve the Nobel Prize for economics?', *London Review of Books*, 3 August 1995

McCombie, Stephen, Josef Pieprzyk and Paul Watters, 'Cybercrime attribution: an eastern European case study', *Proceedings of the 7th Australian Digital Forensics Conference* (2009)

Mączewski, Paweł, 'The visual encyclopedia of Russian jail tattoos', *Vice*, 15 October 2014, https://www.vice.com/en_uk/article/9bzvbp/russian-criminal-tattoo-fuel-damon-murray-interview-876 (accessed 6 October 2017)

Marat, Erica, 'The changing dynamics of state–crime relations in Kyrgyzstan', *Central Asia–Caucasus Analyst*, 21 February 2008

Marat, Erica, 'Impact of drug trade and organized crime on state functioning in Kyrgyzstan and Tajikistan', *China and Eurasia Forum Quarterly* 4, 1 (2006)

Matich, Olga, 'Mobster gravestones in 1990s Russia', *Global Crime* 7, 1 (2006)

Matskevich, I. M., *Mify prestupnogo mira: o zhizni i smerti izvestnykh prestupnikov proshlogo i nastoyashchego* (Moscow: Prospekt, 2015)

Matuszak, Sławomir, *The Oligarchic Democracy: The Influence of Business Groups on Ukrainian Politics* (Warsaw: Ośrodek Studiów Wschodnich, 2012)

Menn, Joseph, *Fatal System Error: The Hunt for the New Crime Lords who are Bringing down the Internet* (New York: PublicAffairs, 2010)

Meráz García, Martín, '"Narcoballads": the psychology and recruitment process of the "narco"', *Global Crime* 7, 2 (2006)

Merlin, Aude and Silvia Serrano (eds), *Ordres et désordres au Caucase* (Brussels: Editions universitaires de Bruxelles, 2010)

Millar, James, 'The Little Deal: Brezhnev's contribution to acquisitive socialism', *Slavic Review* 44, 4 (1985)

Modestov, Nikolai, *Moskva banditskaya: dokumenty khronika kriminal'nogo bespredela 80–90-kh gg.* (Moscow: Tsentrpoligraf, 1996)

Modestov, Nikolai, *Moskva banditskaya 2: dokumenty khronika kriminal'nogo bespredela 90-kh gg.* (Moscow: Tsentrpoligraf, 1997)

Mozgot, V. G., 'The musical taste of young people', *Russian Education and Society* 56, 8 (2014)

Müller, Martin, 'After Sochi 2014: costs and impacts of Russia's Olympic Games', *Eurasian Geography and Economics* 55, 6 (2014)

Mulukaev, R. S., *Obshcheugolovnaya politsiya dorevolutsionnoi Rossii* (Moscow: Nauka, 1979)

Myers, Jeff, *The Criminal–Terror Nexus in Chechnya: A Historical, Social, and Religious Analysis* (Lanham, MD: Lexington, 2017)

Neuberger, Joan, *Hooliganism: Crime, Culture, and Power in St Petersburg, 1900–1914* (Berkeley: University of California Press, 1993)

Neuberger, Joan, 'Stories of the street: hooliganism in the St Petersburg popular press', *Slavic Review* 48, 2 (1989)

Nomokonov, V. A. and V. I. Shulga, 'Murder for hire as a manifestation of organized crime', *Demokratizatsiya* 6, 4 (1998)

Nožina, Miroslav, 'Crime networks in Vietnamese diasporas: the Czech Republic case', *Crime, Law and Social Change* 53, 3 (2010)

OCCRP, 'The Azerbaijani Laundromat', available at: https://www.occrp.org/en/azerbaijani-laundromat/ (accessed 5 January 2018)

Olcott, Anthony, *Russian Pulp: The Detektiv and the Russian Way of Crime* (Lanham, MD: Rowman & Littlefield, 2001)

Oleynik, Anton, review of Valerii Anisimikov, *Rossiya v zerkale ugolovnykh traditsii tyurmy* (St Petersburg: Yuridicheskii tsentr Press, 2003), *Journal of Power Institutions in Post-Soviet Societies* 6/7 (2007)

Organized Crime Observatory, *Ukraine and the EU: Overcoming Criminal Exploitation toward a Modern Democracy?* (Geneva: Organized Crime Observatory, 2015)

Ostroumov, Sergei, *Prestupnost' i ee prichiny v dorevolutsionnoi Rossii* (Moscow: Izdatel'stvo Moskovskogo Gosudarstvennogo Universiteta, 1980)

Ott, Thomas, 'US law enforcement strategies to combat organized crime threats to financial institutions', *Journal of Financial Crime* 17, 4 (2010)

Oushakine, Serguei, 'Aesthetics without law: cinematic bandits in post-Soviet space', *Slavic and East European Journal* 51, 2 (2007)

Ovchinskii, Vladimir, *Strategiya borby s mafiei* (Moscow: SIMS, 1993)

Ovchinsky, Vladimir, 'The 21st century mafia: made in China', *Russia in Global Affairs*, January 2007

Panin, Dimitri, *The Notebooks of Sologdin* (London: Hutchinson, 1976)

Paoli, Letizia, 'The development of an illegal market: drug consumption and trade in post-Soviet Russia', *British Journal of Criminology* 42, 1 (2002)

Patton, Frederick, 'Expressive means in Russian youth slang', *Slavic and East European Journal* 24, 3 (1980)

Parker, W. H., *An Historical Geography of Russia* (London: University of London Press, 1968)

'People Reporting Ancestry', American Community Survey, 2010

Perry, Mark, 'Putting America's ridiculously large $18T economy into perspective by comparing US state GDPs to entire countries', *AEIdeas*, 6 June 2016

Piacentini, Laura, *Surviving Russian Prisons: Punishment, Economy and Politics in Transition* (Abingdon: Routledge, [2004] 2012)

Pilkington, Hilary, *Russia's Youth and its Culture: A Nation's Constructors and Constructed* (London: Routledge, 1994)

Potter, Matt, *Outlaws Inc.: Under the Radar and on the Black Market with the World's Most dangerous smugglers* (New York: Bloomsbury, 2011)

PricewaterhouseCoopers, *Economic crime: People, Culture and Controls – the 4th Biennial Global Economic Crime Survey: Russia* (2007)

Priemysheva, M. N., 'I. I. Sreznevskii ob ofenskom yazyke', *Acta Linguistica Petropolitana* 3, 3 (2007)

Pushkin, Alexander, *The Captain's Daughter and Other Tales* (New York: Vintage, 2012)

Rai-Gonneau, Ecatherina, *Vie de Kain, bandit russe et mouchard de la tsarine* (Paris: Institute d'études slaves, 2008)

Rampton, Vanessa, '"Are you gangsters?" "No, we're Russians": the Brother films and the question of national identity in Russia', *eSharp* special issue (2008)

Razinkin, Vyacheslav, *'Vory v zakone' i prestupnye klany* (Moscow: Kriminologicheskaya assotsiatsiya, 1995)

Razinkin, Vyacheslav and Aleksei Tarabrin, *Elita prestupnogo mira: tsvetnaya mast'* (Moscow: Veche, 1997)

Razzakov, Fedor, *Bandity semidesyatykh, 1970–1979* (Moscow: Eksmo, 2008)

Razzakov, Fedor, *Bandity vremen sotsializma* (Moscow: Eksmo, 1996)

Remnick, David, *Lenin's Tomb: The Last Days of the Soviet Empire* (New York: Random House, 1994)

Resa Nestares, Carlos, 'Transnational organised crime in Spain: structural factors explaining its penetration', in Emilio Viano (ed.), *Global Organised Crime and International Security* (Aldershot: Ashgate, 1999)

Riasanovsky, Nicholas, *A History of Russia* (New York: Oxford University Press, 1999)

Ries, Nancy, '"Honest bandits" and "warped people": Russian narratives about money, corruption, and moral decay', in Carol Greenhouse, Elizabeth Mertz and Kay Warren (eds), *Ethnography in Unstable Places: Everyday Lives in Contexts of Dramatic Political Change* (Durham, NC: Duke University Press, 2002)

Robinson, Jeffrey, *The Merger: The Conglomeration of International Organized Crime* (Woodstock, NY: Overlook Press, 2000)

Robson, David, 'Are there really 50 Eskimo words for snow?', *New Scientist*, no. 2896 (2012)

Rochlitz, Michael, 'Corporate raiding and the role of the state in Russia', *Post-Soviet Affairs* 30, 2–3 (2014)

Rosner, Lydia, *The Soviet Way of Crime: Beating the System in the Soviet Union and the USA* (Boston: Praeger, 1986)

Rossi, Jacques, *The Gulag Handbook: An Encyclopedia Dictionary of Soviet Penitentiary Institutions and Terms Related to the Forced Labor Camps* (New York: Paragon House, 1989)

Rubin, Rachel, *Jewish Gangsters of Modern Literature* (Urbana: University of Illinois Press, 2000)

Rudakov, Artem, *Chechenskaya mafiya* (Moscow: EKSMO-Press, 2002)

The Russian Primary Chronicle: Laurentian text (Cambridge, MA: Medieval Academy of America, [1953] 2012)

Ryazanova-Clarke, Lara, 'Criminal rhetoric in Russian political discourse', *Language Design* 6 (2004)

Šámal, Zdenek, *Ruské Mafie* (Prague: Ivo Železný, 2000)

Santerre, Maximilien de, *Sovetskie poslevoennye kontslageri i ikh obitateli* (Munich: IPI SSSR, 1960)

Satter, David, *Darkness at Dawn: The Rise of the Russian Criminal State* (New Haven: Yale University Press, 2003)

Schneider, Jane, *Reversible Destiny: Mafia, Antimafia and the Struggle for Palermo* (Berkeley: University of California Press, 2003)

Scholmer, Joseph, *Vorkuta* (London: Weidenfeld & Nicolson, 1954)

Schreck, Carl, 'Blood sport: the rise of Russia's gangster athletes', Radio Free Europe/Radio Liberty, 8 May 2016

Semenov, V., 'Krutye parni', *Ekonomika i zhizn'* 1/1991

Semukhina, Olga, 'From militia to police: the path of Russian law enforcement reforms', *Russian Analytical Digest* 151 (2014)

Senate Select Committee on Intelligence, 'Statement for the record: worldwide threat assessment of the US Intelligence Community', 12 March 2013

Seregny, Scott, 'The *nedel'shchik*: law and order in Muscovite Russia', *Canadian-American Slavic Studies*, 9, 2 (1975)

Serio, Joseph, *Investigating the Russian Mafia* (Durham, NC: Carolina Academic Press, 2008)

Serio, Joseph and Viacheslav Razinkin, 'Thieves professing the code: the traditional role of vory v zakone in Russia's criminal world', *Low Intensity Conflict and Law Enforcement* 4, 1 (1995)

Seroka, Mateusz, 'Montenegro: Russia accused of attempting to organise a coup d'état', OSW, 6 March 2017

Sgovio, Thomas, *Dear America! Why I Turned against Communism* (Kenmore, NY: Partners' Press, 1979)

Shalamov, Varlam, *Kolyma Tales* (London: Penguin, 1994)

Shalamov, Varlam, *Sobranie sochinenii v 4-kh tomakh* (Moscow: Khudozhestvennaya literatura, 1998)

Shchekochikhin, Yurii, *Allo, my vas slyshim: iz khroniki nashego vremeni* (Moscow: Molodaya gvardiya, 1987)

Shelley, Louise, Erik Scott and Anthony Latta (eds), *Organized Crime and Corruption in Georgia* (Abingdon: Routledge, 2001)

Shin, Hyon and Robert Kominski, 'Language use in the United States: 2007' (Suitland, MD: US Census Bureau, 2010)

Shoham, Efrat, ' "Signs of honor" among Russian inmates in Israel's prisons', *International Journal of Offender Therapy and Comparative Criminology* 54, 6 (2010)

Shub, David, 'Kamo: the legendary Old Bolshevik of the Caucasus', *Russian Review* 19, 3 (1960)

Shubinskii, S. N., 'Pervyi peterburgskii general-politseimeister', *Istoricheskii vestnik* 28 (1892)

Sidorov, Aleksandr, *Slovar' sovremennogo blatnogo i lagernogo zhargona* (Rostov-on-Don: Germes, 1992)

Sidorov, Aleksandr, *Vory protiv suk: podlinnaya istoriya vorovskogo bratstva, 1941–91* (Moscow: Eksmo, 2005)

Sidorov, Aleksandr, *Zhigani, urkagany, blatari: podlinnaya istoriya vorovskogo bratstva, 1917–1940* (Moscow: Eksmo, 2005)

Siegel, Dina and Frank Bovenkerk, 'Crime and manipulation of identity among Russian-speaking immigrants in the Netherlands', *Journal of Contemporary Criminal Justice* 16, 4 (2000)

Siegel, Dina and Henk van de Bunt (eds), *Traditional Organized Crime in the Modern World: Responses to Socioeconomic Change* (New York: Springer, 2012)

Skoblikov, Petr, *Vzyskanie dolgov i kriminal* (Moscow: Yurist, 1999)

Slade, Gavin, 'No country for made men: the decline of the mafia in post-Soviet Georgia', *Law and Society Review* 46, 3 (2012)

Slade, Gavin, *Reorganizing Crime: Mafia and Anti-Mafia in Post-Soviet Georgia* (Oxford: Oxford University Press, 2013)

Slade, Gavin, 'The threat of the thief: who has normative influence in Georgian society?' *Global Crime* 8, 2 (2007)

Smith, Sebastian, *Allah's Mountains: Politics and War in the Russian Caucasus*, rev. edn (London: I. B. Tauris, 2006)

Smith, Steven, 'The social meanings of swearing: workers and bad language in late imperial and early Soviet Russia', *Past and Present*, no. 160 (1998)

Smok, Vadzim, 'The art of smuggling in Belarus', *openDemocracy: Russia*, 2 February 2015

Soldatov, Andrei and Irina Borogan, *The New Nobility: The Restoration of Russia's Security State and the Enduring Legacy of the KGB* (New York: PublicAffairs, 2010)

Solomon, Michael, *Magadan* (Princeton: Vertex, 1971)

Solzhenitsyn, Alexander, *The Gulag Archipelago*, 3 vols (New York: Harper & Row, 1974–8)

Souleimanov, Emil and Jasutis Grazvydas, 'The dynamics of Kadyrov's regime: between autonomy and dependence', *Caucasus Survey* 4, 2 (2016)

'Spain details its strategy to combat the Russian mafia', US embassy, Madrid, to US secretary of state, 8 February 2010, WikiLeaks.

Spulber, Nicholas, *Russia's Economic Transitions: From Late Tsarism to the New Millennium* (Cambridge: Cambridge University Press, 2003)

Stack, Graham, 'Money laundering in Ukraine: tax evasion, embezzlement, illicit international flows and state capture', *Journal of Money Laundering Control* 18, 3 (2015)

Stavrou, Theofanis (ed.), *Russia under the Last Czar* (Minneapolis: University of Minnesota Press, 1979)

Stephenson, Svetlana, *Crossing the Line: Vagrancy, Homelessness and Social Displacement in Russia* (Aldershot: Ashgate, 2006)

Stephenson, Svetlana, *Gangs of Russia: From the Streets to the Corridors of Power* (Ithaca, NY: Cornell University Press, 2015)

Stephenson, Svetlana, 'The Kazan Leviathan: Russian street gangs as agents of social order', *Sociological Review* 59, 2 (2011)

Stephenson, Svetlana, 'The violent practices of youth territorial groups in Moscow', *Europe–Asia Studies* 64, 1 (2012)

Sterling, Claire, *Crime Without Frontiers: The Worldwide Expansion of Organised Crime and the Pax Mafiosa* (London: Little, Brown, 1994)

Stolee, Margaret, 'Homeless children in the USSR, 1917–1957', *Soviet Studies* 40, 1 (1988)

Stuchka, Pavel (ed.), *Entsiklopediya gosudarstva i prava* (Moscow: Izdatel'stvo kommunisticheskoi partii, 1927)

Sukharenko, Alexander, 'The use of corruption by "Russian" organized crime in the United States', *Trends in Organized Crime* 8, 2 (2004)

Suvorov, Viktor, *Spetsnaz: The Story behind the Soviet SAS* (London: Grafton, 1989)

Svetlichnaja, Julia, and James Heartfield, 'The Russian security service's ethnic division and the elimination of Moscow's Chechen business class in the 1990s', *Critique* 36, 3 (2008)

Sylvester, Roshanna, *Tales of Old Odessa: Crime and Civility in a City of Thieves* (DeKalb: Northern Illinois University Press, 2005)

Taylor, Brian, 'Police reform in Russia: the policy process in a hybrid regime', *Post-Soviet Affairs* 30, 2–3 (2014)

Taylor, Brian, *State Building in Putin's Russia: Policing and Coercion after Communism* (Cambridge: Cambridge University Press, 2011)

Thomas, Bill and Charles Sutherland, *Red Tape: Adventure Capitalism in the New Russia* (New York: Dutton, 1992)

Thurston, Robert W., 'Police and people in Moscow, 1906–1914', *Russian Review* 39, 3 (1980)

Troyat, Henri, *Daily Life in Russia under the Last Tsar* (Stanford: Stanford University Press, 1961)

Turbiville, Graham, 'Organized crime and the Russian armed forces', *Transnational Organized Crime* 1, 4 (1995)

UN Office on Drugs and Crime, *The Global Afghan Opium Trade: A Threat Assessment* (Vienna: United Nations, 2011)

UN Office on Drugs and Crime, *Results of a Pilot Survey of Forty Selected Organized Criminal Groups in Sixteen Countries* (Vienna: United Nations, 2002)

UN Office on Drugs and Crime, *World Drug Report 2012* (Vienna: United Nations, 2012)

UN Office on Drugs and Crime, *World Drug Report 2013* (Vienna: United Nations, 2013)

United Kingdom Parliament, House of Commons All-Party Group, *Parliamentary Human Rights Group (PHRG) Report, Chechnya Fact-Finding Mission*, 10 June 2010, available at: http://www.refworld.org/docid/4cc7ed2a2.html (accessed 5 January 2018)

United States Government Interagency Working Group, *International Crime Threat Assessment* (2000)

Vaksberg, Arkady, *The Soviet Mafia* (New York: St. Martin's Press, 1991)

Varese, Federico, 'Is Sicily the future of Russia? Private protection and the rise of the Russian Mafia', *European Journal of Sociology* 35, 2 (1994)

Varese, Federico, *Mafia Life: Love, Death and Money at the Heart of Organised Crime* (London: Profile, 2017)

Varese, Federico, *Mafias on the Move: How Organized Crime Conquers New Territories* (Princeton: Princeton University Press, 2011)

Varese, Federico, *The Russian Mafia: Private Protection in a New Market Economy* (Oxford: Oxford University Press, 2001)

Varese, Federico, 'The society of the *vory-v-zakone*, 1930s–1950s', *Cahiers du monde russe* 39, 4 (1998)

Vincent, Mark, 'Cult of the "urka": criminal subculture in the Gulag, 1924–1953', PhD dissertation, University of East Anglia, 2015

Viola, Lynne, *Peasant Rebels under Stalin: Collectivization and the Culture of Peasant Resistance* (Oxford: Oxford University Press, 1998)

Volkov, Vadim, 'Between economy and the state: private security and rule enforcement in Russia', *Politics and Society* 28, 4 (2000)

Volkov, Vadim, 'Patrimonialism versus rational bureaucracy', in Stephen Lovell, Alena Ledeneva and Andrei Rogachevskii (eds), *Bribery and Blat in Russia: Negotiating Reciprocity from the Middle Ages to the 1990s* (Basingstoke: Macmillan, 2000)

Volkov, Vadim, *Silovoe predprinimatel'stvo, XXI vek* (St Petersburg: European University of St Petersburg Press, 2012)

Volkov, Vadim, *Violent Entrepreneurs: The Use of Force in the Making of Russian Capitalism* (Ithaca, NY: Cornell University Press, 2002)

Wallace, Donald Mackenzie, *Russia*, 2 vols (London: Cassell, 1905)

Waller, Michael, 'Organized crime and the Russian state', *Demokratizatsiya* 2, 3 (1994)

Waller, Michael and Victor Yasmann, 'Russia's great criminal revolution: the role of the security services', *Journal of Contemporary Criminal Justice* 11, 4 (1995)

Webster, William, Arnaud de Borchgrave and Frank Cilluffo (eds), *Russian Organized Crime and Corruption* (Washington, DC: Center for Strategic and International Studies, 1997)

Webster, William, Arnaud de Borchgrave and Frank Cilluffo (eds.), *Russian Organized Crime and Corruption: Putin's Challenge* (Washington, DC: Center for Strategic and International Studies, 2000)

Weissman, Neil, *Reform in Tsarist Russia: The State Bureaucracy and Local Government, 1900–1914* (New Brunswick, NJ: Rutgers University Press, 1981)

Weissman, Neil, 'The regular police in tsarist Russia, 1900–1914', *Russian Review* 44, 1 (1985)

Weissman, Neil, 'Rural crime in tsarist Russia: the question of hooliganism, 1905–1914', *Slavic Review* 37, 2 (1978)

Wiersma, Jan Marinus, 'European Parliament ad hoc delegation to Moldova 5–6 June 2002', European Parliament, July 2002

Williams, Phil, 'Transnational criminal organizations: strategic alliances', *Washington Quarterly* 18, 1 (1995)

Worobec, Christine, 'Horse thieves and peasant justice in post-Emancipation Imperial Russia', *Journal of Social History* 21, 2 (1987)

Wyatt, Tanya, 'Exploring the organization of Russia Far East's illegal wildlife trade: two case studies of the illegal fur and illegal falcon trades', *Global Crime* 10, 1–2 (2009)

Wyatt, Tanya, 'The Russian Far East's illegal timber trade: an organized crime?', *Crime, Law and Social Change* 61, 1 (2014)

Yaffa, Joshua, 'The double sting', *New Yorker*, 27 July 2015

Yakovlev, Vladimir, 'Kontora "Liuberov"', *Ogonek* 5/1987

Yakubov, Oleg, *Mikhailov ili Mikhas* (Moscow: Veche-Ast, 1999)

Yaney, George L., 'Law, society and the domestic regime in Russia, in historical perspective', *American Political Science Review* 59, 2 (1965)

Yashin, Ilya, *Ugroza Natsional'noi bezopasnosti* (independent expert report, Moscow, 2016) available at: https://openrussia.org/post/view/12965/ (accessed 5 January 2018)

Young, Sarah, 'Knowing Russia's convicts: the other in narratives of imprisonment and exile of the late imperial era', *Europe–Asia Studies* 65, 9 (2013)

Zelnik, Reginald, *Labor and Society in Tsarist Russia: The Factory Workers of St Petersburg* (Stanford: Stanford University Press, 1971)

Zhilin, Aleksandr, 'The Shadow of Chechen Crime over Moscow', *Jamestown Foundation Prism* 2, 6 (1996)

Zuckerman, Fredric, *The Tsarist Secret Police in Russian Society, 1880–1917* (Basingstoke: Macmillan, 1996)

INDEX

Names within quotation marks are criminal nicknames where no proper name is listed. Otherwise, a cross-reference from the nickname directs the reader to the person's real name.